ON GREEK RELIGION

D1525195

A VOLUME IN THE SERIES
Townsend Lectures/Cornell Studies in Classical Philology

Edited by Frederick M. Ahl, Theodore R. Brennan, Charles F. Brittain,
Kevin M. Clinton, Gail J. Fine, David P. Mankin, Sturt W. Manning, Alan J.
Nussbaum, Hayden N. Pelliccia, Pietro Pucci, Hunter R. Rawlings, III, Éric
Rebillard, Jeffrey S. Rusten, Barry S. Strauss

VOLUME LX
On Greek Religion

By Robert Parker

A list of titles in this series is available at www.cornellpress.cornell.edu.

ON GREEK RELIGION

ROBERT PARKER

CORNELL UNIVERSITY PRESS
Ithaca and London

LIBRARY
FRANKLIN PIERCE UNIVERSITY
RINDGE, NH 03461

Copyright © 2011 by Cornell University

All rights reserved. Except for brief quotations in a review, this book, or parts thereof, must not be reproduced in any form without permission in writing from the publisher. For information, address Cornell University Press, Sage House, 512 East State Street, Ithaca, New York 14850.

First published 2011 by Cornell University Press
Printed in the United States of America
First printing, Cornell Paperbacks, 2011

Library of Congress Cataloging-in-Publication Data

Parker, Robert, 1950–
    On Greek religion / Robert Parker.
      . p. cm. — (Townsend lectures/Cornell studies in classical philology)
    Includes bibliographical references and index.
    ISBN 978-0-8014-4948-2 (cloth : alk. paper)
    ISBN 978-0-8014-7735-5 (pbk. : alk. paper)
    1. Greece—Religion. I. Title. II. Series: Cornell studies in classical philology. Townsend lectures.
  ✓ BL790.P37   2011
      292.08—dc22   2010040747

Cornell University Press strives to use environmentally responsible suppliers and materials to the fullest extent possible in the publishing of its books. Such materials include vegetable-based, low-VOC inks and acid-free papers that are recycled, totally chlorine-free, or partly composed of nonwood fibers. For further information, visit our website at www.cornellpress.cornell.edu.

Cloth printing   10 9 8 7 6 5 4 3 2 1
Paperback printing   10 9 8 7 6 5 4 3 2 1

❧ Contents

❧ PREFACE

There has been a remarkable and ever-increasing growth of interest in ancient Greek religion in the last half-century. Doubtless many different factors are partly responsible. In every area of historiography, the study of "kings and battles" has had to surrender its traditional primacy. In relation to Greece, the classicizing approach that sought there models of timeless perfection has largely fallen out of fashion. J. C. Stobart's *The Glory That Was Greece*[1] seems finally to have gone out of print; instead we are urged to remember that, for all its superficial familiarity, the ancient world was "desperately alien" from our own. Where religion used to be neglected as one of the rare domains of life in which the Greeks failed to leave a lasting legacy, it is now attended to as part of their intriguing otherness. E. R. Dodds's matchless study of *The Greeks and the Irrational*[2] has been so thoroughly successful that it is almost time to reemphasize the real achievements of Greek rationalism. A different factor is that in Europe, at least, the social influence of established religion has declined drastically. Many are intrigued, it may be guessed, by a form of life more characteristic of their parents' or grandparents' generation than of their own; certainly many professional scholars of ancient religion are children of pastors,[3] or lapsed believers (not that ancient religion in fact bore much resemblance to the institutional Christianity of the first half of the twentieth century).

New developments in scholarship too have given the subject new impetus. When, late in his life, the great scholar who dominated the field for the first half of the twentieth century, Martin Nilsson, surveyed the history of the discipline in his large German *History of Greek Religion,* he declared that the essential conceptual tools had been forged in the period from 1875 to about 1900, and had not changed since.[4] The exciting and sometimes savage

---

1. First edition London, 1911.
2. Berkeley, 1951.
3. For one explicit statement of the connection, see S.R.F. Price, *Rituals and Power* (Cambridge, 1984), 11.
4. Nilsson, *Geschichte,* 6–10.

splendor of Greek mythology, in Nilsson's conception, had little to do with cult as actually practiced. Myths could teach the modern inquirer about Greek prehistory; the prime purpose of the rituals was, mundanely, to make the crops grow. But that uninspiring picture of a subject where the big questions had all already been answered was drastically challenged in the 1960s and 1970s. Jean-Pierre Vernant adapted the methods of Claude Levi-Strauss to study the implicit mental structures underlying Greek myth and cult and, through them, Greek society; Walter Burkert interpreted Greek sacrificial rituals in the light of contemporary ethological investigations into animal and human aggression.[5] Disagreeing in almost all else, the one asserting the primacy of the mental, the other almost abolishing it, they were at one in turning attention away from the life of the fields and back toward society; they agreed too in reasserting the importance of myth.

The study of the subject recovered the excitement that it had possessed in the period when Nilsson's conceptual tools had been forged.[6] Debate has moved on, but the liberating effect of the great rejection of existing paradigms has remained. There remains, too, a factor that has always made Greek religion interesting: its omnipresence in the art and literature of the Greeks. But this omnipresence raises a point very important for the approach adopted in this book. There is something of a paradox about our access to ancient Greek religion. We know too much, and too little. The materials that bear on it far outreach an individual's capacity to assimilate: so many casual allusions in so many literary texts over more than a millennium, so many direct or indirect references in so many inscriptions from so many places in the Greek world, such an overwhelming abundance of physical remains. But genuinely revealing evidence does not often cluster coherently enough to create a vivid sense of the religious realities of a particular time and place. Amid a vast archipelago of scattered islets of information, only a few are of a size to be habitable.

Two methodological consequences follow. First, if this sprawling field of inquiry is to be unified, it is essential to debate central issues explicitly: we

---

5. See pp. 87–97 and 160–65 below.

6. Witness Gilbert Murray's remarkable claim in 1907: "It seems a bold statement, yet on reflection we are prepared to maintain it, that one of the greatest practical advances made by the human race in the last fifteen or twenty years has been in our improved understanding of ancient and especially of Greek religion. We are not forgetting Japan, or wireless telegraphy, or radium, or the Hague conference, or even flying machines. To understand the meaning of Religion, if mankind could ever attain it, would be a greater end than is suggested by any of these": "Olympic houses," review of L. R. Farnell, *The Cults of the Greek States,* vols. 3 and 4, *Albany Review* 2 (1907): 199–208. The intellectual passion and excitement of a figure often seen as a complacent late Victorian emerge from R. Ackerman, ed., *Selected Letters of Sir J. G. Frazer* (Oxford, 2005).

need "theory" in the sense of a discussion shared by archaeologists, literary scholars, and historians as to how, say, a Greek god is to be analyzed and described, or what a hero might be, or how a religious system that lacks sacred texts and formal religious institutions can operate. Second, the best evidence must be given priority: the whole archipelago cannot be charted, but one can make paths on the larger, well-watered islands. Scraps of information tempt, it is true, the bold explorer; that which is almost knowable exercises a Siren-like lure; but the shores beneath the Sirens' cliff are scattered with the bleached bones of those who yield to it.

The process of interpreting Greek religion began when the practice of Greek religion began. The theories developed in antiquity were in good measure taken over when interest in the subject revived in the Renaissance, and debate has continued with greater or lesser intensity ever since. We are inevitably both beneficiaries and victims of that tradition: beneficiaries in an obvious sense, victims in the sense indicated by J. M. Keynes in his famous observations on the role of theory in practical affairs:

> The ideas of economists and political philosophers, both when they are right and when they are wrong, are more powerful than is commonly understood. Indeed the world is ruled by little else. Practical men, who believe themselves to be quite exempt from any intellectual influences, are usually the slaves of some defunct economist. Madmen in authority, who hear voices from the air, are distilling their frenzy from some academic scribbler of a few years back.[7]

Mutatis mutandis, Keynes's observation is just as relevant to the study of ancient religion: one can see this, for instance, if one observes the confidence with which a concept such as that of the "fertility god" was long accepted by the most cautious scholars as capturing a certified reality—when it is in fact the product of a particular phase of speculation. For a variety of reasons (some relating to the study of all nonscriptural religions, some to the deficiencies of our evidence) the subject is one highly dependent on broad interpretative paradigms that may alter drastically. But even discredited paradigms seldom vanish completely, and may leave traces of themselves in the common conceptual store. There is no escape from this situation: one cannot speak without concepts, and one cannot test the validity of every concept before using it. But a certain awareness of the history of the subject can help to indicate what comes from where, what easy assumption is based on what past theory and is only as valid as that theory.

---

7. *The General Theory of Employment, Interest and Money* (London 1936), 383–84.

This book is an attempt to promote debate on central issues on the basis of reliable evidence and with some attention to the history of the discipline.[8] The topics treated closely resemble those that might appear in an "Introduction to Greek Religion," but this is not a handbook; the emphasis is on problems and approaches, often analyzed in some detail, not on basic factual information. Nor, certainly, do I claim to be comprehensive. I will mention here, to give them a brief moment in the light, some major topics that I merely take for granted in what follows.

Charis: the exchange of gifts and favors as the ideal relationship between man and god.[9] In *Iliad* book 16, about to make a prayer of the utmost solemnity that Patroclus should succeed in the coming battle and come back safe, Achilles pours a libation to Zeus (220–32); the care with which he purifies the libation bowl, a bowl that he reserves for offerings to Zeus, is elaborately described. He does all this because he is about to seek a favor from the god, and the honorific libation is a gift; in an emergency when he lacked time to bring an offering, he could have reminded Zeus of offerings brought in the past, or promised such in the future. He reinforces his present appeal by a reminder to Zeus that the god has already given him aid in the past (236–38). What is at issue is not therefore a simple *"do ut des,"* whereby one gift buys one benefit, but a continuing relationship (what anthropologists call "generalized reciprocity"). Because of the *charis* ideal, the study of Greek religion is inevitably a study among other things of the cult practices that constitute the gifts made by mortals. Exactly what counts as a gift is a further question. Sacrifices (or libations, or incense burning) and objects dedicated to the gods certainly do; prayers do not, being mere accompaniments to gifts indicating which mortals hope to receive what benefits from which gods in return. A hymn, however, or an elaborate choral performance could "delight" a god and so constitute an offering in exchange for which a benefit could be requested.

Locality: the importance of place in the Greeks' relation with their gods. Achilles in the prayer just mentioned addresses Zeus as "lord Zeus, Dodonaean, Pelasgian, living far off, ruling stormy Dodona" (233–34). Though appealing

---

8. I have profited very greatly from Konaris, *Greek Gods.*

9. Cf. in brief p. 95 n. 82 below. P. Veyne objects, in "Inviter les dieux," that "si l'on fait un vœu et qu'on promette à quelque dieu un sacrifice au cas où l'on serait exaucé, ce n'est pas là de l'échange: c'est ce que nous appelons, ici et maintenant, de la corruption, du bakchich... corruption et hommage sont la même chose: on ne se présente pas les mains vides devant les grands" (15), and "ramener à de l'échange ces faveurs, ces négociations, ces ruses, toute cette richesse pittoresque et précise, est toujours possible sans être jamais instructif: c'est lâcher la proie pour l'ombre, tant le mot d'échange est pauvre de sens" (18). Yes and no: the point of the "corruption" was to create at least an illusion of reciprocity, *charis.*

to the ruler of Olympus, Achilles also firmly associates him with a particular cult site on earth. The *Homeric Hymns to Apollo* tell how the god came to be born on Delos (after the long wanderings of his pregnant mother) and how he selected Delphi as the site for his oracle. The *Hymn to Demeter* tells of the foundation of her temple and rites at Eleusis. So these stories of the gods' entry into the human world tell also of how they became associated with particular places; the gods are often known as (for example) Apollo of Delos or Delphi, Demeter of Eleusis (or Cyprian Aphrodite, or Argive Hera...). Even much less important sacred sites have their particularity: the ritual norms in the cult of a single god differ from sanctuary to sanctuary, and each sanctuary of any size will have its own priest. Conversely, it must in large measure have been through sanctuaries and gods that Greeks thought about their environment. It is not chance that Pausanias's journey through Greece is to such an extent a gazetteer of religious sites. The first thing to be done in founding a colony was to mark out sacred precincts; even at the microlevel of the Attic deme we see that sacred sites were not confined to the center but were widely dispersed within the deme's territory. Not just "everything" (as Thales said) but everywhere was full of gods.

Sacred places and sanctuaries: where they were located (a continuation of the previous topic), what they contained (the whole gamut from "just an altar, and awe"[10] to huge enclosures with many temples), how their layout affected the experience of the worshipper, the possibilities of communication with the gods or direct experience of the gods created by the images of various kinds that they contained. The gods were, in a sense, literally present in their sanctuaries. Greeks constantly, in documents and contexts of very different kinds, referred to what we would call a statue of a particular god simply by that god's name; in representations on vases of scenes set in temples, it is often unclear whether we are looking at a statue or at an actual god. To be sure, they knew that statues were made by craftsmen from physical materials; and plain statements that statues are gods, or that gods are statues, are not to be found. To that extent the Christian claim that pagans bowed down to wood and stone is as crude as the claim that they believed their gods to feed on the sacrifices that they brought them. Nonetheless, they constantly behaved and spoke *as if* their statues were gods: when a statue of Dionysus was brought in procession to the theater at the start of the Athenian Dionysia, this was not a "representation of the bringing in of Dionysus" but quite simply "the bringing in of Dionysus"; and so on in numerous other cases. Statues also tended to behave as if they were animate: a recent work of

---

10. *Ara tantum et reverentia:* Tac. *Hist.* 2.78, on Mount Carmel.

reference has sections on "statues that turn, that move, that sweat, that weep, that speak" as well as on "other prodigies" associated with them.[11]

Issues of fate, theodicy, and divine justice. Homer describes Zeus's response to Achilles' prayer in *Iliad* 16 thus (250–52):

> So he prayed, and cunning Zeus heard him.
> One part the father granted, one part he refused.
> He granted that Patroclus should drive back the fighting and battle from the ships.
> He refused that Patroclus should come back safe from the battle.

For Achilles, we are aware, it was no better to have half his prayer granted than to have it rejected wholly, a point that Homer's feigned matter-of-factness brings out with utmost poignancy. We are not told the grounds for Zeus's decision, but the absence of explanation draws attention to itself; it is characteristic of the presentation of religion in high literature both to engage in, and to invite, speculation about divine justice, fate, human responsibility, and the like. There is no reason to exclude such topics from the study of Greek religion: it is implausible to deny that "ordinary Greeks" were interested in the problems of divine justice and fate and the rest, even if such concern is mostly revealed to us through literature. Nor does the comparative fixity of cult rules, as opposed to the ebb and flow of competing opinion about more abstract topics, make the former more real than the latter. We trivialize the Greeks if we do not engage with their thought on these issues. But it is not easy to bring the two things together within a single field of argument. The concentration in this book on cult practice is based not on a judgment about what might constitute "real" religion, but more mundanely on the wish to do one thing at a time. (My relative indifference to the afterlife, by contrast, is designed to mirror theirs.)

Enough of this list of omissions, which could certainly be extended. Though much is taken, much, I hope, abides. The periodization of Greek religion is an open though seldom-discussed question, which might indeed have formed a chapter in this book. One can argue that no single disjuncture occurred that was greater than any other between the earliest evidences of post-Mycenaean religion and the triumph of Christianity; so all division into periods within that long span of time is arbitrary. But, however arbitrary, it is also, in practical terms, hard to avoid. The pressure exerted on the whole structure of Greek society by Roman control arguably caused more change

---

11. See the section index in *ThesCRA* 2.417. The mixed character of divine statues as both matter and god was already stressed by Burckhardt, *Kulturgeschichte,* 408–9.

in the religious sphere than any other factor. I therefore take as my notional time frame the period between the first post-Mycenaean written documents (so the eighth century) and the creation of the Roman provinces of Macedonia in 146 and of Asia in 133 BC. Most emphasis will lie on the middle of that period, because of the clustering of literary sources, and a few intrusions from after its end will occur.

The book lacks a sequential plot, and the seven chapters can be read as self-contained units. But they have a unity of approach and a shared concentration on central issues that make of them, it is hoped, not "essays" but "an essay" on Greek religion.

❧ ACKNOWLEDGMENTS

This book derives from the Townsend lectures that I had the honor of giving at Cornell University during the autumn of 2008. Given my topic, I was pleased to learn, on my first day on campus, that Ezra Cornell had founded the university as a nondenominational, anti-sectarian institution, which in the stirring words of Andrew D. White would be "an asylum for science where truth shall be sought for truth's sake.... where it shall not be the main purpose of the Faculty to stretch or cut Science to fit 'Revealed Religion.'"[1] The hospitality and helpfulness of many colleagues made my stay in Cornell a happy one, and I hope it is not invidious if I single out for thanks Kevin Clinton and Nora Dimitrova, Gail Fine and Terry Irwin, Hayden Pelliccia, Hunter Rawlings III, Jeff Rusten, and most especially Charles and Harriet Brittain. I remember with affection too the nine participants in my graduate seminar. Among those who have worked on this book for Cornell University Press I am especially grateful to Peter Potter for comments on my manuscript, to Marie Flaherty-Jones for admirably attentive copyediting, and to Candace Akins for always helpful manuscript editing. I must also thank the University of Oxford for the year's leave that allowed me to visit Cornell and then prepare the lectures for publication.

I was able to discuss my first ideas for this book with Christiane Sourvinou-Inwood. Our dialogue about Greek religion extended back so far that I can no longer remember precisely when it began. The book would be a better one had that dialogue not been prematurely cut short by her death in May 2007. I dedicate it to her memory.[2]

---

1. Letter of August 1862 to Gerrit Smith, quoted in M. Bishop, *A History of Cornell* (Ithaca, 1962), 41–42.

2. A brief account of her work is forthcoming in the *Oxford Dictionary of National Biography.*

ON GREEK RELIGION

CHAPTER 1

Why Believe without Revelation?

The Evidences of Greek Religion

The great fourteenth-century philosopher of history Ibn Khaldûn, arguing against the view of "the philosophers" that prophecy is a natural human quality, observed that "people who have a (divinely revealed) book and who follow the prophets are few in number in comparison with the Magians [i.e., pagans] who have none."[1] The Greeks, it is a commonplace to observe, were among the many peoples who lacked a book and prophets in Ibn Khaldûn's sense. The Greeks will not have perceived this "lack" as anything of the kind, and to that extent the negative characterization is a bad starting point. But it can be taken as a stepping-stone toward investigating those positive features of their religious system on account of which there was, indeed, no lack. Three questions naturally arise. First, if the basis for sacrifice, dedications, processions, festivals, and all the other apparatus of Greek worship[2] was not a book or prophecy, then what was it? What reason had the Greeks, unenlightened by revelation, to believe in their gods? The second question follows closely from the first. Given,

---

1. *The Muqaddimah: An Introduction to History,* trans. F. Rosenthal (abridged edition by N. J. Dawood, reissued with new introduction by B. B. Lawrence, Princeton, 2005), 47–48. The concept of "People of the Book" goes back to the Qur'an, 5.14–15.

2. Dion. Hal. *Ant. Rom.* 2.18.2 has a useful list of the components of "religion": ἱερά, τεμένη, βωμοί, ξοανῶν ἰδρύσεις...ἑορταί, θυσίαι, ἐκεχειρίαι, πανηγύρεις, πόνων ἀναπαύλαι; cf. 2.63.2, which adds ἁγνεῖαι, θρησκεῖαι, καθαρμοὶ καὶ αἱ ἄλλαι θεραπεῖαι καὶ τιμαί.

again, the absence of revelation, how could the Greeks know what was pious or impious, what pleasing or unpleasing to the gods? And third, if Greek religion was not a religion of the book, then what was the role of all those texts that, beginning as Herodotus noted (2.53) with Homer and Hesiod, evidently played some part in it, without which indeed we moderns could scarcely approach the subject at all?

This chapter will treat those three questions in turn. I will then address two further issues that follow from them. The Greeks lacked sacred books, but they certainly did not lack myths; the role of those myths in religious life needs to be considered. Second, myths imply certain conceptions of the gods' capacities and attitudes, what we might be tempted to term "beliefs" about the gods, were "belief" not a term that has often been declared inapplicable to ritual-centered ancient religions. Yet surely even a ritual is performed in the belief that there is some purpose in doing so.... Some way needs to be found of reconciling the evident truths that, on the one hand, the fixed and regulated elements of Greek religion were ritual acts, and on the other that volumes could be filled with Greek stories about the gods, speculations about them, appeals to them, criticisms of them. One way of mediating between those for whom Greek religion is a matter of things done at or near an altar, and those for whom it is rather the sum of the stories, speculations, and appeals just mentioned, is to argue that, though beliefs were held, only acts were subject to control. That mediating proposal, however, calls for two footnotes or riders: philosophers laid claim not to mere belief but to sure knowledge about the divine, on the basis of a priori postulates as to what a god should be like; and a few incidents, chief among them the prosecution of Socrates, may bring into doubt the notion that thought was free and only action policed. The chapter will therefore move a considerable distance from its starting point. But all the topics discussed are consequences, or qualifications, of the central absence noted by Ibn Khaldûn.

Evidences

Two of the most influential books in the nineteenth century, still in print, were William Paley's *A View of the Evidences of Christianity,* of 1794, and his *Natural Theology; or, Evidences of the Existence and Attributes of the Deity, Collected from the Appearances of Nature,* of 1802. The first question posed above could be reformulated anachronistically as an attempt to establish what Sophocles' or Pindar's *"Evidences"* might have looked like. In a sense there is a single, simple answer to that question, and one evidence that easily outweighs all others, even if Greeks did not often formulate the matter in quite this way. When Nicomachus was charged in 399 with impiety for altering the traditional sacrificial calendar of Athens, the prosecutor argued: "Our ancestors, who only made the sacrifices prescribed in Solon's code, bequeathed to us a city which was the greatest and happiest in all Greece; and so we ought to make the same sacrifices as them if for no other reason, for the good luck that they brought." In the past, when sacrifices were performed more regularly, the weather too was more regular, says Isocrates.[3] Every dedication set up by a Greek in fulfillment of a vow is testimony that the prayer accompanying the vow has been fulfilled. The greatest evidence then for the existence of the gods is that piety works: the reward for worshipping the gods in ways hallowed by tradition is prosperity. The converse is that impiety leads to disaster; and, though the piety-prosperity nexus is not often used as a proof of the existence of the gods, the afflictions of the wicked are indeed a much-cited evidence. "Father Zeus, you gods still exist on high Olympus, if the suitors have really paid the penalty for their reckless insolence," says Laertes in the *Odyssey;* "The gods exist," delightedly exclaims the chef in Menander's *Dyskolos* when his enemy, whom he regards as impious, falls down a well. We seem to catch here the tones of excited colloquial speech.[4]

When fair weather and flourishing crops are seen as a reward of piety, the argument rests implicitly on the assumption that the natural environment is under divine control. Here then potentially is another evidence: if every shower of rain comes from Zeus—and "Zeus" or "god" "is raining" was used more or less interchangeably in Greek with an impersonal "it is raining"—then direct contact with divine power is an everyday experience. It surely will not have felt like that, even for the pious: rain for them was rain, part of normality, as it is for us, not an epiphany. But when rain declined to fall, it could be prayed for; thunderbolts were embodiments of "Zeus who descends," storms could be caused by human pollution, winds could be summoned or averted by sacrifice, an untimely earthquake or eclipse could cause a general to be replaced, military activity to be abandoned or delayed. According to the messenger in Aeschylus's *Persai,* when an unseasonable storm froze the Strymon in the face of the retreating Persian army, "people who hitherto paid no regard to the gods (θεοὺς δέ τις / τὸ πρὶν νομίζων

---

3. Lys. 30.18; Isoc. *Areopagiticus* 29–30. Pindar often attributes an athlete's success to piety, e.g., *Ol.* 3.38–41, 6.77–81, 8.8.

4. Hom. *Od.* 24.351–52; Men. *Dysk.* 639. There was a proverb "Now the gods are blessed" or "Now the blessed gods [exist]" (νῦν θεοὶ μάκαρες) used "of those who received deserved punishment for what they have done" (Diogenianus 6.88). Cf. Aesch. *Ag.* 1578–79; Eur. *Supp.* 731–32, *El.* 583–84, *HF* 841–42.

οὐδαμοῦ)" then turned to prayers; though ascribed to Persians, the psychology is also perfectly Greek.[5]

This was the level at which pre-Socratic philosophy, with the premise of a rule-bound natural order, came into conflict with popular religious assumptions; and, for those educated in the philosophical schools, storms and eclipses ceased necessarily to convey any message about the divine. (But there was always the possibility of a both and/or "double determination" explanation, whereby god worked through the natural order.)[6] Even for the less educated, such messages were only intermittently audible; this was the religion of crisis situations. Nature was a great mechanism for the transmission of communications from, and about, the divine, but the mechanism was only recognized as operating occasionally. The vaguer proposition, however, that piety is the soil in which good crops grow was a permanent if unemphatic presumption.

The "rewards of piety" argument is in principle empirical: the gods' concern for humanity is confirmed by their differential treatment of the good and bad. The pragmatism of this approach leads to the theoretical possibility of abusing the gods when they maltreat the good just as one praises them when they punish the bad. Complaints and even threats against unjust gods are raised by characters in literature, but there are no early Greek parallels for the popular response to the tragic early death of the Roman prince Germanicus, when temples were stoned.[7] Perhaps our sources have censored such incidents; more probably there was a tendency in such circumstances to seek out ritual omissions and so exculpate the gods. The Rewards of Piety is in reality a pseudoempirical argument, deriving its force from selective vision, inertia, and traditionalism. Yet psychologically it doubtless remained for most Greeks among the most potent of all evidences.

5. Aesch. *Pers.* 495–99. Rain and winds: cf. pp. 74 and 77; "Zeus who descends": *NGSL* 1.10 with Lupu's note; storms and pollution: Lhôte, *Lamelles oraculaires,* 14 (*SEG* 19.427); earthquake/ eclipse: e.g., Hdt. 9.10.3; Thuc. 3.89.1, 6.95.1, 8.6.5; Xen. *Hell.* 3.2.24 (all Spartan); Thuc. 7.50.4 (Athenian). On more complicated ways in which the gods were seen as guarantors of an order that was not necessarily moral, see E. Kearns, "Order, Interaction, Authority: Ways of Looking at Greek Religion," in *The Greek World,* ed. A. Powell, 511–29 (London, 1995), at 515–19.

6. See Lloyd, *Magic, Reason and Experience,* chap. 1; for the conflict: Parker, *Athenian Religion,* 209. Double determination: see, e.g., Plut. *Per.* 6.

7. Suet., *Calig.* 5. Complaints and threats: e.g., Eur. *Hec.* 488–91; Hom. *Il.* 22.20; cf. R. Parker in *Greek Tragedy and the Historian,* ed. C. Pelling (Oxford, 1997), 159 n. 60 [+]. The claim of Arr. *Epict. Diss.* 2.22.17 that Alexander instructed the Asklepieia to be burned when Hephaistion died generalizes a story told, but not believed, by Arrian about one particular Asklepieion (*Anab.* 7.14.5). It is difficult to do much with Theocritus's playful allusion to the whipping of Pan by Arcadian boys when portions of meat are small (Theoc. *Id.* 7.106–8).

Can others be found? Paley's second book, the *Natural Theology; or, Evidences of the Existence and Attributes of the Deity, Collected from the Appearances of Nature,* is a presentation of the argument from design. It begins with a famous comparison:

> In crossing a heath, suppose I pitched my foot against a stone, and were asked how the stone came to be there: I might possibly answer, that for any thing I know to the contrary, it had lain there for ever: nor would it perhaps be very easy to show the absurdity of this answer. But suppose I had found a watch upon the ground, and it should be inquired how the watch happened to be in that place; I should hardly think of the answer which I had before given, that for any thing I knew, the watch might have always been there. Yet why should not this answer serve for the watch, as well as for the stone? Why is it not as admissible in the second case as in the first? For this reason, and for no other, viz., that when we come to inspect the watch, we perceive (what we could not discover in the stone) that its several parts are framed and put together for a purpose. . . . The inference we think is inevitable, that the watch must have had a maker.

And exactly the same reasoning applies to the universe as a whole. The ancients had no watches, but from a certain point they certainly had the argument from design: its origins are uncertain, but the phenomenon of providential design is alluded to in several passages in the late fifth century, and the reverse argument (because the world is providentially designed, therefore a provident designer exists) is fully worked out by Socrates in two passages in Xenophon's *Memorabilia*.[8] Thenceforth, "intelligent design" is taken for granted by all philosophers from Plato onward except the Epicureans, who struggle hard to argue against it, and perhaps the Cynics; it forms the core of the Stoic case in Cicero's *De natura deorum,* where a quite close anticipation of the modern image of a "monkey on a typewriter producing the works of Shakespeare" can be found ("If an enormous number of letters were thrown on the ground, could they ever form themselves into the *Annals* of

---

8. Hdt. 3.108.2; Eur. *Supp.* 195–215; Ar. *Thesm.* 13–18; Antiph. *Tetralogy* 3 α 2; ? cf. Critias *TGrF* 43 F 4; Pl. *Prot.* 320C–322E; Xen. *Mem.* 1.4, 4.3. See now D. Sedley, *Creationism and Its Critics in Antiquity* (Berkeley, 2007), chaps. 1–3, who argues, *contra mundum,* that (a) intelligent creation is taken for granted in the pre-Socratic tradition and becomes visible in Anaxagoras and Empedocles (but not, as often assumed, in Diogenes of Apollonia); and (b) it was the historical Socrates who effected the transformation from scientific postulate to theological argument.

Ennius?").[9] In the early mythological cosmogonies, however, the world is not made, but simply happens, and, though in passing allusions the gods may be said to have "made" this or that, there is no elaborated concept of a creator god.[10] One of the central arguments of David Hume's *The Natural History of Religion* is that natural man is not alert to those features of the universe that seem to bespeak designedness; philosophical reflection is required to create such an awareness.[11] That caution is certainly applicable to the Greek case. We cannot allow the argument any very wide diffusion before the fourth century.

Alongside the argument from design, the reality of certain kinds of divination had an important place in Stoic theology, commonly in the form that "since πρόνοια, divine preplanning or care for mankind, exists, the gods must also have granted mortals the possibility of foreknowledge of the future." The reverse form of this argument—since divination exists, so do the gods—may earlier have been an evidence of paganism of some power. A speaker in Xenophon's *Symposium* illustrates the gods' care for him from the guidance they provide through signs of various kinds:

> The gods, whose knowledge and power are absolute, are such friends to me that, because they take care of me, they notice all my doings by both night and day—where I am about to go, what I am about to do; and because they know how every one of these things will turn out, they give me signs, sending as messengers sayings and dreams and omens [literally "birds"], about what I ought to do and what not.[12]

Conversely, when in *Oedipus Tyrannus* Queen Jocasta questions the validity of oracles proceeding from Apollo of Delphi himself (those emanating from human seers are treated as a different matter), the chorus react with horror, and declare, "Religion is perishing" (ἔρρει δὲ τὰ θεῖα). The oracle that finds fulfillment, often in paradoxical ways, despite all human attempts to elude it, is a storytelling motif that was popular throughout antiquity. Such stories were as many proofs that there is a pattern in events visible to

---

9. 2.93. In Plut. *De Pyth. or.* 11, 399E, the Κύριαι Δόξαι of Epicurus are named instead.

10. C. J. Classen, "The Creator in Greek Thought from Homer to Plato," *ClMed* 23 (1962): 1–22.

11. Pp. 27–28 in the edition by A. W. Colver (Oxford, 1976; original 1757). Sedley (2007) argues that it took atomism's explicit postulate of randomness to call forth an explicit statement of the case for design (86).

12. Xen. *Symp.* 4.48; on divination as a benefit, cf. *Mem.* 1.4.14–16, 4.3.12; *Eq. mag.* 9.8–9; *Cyr.* 1.6.46, 8.7.3. Stoics: *SVF* 2.1187–1216. But in Cic. *Nat. D.* 2.7–12 the Stoic Balbus argues from divination to the existence of the gods; cf. Sext. Emp. *Math.* 9.132 (*SVF* 2.1018).

divine intelligence in advance, but to human intelligence only in retrospect.[13] The wise centaur Chiron in Pindar ringingly assures the god of prophecy, Apollo, that:

> You know the appointed end
> of each thing and the ways they are brought to pass;
> and the number of the spring leaves earth blossoms, the number
> of the sands in the seas and the rivers,
> shaken by the waves and the streaming winds; and things to be
> and whence they shall come to pass. All this you know.

And Herodotus stresses that "it is common for there to be signs in advance, when great evils impend for a city or people."[14]

Paley in his *Evidences* was seeking to prove a case. Most of the proofs that I have quoted thus far from Greek authors did not have that function; their authors take the existence of the gods for granted, and the proofs arise unselfconsciously within narratives that have a different purpose. But there are two interesting passages in Herodotus where he explicitly notes that such and such a phenomenon attests the divine thread in events. These passages will help to extend the repertory of evidences.

The first concerns the wrath of Talthybius. When Darius sent heralds to Sparta requesting earth and water, the customary tokens of submission, the Spartans threw them into a well and told them to fetch the earth and water from there. This spirited violation of international law in respect of heralds earned the Spartans the wrath of their own Talthybius, the herald of king Agamemnon who was still honored as a hero in his Spartan homeland and whose descendants still served as heralds in Sparta. Persistent ill omens revealed the hero's anger, and the Spartans appealed for two volunteers to go up to Susa and "pay the penalty to Xerxes for the heralds of Darius who perished in Sparta." But when the two rich and noble volunteers arrived in Susa, Xerxes refused to repay crime with crime or "by killing them release the Spartans from their guilt"; instead he sent them home unharmed. The wrath

---

13. See, e.g., Fontenrose, *Delphic Oracle,* 58–70. Religion perishing: Soph. *OT* 897–910, responding to 707–25, 851–58. Contrast the dismissal of prophecy by human seers at 498–511 (on this distinction cf. Hdt. 2.83).

14. Pind. *Pyth.* 9.44–49, trans. R. Lattimore; Hdt. 6.27.1; cf. 6.98.1, where he infers that a hitherto unexampled earthquake on Delos was a portent of forthcoming evils (Καὶ τοῦτο μέν κου τέρας ἀνθρώποισι τῶν μελλόντων ἔσεσθαι κακῶν ἔφηνε ὁ θεός, where κου is a fine instance of the idiomatic use of that word to make statements about the divine suitably tentative, "doubtless": see J. Wackernagel as cited by Fraenkel in his note on Aesch. *Ag.* 182–83, p. 112).

of Talthybius was allayed for the moment, but "woke up" during the Peloponnesian War. At that time the sons of the two Spartans sent up to Xerxes and released by him were dispatched in their turn to Asia as public messengers, but were betrayed and captured on the way and executed by the Athenians. "This is what seems to me most to show the mark of the gods in the affair. The fact that the wrath of Talthybius struck messengers and did not cease before it found fulfilment is simply what justice required. But the fact that it fell upon the sons of the men who journeyed up to the king because of the wrath makes it clear to me that the event was god-influenced."[15]

What Herodotus here dismisses as "simply what justice required" might in another context have counted as evidence of the efficacy of divine vengeance. But what really reveals the hand of the gods to him in this case is the paradoxical extra twist, the "strange but true" (if not in human terms very obviously just) or "too extraordinary to be coincidental" choice of victims. What is divine is a kind of meaning or pattern, very like that revealed when an oracle finds a paradoxical fulfillment. "SPLENDOUR, IT ALL COHERES," says Heracles (as freely rendered by Ezra Pound) in Sophocles, confronted, fatally, by such a fulfillment.[16]

Herodotus also finds explicit marks of the divine in the circumstances of the battle of Mycale in 479. The battle occurred on the afternoon of the day, the morning of which had seen the victory of Plataea on the other side of the Aegean. Nonetheless, a rumor of the victory at Plataea spread through the Greeks as they advanced at Mycale, bringing them courage, and "a herald's staff was found lying [on the beach] at the tideline." Herodotus takes the heartening (and accurate) rumor as one of "many indicators of the divine element in events," and goes on immediately to note ("it happened that this too was the case") that both battles took place next to sanctuaries of Eleusinian Demeter.[17] Significant coincidence, as seen in the proximity of two sanctuaries of the same goddess, seems here to be one indicator of the divine; another is the spread of news with a speed impossible by ordinary human communication.

---

15. Hdt. 7.133–37; the quotations 7.137.1–2. The phrases rendered above respectively "to show the mark of the gods" and "god-influenced" replace simple forms of θεῖος, the adjective formed from θεός, god: literal renderings would be "This is what seems to me most godly/divine in the affair" and "makes it clear to me that the event was godly/divine." The artificiality of the connection seen by Herodotus (for six Peloponnesian messengers died in all, Thuc. 2.67, and at the hands of the Athenians, not the Persians) is irrelevant to its theological implications.

16. Soph. *Tr.* 1174. "This is the key phrase, for which the play exists," Pound added in a note: *Sophokles: Women of Trachis; A Version by Ezra Pound* (London, 1956), 50.

17. Hdt. 9.100–101.

"A speed impossible by ordinary human communication": Did "miracles" then function for the Greeks, as so significantly for the early Christians, among the evidences for belief? The question requires delicate handling. The text of Herodotus abounds in events that fall outside the humdrum level of everyday causality in a way that suggests to him or at least to a character in his text the involvement of the gods.[18] Some of these events must have represented for Herodotus impossibilities in normal physical terms: fish that come back to life, a great cry emerging from an empty landscape, weapons that move out of a sanctuary of their own accord. Others are merely improbabilities: when the Cnidian workers attempting to channel through their isthmus suffered an abnormal number of eye injuries from chips of stone, they consulted an oracle, and learned that Zeus would have made Cnidus an island had he wished it to be one. The Cnidians judged the level of injury "beyond what was to be expected," and the oracle confirmed their view; but the criterion here is a fuzzy one, not a rigorously defined law of nature.[19] Alongside these physically impossible or implausible events we find what one might term the morally implausible occurrence in which the wrath of Talthybius was embodied. It was not a breach or even a bending of the laws of nature that the two men sent up into Asia and killed were the sons of the two men earlier sent up into Asia and released; it was a meaningful event that revealed the slow and oblique working of divine justice.

Three elements stand out in the language Herodotus uses in these contexts. Sometimes he describes such occurrences as a "wonder," θῶμα,[20] sometimes as a "portent," τέρας (but he would scarcely have described, for instance, the events relating to Talthybius's wrath as a portent); sometimes, as we have seen, he speaks of there being "something divine" about them. But they are not brought together into a single class of "miracles." There is no Greek word for "miracle," and the word is absent because the concept is absent. Instead of miracles, we have a range of unusual occurrences that may have a divine origin.

The closest equivalent to a catalog of miracles surviving from classical Greece is the late fourth-century temple record of Epidaurus.[21] Here we

18. See Harrison, *Divinity and History*, 64–101; for the kind of everyday, untheorized conception of natural laws that is relevant here, cf. Lloyd, *Magic, Reason and Experience*, 50–51. J. Shaw, *Miracles in Enlightenment England* (New Haven, 2006) is a lively introduction to later debate.

19. 9.120.1–2 (fish); 8.65.1 (cry); 8.37.1–2 (weapons); 1.174.3–5 (Cnidians).

20. 6.117.2, 8.37.2, 8.135.1, 9.65.2; for τέρας see the entry in J. E. Powell, *A Lexicon to Herodotus* (Cambridge, 1938).

21. *IG* 4² 1.121–24; for trans. see RO 102 (*stele* 1 only); Edelstein and Edelstein, *Asclepius*, vol. 1, T 423 (*stelai* 1 and 2 only); L. R. LiDonnici, *The Epidaurian Miracle Inscriptions: Text, Translation and Commentary* (Atlanta, 1995). Other sanctuaries displayed similar inscriptions: Strabo 8.6.15, 374

read, for instance, how Asclepius restored sight to a person so blind that the organ of sight itself, the eye, was missing; we are told that skeptical bystanders had initially shared our assumption that such a cure was not merely unlikely but impossible. Like many miracle stories, this story and others similar to it in the same inscription have the specific function of demonstrating the power of the wonder-worker; they are a product of the fervid special atmosphere of a healing cult. But even the most miraculous cures worked by Asclepius are not "miracles"; they are simply some among his many "cures" (the title of the inscription), of very varied character.

In contrast to "miracle," a concept that the Greeks were certainly familiar with is "epiphany." From the third century BC onward there existed as a minor literary genre the collected Epiphanies of a god or goddess.[22] The noun "epiphany" first appears in the relevant sense in the third century, when the minor literary genre too emerges, and quickly becomes common and important; it can indicate not merely a visible or audible epiphany (whether in the light of day or through a dream; whether of the god in its own form or in human form or through its statue—the modalities are extremely numerous[23]) but also any clear expression of a god's favor such as weather conditions hampering an enemy, a miraculous escape, or a cure; it may also be used of the continuing disposition or capacity of a god or goddess to offer manifest assistance. But epiphanies as a phenomenon antedated the creation of the noun "epiphany," the most famous perhaps being that of the god Pan to the message runner Philippides in Arcadia in 490 BC; what happened in the third century was a formal recognition of the concept, which so acquired new potential and importance,[24] but not its creation ex nihilo.

Many stories of sightings of supernatural powers circulated before that: to take only a handful from Herodotus, giant warriors might lend aid in a battle line, the "phantom of a woman" might by contrast reproach mortal warriors

testifies it for Cos and Tricca, and a fragment survives from Lebena in Crete (*IC* 1.17.7, 9–16; Melfi, *Lebena,* appendix 1, nos. 10–19; an extract at Edelstein and Edelstein, vol. 1, T 426); cf. M. Girone, Ἰάματα: *Guarigioni miracolose di Asclepio in testi epigrafici* (Bari, 1998: non vidi). Fervid atmosphere: R. Herzog, *Die Wunderheilungen von Epidauros* (Leipzig, 1931), 59–64, rightly denying that the phenomenon is primarily one of priestly propaganda.

22. Istros *FGrH* 334 F 50–52, *Epiphanies of Apollo;* ibid. 53, *Epiphanies of Heracles; IPE* 1² 344 = Syriskos *FGrH* 807 F 1, *Epiphanies of the Maiden of the Cherronesos* (for a later epiphany of this goddess see *Syll.*³ 709.23–25); later, a section of the Lindian Chronicle is headed "epiphanies" (*FGrH* 532 D).

23. See H. S. Versnel, "What Did Ancient Man See When He Saw a God?" in *Effigies Dei: Essays on the History of Religions,* ed. D. van der Plas, 42–55 (Leiden, 1987).

24. Cf. H. S. Versnel, *Ter Unus* (Leiden, 1990), 190–91: "miracles" and epiphanies had always been noted, but only came to be systematically deployed as proofs of divine power from the late fourth century. Philippides: Hdt. 6.105.

for their cowardly behavior, a hero might assume the form of a mortal in order to impregnate a mortal woman, a goddess disguised as a woman might transform an ugly little girl into a radiant beauty....[25] For most individuals, epiphanies were a matter of report, which they might or not believe, rather than of personal experience, but the same is true of many religious phenomena, such as exemplary stories of wickedness punished. Herodotus believes that the Athenians accepted the reality of Philippides' experience, and founded a cult on its basis. An inscription of 39 BC from Stratonicea in Caria records the interventions of Zeus Panamaros (through mist, thunder, and the like) that repelled an invading force without a single Stratonicean life being lost. What is most remarkable about this text is that the pious narrative is embedded within a decree of the assembly (though the actual decision is lost): since the god gave aid in all these ways, therefore...[26]

Have we really got to the bottom of the matter with the four or five evidences so far identified? At a psychological level a further motive must have been powerful, though only with difficulty could it be formulated as an explicit argument. Put explicitly in its simplest form, it becomes absurd: "the gods exist because we worship them." But in an outburst of majestic indignation in the *Laws*, rumbling throughout a sentence that lasts more than 175 words, Plato says something very similar.

> How one can argue that the gods exist without getting angry? It's inevitable to resent and hate the people who have forced us and still force us to make this argument, people who will not accept the stories which from the time they were little children at the breast they heard from nurses and mothers, stories told both playfully and seriously as a kind of soothing charm—stories which they also heard in prayers accompanying sacrifices, while at the same time seeing sights accompanying them such as a child most loves to see and hear being

---

25. Hdt. 8.38–39, 8.84.2, 6.69.1–3, 6.61. For epiphany as an argument for the existence of gods see Cic. *Nat. D.* 2.6 *praesentes saepe di vim suam declarant*. On epiphany see F. Pfister, *RE Supp.* 4 (1924): 277–323; W. K. Pritchett, *The Greek State at War* (Berkeley, 1979), 3:11–46 (military epiphanies—a huge category); Lane Fox, *Pagans and Christians,* 102–67; Versnel, 1987 in n. 23; Harrison, *Divinity and History,* 82–92; F. Graf, *ICS* 29 (2004): 111–27, and M. Dickie, ibid., 159–82. Graf argues that, whereas individuals see gods in person, epiphanies experienced by a group tend, as first identified, to occur through natural processes (such as the incident at Stratonicea mentioned in the text), though narrative elaboration may follow. Dickie analyzes culturally prescribed responses to supposed epiphanies (some already seen in Hom. *Od.* 3.371–84).

26. *IStraton.* 10. Philippides: Hdt. 6. 105. For the possibility that the Athenians' belief was reinforced by a second, military intervention of Pan, see S. Hornblower, "Epic and Epiphanies," in *The New Simonides,* ed. D. Boedeker and D. Sider, 135–47 (Oxford, 2001), at 143–45.

performed at a sacrifice—and their own parents showing the most intense earnestness for their well-being and their children's, addressing the gods with prayers and supplications as beings who most certainly exist, and seeing and hearing the prostrations and supplications as sun and moon rise and set of Greeks and barbarians without exception both in crises of all kinds and in good times, not as if the gods don't exist but as if they most certainly do and allow not even a hint of a suspicion that they don't: when dealing with people who scorn all this for no good reason at all—as people with even a grain of good sense would say—and force us to argue as we are now arguing, how can one adopt a gentle tone in correcting these people and teaching them, first of all, that the gods exist?[27]

The Stoics too tried to use the reality of "piety" (εὐσέβεια), "respectful behavior" (ὁσιότης), and cult practice as an argument for the reality of "gods"; in its most concrete (perhaps parodied?) form, "because there are altars, the gods exist," this argument proved a ready target for Cynic scorn.[28] But the motive may have been effective psychologically however weak it was logically. The thought can have two forms, one more inert, one more dynamic. The inert form is that the endless rituals, with whatever indifference they are performed, carve a channel in the mind, like water in a rock. Cult is too omnipresent a feature of how things are for the possibility that it has no object to make sense. The more dynamic form is that some rituals for some worshippers created a sense of contact with the divine. One knows that the gods exist because one feels their presence during the drama of the mysteries or the elation of the choral dance.

These evidences have been garnered from a variety of remarks made en passant by writers with different concerns. But the attempt to prove the existence of gods eventually entered the philosophical agenda and brought with

---

27. Pl. *Leg.* 887C–888A. One might compare Polybius's description (4.20.8) of Arcadians performing hymns and paeans to their local gods and heroes from earliest childhood.

28. Sext. Emp. *Adv. Math.* 9.123–24 = *SVF* 2.1017 (εὐσέβεια and ὁσιότης: cf. Zeno's argument that gods can be "reasonably" [εὐλόγως] honored, ibid. 133, *SVF* I 152); *SVF* 2.1019 (altars, an argument attributed to Chrysippus by the Aristotelian commentator Themistius); Cynic mockery: Lucian *Hermotimos* 70, *Zeus Tragoedus* 51. The argument from the facts of cult plays a multiple role in Carneades' soritic arguments against Stoic rationalized theology in Sext. Emp. *Adv. Math.* 9.182–90 and, still more, Cic. *Nat. D.* 3.43–52 (cf. chap. 3 n. 84), in a way that might seem to suggest that Stoics had deployed it not only to show that gods exist but also to determine their character. But the unacceptable consequences extracted from it by Carneades (unhealthy passions such as love and pity are gods; barbarian theriomorphic gods are gods) are so obvious that it is hard to believe the Stoics would not have anticipated them.

it the attempt to analyze the origins of human belief in the gods. The Stoic Cleanthes identified four such sources: the reality of divination; the "greatness of the benefits which derive from the balance of the climate, the fertility of the earth, and the abundance of numerous other advantages"; the fear caused by thunderbolts, storms, plagues, portents, and like phenomena; and fourth and greatest, the splendor of the cosmic order. (The first, second, and fourth of these sources of belief would also have constituted for a Stoic valid grounds for belief; most philosophical theologians would have added the agreement of mankind, throughout time and space, that gods exist.)[29]

The emphasis in Cleanthes' list differs somewhat from the one attempted above. The argument from cosmic order and design has a prominence that, we have noted, it acquired only in the fourth century. Cleanthes' mortals are very passive vis-à-vis the gods, mere recipients of benefits conferred or terrors inflicted by them; he neglects the way in which cult practice, the mortal's relation with the divine, the answered prayer, might reinforce belief. His mortals experience gratitude and fear, but not the moral satisfaction of seeing piety rewarded and villainy brought low. (But perhaps he does well to give fear its place.)[30] We can, however, surely endorse his founding assumption that any Greek challenged to adduce evidences for divinity would have looked for them in experience (his own, and the reported experience of others), in the workings of the world in the here and now. The Greeks traced the origins of most of their rituals to the distant past. But the point was that the efficacy acquired then was still operating in the present.

Oracular Revelation

None of these evidences was of a character to reveal very much about the nature, wishes, or disposition of the gods: they display their power, but beyond that they show little more than that the gods reward the pious, chastise the impious, and protect communities that pay them due honors. How then could Greeks acquire more accurate information? At a global level, one embracing the totality of potential divine powers as laid out, for instance, in Hesiod's *Theogony,* the answer is, rather simply, that they could not. Hesiod claims that he is inspired

---

29. Cleanthes: Cic. *Nat. D.* 2.13–15 (*SVF* 1.528). Agreement of mankind: e.g., Cic. *Nat. D.* 1.43–44 (space); ibid. 2.5 (time).

30. *Primus in orbe deos fecit timor,* "Fear first created gods in the world" (opening of a poem of Petronius, xxvii Buecheler = *Anth. Lat.* 466 Riese, 464 Shackleton Bailey; quoted in Stat. *Theb.* 3.661): one-sided, but not wholly wrong.

by the Muses, but, even if we believe his claim, he also tells us that the Muses themselves admit to "knowing how to speak many lies that resemble the truth," as well as the truth itself.[31] Every listener could observe that different poets claiming inspiration from the Muses might give differing accounts. But the impossibility of acquiring a dependable *summa theologiae* led to no epistemological crisis. "Ancestral traditions, coeval with time"[32] prescribed in a general way the forms of cult with which individual gods were honored. Particular problems thrown up by changing circumstances could be dealt with by consultation of an oracle; many examples will be cited in appendix 1.

Such ad hoc consultation of oracles about cultic matters was of fundamental importance for the whole Greek religious system. It is a seldom-noted exception to the proposition that revelation has no place in Greek religion: revelation of the divine will is precisely what an oracular response provides, though only in relation to the very specific question presented to the god. One of the earliest sacred laws prefaces its prescriptions with "(the) god decreed" (θεὸς ἔπεν): in answer, we can safely assume, to an inquiry.[33] It was possible to check that particular cultic innovations were satisfactory to the gods, or that they were being adequately tended in other ways. After the Greek victory in 480, the Greeks asked Apollo of Delphi whether the spoils sent to him "were full and pleasing"; the god was generally satisfied but requested a little more from the Aeginetans. Communities could also pose rather vague questions such as "by sacrificing and praying to what god or hero they might inhabit their city best and most safely and have fair harvests and abundant harvests and enjoyment of the good harvest."[34] Inquiries of this kind invited, and often received, the instruction to introduce the cult of a new god or an existing god under a new epithet; gods introduced in these circumstances might bear the epithet "ordained at Delphi." Such advice to a community provided a reassurance that its cultic arrangements would be, that adjustment having been made, in good order.

---

31. Hes. *Theog.* 26–28.

32. Eur. *Bacch.* 201; cf. Hes. fr. 322 M/W ap. Porph. *Abst.* 2.18.3, νομὸς δ᾽ἀρχαῖος ἄρισ-τος. On tradition see, e.g., the texts cited by Rudhardt, *Essai,* 99, or Mikalson, *Athenian Popular Religion,* 95–98.

33. *LSA* 42, Miletus, c. 500. Seldom-noted: see, however, Rudhardt, *Essai,* 66; the point is also stressed in J. D. Mikalson, *Greek Popular Religion in Greek Philosophy* (Oxford 2010), 139–39. Rudhardt (*Essai and RHR* 209 [1992]: 231–32) contrasts Greek religion as based on "inspiration" (poets, oracles)—an inspiration that is partial and can always be supplemented—with religions based on revelation, which is final and total. The point about the partiality of Greek revelation is well-taken, but he overvalues poets by assimilating their authority to that of oracles.

34. Lhôte, *Lamelles oraculaires,* 2; cf. 1, 4, 5, 7; there are many similar private inquiries, e.g., 8. "Ordained at Delphi" (πυθόχρηστος): p. 265 n. 2 below. 480: Hdt. 8.122.

Psychologically, it is hard to imagine how the Greeks could have lived their religion without this control, this narrow window of revelation. No human body was empowered to provide reassurance or to legitimate change in the same way. But the window was narrow, and no attempts were made to broaden it until the second century AD. Perhaps around the year 200 Apollo of Claros was asked, "Who or what is god?" or something similar (another version, or perhaps another question, runs delightfully, "Are you god or is someone else?"); his answer or part of it survives written on a wall in Oenoanda.[35] To anyone who has perused the records of oracular consultation of the previous eight hundred or so years, that question and others like it from the same period mark an astonishing break with tradition. By inviting the oracular god to pronounce on the very nature of godhead, they violate one of the unwritten laws of consultation. Oracles as traditionally understood were not there for that, but to adjudicate particular problems of cult practice. One needed to know how to worship the gods in ways pleasing to them; one did not need to know precisely what those gods were like. The ability to carry on without such knowledge was a defining characteristic of this untheological religion.[36] But the Greeks believed that their practices had a secure foundation and were even in a certain sense based on revelation. In a remarkable passage of *Laws* Plato writes that

> whether one is founding a new city from scratch or restoring a cor-
> rupted old one, in the matter of what gods and shrines should be estab-
> lished by each group and what gods or spirits (δαίμονες) the shrines
> should be named in honor of, no one with any sense will alter what
> has come from Delphi or Dodona or Ammon, or been occasioned
> by stories of old—however these stories convinced people, whether
> on the basis of apparitions or a report of divine inspiration; since they
> were convincing, men established blends of sacrifices and rites whether

35. See Lane Fox, *Pagans and Christians,* 168–77, 191–96, building on L. Robert, *CRAI* (1968): 568–99 and (the Oenoanda inscription) *CRAI* (1971): 597–619 (together = Robert, *OMS* 5, 584–639); the text is now *Steinepigramme,* vol. 4, 17/06/01; cf. R. Merkelbach and J. Stauber, *Epigraphica Anatolica* 27 (1996): 41–45 (arguing for multiple questions and responses). The supposed inquiry of Apollophanes the Arcadian (otherwise unknown) to Apollo whether Asclepius was a son of Arsi-noe and so a fellow citizen of the Messenians (Paus. 2.26.7) is very unusual, even if a forgery (so Fontenrose, *Delphic Oracle,* 324, dating it "c. 350–300": *LGPN* 3A has Apollophanes "? 370 B.C."). The question put to Sarapis by Nicocreon, king of Cyprus, as to "which god he was" (Macrob. *Sat.* 1.20.16–17) is surely not genuine.

36. A religious psychologist, J. H. Leuba, quoted by W. R. James, *The Varieties of Religious Experience* (London, 1902), 506, maintained that, in religious experience in general, "God is not known, he is not understood; he is used."

native or Etruscan or Cypriot or from any other source whatsoever, and on the strength of these reports they consecrated oracles (?) and statues and altars and temples, and furnished each of these with precincts.[37]

None of all this, Plato insists, should be altered in the slightest. For Plato, then, tradition ultimately rests on communication from the gods, whether that came through oracles or through visual or auditory epiphany. This may be an exaggeration of popular assumptions, but it is not a travesty of them.

The Role of Books

This chapter started from Ibn Khaldûn's distinction between religions that are guided by a sacred book and those that are not. What is at issue is not the book as an item in the technology of communication, but the specific authority assigned to certain books, their power to validate religious practice and belief. For the Greeks, as we have just seen, such validation came partly from tradition, partly from the limited revelation provided by specific oracular responses. But texts that spoke of the gods of course existed in Greece—the poems of Homer and Hesiod, for instance; and, in addition to specific texts with a more or less fixed form, there were all the stories that we bundle together under the rubric of "myth." The relevance to Greek religion of all these texts and stories must now be addressed.

A first observation is easily made.[38] The religion of the Greek cities derived its authority from tradition; one function of written texts was as an alternative source of authority for religious practices that could not appeal to "the custom of the city" for their validation. The classic illustration of this point is a passage in *Republic* where Plato speaks disapprovingly of begging priests and seers (ἀγύρται καὶ μάντεις) who go to the doors of the rich and "present a hubbub of books of Musaeus and Orpheus, offspring of the Moon and the Muses, as they say, in accord with which they conduct sacrifice" (364E). Plato's phrase "by which they conduct sacrifice" is helpful because it isolates

---

37. Pl. *Leg.* 738B–C (cf. *Epin.* 985C). "Oracles": φῆμαι of the mss. is so taken by editors and translators and now by the 1996 supplement to LSJ, but in the one parallel quoted, Eur. *Hel.* 820, the word can comfortably be understood as "voice." I suspect corruption.

38. See Burkert, *Mystery Cults,* 70–72; R. Baumgarten, *Heiliges Wort und heilige Schrift bei den Griechen* (Tübingen, 1998); A. Henrichs, "*Hieroi Logoi* and *Hierai Bibloi:* The (Un)Written Margin of the Sacred in Ancient Greece," *HSCP* 101 (2003): 207–66; Henrichs in *Written Texts and the Rise of Literate Culture in Ancient Greece,* ed. H. Yunis, 38–58 (Cambridge, 2003); Graf and Johnston, *Ritual Texts,* 175–84.

so precisely a form of ritual unknown in public cult: sacrifices there were never conducted "in accord with" any book. The "books" of Orpheus and Musaeus (but "books" of what scale?—we would perhaps call them booklets or pamphlets) are pseudonymous poems ascribed to them, and the claim of the "collectors and seers" will have been that these, the greatest singers of the legendary period, did indeed possess inspired insight into divine matters.

Euripides' Theseus, too, in *Hippolytus* contemptuously accuses his step-son Hippolytus of a hypocritical involvement with Orphic rites that in-volved "honoring the smoke of many books." Similarly, Demosthenes paints a scornful picture of the young Aeschines acting as assistant to his mother in her shady ritual activities and "reading out the books for her as she per-formed initiations." The attempt to reconstruct real ritual activities from Demosthenes' description is a hopeless task, because we have no control on the extent to which he has exaggerated, combined, and distorted; but for our purposes the central point remains that he is making these rites out to be as disreputable as possible, and so gives the book a prominent place. The question "what was this book?" is unanswerable for the reason just given, but, if one asks what kind of thought Demosthenes was seeking to implant in his hearers' minds, the answer will doubtless be not "Rituals for Sabazius: A Practical Guide" but, again, a supposedly inspired writing by some an-cient sage: the book's function will have been to provide not instruction, but authentication.[39]

There survives a papyrus decree issued by one of the Ptolemies, prob-ably Ptolemy IV, ordering all those who performed initiations for Dionysus in Egypt to present their "sacred accounts," ἱεροὶ λόγοι, to an official in Alexandria for control and authentication. The text is as problematic as it is important, and it is not even agreed that these "sacred accounts" are religious texts at all, as opposed to accounts in the financial sense relating to the cult. But the majority view is that they are sacred writings, and the remarkable implication follows that in Egypt any Dionysus-initiator owned such a sacred account as an indispensable part of his equipment. Our ignorance of these rites of Dionysus is very deep, but again we are clearly not dealing with civic cult but with wandering initiators. Only disreputable priests need books. We may assume that the contents of all such books were jealously guarded by their owners.[40]

---

39. Eur. *Hipp.* 952–54; Dem. 18.259. For the oddity in Greek eyes of book-guided rituals, see Paus. 5.27.6; a sacrifice over which a "theogony" is recited is odd too, Hdt. 1.132.3.

40. *BGU* 1211 (= the Loeb *Select Papyri,* vol. 2, ed. A. S. Hunt and C. C. Edgar, no. 208; Graf and Johnston, *Ritual Texts,* 189–90), on which see A. Henrichs, *HSCP* 101 (2003): 224–31.

A similar contrast applies in relation to divination. Apollo's priestess at Delphi pronounced the god's will orally in answer to an oral question, though in public inquiries the answer was often then written down in order to be transmitted back to the city reliably. At Dodona writing intruded into the consultative process, because questions were often written and apparently answered on lead tablets, of which many survive; but the answer was deemed to derive directly from the mind of the god, not from a book.[41] Another popular form of divination in cities was that provided by *chrēsmologoi*, oracle-speakers or oracle-collectors. They seem mostly to have worked with collections of oracles ascribed to ancient figures such as Musaeus or Bakis or Glanis, and the "book" was fundamental to their practice. A delightful scene in Aristophanes' *Birds* shows a *chrēsmologos* reciting impossibly self-serving oracles to the hero, and urging him repeatedly when he expresses doubt to "take the book" and see for himself. The *chrēsmologoi* are a good example of the inseparability of written and oral, because they did not merely read out but actually performed their oracles: "oracle-singers," *chrēsmōdoi*, is another word for them. The written text was a fallback, but an essential one: the authority of these oracles was that of Musaeus and Bakis who supposedly first uttered them, and it was the written text that permitted the claim that the actual words of these ancient seers were still accessible. It is a traditional mistake to apply the derogatory mistranslation "oracle-mongers" to the *chrēsmologoi* and to treat them as inherently disreputable or marginal. They had much more of a role in Athenian public life than, say, Orpheus initiators did, and the *chrēsmologos* Hierocles was an influential figure. All the same, an oracle specially sought out and brought back from Zeus or Apollo at Dodona or Delphi had an authority that an oracle sung by a *chrēsmologos* lacked: the latter might or might not influence opinion, whereas the former was truly authoritative. The book shored up the authority of *chrēsmologoi*, but with imperfect success.[42]

Books are never mentioned in connection with the Eleusinian Mysteries, and this absence seems to have been the norm for mystery cults that had fixed locations. Two exceptions, however, must be noted, one certainly falling into the class of "exceptions that prove the rule," the other perhaps an authentic exception. (Of a third too little is known to invite discussion.[43]) The exception

---

41. Delphic responses written: e.g., Hdt. 7.142.1, and evidently at Sparta, Hdt. 6.57.4. Dodona: Lhôte, *Lamelles oraculaires,* passim.

42. On *chrēsmologoi* see references given p. 47 n. 20 below. The scene in Ar. *Av.* is 959–91.

43. In connection with the Mysteries of Demeter and Dionysus at Lerna, Pausanias reports (2.37.3) the brilliant proof by his contemporary Arriphon that the "writings on the heart of oreichalc" were not written by the supposed founder, Philammon. That gives no clue as to their content or actual date. On the pretension refuted by Arriphon, see Pirenne-Delforge, *Pausanias,* 300–301.

that proves the rule concerns the Mysteries of the Great Gods (or Goddesses) at Andania in Messenia. The rites still practiced in Pausanias's day were supposedly those brought thither from Eleusis in mythical time by Caucon. But the problem was to explain how there could be continuity between the rites of the Hellenistic period and those established by Caucon, given that for much of the intervening period Messenian culture had been blotted out by the Spartan conquest. The answer was that, with defeat in the second Messenian war impending, the national hero Aristomenes had recorded the rites on tin tablets and buried them; these tablets were rediscovered, with divine aid, at the liberation of Messene in the fourth century and transcribed by priests into books.[44] Writing is here an indispensable postulate in order to preserve the fiction of continuity. And, as usual, its function is not practical, but one of validation.

The exception that may be a true one is that of the Mysteries of Demeter Eleusinia at Pheneai in Arcadia. Pausanias writes:

> Beside the shrine of Demeter Eleusinia is the so-called "Stone building," two big stones fitted against one another. Every second year when they celebrate what they call the Great Rite they open these stones. They remove certain writings that relate to the rite and read them in the hearing of the initiates; then they deposit them again the same night. (Paus. 8.15.1–2)

What the books contained we are not told. The mundane view that they listed rules to be observed by the initiates would render them unremarkable—they would become merely a sacred law of familiar type in an unusual medium—but scarcely seems to fit the ceremonial solemnity with which they are treated.[45] They should have contained either a secret myth or instructions for the conduct

---

44. Paus. 4.1.5 (Caucon); 4.20.1–4 (burial); 4.26 (recovery); cf. N. Deshours, *Les Mystères d'Andania* (Bordeaux, 2006), 191–95. The books mentioned in the long inscription of 91 BC relating to these mysteries (*LSCG* 65.12) are very likely to be the same: so Baumgarten, 1998, 128, and Deshours, 2006, 73–75, 121. Cf. in general W. Speyer, *Bücherfindung in der Glaubenswerbung der Antike* (Göttingen, 1970).

45. So Jost, *Arcadie*, 319. Note, however, the "written tablet, containing matters relating to the rite" (πινάκιον γεγραμμένον, ἔχον τὰ ἐς τὴν τελετήν, Paus. 8.37.2) on public display in the sanctuary of Despoina at Lycosoura and perhaps identical (but Jost, *Arcadie*, 329, has doubts) with the sacred law *LSCG* 68. Pausanias's language in the two cases is very similar. A. Henrichs, *HSCP* 101 (2003): 243, raises the possibility that the book "contained the *hieros logos* that explained the bean prohibition" attested in the cult (Paus. 8.15.4). Nilsson, *Griechische Feste*, 344, treats a written text used in mysteries as proof of a (Hellenistic or later?) reform. Note, however, that an Oscan ritual text relating to the cult of Ceres was found between two large stones as in the installation described by Pausanias: H. Rix, *Sabellische Texte: Die Texte des Oskischen, Umbrischen, und Südpikenischen* (Heidelberg, 2002), 82, Sa 1; for the find context, F. S. Cremonese, *Bullettino dell' Instituto* (1848): 145–51 (*non vidi*: I owe the reference to Michael Crawford).

of a ritual of very unusual kind. Perhaps here, exceptionally, the fixity of a written text was held to out-trump oral tradition in prestige even in a cult that professed to go straight back uninterruptedly to mythical times. But the Pheneates maintained, according to Pausanias, that their mysteries were a replica of those of Eleusis, introduced by one Naos, a descendant in the third generation of the primeval Eleusinian Eumolpos. Possibly, then, the writings claimed to be the mechanism by which sacred lore was transferred by Naos from Eleusis to Pheneai. They would then be an equivalent, mutatis mutandis, to the tin tablets of Aristomenes.

Whatever the truth about that particular case, the general proposition that texts had no direct place in the conduct of the vast majority of Greek rituals is unaffected. When, in the Hellenistic period, the city of Priene established a public cult of Sarapis, there was no question of conducting the ritual in accord with books: the priest had to supply a live Egyptian to perform the rites with the proper expertise. We do not know whether the most famous of all Greek priestesses, that Lysimache who conducted the rites of Athena Polias on the acropolis at Athens for sixty-four years, was able to read: what is clear is that she had no need of that skill to discharge her high function—except possibly to deal with temple accounts.[46] In the rare cases where an inscribed "sacred law" gives instructions for the conduct of a ritual, a special explanation is usually available. As far as we can see, it is not that the traditional guardians of sacred lore, like Caesar's Druids and the early Roman aristocracy, actively resisted the use of writing in order to keep their special knowledge exclusive.[47] The cultural convention simply followed a different channel.

Where Myths Were Told

A further wedge can be driven between texts and religious practice. Poems that described the doings of the gods were, it is not in doubt, extremely common in Greece: the lack of sacred texts by no means entails a lack of

---

46. Egyptian: *LSA* 36 (*RICIS* 304/0802). Accounts: Lycurgus fr. 31 Blass (6.4 Conomis), from "On the Priestess," reveals that the priestess in question was required by decree to "join in sealing the account-books (?)" (συσσημαίνεσθαι τὰ γραμματεῖα). The probable priestess Menophila of Sardis was praised on her funerary inscription for her literacy (*Steinepigramme* vol. 1, 04/02/11, late second century BC?; Connelly, Portrait of a *Priestess*, 251–52), but without any connection being drawn with priestly functions.

47. Special explanation: cf. R. Parker, "Epigraphy and Greek Religion," in *Epigraphy and the Historical Sciences*, ed. J. K. Davies and J. J. Wilkes, forthcoming in the *Proceedings of the British Academy*. Traditional guardians: Livy 9.46.5, with the commentary of S. P. Oakley (2005, 609–13); Caes. *Bell. Gall.* 6.14.3–4.

texts treating sacred matters. Hesiod's *Theogony* and the Homeric Hymns are the most tangible representatives of the whole large class. But the context in which such poems were recited needs to be noted. It is widely accepted that Hesiod's *Theogony* is the poem that he himself in *Works and Days* (654–57) says that he performed at the funeral games for King Amphidamas in Chalkis. The performance context of the Homeric Hymns is uncertain, but it is not at all clear that we can assign the *Hymn to Hermes,* for instance, to a festival of Hermes, the *Hymn to Apollo* to a festival of Apollo, and so on systematically; some at least seem to belong in the kind of rhapsodic contests where epic was performed.[48] So here we have religious poetry performed in a festival context but without any direct relation to ritual; tragedy too is a genre shot through with religious content and performed at a festival, but not in immediate association with the cult acts.

As for the telling of myths as part of the ritual activity at festivals, the only regular mechanism that can be identified is the choral performance of hymns, paeans, and the like. This was indeed both common and important; its significance, as the central point of intersection between myth and ritual, has been greatly underestimated in the debate on the relation between those two things.[49] But not all festivals included choral performances. At one, the Attic Oschophoria, we happen to be told that at a certain stage in the proceedings the participants told each other myths.[50] The detail is isolated, and even here it is not priests or priestesses who do the telling. The idea of an Attic priest or priestess recounting myths to the faithful is just as unfamiliar as the idea of their using books in the conduct of ritual. At the Panathenaea a robe was presented to Athena on which was depicted that Battle of the Gods and Giants in which she played a conspicuous role.[51] But parallels are not easy to find for such an active deployment of visually depicted mythology in ritual.

Mysteries perhaps represent a special case; for one of their distinctive features seems to have been that communication of some kind took place between initiators and initiates; and though, at Eleusis at least, the central medium of

---

48. On this problem see my comments in *GaR* 38 (1991): 1–2.

49. Cf. W. D. Furley, "Praise and Persuasion in Greek Hymns," *JHS* 115 (1995): 29–46, at p. 46: "Hieratic texts point to the unity of purpose between tales about the gods and worship of the gods through ritual which the myth-and-ritual school of religious interpretation has always assumed." This is a central argument of Kowalzig, *Singing.*

50. Plut. *Thes.* 23.4. Whether the statement of Σ Lucian p. 280.25–29 Rabe that at the Attic Haloa the magistrates spend time "displaying (ἐπιδεικνύμενοι) to all the visitors that civilized food was first discovered among them and shared out to all mankind from them" implies a formal speech (on myth?) is very doubtful: Parker, *Polytheism,* 167, n. 45 (citing Lowe).

51. Cf. p. 201 n. 104.

communication was "showing," not "telling," some element of telling can perhaps not be ruled out. On the one occasion where Herodotus speaks of a "sacred story" or "sacred account" (ἱερὸς λόγος) in relation to a Greek cult,[52] he says, rather ambiguously, that a ἱερὸς λόγος that was "told by the Pelasgians" is now "revealed" in the Samothracian Mysteries (2.51.4). We hear of "sacred stories" or similar things in relation to mysteries rather than to ordinary cults simply, it has been suggested, because in these cases rules of secrecy applied: stories about origins were regularly told in relation to all cults, but could normally be mentioned freely.[53] The point is true, but its correlate seems to be that the myths attached to ordinary cults were not formally recounted by priests as a part of the ceremony. It was the special secrecy attaching to mysteries that required associated myths (or some of the associated myths, for not all were secret) to be sucked in and incorporated in the ceremony itself.

There is a sense then in which myth and ritual occupied a different *Sitz im Leben*. There were many festivals at which no space was available for the explicit evocation of myth;[54] equally, many of the most important contexts in which myths were re-performed, the theater above all, were not directly connected to ritual. Many of the words that were most relevant to Greek festivals and Greek rituals were spoken outside the festival and ritual context.

Myth and Religion

Few subjects have been more contested than the relation of Greek myth to Greek religion.[55] In the eighteenth and nineteenth centuries many scholars saw myth as the main medium through which Greek religious ideas were expressed: the study of Greek religion was therefore the study of the gods

---

52. He mentions Egyptian ἱεροὶ λόγοι in 2.48.3, 2.62.2, and 2.81.2, and the plain λόγος of 2.47.2 is clearly no different. He never recounts them, not apparently because they were told him as secrets, but perhaps as Harrison suggests (*Divinity and History*, 189; see ibid., 184–86 for other religious silences in book 2) because these stories were comparable to those recounted in Greek mysteries. Pausanias twice borrows the concept: the Phleiasians (2.13.4) have a ἱερὸς λόγος as to why their cult of Hebe lacks a statue, and the Pheneatai (8.15.4) as to why they regard the bean as impure. The context of this last reference is one of Mysteries of Demeter; the Phleiasian λογός is the only usage relating to a Greek nonmystic cult.

53. W. Burkert, in *Oxford Readings*, 228, n. 5. Graf and Johnston, *Ritual Texts*, 182, argue that ἱεροὶ λόγοι were normally standard myths with added elements, not wholly new myths.

54. "La Grecia antica non ci ha lasciato un solo mito in un contesto rituale": Brelich, *Eroi*, 35.

55. See especially Versnel, *Transition and Reversal*, 15–88; E. Csapo, *Theories of Mythology* (Oxford, 2005), 132–80. The extent to which the Greeks ever recognized a distinctive class of myths comparable to the "Greek myths" familiar to us is controversial (for a denial see, e.g., C. Calame, *Myth and History in Ancient Greece*, trans. D. W. Berman [Princeton, 2003], 12–27; R. L. Fowler will argue the other case in a forthcoming article, "Mythos, Logos, Herodotos"); the point is irrelevant to my concerns here.

as represented in mythology. With growing interest in ritual, the pendulum swung from myth to cult at the end of the nineteenth century. Myth reclaimed some of its rights with the argument of the "myth and ritual" school that rituals were reflected or interpreted or paralleled in myths, even if in this conception ritual tended to be the master and myth the servant. A compromise position was that myths and rituals were distinct but parallel phenomena, fulfilling comparable functions in different media.[56] One stepping-stone within the quagmire is to recognize that "Greek myths" are not a unified category about which we have any reason to expect that general statements can be made. We are not confronted by all-or-nothing choices; by allowing that some myths have religious content or relate to ritual in some way, one is not required to argue the same for all. All the same, it may seem that the argument above about the largely different contexts of myth and ritual must lead to a rather extreme downplaying of the importance of myth within religion.

The conclusion would be quite wrong, however. Myths, or some myths, were of fundamental importance to the Greeks, whether or not they were recited during the rituals they performed, whether or not they mirrored or echoed or derived from those rituals in whatever way. The preoccupation with particular connections has obscured the more fundamental relation between the two spheres. Let us take a counterexample to illustrate the point. In his celebrated study of the Alpine cult of St. Besse, Robert Hertz stated:

> If you ask local people who St Besse was, when he lived and what he did, you will usually obtain from them only vague and incoherent replies. However, as far as the status of the saint at present is concerned, they will answer you with unanimity and precision: St Besse is a saint who has 'great powers' and who performs 'many miracles'. His name arouses in them above all, not intellectual curiosity, but feelings of tender veneration, gratitude and hope.[57]

The possibility that Hertz here presents to us is that of a cult without myth, one based exclusively on the belief in the presence of an active power for good. One can certainly conceive that some cults have been in large measure of that type, including some Greek cults (those of anonymous Attic heroes,

---

56. On this *pari passu* (Jane Harrison's term) approach as developed in particular by Burkert, see Versnel, *Transition and Reversal*, 74–79; Csapo, 2005, 180.

57. "St. Besse: A Study of an Alpine Cult," in *Saints and Their Cults: Studies in Religious Sociology, Folklore and History,* ed. and trans. Stephen Wilson, 55–100 (Cambridge, 1983), at p. 59 (first published in *RHR* 67 (1913): 115–80, subsequently in R. Hertz, *Sociologie religieuse et folklore,* Paris, 1928 and 1970, 110–60).

for instance). In the Hellenistic period, admirers of the Egyptian gods boasted that their divinity was revealed not through myths but through manifest present power.[58] But it is not at all plausible that a worshipper of Heracles, say, approached the hero with a mind wiped clean of all recollection of the labors recounted in so many poems and plays, depicted in so many works of painted and plastic art. Nor is it credible that the various demesmen of Attica who performed sacrifices to the Herakleidai did so without thinking of the good services done by their ancestors to those victims of oppression and so frequently evoked in the state funeral orations and on the tragic stage.

The argument is particularly potent in relation to heroes (for all that there may have been a few sunk in anonymity), since their title to worship rested on the events of their lives. In their case, it is often plausible that myth came first and cult followed afterward; we recently learned, for instance, that a sanctuary of the Seven against Thebes was founded by Argos in the sixth century, well after the first attestation of the myth.[59] Asclepius too was a doctor in story long, as far as we can see, before he became the greatest of healers in cult. But it is not credible either that a worshipper of any of the major gods was ignorant of their parentage and powers. Even in the case of St. Besse, Hertz modifies his own position later in his study when he contrasts "the glorious career of St Besse as it is told from the pulpit by the curés" with the much homelier versions that he heard "among the simple faithful of Cogne."[60] "The simple faithful of Cogne" were not then, after all, exempt from the human impulse to tell stories about the things that matter. Nor certainly were the Greeks.

The simple but basic truth about the relation of myth to ritual in Greek religion is that, without myth, the rituals would be addressed to powers without histories or attributes and even at the extreme without names. Herodotus wrote that:

> Not till the day before yesterday, so to speak, did the Greeks know the origin of each of the gods, or whether they had all existed always,

58. Diod. Sic. 1.25.4; Aristid. Or. 45.15; cf. O. Weinreich, *Ausgewählte Schriften* (Amsterdam, 1969), 1:418–19. Cf. the pre-personal, pre-mythological "Sondergötter" postulated by H. Usener, *Götternamen* (3rd ed., Frankfurt, 1948, ed. 1 1896), 279.

59. *SEG* 37.283 (cf. 52. 312). Bremmer, *Greek Religion,* 62, mentions the cult of the Agamemnonidai at Tarentum (*Mir. ausc.* 106, 840 a 6–10), at which women were forbidden to eat of the sacrifices, as a clear, if unusual, example of direct influence of myth on cult. Lovers made oaths on the tomb of Iolaos, lover of Heracles (Plut. *Amat.* 17, 761D). Heraclidae: M. H. Jameson, "The Family of Herakles in Attica," in *Herakles and Hercules,* ed. L. Rawlings and H. Bowden, 15–36 (Swansea, 2005), argues that the cults celebrated an ideal image of the Athenians' humanity toward the oppressed.

60. Hertz, 1983, 73.

and what they were like in appearance....It was Homer and Hesiod who created a theogony for the Greeks, gave the gods their epithets, divided out offices and functions among them, and described their appearance. (2.53)

If for "Homer and Hesiod" we substitute "the myths, as told or represented in whatever medium," Herodotus's statement is perfectly correct. It is not that myths explain rituals in detail but that, without myths, the gods and heroes lose shape and attributes and differentiation. They cease to be the gods known to us, or to the Greeks. Not all myths, to repeat a point, reveal the gods in this way. Why should they? Real progress has been made in the last two decades or so in appreciating how myths gave a sense of identity to human groups, rooted them in a landscape, placed them in history, mapped out their interrelationships with other such groups.[61] The tragedies based on myths of a different type retain their appeal because of their stark depiction of the horrors of family life. And one could identify many further functions little related to religion.

But some myths dealt specifically with the history of the gods. Enormous weight was borne by a limited number of myths, those "archmyths" as they have been called,[62] narrated, for us, in Hesiod and the *Homeric Hymns* and telling how gods were born, acquired their powers, and arrived at their principal sites of cult. Such were the core themes of poems sung by choruses in actual cult contexts. Songs sung at Delphi told how Apollo arrived at the site and how he slew the dragon Pytho; more recherché variants told how Neoptolemus too acquired a place in the cult, or detailed the history of Apollo's four temples. Songs sung on Delos told, again and again, of the events culminating in the birth of Apollo on the island. Dithyrambs for Dionysus reserved a place of privilege for the god's mother, Semele.[63] What was at issue was not primarily the particular ritual about to be performed. It was the sanctity of the god and of the cult site. Many of the surviving cult songs were written for choruses dispatched by their cities to the great religious centers such as Delphi and Delos. The myths they sang explained why it was indeed appropriate to make the journey.

---

61. I am thinking of such works as I. Malkin, *The Wanderings of Odysseus* (Berkeley, 1998); C. P. Jones, *Kinship Diplomacy in the Ancient World* (Cambridge, Mass., 1999), and many studies by C. Calame. The one criticism one might make of Csapo's superb *Theories of Mythology* (n. 55 above) is a relative neglect of this trend in studies and the "charter" role of myth that makes it possible.

62. J. S. Clay, *The Politics of Olympus* (Princeton, 1989), 13.

63. See, e.g., Rutherford, *Paeans,* and Kowalzig, *Singing,* passim; for sources, J. N. Bremer and W. D. Furley, *Greek Hymns,* 2 vols. (Tübingen, 2001).

Another class of myth concerned the relations between particular gods and particular cities. The point was to establish a city's "dearness to the gods" by grounding through myth the affection for it of an individual god. The best-known instance is the story of Athena's and Poseidon's competition for Attica, depicted on the west pediment of the Parthenon, but most cities had something equivalent. Plato in *Menexenus* (237c–d) draws out the obvious implication: "All men should praise our land ... first and above all because it is dear to the gods. The quarrel and trial of the gods who disputed for it bear witness to what I say." These were, one might say, "comfort myths." Mortals needed to know not only who the gods were, but why they might hope for their favor.[64]

There is another very general level at which myth underlay religion. Again it is so familiar to any reader of Greek texts that its importance can easily be overlooked. Festivals, cult titles, unusual practices, topographical features, place-names, and many other phenomena have explanations of origin attached to them, and these explanations typically derive from incidents that occurred in the period that the Greeks themselves by the fifth century distinguished from "the age of men."[65] Not all such aitia (to use the Greek term) relate to cult and religion, but a clear majority do. A few rituals had, it was said, been established by the gods themselves present in person on earth. (These revelations of rites by—typically—Dionysus and Demeter are a further exception to the generalization that Greek religion was a religion without revelation.) Other rituals commemorated events in divine biography; the Delphic Septerion, for instance, supposedly mimicked Apollo's flight to Thessaly after the killing of the dragon Pytho. Others were simply associated with incidents in the myths of heroes. A passage in Apollonius's *Argonautica* deploys a single mythological incident to explain the name of the island Anaphe, the cult title Aigletes borne by Apollo on the island, and the custom whereby women and men exchange insults at Apollo Aigletes' annual festival; they all had their origin in the stay of the Argonauts on the island on the return voyage from Colchis.[66]

For various reasons, scholarship is disposed to be tentative in its dealings with such aitia. Often the link between aition and practice seems slight and artificial, a similarity of mood[67] (and not always even of that), not of detail. Normally the mythological event is not an intrinsic part of a larger

---

64. See Sourvinou-Inwood, "Polis Religion," 23–24, on what she calls "guarantee myths."

65. Hdt. 3.122.2; cf. for Pausanias, Pirenne-Delforge, *Pausanias,* 43–47. The distinction exists, even if, as Harrison argues, *Divinity and History,* 198–207, Herodotus in many respects ignores it.

66. Ap. Rhod. *Argon.* 4.1711–30, based on Callim. *Aet.* fr. 7–21 Pfeiffer; cf. Conon *FGrH* 26 F 1 (49). Septerion: n. 68 below.

67. F. Graf, *Greek Mythology* (Baltimore, 1993), 115.

myth but has been added to it ad hoc to generate an explanation; these are branchlines leading off from the great routes of myth. Aitia are very unstable: incompatible explanations for a single rite compete,[68] or replace one another over time. And the simple question as to how many of those who participated in a particular rite would have heard a particular account of its origin, and in what context, is one that we are usually not in a position to answer. Despite all this, the central point remains that tracing the origins of their religious practices to the heroic period had an instinctive rightness for Greeks; it was the default setting of their mind, and any Greek with a modicum of ritual knowledge would have been familiar and comfortable with explanations of this kind. Even if the contexts in which aitia were repeated are often uncertain, in cults that hosted choral performances the relevant aitia will surely have been heard in association with the rituals that they explained. What this default setting of the mind, this general familiarity, said was "in their broadest outlines, our religious practices date back to the generation of heroes." This is, once again, tradition or antiquity substituting for revelation as a source of legitimacy for those religious practices. It did not matter that particular aitia were unpersuasive or unstable. What mattered was the rooting of the whole system in heroic time.

Even the myths that had a primarily human focus—and this is the case with many of the best known, those of Oedipus and Orestes, for instance, or the Trojan and Theban cycles—reinforced the underlying conception of a heroic generation. (So a limited modification is needed to the assertion that no generalizations about "Greek myths" are possible.) The "compromise position" mentioned above in the myth-and-ritual debate also has its relevance here. According to this, myths and rituals are distinct media that may nonetheless deal with the same human problems. "Growing up," for instance, is a common theme of stories, and the transition from childhood to adulthood is a central concern of many ceremonies. The mythical theme that Walter Burkert terms "the maiden's tragedy" can be juxtaposed with what we know of girls' maturation rituals in Greece.[69] There is no need to suppose (a common fallacy) that growing-up stories in some sense derive from growing-up rituals. But through etiology the two strands could be-

---

68. See, e.g., Callim. *Aet.* fr. 79, where three possible reasons are offered why women in childbirth invoke a virgin helper (Artemis). In *De def. or.* 15, 418A Plutarch points out that the received aition for the Delphic Septerion (cf. p. 191) fails to fit the ritual practices; in *Quaest. Graec.* 12, 293C he had casually spoken of the rite as imitating events relating to the killing of the dragon (the received version) "or something of the kind." On the progressive "Theseus-ization" of Attic etiology (the consequences of which are displayed throughout Plut. *Thes.*), see n. 70 below.

69. *Structure and History,* 6–7, and on the comparison with initiation rituals, p. 16.

come entangled and influence one another in complicated ways. The myths of Theseus and Perseus, for instance, are, among other things, instances of the story pattern identified by Otto Rank as "the myth of the birth of the hero": the story of a young man of noble birth oppressed and deprived of his rights in early years who wins through to kinghood. Perhaps the story pattern appeals to a general childhood fantasy (to which adults still respond) that one is oneself an unrecognized prince or princess. It is, then, a story, fulfilling imaginative and emotional needs. But it is certain in the case of Theseus and plausible in that of Perseus[70] that the myths became associated etiologically with growing-up rituals, and in such a situation the participants will not have perceived the link between myth and rite as trivial. On the contrary, Theseus and his companions became role models for their successors. The Athenian youths who traveled annually to Delos to sing for Apollo were explicitly identified with the youths who made the same journey in company with Theseus in mythological time: the same specialized term, ἤθεοι, was applied to both.

If contemporary performers and mythological models can blend into one another in this way, it is evidently a mistake to separate myth from ritual too sharply. This phenomenon of "blending" will be discussed in another chapter. In a few cases (particularly in the cults of Demeter and Dionysus) the participant's experience of the ritual must have been so shaped by knowledge of the myth that the myth was close to constituting the plot of the ritual.[71] But for the moment I turn instead to a different issue concerning etiologies, which may seem to lead in a different direction. Though most explanations of the origin of festivals related to the generation of heroes, some did not. Herodotus (3.48) tells, for instance, how the tyrant of Corinth Periander dispatched three hundred Corcyraean children to the Lydian king Alyattes to be castrated. The good people of Samos, where the ship touched en route, told the children to take sanctuary in the temple of Artemis, and in order to feed them "they established a festival that they observe even now in the same way. At nightfall, throughout the period the children were suppliants, they organized choruses of maids and youths, and when they did so they made a

---

70. O. Rank, *Der Mythus von der Geburt des Helden* (Leipzig and Vienna, 1909). Theseus: Kearns, *Heroes of Attica,* 120–24; C. Calame, *Thésée et l'imaginaire athénien* (Lausanne, 1990), chap. 3; on ἤθεοι p. 200 below. Perseus: see the study of the Mycenaean inscription *IG* 4.493 (*LSAG*² p. 174 no. 1) by M. H. Jameson, in R. Hägg and G. Nordquist, eds., *Celebration of Death and Divinity in the Bronze Age Argolid* (Stockholm, 1990), 213–23 (summarized by Bremmer, *Greek Religion,* 62).

71. But these cases are the exceptions: there is a real gap between the loose myth-ritual relation characteristic of Greek religion and the deliberate reenactment of myth in rites found in Christianity and, it has been argued (R. Beck, *JRS* 90 (2000): 172–75), in Mithraism. Blending: p. 200 below.

rule that the choruses should carry honey and sesame cakes, which the Corcyraean children could snatch and so be fed."[72]

Herodotus's explanation of the origin of the festival is most unlikely to
be true, yet the "mythical" explanation chosen dates not from the age of
heroes but from a few generations before his own birth. Do such cases sub-
vert the claim that, for the Greeks, the rightness of their festival system lay in
its grounding in the generation of heroes? They introduce a complication,
rather. There never either was, or was felt to be, a ban on the introduction
of new rituals. Additions could be made either on the basis of remarkable
events, such as epiphanies, or on the instruction of an oracle. But taken in
the round the ritual system was still felt to be traditional. The mixture of
mythological and post-mythological aitia is simply a reflection at the etiological level of the general perception that a city's ritual calendar was a blend
of "ancestral" rites and others added in particular, remarkable circumstances.
Mythological aitia were qualified for their function by the mere fact of belonging to that special time. The Samian ritual mentioned above traced its
origin to a humane intervention against a monstrous and un-Hellenic act
of cruelty by a tyrant. Post-mythological aitia probably demanded a strong
relation of this kind either to accepted values or to a city's safety.[73]

The Instability of Myth

Myth is integral to religion, therefore; it is not a fancy wrapping paper which
must be taken off in order to get down to the realities of cult. Yet the role
of Greek myths, it need scarcely be stressed, is very different from that of
sacred books. At the most drastic, intellectuals felt able to dismiss the whole
mythic representation of deity as what came to be called *theologia fabularis,*
"mythical theology," an invention of poets, while still treating the cults as a
valid mode of access to the divine. For them the myths were indeed just a
wrapping, and a very deceptive one. The only alternative to rejection, for the

---

72. Hdt. 3.48, on which see C. Sourvinou-Inwood, *OpAth* 17 (1988): 167–82 = *"Reading"
Greek Culture,* 244–84, and now Ducat, *Spartan Education,* 256–58.

73. The famous whipping ritual of ephebes at the altar of Artemis Orthia in Sparta, and the
otherwise unknown "procession of Lydians that followed it," are explained by Plut. *Aristid.* 17.10
as deriving from an incident during the battle of Plataea, a heroic moment in Spartan history. (The
whipping also had a mythological aition, Paus. 3.16.7–11; cf. Graf, *Nordionische Kulte,* 87–88). A
stealing custom on Samos is explained by a period when the islanders had to live by pillage on the
mainland, followed by a triumphant return (Plut. *Quaest. Graec.* 55, 303D). The greatest Phocidian
festival was said to commemorate the great victory that saved the ethnos from destruction by the
Thessalians: Plut. *De mul. vir.* 2, 244D, *Non posse* 18, 1099E–F. Cf. pp. 219–220 below.

philosophically trained, was allegorical reinterpretation.[74] But even for those outside those very restricted circles there was little about the myths that was stable or dependable, or so at least it appears to an outside observer. Stories about the birth of deities, we have seen, were fundamental, the staple of cult hymns. But the poet of the early *Homeric Hymn to Dionysus* already contrasts what he declares to be his own true account of the god's birth with no fewer than five "lying" counterclaims.

That was one way to navigate the currents of endless variants without being swept into skepticism: one account is true, all others false. To a large extent the variants are regional, and we can suppose that worshippers accepted the version of the myth that they were born to; the claim that Apollo was born in Lycia will not often have been heard on Delos. Similarly, though we may be aware that the myths associated with a particular sanctuary change over time, we should not necessarily project that awareness onto those who frequented it. But it is very uncertain to what extent we can postulate mythological consensus, an agreed local version, even at a particular place and time. Since priests did not recount myths, there was no obvious mechanism by which even a powerful cult could communicate a standardized account from the center. Temple sculpture, where it existed, could scarcely alone carry such narrative weight. In some cults, as we have seen, foundational myths were repeated again and again by pious choruses. If the same hymn was rendered on all occasions year in, year out, its version could indeed establish itself as standard. But at great sites such as Delphi and Delos, frequented by sacred missions from afar, different choruses sang different hymns. Stability is likely to have been the exception rather than the rule.[75]

Myths lacked fixed form; nor was there anything resembling a canon of myths known to everybody even if in divergent forms. Two consequences follow from the absence of a canon. On the one hand, the question of what myths were known to whom is always an open one. One can guess at a core of "archmyths" that were very generally familiar, because often alluded to or depicted. But that criterion can produce surprising results. At Greek sacrifices, mortals received the best meat, and the gods had to be content with

---

74. *Theologia fabularis:* see, e.g., W. Jaeger, *The Theology of the Early Greek Philosophers* (Oxford, 1947), 2–4; Babut, *Religion des philosophes,* 195; G. Lieberg, *Rh. Mus.* 125 (1982): 25–32 [+]; Plut. *Amat.* 18, 763C–E is a clear presentation in Greek. On allegory most recently, L. Brisson, *How Philosophers Saved Myths: Allegorical Interpretation and Classical Mythology,* trans. C. Tihanyi (Chicago, 2004).

75. Graf and Johnston, *Ritual Texts,* 176: "'Canonical' sacred histories were therefore unlikely to exist even at the local level." Note, e.g., that "Pindar consistently makes Apollo and Artemis twins, but elsewhere this detail is rare": Rutherford, *Paeans,* 368. We cannot, it is true, prove that all the variants on this central Delian myth were to be heard on Delos itself.

fat and bones. Hesiod explained that the unequal division had its origin in a deception exercised by Prometheus "at the time when the gods and mortal men had a dispute" (or "were separated"—the force of ἐκρίνοντο is unclear) "at Mekone" (*Theogony* 535–36). Hesiod's myth relates the practice, satisfyingly, to a time of interaction and perhaps of division between gods and mortals, a time therefore when the order of the universe is being constituted; he also links it to Prometheus, the central figure in other myths that concern dealings between mortals en masse and gods. But though allusions to the unequal division are quite common,[76] no other source of the classical period appears to relate it to Prometheus or Mekone or a dispute/division between gods and men.[77] Are we then entitled to say that "the Greeks" explained the division of meat at sacrifice by reference to the trick of Prometheus? The core of myths universally or all-but-universally known may be very small. But if the core is small, the periphery is uncontrollably large. Any story about gods and heroes that any Greek heard or saw and remembered on any occasion was a part of their conception of the gods. Many Greeks from very early on rejected many stories about the gods as untrue, because unworthy of divine dignity or morality, and they were free to do so; but there was no mechanism whereby stories of "gods in sundry shapes, committing heady riots, incest, rapes" could be put under a ban as uncanonical. Since there was no canon, it was equally possible for moralists to reject such stories, and for unreclaimed man to revel in them.

Ritual and Belief

An ancient debate, older even than that on the relation between myth and ritual, concerns the relation between cult-act and belief in ancient religion. Bernard de Fontenelle wrote in *Histoire des oracles* in 1686: "Il y a lieu de croire que chez les payens le religion n'estoit qu'une pratique, dont la speculation estoit indifferente. Faites comme les autres, et croyez ce qu'il vous plaira.... Aussi voit-on que toute la religion payenne ne demandoit que des ceremonies, et nuls sentimens du cœur."[78] If Fontenelle's position has been

---

76. Cf. p. 136 n. 53.

77. Callim. *Ait.* fr. 119 refers to a different incident from primeval time set at Mekone; later allusions (see M. L. West's notes on Hes. *Theog.* 538 and 551) simply derive from book knowledge of Hesiod.

78. Première dissertation, chap. 7 (pp. 69–70 in the critical edition by L. Maigron, Paris, 1934). Cf. W. v. Humboldt, "Über das Studium des Alterthums und des griechischen insbesondre" (1793), in A. Leitzmann, ed., *Wilhelm von Humboldts Werke, 1785–1795* (Berlin, 1903), 1:255–81, at 274 (32),

much more influential among students of Roman than of Greek religion, that is perhaps largely a consequence of the notorious scarcity of Roman mythology: one needs to put the *Iliad,* say, or Euripides' *Troades* rather firmly out of mind in order to envisage Greek religion as purely a matter of the performance of cult acts. A religion whose principal rule is "Faites comme les autres, et croyez ce qu' il vous plaira" may sound a poor kind of thing: external conformity to social convention while one's mind is on other things (or on nothing at all). Fontenelle's tone is, indeed, rather dismissive. But it can be supplemented and glossed in a way that makes it applicable to Greece too.

First, a supplement. In its subtlest form, a neo-Fontenellian approach allows that pagan cult is grounded in a belief in its own efficacy: one worships the gods because, experience shows, benefit derives from doing so. The gods are there. At this very basic level there is indeed belief, a belief very generally shared, or at least feigned, and in social terms not wholly safe to repudiate. (But perhaps this foundational belief should rather be treated as certainty or knowledge.)[79] Without acknowledging this level of belief one cannot make sense of the innumerable literary texts and inscriptions in which individuals turn to the gods with requests, apologies, expressions of hope and gratitude (or conversely, doubt and disappointment). Second, a gloss. Fontenelle did not deny, it should be noted, that a pagan might hold beliefs or indulge in speculation about the gods. Again, it would be absurd to do so; the whole of Greek literature proves the contrary. Many Greek worshippers no doubt approached the altars with their heads full of notions, fears, hopes, and stories

---

"Die Religion übte schlechterdings keine Herrschaft über den Glauben und die Gesinnungen aus, sondern schränkte sich auf Cärimonien ein, die jeder Bürger zugleich immer von der politischen Seite betrachtete"; Burckhardt, *Kulturgeschichte,* 390: "Endlich würden die Griechen mit einer lehrenden Religion schon frühe Streit angefangen haben, die ihrige aber war lauter Dienst, lehrte nichts und war deshalb auch nicht zu widerlegen"; Robertson Smith, *Religion of the Semites,* 19: "Belief in a certain series of myths was neither obligatory as part of true religion nor was it supposed that, by believing, a man acquired religious merit or conciliated the favour of the gods. What was obligatory or meritorious was the exact performance of certain sacred acts prescribed by religious tradition." Contrast the similar but significantly broader formulation of A. D. Nock, *Conversion* (Oxford, 1933), 161: "To the ancients the essence of religion was the rite, which was thought of as a process for securing and maintaining correct relations with the world of uncharted forces around man, and the myth, which gave the traditional reason for the rite and the traditional (but changing) view of those forces." This adds both belief in the efficacy of the rite, and myth.

79. Neo-Fontenellian approach: see M. Linder and J. Scheid, "Quand croire c'est faire: Le problème de la croyance dans la Rome ancienne," *Archives de sciences sociales des religions* 81 (1993): 47–62; J. Scheid, *Quand faire, c'est croire* (Paris, 2005), 275–84; J. Scheid, "Le sens des rites: L'exemple romain," in *Rites et croyances dans les religions du monde romain* (*Entretiens Hardt* 53, Vandoeuvres, 2007), 39–63; cf. I. Gradel, *Emperor Worship and Roman Religion* (Oxford, 2002), 23–25. Knowledge, not belief: Linder and Scheid, 1993, 54; C. Ando, *Roman Religion* (Edinburgh, 2003), 11; C. Ando, *The Matter of the Gods* (Berkeley, 2008), 13–15.

about the divine. Fontenelle's point was that no attempt was made to control or police the contents of those mental lumber rooms.

Finally and crucially, the epistemological underpinning of the Greek attitude needs to be brought out. Early in book 2, Herodotus says that, of the various accounts he heard from Egyptian priests, he proposes to omit as much as possible those concerning the divine (τὰ θεῖα τῶν ἀπηγημάτων) because he believes all men to have equal knowledge of these matters, that is to say, no knowledge. Rituals he describes; it is the accompanying myths that he chooses to omit. The impossibility for mortals of making confident statements about the intentions or nature of the gods is a commonplace in Greek texts; where a claim is made, it will often be introduced with a formula such as "if one may speculate about the affairs of the gods," "if a mortal may guess about the intention of the gods."[80] Myth, we have seen, was unstable, and in many aspects for many worshippers incredible. Oracles revealed the proper ritual conduct to adopt in particular situations, not the nature of the gods. The correct way to sacrifice one could know. But as to the attributes and histories of particular gods, the origins of particular cults, the purpose of particular festivals, the very nature of deity, there was nothing but a flux of opinions, stories, speculations. All that was firm and established and secure, all therefore that it made sense to regulate, was the ritual act. The hubbub of conflicting claims did not arise when old certainties broke down, but was the permanent and inevitable consequence of the lack of a basis for such certainties.[81]

Does this mean that Greek religion was merely ritualist? The pejorative connotations of "merely ritualist" demand challenge.[82] As we have seen, this ritualism understands itself as empiricism and has an epistemological basis. It may also be appropriate to evoke here the often-repeated truth that there was no Greek word for "religion." The answer to the question whether Greek religion was "merely ritualist" will depend on what selection from things said and done by the Greeks in relation to the gods one chooses to include within the term "religion." We can agree that "sacred laws" posted outside sanctuaries told worshippers what to do, not what to think. But it does not

---

80. And. *Myst.* 139: εἴπερ οὖν δεῖ τὰ τῶν θεῶν ὑπονοεῖν; Isoc. 1 (Demonicus) 50: εἰ δὲ δεῖ θνητὸν ὄντα τῆς τῶν θεῶν στοχάσασθαι διανοίας; cf. the texts cited by Harrison, *Divinity and History*, 191 nn. 31 and 33; 258 n. 29. On Hdt. as a reporter of rites, not beliefs, see J. Gould, "Herodotus and Religion," in his *Myth, Ritual, Memory and Exchange* (Oxford, 2001), 359–77 (first in S. Hornblower, ed., *Greek Historiography* [Oxford, 1994], 91–106).

81. Cf. E. Kearns, "Order, Interaction, Authority" (in n. 5 above), 525.

82. On the tradition of deprecating "mere ritualism," which he traces back to the sixteenth century, see J. Z. Smith, *To Take Place* (Chicago, 1987), 96–103; he says that this tradition "marked the study of religion as, essentially, a protestant exercise" (98).

follow that opinions about the divine were not held and were not important to those who held them. (As for the vocabulary with which these opinions should be described—opinion, belief, faith—this too is largely a question of the meaning we choose to ascribe to English words.)

Because the gods are unknowable, myths concerning them are inevitably unreliable. But in a paradoxical way they are also, for the same reason, essential. Myth for Plato was a way of talking about that which could not be talked about in analytic language but which was too important to be passed over in silence. Myth had always been used, if in a less self-conscious way, as a means of representing in word and image what was unrepresentable and, in a strict sense, unknowable. Its lack of binding force was essential to its role. It was not a description of the observable but a figuration of what was imprecisely but powerfully felt. Without it, on the most important matters, there was silence.[83]

Moral Intuition as Revelation: How God Ought to Be

Two complications need to be introduced in conclusion. There is no shortage of texts in which Greeks make just the kind of confident claims about divine matters that, as we have just seen, in other contexts they declare to be impossible. In particular, the fragment of Euripides that runs "If gods do anything base, they are not gods"[84] is an example of a very common form of argument: the gods are no worse than they ought to be; we can use a definition of what is necessarily inherent in a god to judge and make claims about how gods have behaved or will behave. The argument is particularly at home in philosophy, where it underlies the moral critique of traditional myth; and philosophers who saw the regularity of the natural order as divine had an external underpinning for the attempt to stipulate how "the divine" might or might not comport itself.[85] But the unphilosophical Greek who expressed confidence that, because his cause was just, it would be supported by the gods,

---

83. So J. Rudhardt in many writings, e.g., *Thémis,* 159: "Le mythe est en effet un langage particulier: il ne définit pas ce dont il parle, il ne l'enferme dans nul concept; il ne le décrit pas d' une manière contraignante, il le suggère. Il joue d'images qui evoquent leur objet sans exactement le représenter."

84. Fr. 286b.7 Kannicht; within Eur. cf., e.g., *Hipp.* 120, *Bacch.* 1348, *Ion* 436–51. An argument of this form is central to much Christian apologetic; so, e.g., Arnobius contrasts the gods of pagan mythology with gods worthy of the name (*nominis huius appellatione dicendi, Adv. nat.* 7.2), "gods such as, if they exist, they ought to be" (*dei quales, si sunt, debent esse,* ibid. 7.15).

85. Cf. G. Betegh in *A Companion to Ancient Philosophy,* ed. M. L. Gill and P. Pellegrin, 625–39 (Oxford, 2006), at 631–32; on p. 628 he observes that "in the absence of a separate clerical class the

was arguing in the same way. So there was a kind of third, a priori source of knowledge about the gods, alongside tradition and oracular responses.

This possibility of reimagining the divine as the divine ought to be was crucially important in one way, largely irrelevant in another. It was important for the scope for free thought that it allowed; from it emerged the god of the philosophers. But it was irrelevant in the sense that the morally reconstructed god was just one image of the divine in competition with others; it entered the vortex of opinions and speculations, and, though for its adherents it may have had the status of certainty, it had no power of constraint over the attitudes of others. And this a priori moral knowledge of the divine largely related to different areas from those covered by oracular responses and tradition. It adjudicated what stories should be believed about the gods, not, in the main, what forms of worship might please them.

Philosophers, it is true, to some extent deployed it even in relation to cult. Thus they often insisted that the gods "took no pleasure" in expensive offerings (how did they know?) and cared much more for the attitude of mind with which an offering was brought.[86] Theophrastus in On Piety even presented a vegetarian critique of animal sacrifice. But such arguments were intended to adjust the attitude of individual worshippers, not to reform the traditional practices of cities. It had always been a matter of choice for individuals whether to sacrifice modestly or ostentatiously, with animal or with vegetarian offerings. The dominant philosophical tradition on cult might be crudely summarized in two propositions: sacrifice modestly, for the gods care nothing for show; observe the traditions of the city, for we know too little about the nature of the gods to change what in the past has pleased them.[87] Thus the third source of knowledge about the divine, a priori moral knowledge, failed to prove a lever with which to shift that which was fixed and established by the other two.

Surprisingly, there was one current within Stoicism that might seem to have challenged the philosophical consensus in favor of traditional cult; it

philosophers were confident that it was *their* special competence to inquire into the nature of the divine and to define the correct human attitude to the gods."

86. Xen. *Mem.* 1.3.3; Porph. *Abst.* 2.14–20 (largely from Theophr. *On Piety:* cf. fr. 523 Fortenbaugh); Crates *Suppl. Hell.* 358. 10–11; Lucr. 5.1198–1203; Seneca fr. 123 Haase ap. Lact. *Inst. Div.* 6.25.3. Closely connected is the insistence going back to Plato that the unjust cannot bribe the gods by offerings: Pl. *Resp.* 365E; *Leg.* 905D–907B, and often.

87. On respect for tradition see, e.g., Xen. *Mem.* 1.3.1, 4.3.16; Pl. *Epin.* 985D; Babut, *Religion des philosophes,* 157, 165, 181 (Epicureans and Stoics); Sext. Emp. *Pyr.* 3.2; *Math.* 9.49 (Pyrrhonists); above all Plut. *Amat.* 13, 756B–D, where inquiry into religious matters (in this case the motives of those who first declared Eros a god) is deprecated in favor of adherence to "inherited and ancient belief" (ἡ πάτριος καὶ παλαιὰ πίστις).

derived from Cynicism, the most drastic of all the philosophical schools in its attitude to religion. Zeno in his *Politeia* argued that there was no need in the ideal city for sanctuaries and divine images, since they were the work of human hands and, as such, of little value and not sacred. Chrysippus pointed out that the bans on having sexual intercourse in temples and on approaching them after contact with birth or death were unnatural, since not observed by animals. But the Cynic-influenced radicalism of Zeno's *Politeia* was an embarrassment to later Stoics and abandoned by them.[88] As for Chrysippus's observation, it is unlikely that he drew any conclusions for conduct from his observation; we know it only because Plutarch juxtaposes it, as a "Stoic self-contradiction," with a different remark of Chrysippus' that in fact enjoined respect for sanctuaries. So the argument from nature did not provide a lever to upset traditional usages either.

How Free Was Speech about the Gods?

The second complication concerns the often-repeated claim that the Greeks insisted on orthopraxy, "right doing," in relation to the gods, whereas orthodoxy, "right belief," did not exist even as a concept—a claim that is just a translation into a more modern idiom of what Fontenelle stated long ago. Anyone who has ever lectured on Greek religion and has veered toward that position will have been asked, "But what about the trial of Socrates?" Even if one believes that Socrates was convicted for political reasons, the fact will remain that the indictment was that "Socrates does wrong by not acknowledging (νομίζειν) the gods the city acknowledges, and introducing other, new powers (*daimonia*). He also does wrong by corrupting the young." "Acknowledge" is designed to catch the ambiguity of νομίζειν, which is on the cusp between "believe in" and "habitually pay cult to." A possible answer to the question is to stress the just-mentioned ambiguity of νομίζειν, and to note that Xenophon thought that the accusation could be met by emphasizing that Socrates could regularly be seen making sacrifice on the public altars. The issue would then come down to one of behavior after all. But we do not know that jurors would have been satisfied by Xenophon's counter; and there

---

88. Zeno: *SVF* 1.264–67; cf. Babut, *Religion des philosophes,* 178 n. 3; M. Schofield, *The Stoic Idea of the City* (Chicago, 1991), 17. Chrysippus: Plut. *De Stoic. repugn.* 22, 1044F (*SVF* III 753). On Zeno's *Politeia* and its reception, see O. Murray, "Zeno and the Art of Polis Maintenance," in *The Imaginary Polis,* ed. M. H. Hansen, 202–21 (Copenhagen, 2005); on the Cynics and religion, cf. M.-O. Goulet-Cazé, "Religion and the Early Cynics," in *The Cynics,* ed. R. Bracht Branham and Goulet-Cazé, 47–80 (Berkeley, 1996).

is a long list of claims in sources that the supposed teachings, not the doings, of natural philosophers in relation to the gods came under attack in Athens in the second half of the fifth century. Every item in that list (such as the trial of Anaxagoras for impiety, or the decree of Diopeithes rendering teaching of astronomy illegal) is controversial, but the cumulative evidence for suspicion and resentment, if not actual legal action, is very strong.[89]

Probably then, just as the neo-Fontenellian position acknowledges a single bedrock belief in the existence of the gods and the efficacy of the cultic system, so it should be acknowledged that perceived challenges to that bedrock belief by influential teachers were not a matter of indifference. Public action against philosophers deemed atheistical is occasionally reported after the fifth century too, though never very reliably. In a general way, there are occasional allusions to philosophers declining to discuss religious matters "in the street." There are also anecdotes, if of the most unreliable kind, telling how Stilpon the Megarian and Theodorus "the atheist" of Cyrene were expelled from Athens by the Areopagus.[90] The position of the Epicureans is intriguing. Epicurus taught that gods existed and should be honored in traditional ways, but simply as a mark of respect: cult made no difference. Their philosophical enemies charged Epicureans with being closet atheists. Two cities (Messene; Lyttos in Crete) are said to have expelled them with obloquy, though the objection was as much their "effeminate," i.e., pleasure-oriented, value system as their godlessness.

Also relevant is the tenor of permissible public discourse about the gods. The only systematic censoring of speech about the gods that occurred or that could occur (for there were no mechanisms to sustain anything else) was that of social convention, the codes governing the very different things that could appropriately be said in different contexts. No competent speaker in a courtroom or before an assembly would dream, for instance, of questioning the gods' existence, justice, or care for the city, whatever doubts he might nourish

---

89. See Parker, *Athenian Religion,* 207–10 [+]; on the trial of Socrates, ibid., 199–207, and on the exploitation of impiety charges against later philosophers who were unpopular for political reasons, ibid., 276–78. It is not clear how seriously Cleanthes meant his claim that Aristarchus of Samos should have been prosecuted for impiety for his astronomical views: Plut. *De fac.* 6, 923A (*SVF* 1.500; cf. ibid. 481 p. 107.2). The charge against Socrates: Favorinus ap. D.L. 2.40. Xenophon's defense: *Mem.* 1.1.2. Ambiguity of νομίζειν: see W. Fahr, *ΘΕΟΥΣ ΝΟΜΙΖΕΙΝ* (Hildesheim, 1969); H. Yunis, *A New Creed* (Meisenheim, 1988), 62–66: for cases where the sense "customary practice" prevails over belief, see, e.g., Hdt. 2.50.3, 4.59.2; Paus. 9.22.2.

90. "In the street": D.L. 2.117, with J. F. Kindstrand, *Bion of Borysthenes* (Uppsala, 1976), 225. Stilpon and Theodorus: see Parker, *Athenian Religion,* 277–78. Epicureans expelled: Aelian fr. 39, p. 201.13–202.9 Hercher (from Suda ε 2405 s.v. Epikouros). Closet atheists: Posidonius fr. 22 Kidd; cf. Cic. *Nat. D.* 1.85 with A. S. Pease's note.

and reveal in private.[91] The nuances of this social censorship of speech about the gods are difficult for us to become attuned to. Plato makes Socrates raise the possibility that he has been prosecuted for impiety for criticizing myths that told of conflict among gods. How whimsical is this suggestion? Such criticism already had a long history by Socrates' day, and surely never formed the sole grounds for a prosecution; but one can see that it might have been tactless to talk in these terms during the Panathenaea, as the splendid *peplos* embroidered with the victory of the gods over the giants was carried past. It is hard to know what to make of "Aristodemos the small," a man who, as presented to us by Xenophon, deemed cult to be unnecessary because the gods were too magnificent to concern themselves with mortal affairs.[92] He is an instance not just of an unmolested freethinker but also, which complicates the picture, a free-doer: he "neither sacrificed to the gods nor engaged in divination and laughed at those who did." Perhaps he was docketed as a fairly harmless eccentric, the kind of person who only became a source of anxiety if one found oneself on a ship with him in a storm.

Where does all this leave us? The view that it mattered not at all what one said about the gods or was believed to think about them, provided one paid them cult, is too extreme: prosecution of an individual for impiety could occur, as could (probably) legislation against a group such as astronomers or Epicureans. But these were very drastic measures, employed, it seems, and then only occasionally, against persons suspected not just of entertaining but also of propagating views that threatened the bedrock belief in the efficacy of cult. One should remember that if two cities supposedly expelled Epicureans, all the others put up with them; Zeno was not attacked for declaring sanctuaries unnecessary, nor Euhemerus for reducing the traditional gods to deified mortals, nor the later Cynics for their remorseless critique of divination in all its forms.[93] More pervasive as a form of control than spasmodic prosecutions were the norms of acceptable speech about the gods. But opinions

---

91. Cf. R. Parker "Gods Cruel and Kind: Tragic and Civic Theology," in *Greek Tragedy and the Historian,* ed. C.B.R. Pelling (Oxford, 1997), 143–44, 155–56.

92. Pl. *Euthyph.* 6A; Xen. *Mem.* 1.4.2, 10–11.

93. Several Epicureans holding priesthoods are attested under the Roman Empire, though the anomaly of their position might attract comment (Lucian *Symp.* 9, 32), and images of Epicureans were dedicated in Athenian sanctuaries in the first century BC: R. Koch Piettre, "Des Épicuriens entre la vie retirée et les honneurs publics," in Ἰδίᾳ καὶ δημοσίᾳ, 259–72. The views of Euhemerus were by some perceived as impious (so already Callim. *Ia.* 1.9–11: cf. T 14–23 in Winiarczyk's edition), rightly or wrongly (cf. M. Winiarczyk, *Euhemeros von Messene* [Munich, 2002], 107–18), but had enormous influence (Winiarczyk, ibid., 136–67). Cynics: J. Hammerstaedt, "Der Kyniker Oenomaus von Gadara," *ANRW* 2.36.4 (1990): 2834–65, at 2853–62 (whether early Cynics were so severe on, e.g., Apollo of Delphi, is unclear).

unthinkable in a public speech could be aired not only behind closed doors but also in a work of philosophy or even on the tragic stage.

As was noted earlier, all the topics treated in this chapter emanate out, like spokes of a wheel, from the absence, noted by Ibn Khaldûn, of authoritative sacred texts. A close correlate is the absence of a priestly class entrusted with the exegesis of such texts, and more generally of anything resembling a church. The next chapter will consider why this "absence" too was one that the Greeks had no reason to feel as such.

 CHAPTER 2

Religion without a Church

Religious Authority in Greece

In the posthumously published lectures commonly known as *Weltgeschichtliche Betrachtungen,* Jacob Burckhardt distinguished between societies in which "religion is determined by the state" and those in which "the state is determined by religion"; and he described the transition from the one form to the other occasioned by the triumph of Christianity as "a revolution of which we may say that it was the greatest that ever happened."[1] That, at all events, is the apocalyptic proposition that faced readers of the *Weltgeschichtliche Betrachtungen* as they were first published; the scholarly re-edition of his lecture notes that appeared in 1982 suggests that the intended claim was less extreme, namely that the transition to Christianity was the greatest transformation ever to occur in the relation between state and religion, not in the absolute. But even in that mitigated form Burckhardt's claim pinpoints something crucial to Greco-Roman religion: the absence of institutional structures independent of the state. One might almost say that Greek religion operated without institutions altogether. The Delphic oracle,

---

1. Quoted from the translation edited by J. H. Nichols, *Force and Freedom: Reflections on History* (Boston, 1943), 202. The relevant pages in the edition of the lecture notes (*Über das Studium der Geschichte,* ed. P. Ganz [Munich, 1982]), are 191, 311. Cf. W. Burkert, "Jacob Burckhardt über griechische Religion," in *Jacob Burckhardt und die Griechen,* ed. L. Burckhardt and H. J. Gehrke, 209–27 (Basel, 2006).

it is true, had enormous prestige and was almost invariably obeyed when consulted; but Apollo (or the Delphic priesthood) could not force states to consult the oracle. How then did this religion without a church work?[2]

Sacred Business in the Assembly

I start with a concrete case, a humdrum one, deliberately chosen to illustrate a routine procedure. A fragmentary inscription of the third century BC from Miletus reads as follows:

> [Whether] it will be agreeable to the goddess and beneficial to the people both now and henceforth if [the people] conducts the collections for Artemis Boulephoros Skiris as the Skiridai expound and propose or as now occurs. Whatever the god pronounces let the sacred messengers report to the assembly, and let the people, having heard, deliberate, in order that everything may be done in accord with the advice of the god. As sacred messengers were chosen [4 names]. The Milesian people asks whether it will be agreeable to the goddess and beneficial to the people both now and henceforth if [the people] conducts the collections for Artemis Boulephoros . . . [the stone breaks off][3]

So the assembly has decided to consult a god, who will certainly be the local oracular god Apollo of Didyma, on a proposed reform in organizing the collections that financed the cult. What the reform was we do not know, but the presumption is that it was approved by Apollo, or the transaction would scarcely have been recorded on stone. Four significant agencies or factors are in play in the inscription: the assembly; the oracle; a group of specialists, the Skiridai, attached to a particular cult; and the activity of "expounding" (ἐξηγεῖσθαι), which the Skiridai are said to perform. The assembly is involved twice: it first resolves to consult an oracle, and it will then make a decision on the substantive issue on the basis of the oracle's advice. (The language

---

2. For one city see R. Garland, "Priests and Power in Classical Athens," in *Pagan Priests,* 73–91.

3. *Milet* 6.3.1225 (*LSA* 47), "before 234/3?." No. 1224 is a newly published, slightly earlier text of similar content. The issue was quite often of concern. In *IG* 12.6.3 ("s. III² a.": = *LSCG* 123) a priest of Isis asks the Samian assembly for permission to collect as before; in ibid. XII.6.2 ("c. med. s. III a") priests (?) of the Syrian goddess are given collecting rights; *SEG* 6.775 (Tlos, "s. ii. a": = *LSA* 77) forbids unauthorized collection.

of advice, the god being treated exactly like a human counselor, is regular.[4])
In this case the assembly has predetermined to do as the god counsels, and
assemblies as far as we know always did follow oracular advice in such cases;
but formally both decisions were made by the assembly, and the decision to
take the matter to the god was a real one.

Two points are to be noted here. The Skiridai do not consult the god
on their own initiative. No private individual or interest group can approach a god about a matter of public concern and then spring the result on
the assembly; the decision to consult has to come from the assembly itself.
When Asander as satrap of Caria in 321/0 proposed to the Amyzonians that
"Bagadates, whom the oracle of Apollo has designated for him, should be
neōkoros of Artemis," he was not observing the norms of Greek polis life in
presenting a Delphi-sanctioned fait accompli. The nearest approach to an
exception from the polis world comes from Anaphe in the second century
BC, where one Timotheus decided to build a temple of Aphrodite, evidently
at his own expense, and donate it to the city, but was in doubt whether it
should be located within the existing precinct of Apollo Asgelatas or of
Asclepius. He consulted the god on this point, but the form of his question
was not "Where should I build the temple?" nor "Should the city build this
temple?" but "Where should I ask the city's permission to build the temple?"[5]
De facto the god's positive response must have been influential, but de jure
his question had only concerned his own conduct ("What request shall I
make?"), not the city's.[6] The second point to note is that the decision to
consult is not a referral from a human body with secular competence to one
with spiritual competence: it is a referral to a god. No body comparable to
a church intervenes.

Taking such questions to a god was common but far from invariable. In
the late fourth century (?) a group of "Bacchoi" approached the Cnidians
with a proposal to ban all lodging in the sanctuary of Dionysus Bacchus,
"in order that it may be kept pure."[7] Procedurally this case is exactly like the
Milesian one, a reform proposed to the assembly by a group closely involved
with a particular cult (whatever these "Bacchoi" may have been, which is

---

4. See the commentary in *Milet* 6.3 ad loc. In Xen. *Anab.* 3.1.5 Socrates, when consulted by Xenophon, advises him to consult Apollo: forms of the same verb ἀνακοινόω are used in both cases.

5. *LSCG* 129. Asander: *Amyzon* 2.

6. For the distinction, cf. Xen. *Anab.* 5.6.27–8: Xenophon is accused of making a consultative
sacrifice about a matter of public concern without consulting the army; he replies that he was merely
inquiring whether to raise the issue with the army at all. The private initiatives of the prophet Da-
mianos at Didyma at or beyond the end of the third century AD (*Didyma* 504.15–16, 29–31) belong
to a different world: L. Robert, *CRAI* (1968): 593–94.

7. *IKnidos* 160 (*LSA* 55; Jaccottet, *Choisir Dionysos,* no. 154, where see the commentary).

obscure). But it seems simply to have been accepted without more ado. Most of the texts collected in volumes entitled "Sacred Laws of the Greeks" are regulations passed by ordinary legislative assemblies of Greek cities. "Sacred" indicates the topic of the laws in question but reveals nothing about the issuing bodies. Greek legislative bodies devoted much time and attention to sacred matters. Twenty meetings of the Athenian assembly each year had a compulsory space at the start of the agenda for three items of sacred business, and such formal division of the business occurred in other cities too.[8] About most such business, as in the Cnidians' response to the Bacchoi, the assembly made up its own mind without reference to an oracle. Many such autonomous decisions of the assembly, including this one, concern matters of discipline and good order within sanctuaries and at festivals; the rationale may have been that there was no need to consult a god about proposals that were manifestly in the gods' interest. But autonomous decisions penetrate well into the area of sacred finance, about which one might suppose that the gods would have views. The issue is perhaps one of the special sensitivities that provoked referral to an oracle in a particular case; it is discussed in appendix 1 below.[9]

I turn now to the Skiridai of the Milesian inquiry from which I began. Though otherwise unknown, their name shows them to be a group closely concerned with the cult of Artemis Skiritis. Groups of this type are best known from Attica, where many cults were attached to the hereditary associations known as *genē:* the priest or priestess was invariably recruited from within the *genos,* and the other members often had some role in running of the cult. The Skiridai must have been a society roughly of this type, one of several known in Miletus.[10] One of the problems of Greek religion concerns

---

8. Twenty meetings: Ar. *Ath. Pol.* 43.6. The formula that such-and-such a person is to be allowed first access to the assembly μετὰ τὰ ἱερά, found frequently in Athens and sometimes outside, refers to the division (see P. J. Rhodes, *Chiron* 25 [1995]: 195 n. 33 [+]; *BÉ* [1996] no. 157; *BÉ* [2008], no. 399); so too do such formulas as χρηματίσαι περὶ τούτων ἐν ἱεροῖς (*LSCG* 40.16). On the Argive 'Assembly for Sacred Matters' see C. Kritzas, *CRAI* 2006, 424, with references. The distinction made in some cities between laws and decrees needs not concern us here. Compare in general R. Parker, "What Are Sacred Laws?" in *The Law and the Courts in Ancient Greece,* ed. E. Harris and L. Rubinstein, 57–70 (London, 2004).

9. See p. 265.

10. Branchidai: Hdt. 1.46.2, and often; Molpoi: *LSA* 50 passim, and often; Onitadai: *LSA* 50.31, 37, 40; ? Xynchidai (*Milet* 6.3.1385); Euangelidai, Conon *FGrH* 26 ¶44. Evidence from elsewhere in the Greek world is sparse, perhaps deceptively so: see, e.g., Callim. *Aet.* fr. 75.32–38 (Keos); Tac. *Hist.* 2.3 and Hesych. κ 2744, τ 1107 (Cyprus); Arist. fr. 549 Rose (Massilia); ? RO 62 (*LSCG* 151) A 52 (Cos). Hereditary transmission of priesthoods within individual families (Hdt. 7.153.2–3; cf. 3.142.4; for a probable Istrian case, Chiekova, *Pont gauche,* 18–19), particularly royal families (Hdt. 4.161.3; 6.56.1), also occurs, and in the Hellenistic period recurs (see, e.g., *IHistriae* 1.15–20; ibid. 19.20–23; *Iscr. Cos* 82.6–11; *Syll.³* 1007 n. 4 with *IG* 4 (1)² 60; for the act of handing over see *LSCG*

sources of expertise or traditional knowledge. Since the details of procedure at particular festivals were not normally published, the question arises of where the memory of proper procedure at elaborate rites performed once a year only was lodged. The most plausible answer is often the collective expertise of *genē*-like groups.[11]

Not all cults, however, had such groups associated with them; indeed it is very unclear how common they were other than in Attica. Often the know-how must have rested more precariously, particularly precariously when tenure was annual, with a single priest; perhaps to mitigate this difficulty, successive holders of such priesthoods occasionally constituted themselves as boards of "those who have held the priesthood of x." From our present point of view the single priest and the group are analytically interchangeable, since single priests can approach an assembly with a proposal concerning their cult just as do the Skiridai.[12] In both cases what we are seeing is the role of specialists in initiating and influencing action in the religious sphere. But though specialists may advise, the assembly decides. The same relation applies in the military sphere: the seer reads the omens, but it is the general who decides what action to take on the basis of them. Experts have a role, but that role is separated from the power of actual decision making.[13]

61; *LSA* 13 [on the latter see E. Stavrianopoulou in *Norme religieuse,* 220–24, with refs.]); priesthoods held διὰ γένους are common under the Roman Empire (for some references, see A. Chaniotis in *Practitioners of the Divine,* 22 n. 24). On Athenian *genē,* see Parker, *Athenian Religion,* chap. 5 and appendix 2.

11. Three sacred laws reveal these difficulties: one from Tlos (*LSA* 78 B, "c. 100 BC") appoints one of the city's priests to "attend all the sacrifices conducted by the *hierothutēs* and the other magistrates on behalf of the people in order that the sacrifices handed down from the forefathers be conducted piously"; the position was a recurrent one, as side A of the stone contains traces of similar appointments. In *LSA* 121.10–12 from Ephesus ("3rd c. AD") the "publicly financed hierophant" is to teach the *prytanis,* who has sacrificial duties, "what is customary for the gods on each point." A different solution is found in *LSA* 33 B 74–84 (Magnesia on the Maeander, early second century BC): the decree establishing the festival of the Eisiteria is to be read out in the assembly each year. Sale of priesthood contracts specified general duties but not fine points of ritual. On the problem, cf. A. Chaniotis, "Priests as Ritual Experts in the Greek World," in *Practitioners of the Divine,* 17–34. A decree of 20–19 honoring an Eleusinian daduch speaks of his endeavors to restore lost traditions not just from family memory but also from documentary research (if that is what περὶ τὰς ἀπογραφὰς ζήτησις means): *IEleusis* 300.63–68. Herodotus constantly ascribes special learning to Egyptian priests: similar statements about their Greek counterparts are much rarer (but see Hdt. 2.55.3; Pl. *Meno* 81A–B, on which see Parker, *Polytheism,* 99; Paus. 1.22.3; and note especially the two "letters" by priests of Athena Lindia often cited in the Lindian chronicle, e.g., *FGrH* 532 B–C 1; Dignas, "Rhodian Priests," 44).

12. See *LSS* 11 with *LSCG* 21 (*IG* 2².47.23–30 with ibid. 4962); *LSCG* 41, 42, 44, 102, 123. Boards of past priests: Dignas, "Rhodian Priests," 43–44 (Rhodes, Cos, and perhaps Cyrene; the Mantinean society of priestesses of Demeter, n. 31 below, could be similar).

13. Cf. for Rome, M. Beard in *Pagan Priests,* 42–43. General and seer: Pl. *Lach.* 199A.

The Skiridai in the inscription are said not merely to have made a proposal but to have "expounded" it. The verb in question, ἐξηγεῖσθαι, is the quasi-technical term that indicates discussing a religious issue on the basis of specialized knowledge; it is used again, for instance, of a proposal about sacrifices made to the Athenian assembly by the priest of Asclepius Euthydemus.[14] Exegesis has two aspects. In Attica and probably elsewhere there were special functionaries known as exegetes whose role was to advise individuals on religious questions, particularly those relating to pollution. In the other polis where exegetes are explicitly attested, Cos, we find them bringing to the assembly a proposal that "sacred and ancestral laws" concerning purification be codified; it is surely plausible, though as it happens unrecorded, that the Attic exegetes too on occasion advised the assembly, whether spontaneously or on request.[15] The other form of exegesis is that which is found here, the one that occurred when priests or priestly groups spoke with authority about the practices or traditions of their cult. Such was apparently the role of the "Eumolpid exegetes" in Athens, to expound the traditions of the great cult at Eleusis. Exegesis of this kind doubtless occurred throughout Greece, even if the random scatter of our evidence seldom reveals it. In contrast to the punitive disciplinary "sacred laws" emanating from assemblies, those that merely advise worshippers on the etiquette of a cult (what to sacrifice; what rules of purity to observe) must have their origin in such exegesis.[16]

The decisions to be taken by the assembly, those concerning a revised sacrificial calendar or the rights and duties attached to a priesthood, for instance, might be of some complication, and in these cases an individual or a commission was often appointed to draft proposals. The best-known such religious draftsman was Nicomachus, who prepared a new sacrificial code for Athens and was prosecuted for his pains.[17] Nicomachus was (to speak anachronistically) a civil servant, not a man of god.

At this point the question "Who took decisions about religious matters in Greece in the absence of a church?" has found an answer, a simple one: in a democracy, the citizen assembly (heavily guided, no doubt, by the prior

---

14. *LSS* 11.4.

15. See F. Jacoby, *Atthis* (Oxford, 1949), 8–51; J. H. Oliver, *The Athenian Expounders of the Sacred and Ancestral Law* (Baltimore, 1950). Coan exegetes: *LSCG* 154 A 4; *SEG* 55. 931.24. Eumolpid exegesis: Parker, *Athenian Religion,* 295–96.

16. See "What Are Sacred Laws?" n. 8 above; cf. Jacoby, *Atthis* (in previous note), 237 n. 2.

17. See Lysias 30; cf., e.g., the committee that drafted the proposals of the firstfruits decree (*IEleusis* 28a [*IG* 1³.78; ML 73]). For committees drafting job descriptions for priesthoods in Cos, see *Chiron* 30 (2000): 424.

deliberations of the council, but for the present purpose the distinction is unimportant); under other constitutions, we assume, whatever body governed the state: the principle is the same under all constitutions that the same body took decisions on both sacred and non-sacred issues. The important special case of decisions to accept a new cult into the civic pantheon is discussed in appendix 2;[18] those decisions too were taken in the assembly.

The question "On what basis were such decisions taken?" has also been partly answered. It remains to ask what influence individuals other than priests and priestly groups might have had over the assembly, both by making proposals and in contributing to debate where there was controversy. Regrettably but inescapably, the evidence is almost entirely Athenian. In principle, under a democracy, anyone could contribute, but in practice three groups are chiefly in question. First there are interest groups. It was through pressure from Thracians, Egyptians, and Citians resident in Athens that land was assigned for shrines of Bendis, Isis, and the Citians' Aphrodite; though foreigners could not address the assembly, they could make requests to it and so initiate a process.[19]

Second come religious specialists other than priests, above all *manteis,* seers, and *chrēsmologoi,* oracle-singers. These two branches of diviner must be sharply distinguished from priests; in many ways they and not the priests are the true religious specialists of Greece. Unlike most priests, seers lived by their craft (the case with oracle-singers is less clear), and, because they were not tied to particular cults, they could claim a much broader competence. There is no reason to think that priests would have felt authorized to approach or advise the assembly on any cult other than their own; but an inscription shows Athens' most famous seer, Lampon, operating on a wide front: he recommends that proposals made by a commission on summoning firstfruits of corn to Eleusis be accepted; he goes on to propose that a month be intercalated, that regulations be introduced to prevent the establishment of altars in the region known as the Pelargikon, and that he himself be commissioned to draft proposals for collecting firstfruits of olive oil. Lampon's enormous political prestige was doubtless unusual, but the *chrēsmologos* Hierocles was prominent too, and it must have been through political activity that another *chrēsmologos* Diopeithes acquired his sobriquet of "mad." The seer Euthyphro in Plato may complain that he is laughed at when he "speaks in the assembly on religious matters, predicting the future," but his complaint confirms that he spoke; had he concentrated more on "speaking

---

18. See p. 273.
19. *LSCG* 46 (*IG* 2².1283) 6; RO 91 (*LSCG* 34).

about religious matters" and less on "predicting the future," there might have been less laughter.[20]

Finally and most importantly there were politicians. According to Plutarch, Themistocles became unpopular for founding a shrine of Artemis Aristoboule, Artemis of best counsel, after the repulse of the Persian invasion: people saw in the epithet a bragging allusion to Themistocles' own bright ideas. Doubtful though the details of that incident are, it can serve as an emblem of the politician's role in shaping religious policy. A decree of 421/0 regulating the festival of Hephaestus was proposed by Hyperbolus, a demagogue much despised by Thucydides. When in the 330s the merchants of Citium in Cyprus sought permission to buy land to establish a shrine of their Aphrodite, it was the leading politician of the day, Lycurgus, who supported their cause in the assembly. Further proposals on religious matters, some extending down to very minute details, bear Lycurgus's name; many more evidently emanate from his circle.[21] One can even speak of Lycurgus's religious policy, not a thing that can be ascribed to many Greeks,[22] and certainly not to any priest acting as such. (Lycurgus in fact belonged to the *genos* that supplied the priest of Poseidon Erechtheus and may himself have held that prestigious office. These associations possibly enhanced his authority in speaking of religious matters; but it was as politician, not as priest, that he steered the assembly.) Other factors aside, the intermeshing of sacred and public finance was so close that no politician could avoid becoming involved in the affairs of the gods, as a fourth-century rhetorical handbook makes clear. Androtion's involvement with the melting down of old dedications to make processional

---

20. Lampon's proposals: *IEleusis* 28a (*IG* 1³.78; ML 73). Euthyphro: Pl. *Euthphr.* 3B–C (Socrates calls him a *mantis* in 3E: so rightly Flower, *Seer*, 142). On these figures see Parker, *Polytheism*, 92, 111–18; Flower, *Seer*, 58–65, 122–26 (but I doubt his argument that the designation of Hierocles as a *chrēsmologos* in Ar. *Pax* 1047 is just an Aristophanic joke). Diviners were influential at Sparta too, as the fame of Tisamenus of Elis and his grandson Agias shows (Flower, *Seer*, 94–95), but it is not clear that any will have belonged to crucial decision-making bodies: the role of the *chrēsmologos* Diopeithes in the succession dispute between Leotychidas and Agesilaus (Xen. *Hell.* 3.3.3) may have been simply to provide an oracle that was then deployed by Leotychidas; or he may have been adduced by Leotychidas as an expert witness before (probably) the *gerousia* (P. Cartledge, *Agesilaos* [London, 1987], 111); if, as is probable, he is identical with the Athenian Diopeithes (for opinions see Flower, *Seer*, 124 n. 47), he certainly operated as an outsider.

21. Themistocles: Plut. *Them.* 22.2 (cf. Parker, *Athenian Religion*, 155 n. 8). Hyperbolus: *IG* 1³.82. Merchants: RO 91 (*LSCG* 34). Further proposals: *IG* 2².333 (S. Lambert, *ZPE* 154 (2005): 137–44); two separate proposals in *IEleusis* 177.431–32. His circle: cf. Parker, *Athenian Religion*, 242–55. Priesthood of Poseidon Erechtheus: [Plut.] *XOrat.* 843E–F; the statement that Lycurgus himself held it in Parker, *Athenian Religion*, 242, is too confident.

22. The tyrant Clisthenes of Sicyon might be an exception, as Hayden Pelliccia pointed out to me: again, not a religious specialist.

vessels was represented by his political enemy Demosthenes as dire impiety; but it was routine administrative activity, routinely carried out.[23]

Politicians influenced religion. Did religion also influence politics? At a level of shared goals and values it did so very profoundly, since, it was agreed, no city could prosper that failed to maintain right relations with the gods. But nobody rose to political prominence through holding religious office. Lampon was influential, but, as far as we know, in the religious sphere only; important citizens who also held priesthoods are easy to find, particularly in the Hellenistic period, but the priesthoods were an appurtenance of high standing, not its foundation. Interventions in public debate in the name of religion are rare, and usually relate to cults of Demeter, which, as mysteries, invested the cult officials with especial authority. The *genē* associated with the Eleusinian Mysteries tried but failed to prevent the recall to Athens of Alcibiades, who had supposedly profaned their cult. During an interval of hostilities in the civil war of 403 the Sacred Herald of the Mysteries, "a man of powerful voice," appealed to his fellow citizens in the name of the sacred rites they had participated in together to abandon the cause of the "most impious" Thirty. Serving as an envoy in 371/0, Kallias, the Daduch of the same cult, reminded the Spartans of the privileges in relation to the Mysteries that they had enjoyed since mythical times.[24] On particular occasions, then, a cult official might be able to make appropriate appeal to shared religious traditions. But this was not a basis for lasting authority. Herodotus, it is true, seems to see the power of Gelon, tyrant of Gela and Syracuse, as partly resting on his family's hereditary role as "hierophants of the chthonian gods."[25] But the claim is enigmatic, and isolated.

Priests and Priestesses

Priests and priestesses had, we have seen, a certain input into the decision-making process, but far from a dominant role. What of their other functions? In contrast to the Roman situation, priests and priestesses are at least clearly identifiable.[26] It is true that an enormous number of cultic roles were

---

23. Handbook: [Arist.] *Rh. Al.* 1423a20–1424a8. Andronion: Dem. 22.69–78; 24.176–86; cf. D. M. Lewis, *BSA* 49 (1954): 39–49.

24. Alcibiades: below, p. 52. Sacred herald: Xen. *Hell.* 2.4.20–22. Callias: ibid. 6.3.3–6. Cf. T. Wareh, "Hierophantic performances," in *Horkos,* ed. A. Sommerstein, 161–78 (Bristol, 2007).

25. Hdt. 7.153.

26. For excellent syntheses, see V. Pirenne-Delforge, *ThesCRA* 5:1–31 (priests/priestesses), S. Georgoudi, ibid. 31–60 (*hieropoioi* and the like). My focus in what follows is on priests in cults of the city or its subdivisions; but note that private associations also had priests.

discharged by non-priests: by children and young people charged with special tasks and sometimes bearing special titles; by choruses, of all ages; by "performers of sacred rites" (*hieropoioi*) appointed by the city; by magistrates; and by others besides. Priests were also often flanked by boards of "supervisors" (*epistatai; epimelētai*) and "treasurers of sacred monies" and "temple builders" and, again, magistrates: details vary from city to city, and a list of the parapriestly functionaries both on the cultic and the administrative side from the whole Greek world would be unmanageably long.[27] Nonetheless, a function exists clearly identified by the Greek words ἱερεύς and ἱέρεια, normally and reasonably translated priest and priestess.

The dominant tradition has long been to downplay the importance of this function in Greek religion, to stress the lack of special training for what was usually a part-time post, to note that priests from different cults never met together to discuss matters of common concern; Isocrates' statement is often quoted that men wrongly regard kingship, like priesthood, as something that any man is fit for.[28] Early in the first century BC the people of Herakleia under Latmos in Caria asked an oracle whether the most important priesthood of their city (that of Athena Latmia) should henceforth be sold by auction for life or whether a new occupant should be elected annually. Both alternatives may seem to modern eyes to devalue the office, the one by making the criterion of choice ability to pay, the other by imposing too short a tenure to allow for acquisition of expertise; yet both systems were very widely applied. The oracle pronounced in favor of annual election of the person preeminent in "birth and orderliness of life" (ὃς γένει ἠδὲ βίου τάξει προφερέστατος ἐστίν): the criterion therefore was civic standing and respectability, not religious commitment. Priesthoods that were open to children and even, in a few cases, confined to them cannot have carried heavy duties or responsibilities.[29]

27. For Attica see R. Garland, *BSA* 79 (1984): 75–123; for other cities, S. Georgoudi (previous note).

28. Isoc. 2 (*Nicocles*) 6 τὴν βασιλείαν ὥσπερ ἱερωσύνην παντὸς ἀνδρὸς εἶναι νομίζουσιν, ὃ τῶν ἀνθρωπίνων πραγμάτων μέγιστόν ἐστι καὶ πλείστης προνοίας δεόμενον. It is the valuation of kingship, not of priesthood, that Isocrates rejects; cf. Isoc. *Antid.* 71.

29. Herakleia: *SEG* 40.956: cf. p. 268 below. Sale of priesthoods was commonplace from c. 400 BC in Greek Asia Minor and islands (e.g., Chios, Cos) off its coast: see *ThesCRA* 5:7 and for what may be the earliest instances (on Chios), R. Parker in Χιακὸν Συμπόσιον εἰς μνήμην *W. G. Forrest*, ed. G. Malouchou and A. Matthaiou, 69–72 (Athens, 2006). Annual tenure was normal for priesthoods created in Athens from the fifth century onward (selection for life from *genē* remained the system for older-established priesthoods). The terms of tenure of priesthoods outside Athens in the archaic and classical priods are scarcely known, while for the Hellenistic period we lack a synthesis; but annual tenure is certainly not rare. Children: some contracts of sale for priesthoods

A reaction against the consensus has begun of late, and one good consequence should be to overcome the vagueness and overgeneralization that tend to prevail on an under-researched topic. It is obviously rash, for instance, to compare the experience of a priestess who served for one year in a minor cult with that of Lysimache, priestess for sixty-four years in the most important state cult of Athens;[30] that Lysimache was a part-timer is not at all clear, that she was emotionally deeply committed to the goddess whom she served is surely highly likely. A Mantinean ex-priestess in the 40s BC made arrangements for her support for the cult of Demeter and the "society of priestesses of Demeter" (itself a noteworthy rarity) to be maintained by her daughter and granddaughter after her death. A minimal counterclaim to the traditional downplaying of the role of priests and priestesses is to observe that they were evidently necessary to the working of the religious system.[31] Just how necessary is shown by a famous list of priesthood sales from Hellenistic Erythrae, which shows that that small place had at least fifty-four. A newly discovered text from Attica issued not by the city but a subgroup, probably the deme Aixone, listed at least ten separate priesthoods. Two further priesthoods of that deme are independently attested; if we accept the attribution of the new text to Aixone, add the two to the ten and extrapolate in proportion for the whole of Attica, we reach the startling figure of at least 545 deme priesthoods.[32] Completely irresponsible and fantastic though that calculation is, the point that priesthoods were very abundant remains. Burkert's remark that "Greek religion could almost be defined as a religion without priests" looks very bold in the light of such facts (of which, of course, he was well aware); and when Jacob Burckhardt claimed that "the Greeks occupied a world of laymen...they simply did not know what a priest was," he was using language in a very humpty-dumptyesque way.[33]

Some priests were depicted on their tombstones holding the symbols of priestly office (for a man the sacrificial knife, for a woman the temple key);

---

impose minimum age limits as low as eight or ten: *Chiron* 30 (2000): 424 cf. SEG 55. 926. 7; for priesthoods restricted to maidens or boys, see *ThesCRA* 5:6.

30. Pliny *HN* 34.76 with *CEG* 757.

31. So Price, *Religions,* 68: other revisionist works are Connelly, *Portrait of a Priestess;* Dignas, *Economy of the Sacred; Practitioners of the Divine.* On priestesses note too S. Georgoudi, "*Athanatous therapeuein:* Reflexions sur des femmes au service des dieux," in Ἰδίᾳ καὶ δημοσίᾳ, 69–82. Mantinean priestess: *IG* 5.2.266. On colleges of ex-priests, see n. 12 above.

32. *IErythrae* 201 (cf. p. 98); *SEG* 54.214, with Parker, "Aixone," 197.

33. Burkert, *Greek Religion,* 95: the paradox is explained in what follows: "There is no priestly caste as a closed group with fixed tradition, education, initiation and hierarchy." Burckhardt: *Über das Studium* (n. 1 above), 198, 326: "Eine völlige Laienwelt...sie wußten eigentlich nicht was ein Priester sei." In *Kulturgeschichte,* 325, Burckhardt more reasonably distinguished between priests, which the Greeks had, and *Priesterstand/Priestertum,* which they lacked.

they or their kin evidently saw the office as an integral part of what they were. That argument is double-edged, however, because only a small proportion of tombstones bear priestly emblems: more people must have held priesthoods at some time in their lives than chose to advertise it on their graves. Some arguments for marks of separation between priests and laity are similarly double-edged: priests might wear distinctive dress, but normally only on ceremonial occasions; some priests were bound to chastity, but most were not.[34]

What is fairly clear is that at most times and places in the Greek world priesthood was not, despite Isocrates' dictum, something for anybody; prestige attached to the office, and it was therefore dominated by a social elite. For Cicero it was proof of the wisdom of the Roman ancestors that they "wished the same people to be in charge of the cult of the immortal gods and the supreme interest of the state"; the situation was not so different in Greece. In the two Greek cities that retained kings, priesthoods were attached to the office, and where priesthoods were allocated by election or auction they were mostly held by men of the governing classes and their wives and daughters, those "preeminent in birth and orderliness of life" in the words of the oracle. In Hellenistic Rhodes, a kind of priestly cursus honorum developed whereby leading citizens occupied the main annual priesthoods in a fixed order.[35] Anyone who has looked carefully at the theater of Dionysus in Athens knows that the public priests had specially designated front seats. On occasions of civic display in the Hellenistic city, the "priests and priestesses" were frequently required to participate as a group; they existed as a ceremonial body though not as a deliberative one.[36] They were part of the establishment.

34. Tombstones: A. Scholl, *Die attischen Bildfeldstelen des 4. Jhs. v. Chr.* (Berlin, 1996), 135–48; A. Kosmopoulou, *BSA* 96 (2001): 292–99; Connelly, *Portrait of a Priestess,* chap. 8. Double-edged: I owe this observation to Marietta Horster. Dress: Connelly, *Portrait of a Priestess,* chap. 4; A. G. Mantis, Προβλήματα της εικονογραφίας των ιερειών και των ιερέων στην αρχαία Ελληνική τέχνη (Athens, 1990), 82–96; *ThesCRA* 5:29–31; for epigraphic evidence, *Chiron* 30 (2000): 425. Chastity: Parker, *Miasma,* 86–91; for other purity requirements, ibid., 175 n. 177.
35. Cicero: *Dom.* 1. Kings as priests: Hdt. 4.161.3; 6.56. Rhodes: Dignas, "Rhodian Priests." Priesthood and the governing class: the issue is too large to document here, but see, e.g., R. van Bremen, *The Limits of Participation* (Amsterdam, 1996), 22, 29–30, 44; Dignas in *Practitioners of the Divine,* 78–80. Prestige: R. van den Hoff, "Images and Prestige of Cult Personnel in Athens," in *Practitioners of the Divine,* 107–41 (much of which has parallels throughout Greece).
36. Cf. S. Dmitriev, *City Government in Hellenistic and Roman Asia Minor* (New York, 2005), 25: "The occasions mentioned above required the presence of priests, as almost everything in Greek cities did, but they were not religious events." Front seats: M. Maass, *Die Prohedrie des Dionysostheaters in Athen* (Munich, 1972); outside Athens, *Chiron* 30 (2000): 425 (8). Priests and priestesses: see, e.g., RO 85 B 42-3; *LSA* 15.40–41; 32.36–37; 81.11; *LSS* 44.9; *IPriene* 14.17–20; *OGIS* 332.33; *RPh* 63

Did being part of the establishment mean that they had to do as the rest of the establishment wished? According to the standard view, the priest, to speak bluntly, took orders from the assembly: the terms of office were often determined by the assembly (as we see from the advertisements for priest-hood sales from the eastern Greek world), and at Athens priests even had to undergo audit, *euthynē*, like ordinary magistrates.[37] The most powerful attempt to show priests occupying a more independent position is an impor-tant study from 2002 by Beate Dignas. She investigates several cases in Asia Minor where priests and civic authorities seem to be in conflict, a dispute, for instance, that lasted at least twenty years (c. 240 to 220) between the priests in the important cult of Zeus at Labraunda in Caria and the authorities of the neighboring city of Mylasa; what was at issue was the control of sacred revenues, and three Hellenistic monarchs as well as several of their officials were sucked into the affair.[38] She argues that we need to conceptualize the situation in terms of a triangle of interests, constituted by city, priests, and king: the interests of city and priests do not blend into one.

The crucial difference between these cases and the situation in archaic and classical Greece is the existence of a king as an external third party to whom appeal could be made. The leverage that the king gave the priests was not available in the classical city. At Athens, when the assembly in 411 discussed the recall of Alcibiades, who had supposedly profaned the Mysteries of Eleu-sis in 415, members of the two sacred *genē* who controlled the cult protested in the name of religion. The case shows that, as Dignas argues, priestly groups might internalize the values of a cult and come to see themselves as more committed to their god than to their city.[39] But protest was all they could do—protest, and be outvoted. Alcibiades did eventually return, though not,

---

(1937): 337–38 no. 10, lines 12–14; cf. Plut. *Pelop.* 33.5. For joint dedications by the συνιερεῖς of a given year in Lindos, see Dignas, "Rhodian Priests," 43.

37. Priesthood sales: above n. 29; but terms of tenure were also determined by the assembly at Athens, *IG* 1³.35 (M/L 44, *LSCG* 12 A). Audit: *IG* 2².354.21–22; 410.22; Aeschin. 3.18. Priesthoods were not formally magistracies (M. Hansen, *GRBS* 21 [1980]: 170), but the gap was not great (Arist. *Pol.* 1299a 15–19; Dmitriev, 2005, in n. 36, 25–26).

38. Dignas, *Economy of the Sacred;* for the Labraunda case, known from *ILabraunda* 1, see 59–66. In fairness to Dignas's admirable monograph I should stress that her model well fits the region and time frame it is designed to fit.

39. "The sanctuaries were run and their activities shaped by individuals who identified them-selves with this task and saw themselves *interacting* with the secular world of the *polis*": Dignas, *Economy of the Sacred,* 33; cf. 30 on "administration from within." Alcibiades: Thuc. 8.53.2 (411); cursing and uncursing: Plut. *Alc.* 22.5, 33.3; [Lys.] 6.51. But it should be noted that the strength of involvement of the two Eleusinian *genē* with their hugely prestigious cult was scarcely typical. *SEG* 48.1037.17 ("c. 180–166 B.C.") instructs priests and priestesses to curse offenders against the Delian sanctuaries.

as it happens, on that occasion, and the *genē* were instructed to uncurse the curses that they had earlier pronounced against him (again on the instructions of the assembly). Dignas sums up her position by quoting a brief letter of the Macedonian king Demetrius II concerning Beroia:

> Demetrius to Harpalus greetings. The priests of Heracles say that some of the god's revenues have been diverted to the public funds. Take care now that they are restored to the god. Farewell.

The king intervenes for the god against the city, on appeal by the priests. But, again, without a monarch the city would have been free to appropriate Heracles' funds for its own uses.[40]

If priests could not stand up effectively for their god against secular interests, what were they for? What function did they exercise that no one else did?[41] It proves strangely difficult to answer that question. Two limiting positions are possible here. One would start from the point that there was no such thing as a priest or priestess *tout court,* a person who served all the gods, nor even a priest or priestess of Apollo or Artemis or Dionysus; one was always priest in a particular cult in a particular sanctuary, with the added epithet (Athena *Polias* or Dionysus *Thyllophorus* or whatever) usually required to identify the site in question.[42] One might then see the priest or priestess as essentially a glorified sacristan or churchwarden, a person who presides over a particular sanctuary and ensures that property is not stolen and sacrifice is made in accord with the specific local norms.[43]

The opposite approach would start from the statement in Plato that "the class of priests, as tradition says, is skilled in giving gifts from us to the gods through sacrifices in accord with their wishes, and in beseeching from them for us through prayers the acquisition of benefits."[44] Since prayer accompanies sacrifice, what Plato's claim amounts to is that priests are experts in sacrificing; and, since sacrifice was the most important means of communication

---

40. *Syll.*[3] 459, M. B. Hatzopoulos, *Macedonian Institutions under the Kings* (Athens, 1996), vol. 2, no. 8: 248 BC. For the pressures to divert funds, see the case study of first-century AD Miletus by Chaniotis in *Practitioners of the Divine,* 23–25; note too the interventions by priests to protect funds that he cites, ibid., 26 n. 35.

41. Thirty attempts at definition are helpfully cited and discussed by A. Henrichs in *Practitioners of the Divine,* 1–14.

42. Burkert, *Greek Religion,* 95—and already Burckhardt, *Kulturgeschichte,* 394.

43. Cf. Arist. *Pol.* 1322b 18–25.

44. Pl. *Plt.* 290c–d καὶ μὴν καὶ τὸ τῶν ἱερέων αὖ γένος, ὡς τὸ νόμιμόν φησι, παρὰ μὲν ἡμῶν δωρεὰς θεοῖς διὰ θυσιῶν ἐπιστῆμόν ἐστι κατὰ νοῦν ἐκείνοις δωρεῖσθαι, παρὰ δὲ ἐκείνων ἡμῖν εὐχαῖς κτῆσιν ἀγαθῶν αἰτήσασθαι; cf. Pl. *Symp.* 202e.

between gods and men, one might extend the claim a little to the proposition that priests were the privileged mediators between the two breeds. In the Hellenistic period, we find priestesses in leading cults of Pergamum who are "pleasing to the gods" praised for contributing to the "safety of the city" by their piety. There develops (explicitly in Cyrene, by implication in some other places) the conception of the "fair year" priest, during whose term of office the city enjoyed "peace and prosperity" or "plenty and fair crops" or the like.[45]

One difficulty with this approach is that, even though the commonest Homeric word for "immolate an animal," ἱερεύω, is etymologically just "do what a priest does," priests were far from having an exclusive right to sacrifice. It is not just that individuals were free to sacrifice for themselves in their own homes, nor even just that priests did not have a monopoly on sacrificing even within their own sanctuaries: an early Chian sacred law prescribes, for instance, that "if the priest isn't there, let him [the worshipper] call out three times, trying to make himself heard, and perform the rite himself."[46] The real objection is that, even at public rites conducted for the well-being of the city, sacrifices were just as likely to be conducted by magistrates as by priests. Just after the passage quoted above on the role of priests, Plato adds that "in many places in Greece one finds the chief magistrates required to fulfill the chief role in such sacrifices"; he goes on to mention the ritual role of the annual "king archon" at Athens. Aristotle explicitly distinguishes between two types of public sacrifice: those "assigned by convention to priests" and those performed by officials who "derive their authority from the common hearth." At Athens the nine main magistracies were described as "crown-wearing": the crown was a symbol of sacredness, which assimilated magistrates to priests; in many Hellenistic cities the eponymous magistrate came to be known as just that, Stephanephoros, crown-wearer, and the crown that he wore was apparently sacred to a specific god.

Both priests and magistrates regularly sacrificed and prayed on behalf of the city, often together; and numerous texts show them closely associated on ceremonial occasions. In a calendar from Mykonos we not only find the choice of the most beautiful sows entrusted to the boule, but also an

45. Pergamum: OGIS 299.1–12 (149 BC, according to C. P. Jones, Chiron 4 [1974]: 188–89); SEG 4.687 (c. 60s BC, according to Jones [in this note], 200). "Fair year priest": L. Robert, Hellenica, vol. 1 (Limoges, 1940), 7–17; vol. 2 (Paris, 1946), 142–45; vols. 11–12 (Paris, 1960), 542–55, on what is now SEG 26.1835.

46. LSS 129.7–11; cf. IOropos 277 (LSCG 69; RO 27) 25–27. Persians, by contrast, supposedly could not sacrifice without a magos: Hdt. 1.132.3; so too Indians needed a "sophist," i.e., Brahman (Arrian, Indica 11.3).

instruction that "the magistrates and priests shall ensure that the rites are conducted well."[47] "Performers of rites" too (*hieropoioi*), boards of citizens often recruited from the boule, not only provided organizational assistance but could also be said to perform public sacrifices. Honored guests too might be given the privilege of sacrificing an animal.[48] Even the conception of the "fair year" priest has its origin in the practice of noting that, in the year of particular magistrates, a city flourished: we read, for instance, that "in the archonship of Aristokritos" (284 BC) there was "health and prosperity" on Delos, almost two and a half centuries before the year of a priest of Athena Lindia on Rhodes was credited with "peace and prosperity."[49]

From a theoretical point of view this near equivalence of priest and magistrate is of fundamental importance. Future research needs to address the question of whether and how their roles can be differentiated. One can argue that magistrates had organizational responsibility for sacred events within which priests provided more specialized services of expert prayer and sacrifice.[50] On similar lines, it has been suggested that we could separate the

---

47. Pl. *Plt.* 290E; Arist. *Pol.* 1322b 26–8 (cf. p. 62 below on the "sweeper" role of Spensithios, and many allusions to sacrifices performed by demarchs, e.g., *IG* 2².1183.33; *SEG* 50.168 A 2.1–2, 23). Crown-wearing at Athens: Parker, *Polytheism,* 98. Stephanephoroi: B. Dignas, *Kernos* 20 (2007): 173–87. The stephanephorate blurs the distinction of magistrate and priest; so too does the role of the priest of Zeus Akraios as chief magistrate of Demetrias (F. Stählin, *AM* 54 [1929]: 204–5; E. Meyer in F. Stählin et al., *Pagasai und Demetrias* [Berlin, 1934], 184). Magistrate and priest at Athens: Parker, *Polytheism,* 95–99 [+]. A few examples from outside Athens: magistrates and priests co-involved in processions: *LSA* 32.31–40; 81.9–13; *LSS* 44.8–11; *IPriene* 14.21; *Iscr. Cos* 82.20–23; Paus. 2.35.5; in prayers *LSA* 15.39–48; and cf. n. 50. Mykonos: *LSCG* 96.13, 19–20.

48. *Hieropoioi:* Arist. *Ath. Pol.* 54.6–7 (mentioning sacrifices: cf. *IEleusis* 13 [*IG* 1³.5; *LSCG* 4]), with P. J. Rhodes's commentary ad loc.; S. Georgoudi, in *ThesCRA* 5:32–40. Guests: L. Robert, *Hellenica,* vols. 11–12 (Paris, 1960), 126–30.

49. *IG* 11.2.105; *Lindos* 347 (*Syll.³* 765) a 4. On such formulas, see Robert, *Hellenica,* 2:142 [+]; *Lindos,* p. 91.

50. Note the vocabulary of supervision (ἐπιμελεῖσθαι) and organization (διοικεῖν) used of magistrates in Arist. *Ath. Pol.* 57.1. This distinction is one strand in a rare article addressing the problem, F. Gschnitzer, "Bemerkungen zum Zusammenwirken von Magistraten und Priestern in der griechischen Welt," *Ktema* 14 (1989): 31–38. Among his observations are (1) that public curses are often solely the responsibility of magistrates (Plut. *Sol.* 24.1; Schwyzer 688 C 6–9; ML 30 + *SEG* 31.985; *Syll.³* 578.60–64; *LSA* 16.17–27), sometimes of magistrates in association with priests (*IC* 3.4.7; *SEG* 33.679.7–13), once of priests apparently under instruction/supervision from magistrates (*IG* 11.4.1296A and B); one ad hominem curse is added to the prayers uttered by public priests (Livy 31.44.6; on the cursing of profaners of the Eleusinian Mysteries, a special case, see n. 39); (2) that in *Syll.³* 180 (*IG* 2².114) and 181 (*IG* 2².112) public vows are pronounced by heralds, not priests; (3) that in *Illion* 32 (*OGIS* 219) priests and magistrates are involved throughout, but emphasis falls on priests in relation to prayers (20–27) and on magistrates in organizing a sacrifice (27–30) [but the latter hierarchy is reversed in *OGIS* 309.4–7!]; (4) that sacrifices to ensure the success of a sympolity are conducted in *Milet.* 1.3.146.50–55, 73–78 by priests and the Stephanephoros, whereas in *Milet.* 1.3.150 (*Syll.³* 633) 17–24 an offering by *prytaneis* is added, with the priest in a subordinate role [cf., e.g., *SEG* 41.1003, 2.33–36]. His conclusion (translated) is "The sphere reserved for the

roles by varying the emphasis in the two cases: priests *pray and sacrifice* for the city; magistrates pray and sacrifice *for the city*: they come from different directions but converge at one point.[51] Part of our difficulty lies in the distinction drawn by Hubert and Mauss between "le sacrifiant," the person who sponsors and pays for the sacrifice, and "le sacrificateur," the specialist who performs the ritual actions. Since Greek fails to make any such distinction, both magistrate and priest might "sacrifice" on the same occasion, the magistrate as "sacrifiant" (representing the city, which pays for the victim), the priest as "sacrificateur." It is very plausible that, could we observe the rites more closely, such a complementarity of roles would often be revealed; and in such cases the priest retains a distinctive sacral function.[52] But the passage from Aristotle cited above shows that certain rites were wholly in the charge of magistrates. And there is never any effort in Greek allusions to these topics to reserve to priests the dignity of representing the city before the gods. Greeks were always happy to speak of both classes praying and sacrificing for the city without making the distinctions teased out above.

To return to the question of the specific function of the priest or priestess, they certainly had special rights and responsibilities in relation to particular sanctuaries, the cult images that they contained, and the cult acts there conducted.[53] They also probably had an exclusive role in certain sacrifices made within that cult: it will not have been arbitrary whether a particular sacrifice was performed by a priest or a magistrate; the priest will have been a privileged intermediary between gods and men on particular occasions and in a

---

specific cult personnel is evidently small, and its boundaries permeable, at least for the authority of the state, which in the last analysis covers religious activity as a whole (*die staatliche Autorität, die am Ende doch das ganze Sakralwesen mit umspannt*). There can be no talk of autonomy of the religious sphere among the Greeks."

51. Anonymous Oxford University Press reader cited in Parker, *Polytheism,* 98 n. 32.

52. In *Iscr. Cos* 145.12–20 the *monarchos* and the *hieropoioi* are instructed to make certain sacrifices to Hermes Enagonios and the priest to "process with them." But earlier it has been said (10–11) that the priest is to "place the sacred portions on the altar" for all those sacrificing in the shrine. The case is doubtless similar, though less clear, in ibid. 180.24–27; 215.24–44; the new texts *SEG* 55. 926.8-9, 928 A 13-14, B 14, 931. 17-18 suggest that such placing of the sacred portions on the altar by the official priest was the Coan norm. For a strong assertion of the primacy of the priest in ritual, see A. H. Rasmussen in *Religion and Society,* ed. A. H. Rasmussen and S. W. Rasmussen, 71–80 (Rome, 2008). Sacrifiant/sacrificateur: Hubert and Mauss, *Sacrifice,* chap. 1.

53. Dignas, *Economy of the Sacred,* 33: "We know that their job was to perform or assist in public or private sacrifice, to maintain order and respect for the sacred laws, to organize the religious festivals, to look after the cult statue and the relevant cult-buildings and also to check the revenues and expenditures of the sanctuary." Legends concerning transfer of cult statues tend to have them carried by the priestess (*ThesCRA* 5:16). Tendance of the statue is stressed in the epitaph for the first priestess of Athena Nike at Athens, *IG* 1^3.1330 = *CEG* 93, sacrifice in one for a priest from Cnidus, *SEG* 44.904 (*Steinepigramme* 1, 01/01/10; *ThesCRA* 5:19 no. 71).

particular context. As a group, as we have seen, they symbolized the collective piety of the city on ceremonial occasions. In a crisis too, where a desperate supplication had to be made to the gods, or in the name of the gods, or to a monarch, they would often be deployed.[54]

They were rather closer to the gods than ordinary people. The requirements of purity imposed on them were somewhat more stringent than on others; they had to be "healthy and intact in body," like the gods themselves; there were stories of priests and priestesses (but down to what level?) being spared enslavement or payment of ransom by victorious enemies. Their dreams had especial weight: speaking in the Athenian assembly, Demosthenes cited a Sicilian priestess's dream about the tyrant Dionysius, and significant dreams of the priest or ex-priest of Athena Lindia are recorded in a notable document of Rhodian local history, the Lindian chronicle.[55] The crowns they wore perhaps imitated those of the gods they served and (occasionally) embodied. On the other hand, the most important channel of communication between gods and men was through divination, and ordinary priests had little to do with that; it was the sphere of seers and, at oracular shrines, of "prophets" and "prophetesses." (How to classify these figures is one of the ambiguities at the margin of the class of priests; but, even if prophets are priests, it does not follow that priests are, in general, prophets.) We cannot therefore in any general way treat priests as the mediators between gods and men. As we have seen, they did not even have a monopoly on mediating through sacrifice. In private, ordinary heads of household did it; on a public level, priests shared the role with magistrates.[56]

Polis Religion

That sharing is an emblem of the Greek intermingling of church and state, what it has become fashionable to call "polis religion." The expression "polis

---

54. Pirenne-Delforge in *ThesCRA* 5:17, citing Plut. *Pelop.* 12.6, Polyb. 16.33.5 (cf. ibid. 16.31.7, where they administer solemn oaths); cf. the priest of Zeus in Soph. *OT* 18.

55. Purity: above, n. 34. Intact: J. Wilgaux, in *Norme religieuse,* 231–41. Priests spared: Arrian *Anab.* 1.9.9, cf. Plut. *Alex.* 11.12; Plut. *Alc.* 29.5. Dreams: Aeschin. 2.10; *FGrH* 532 D 2 and 3; note too the dreams sent by Demeter to her priestesses at Corinth relating to Timoleon, Diod. Sic. 16.66.4; Plut. *Timol.* 8. 1, and the interpretation of omens before Leuctra by Theban priestesses, Xen. *Hell.* 6.4.7. But I have found only one priestly dream in Pausanias, 4.26.3. Crowns: B. Dignas, *Kernos* 20 (2007): 184, with bibl.

56. A. Henrichs in *Practitioners of the Divine,* 8, plausibly suggests that "in the case of animal sacrifice, it was the ritual performance itself rather than the performer that mediated between gods and men."

religion" had no doubt been casually used previously, but it became a term of art, the summation of an approach and a theory, only with the publication of Christiane Sourvinou-Inwood's article "What Is Polis Religion?" in 1990. That article, probably the most influential single item in the study of Greek religion since the early studies of Burkert and Vernant in the 1960s, has been widely seen as proposing a new paradigm, one that is much debated. For some, it gives the polis too much control over religion; for others, religion too much control over the polis.[57] But it does not introduce a new paradigm in the sense of replacing existing ones, to which it is, in fact, complementary. And it is certainly not a denial of the role of individuals and of groups, of private sacrifices and dedications, in Greek religion. Nor is it a denial that individuals went outside the confines of their city for religious purposes, to consult an oracle for instance, and that certain religious events were organised by supra-polis bodies such as amphictionies.

What the article does do is focus attention on the questions of decision making and authority discussed above; and it argues much more emphatically and incisively than had been done before that "it was the ordered community, the *polis*, which assumed the role played in Christianity by the Church."[58] It is not primarily a thesis about religion as a matter of imagination, conceptualization, belief; it is about organization, policing, control. "The polis provided the fundamental framework in which Greek religion operated," it claims; "the polis anchored, legitimated and mediated all religious activity." The statement "polis religion embraces, contains and mediates all religious discourse" may seem to go further, because it introduces discourse, the world of ideas.[59] But the claim is not that the polis generates all religious ideas. Sourvinou-Inwood stresses that many myths and practices were Panhellenic and does not deny that religious ideas floated freely from one city to another; the claim is merely that, in the long term, it was the city that determined whether a particular religious conception, at least insofar as it affected actual

---

57. Sourvinou-Inwood, "Polis Religion." For the latter criticism, see M. H. Hansen and T. H. Nielsen, *An Inventory of Archaic and Classical Greek Poleis* (Oxford, 2004), 130–34; for variants of the former, G. Woolf, "Polis-Religion and Its Alternatives in the Roman Provinces," in *Römische Reichsreligion und Provinzialreligion,* ed. H. Cancik and J. Rüpke, 71–84 (Tübingen, 1997), repr. in *Roman Religion,* ed. C. Ando (Edinburgh, 2003), chap. 2 (with the comments of J. Scheid, *Quand faire, c'est croire* [Paris, 2005], 125–28); A. Bendlin, "Looking beyond the Civic Compromise: Religious Pluralism in Late Republican Rome," in *Religion in Archaic and Republican Rome and Italy,* ed. E. Bispham and C. Smith, 115–35 (Edinburgh, 2000). A "symposium in memory of Christiane Sourvinou-Inwood" at the University of Reading (July 4–6, 2008) took as its theme "Perceptions of Polis-Religion: Inside-Outside"; cf. J. Kindt, "Polis Religion: A Critical Appreciation," *Kernos* 22 (2009): 9–34.

58. Sourvinou-Inwood, "Polis Religion," 19–20 (though she goes on at once to point out the danger inherent in all such comparisons).

59. These three citations: Sourvinou-Inwood, "Polis Religion," 13, 15, 20.

RELIGION WITHOUT A CHURCH 59

practice, was to be granted right of residence within its walls. In most parts of the Greek world,[60] individuals lived their lives within city-states, even if they went outside them occasionally to Panhellenic sanctuaries. For organization and control, the crucial body was the city.

Of the various critiques that have been offered, the most interesting perhaps concerns the scope of the control exercised by the polis. Rites were conducted at many different levels: by the city itself, by the formally recognized subunits of the city such as demes, tribes, and phratries, by long-established hereditary cult groups such as *genē*, and also in various cult societies of differing levels of stability that the individual joined by choice: worshippers of the Mother, of Sabazius, of Adonis, of Dionysus, of the Corybantes, initiates of Orpheus, and so on. It can be argued that at this bottom level in particular, the level of elective cults, there was a freedom and a scope for creativity that the polis–religion model seems to disallow. But even at the intermediate level there can have been very little real regulation except by group convention: if a particular set of worshippers chose to adjust sacrificial rules in the cult, to change a particular offering, say, from a holocaust to one yielding edible meat, it is hard to see how the polis could have stopped them.[61] As for what could happen below the level of the group, a famous passage of Plato's *Laws* on what he strikingly calls "illegal god business (θεοπολεῖν παρὰ νόμον)" must be quoted (the general sense is clear though all translators struggle with details of Plato's impressionistic late style):

> No one shall possess a shrine in his own house: when anyone is inclined to sacrifice, he shall go to the public shrines to sacrifice, and he shall hand over his offerings to the priests and priestesses who care about the relevant observances; and he shall join in the prayers along with anyone else he wishes to have join in with him. This shall be done for the following reasons. It is not easy to establish shrines and gods, and to do it properly needs much thought; yet it is typical of all women, in particular, and of the sick everywhere and those in danger and in any kind of difficulty, and on the other hand when people come into

---

60. Where political organization was not based on the city, religious organization was necessarily also different. Sourvinou-Inwood does not make this point, but as I know from conversation certainly acknowledged it. She can perhaps be charged with reducing the role of the poleis Delphi and Elis at the great Panhellenic sanctuaries that they controlled to ordinary polis business, when these were in fact special relationships: S. Hornblower, *A Commentary on Thucydides,* vol. 3, *Books 5. 25–8.109* (Oxford, 2008), 125.

61. Self-regulation was discussed by F. S. Naiden in an interesting paper at the Reading conference (n. 57 above), "How Athens Regulated Sacrifice by Individuals and Associations."

any kind of wealth, to consecrate whatever they have to hand and vow sacrifices and promise foundations to gods and *daimones* and the children of gods—they do this because of fears in visions when awake and in dreams, and similarly, remembering many apparitions and treating altars and shrines as remedies for each of them, they fill every house and every village, siting them in open spaces too and wherever anyone in such a state of mind hits upon [*or*, wherever any has had such an experience].[62]

Plato's view is evidently that the polis should indeed "anchor, legitimate, and mediate all religious activity," but in the real city of Athens regrettably failed to do so.

It is important here to consider mechanisms. Greek cities no more had a public religious prosecutor than they had a public prosecutor of any kind. The only way in which most kinds of religious misbehavior could be controlled was through the willingness of a volunteer prosecutor to lodge an accusation of impiety. The counter that can then be made from the polis-religion side is to point to occasions when prosecutions were in fact brought against organizers of elective cults. Three cases are known from the fourth century where women (always women) who led revel bands were prosecuted on charges (unfortunately not known in detail) relating in some way to those bands; two of the prosecutions ended in execution.[63] A rare detail attested from outside Athens is that at Thebes, probably in the fourth century, legislation was passed to prohibit "nocturnal rites"(probably of women). One can also point out that most scholars believe that impiety, *asebeia,* like pornography according to Justice Stewart, was an "I know it when I see it" kind of thing.[64] (But it was not unique in this among offenses known to Greek law; underspecification seems to have been the norm.) Since it was undefined, it was unlimited: one could never know what a prosecutor might not try to bring under the heading. The polis, it can be argued, by allowing prosecutions for an undefined crime of impiety, claimed a right of control over all

62. Pl. *Leg.* 909d–910. Did Plato really wish to abolish such familiar domestic cults as that of Zeus Ktesios? My guess is that they were too accepted and unexceptionable for him to think of them here; if so, there is some justification for treating them as de facto though not de jure aspects of "polis religion" in the sense of "practices dictated by communal norms," not by individual preference. But for critics of Sourvinou-Inwood in this area, see n. 57.

63. See Dickie, *Magicians,* 50–54, on the prosecutions of Phryne, Theoris, and Nino.

64. See references in Parker, *Athenian Religion,* 215 n. 63. Thebes: Cic. *Leg.* 2.37 (in a context concerning women's rites and Bacchic rites) *omnia nocturna in media Graecia Diagondas* (mss: *Daitondas* Knoepfler) *lege perpetua sustulit:* see two studies by D. Knoepfler cited in *SEG* 39.435, 50.481.

religious activities that occurred on its territory. It did not and in fact could not exercise this right of control in all cases, and as a result there was de facto a good measure of freedom; but that freedom was never acknowledged as a principle, and could be withdrawn.

Both sides in the debate have some right on their side. Those who object that the polis-religion model is making the Greek city into a 1984 or Brave New World society are right that it was not like that at all. In Rome, not a notably intolerant place in religious terms, we know of bans/restrictions/expulsions relating to rites of Bacchus, Isis, and Cybele, and others striking Jews and astrologers; in Athens, by contrast, it was only in a comedy of Aristophanes that "Sabazius and other foreign gods" were expelled from the city.[65] Even in Athens, however, there was no ideal of "religious freedom," and there were limits to religious laissez-faire. The modern perspective in which religion is a sphere distinct from the state and not to be intruded on by it is wholly alien to the Greeks.[66] They had no way to conceive of religious practice except as intertwined with the broader structure of life in the city.

Was It Ever Thus?

Most of the evidence in this chapter has been taken from classical Athens, with some supplementation from Hellenistic cities. About earlier times and other places one is largely reduced to the negative observation that nothing suggests a radically different principle of organization. At most one might wonder whether there might once have been a closer connection between control over cults and political power: the Attic *genē*, religious bodies only in the classical period, may once have had a place in the political structure; in the Molpoi of Miletus we can observe an instance (but a unique one) of a religious association that retained some influence over access to the citizenship into the Hellenistic period.[67] Were this uncertain speculation correct,

---

65. Cic. *Leg.* 2.37, perhaps referring to Ὧραι (cf. K/A p. 296). Rome: Beard, North, and Price, *Religions of Rome,* 91–96, 228–36; *ThesCRA* 3:275–77.

66. Sourvinou-Inwood, "Polis Religion," 18. Dignas, *Economy of the Sacred,* 1, notes the complex relation between church and state that exists in many modern countries, but adds as a crucial difference "the Greeks never even *claimed* a separation of church and state." See now the well-judged conclusion to P. J. Rhodes, "State and Religion in Athenian Inscriptions," *Greece and Rome* 56 (2009): 1–13. "Der Form nach behielt sich wohl der Staat die Verfügung über fremde Kulte vor, allein die Praxis war eine ungleiche": Burckhardt, *Kulturgeschichte,* 324.

67. *Genē*: Parker, *Athenian Religion,* 65. Molpoi: V. B. Gorman, *Miletos, the Ornament of Ionia* (Ann Arbor, 2001), 94–97 (who, however, underestimates the importance of their involvement with citizenship).

the conclusion should doubtless be that one elite controlled both religious life and the affairs of the city (as in the Hellenistic period) rather than that there was an independent route to power through religious office. In Athens, the annual magistrate known as "king" had especial responsibility for sacred matters: he adjudicated disputes relating to priesthoods, "administered" most of the ancestral sacrifices, and selected junior officiants in several cults; trials for impiety and deliberate murder were heard in his court. Magistrates of the same name existed in other cities, very likely with similar functions. Whether or not these annual kings were descendants of actual kings, they were understood to be so; secular and sacral were believed to have been inseparable in the archaic as in the classical city. In classical Athens again, the Areopagus council exercised an ill-defined power of supervision over the religious life of the city, probably a vestige of its greater general competence in earlier times.[68] The Areopagus was made up of ex-magistrates, not of priests.

I finish with some historical snapshots. In the one mention of the mechanism of the appointment of a priest in Homer, it is said that "the Trojans" made Theano their priestess. Thus the idea of the priest as a servant and appointee of the people is already visible, long before the emergence of democracy. The second snapshot is from an archaic oligarchy, an otherwise unknown city or subdivision of a city in Crete c. 550 BC. This body, the Dataleis, appointed one Spensithios as its public scribe, entrusting him with recording all "public, divine, and mortal affairs." As in the Athenian assembly, divine and mortal affairs were distinguished conceptually, but not separately handled. The text also lays down that in public cults that lack a priest of their own Spensithios is to perform the sacrifices. So the blurring of roles between civic official and priest is already attested in sixth-century Crete: appointed as a specialist in writing, Spensithios serves as a sweeper up of stray priestly functions too.[69]

The final snapshot is of the first known Greek chief priest, *archiereus,* one Nikanor, appointed chief priest of all shrines on this side of the Taurus Mountains by Antiochus III in 209 BC.[70] We see here on the one hand the real change brought by Hellenistic monarchy. The new kings had a power over religious affairs unthinkable for individuals in previous

68. *Basileus* in Athens: Arist. *Ath. Pol.* 57.1–2, with P. J. Rhodes's commentary ad loc.; P. Carlier, *La royauté en Grèce avant Alexandre* (Strasburg, 1984), 329–50. *Basileis* outside Athens: ibid., 487–91. Areopagus: Parker, *Athenian Religion,* 130.

69. Theano: Hom. *Il.* 6.300. Spensithios: A. M. Davies and L. H. Jeffery, *Kadmos* 9 (1970): 118–54 (= *Nomima* 1:22).

70. *SEG* 37.1010 (for a new copy see ibid. 54.1353) with *SEG* 46.1519 (Ma, *Antiochos III,* dossier 4 and 49); cf. H. Müller, "Der hellenistische Archiereus," *Chiron* 30 (2000): 519–42.

centuries: Alexander decreed that the dead Hephaestion was to be a hero throughout his empire; Ptolemy Soter created a new Greco-Egyptian god, Sarapis; Attalus III elevated Zeus Sabazios to the highest honors in Pergamum because of his mother's devotion to that cult.[71] We have already seen how sanctuaries could appeal to kings against cities. Outside the Greek cities, new, more centralized organizational structures were set in place, of which the creation of the chief priesthood was one; an inscription first published in 2007 showed that it was the Seleucid aim of bringing religious activity under bureaucratic control that underlies the story of Heliodorus's impious attempt on the temple treasures of Jerusalem, the miraculous repulse of which is related in the second book of Maccabees and dramatized by Raphael in *La cacciata di Eliodoro dal Tempio* in the Vatican.[72] The chief priesthood is therefore symptom of a transformed world.

But though a chief priest sounds like a symbol of distinctively religious authority, he was nothing of the kind. We happen to know that both Nikanor and another chief priest appointed by Antiochus[73] were men grown grey in royal service now taking up the priesthood as a kind of pensioned retirement post, but that is not the essential point. What is more important is that these were still administrative positions within the Seleucid bureaucracy, posts to which the king appointed and from which he could no doubt have dismissed if need arose. There was little danger of a meddlesome priest emerging in these conditions, none of his standing out effectively against the king. The chief priest was a servant of the king just as the priests of the classical period were servants of the people.

---

71. Arr. *Anab.* 7.14.7, with Hyperides, *Epitaphios* col. 8.21; *OCD*³ s.v. Sarapis; *RC* 67.

72. H. M. Cotton and M. Wörrle, "Seleukos IV to Heliodoros: A New Dossier of Royal Correspondence from Israel," *ZPE* 159 (2007): 191–203.

73. *RC* 44.

✎ CHAPTER 3

Analyzing Greek Gods

It is, the reader may feel, high time to popu-
late the religious system described in the previous two chapters with gods.
But the traditional approach of describing the gods one by one obscures
some of the most important questions, and it is these that this chapter will
confront. To what extent was the divine world, as perceived by the Greeks,
full of the sharply differentiated figures so familiar from myth and art
but inaccessible to actual experience? Ordinary speech tends to be vaguer,
whereas in cult practice the gods are commonly differentiated still further
by the addition of epithets. What kind of thing is a god if a river or an
abstraction such as "Righteous Indignation" or a living monarch can be
one? How important is the differentiation between gods of the heaven
and gods of the earth? The first half of the chapter will treat issues such as
these. The second will confront the simple-seeming question of how gods
differ from one another, if they do. When speaking of individual gods, the
ancients ascribe to them "honors," or spheres of activity, apparently specific
to themselves; but, as described by ancients and still more by moderns, those
spheres of activity seem very frequently to overlap. Was the divine world
a market system in which encroachment by a competitor could always
occur, or is it the task of scholarship to uncover distinctions that, if at a not
fully articulated level, yet structured Greek thought and kept the different
powers apart?

"The Gods" as Anonymous Collective; Named Gods; Gods with Epithets

At one level, the question "What is a Greek god?" scarcely seems a difficult one to answer. On the pediment of the temple of Zeus at Olympia, Apollo stands forth plastic, majestic, a superb type of imperious young manhood. Gods are mortals without their limitations. And such they are for the most part in myth too. But when gods are spoken of other than in tellings of myth, the perfect clarity of the sculptural image tends to dissolve, even if we set aside as an eccentric minority opinion the view of those who denied that they had human form at all. On the one hand, just as no mortal ever in fact saw Apollo's unshorn locks tossing on his shoulders, so too it was rare in ordinary speech to speak of individual named gods, except in expressions such as "by Zeus." An orator addressing the Athenian assembly would assure his audience of the favor of "the gods" to Athens; he would not tell them of the particular attitude of Zeus or Athena. So too juries were warned of the danger of offending "the gods" by an unjust verdict.

It is in oratory that the preference for this anonymous form of expression is most obvious. But we have every reason to think that oratory is here merely reflecting the norms of everyday speech. Tragedy is full of named gods, but they mostly appear in contexts such as choral odes which are furthest removed from the representation of ordinary language. In the more realistic portions, anonymous "gods" again predominate. In the most mimetic of all genres, the New Comedy of Menander, individual gods are indeed named frequently, but almost without exception in oaths or curses or prayers or with reference to their sanctuaries or cult acts addressed to them; they are not adduced by characters as an explanation for events in the human world. There is in fact no kind of Greek writing in which "the gods" are not often spoken of as a nameless collective.[1]

The distinction between the named gods of myth and the anonymous gods of daily discourse derives, it may be objected, not from a different belief about the nature of the gods but from the limitations of human perception. Mortals may believe in named deities, but they have no way of identifying their individual interventions in the world of experience; the issue is not one of ontology but of epistemology. In one scene in Homer, Diomedes is allowed to see gods present on the battlefield at Troy, but that is temporary

---

1. Oratory: see Mikalson, *Athenian Popular Religion,* 66–68. I know no general study for tragedy, but see, e.g., my comments in *Sophocles Revisited,* ed. J. Griffin (Oxford, 1999), 16; and cf. J. D. Mikalson, *Honor Thy Gods* (Chapel Hill, 1991), 25. Menander: *Dysk.* 643–44 is an exception, but one readily explicable from the plot.

poetic fantasy. In "reality" only oracles directly inspired by the gods, or poets claiming the inspiration of the Muses, can draw back the veil to reveal the divine agents behind events. Thus, in Herodotus, it is through oracles that we learn of Apollo's negotiations with the Moirai over the destiny of Croesus, of Athena's urgent supplications to Zeus at the time of the Persian invasion.[2] And though in daily speech mortals are chary of claims about the wishes of individual gods, once they turn to cult activity it is always to them that they address themselves. One prays and makes dedications to Athena or Artemis, not "the gods." In sleep too one may see individual gods, because in sleep every individual becomes a kind of seer.[3]

The objection is well made. But another linguistic phenomenon may seem to relate more truly to the very nature of the gods. In many authors, generalizing references to "the gods" alternate with references to "god" or "the god" or "the divine." A detailed study has shown that in a majority of cases singular and plural are interchangeable.[4] One of the central controversies in the study of Greek religion in the nineteenth century concerned polytheism and monotheism: some held that an original monotheism had been corrupted into the polytheism that we know, others saw monotheism struggling to emerge from the polytheistic mire. But no development in either direction in fact occurs. The culture is always polytheistic—it was well said long ago that Greeks typically prayed not to individual gods but to "chords of gods"[5]—but always one in which references to a singular god are entirely normal. It has come to be recognized that the terms of the nineteenth-century controversy were anachronistic: though many issues about the nature of gods (anthropomorphism for instance) were indeed objects of debate, the choice between "one god or many" was not one that even philosophers felt it necessary to worry very much about; it was Christian proselytizing monotheism that first polarized the one and the many.[6] The Greeks were not crypto-monotheists;

---

2. Hdt. 1.91.2–3; 7.141.3. Scene in Homer: *Il.* 5.127–28.

3. So Sostratus's mother's dream about Pan (Men. *Dysk.* 411–18) is not an exception to the general point made above about Menander.

4. G. François, *Le polythéisme et l'emploi au singulier des mots* θεός, δαίμων (Paris, 1957). On the occasional multiplication of individual gods ("Demeters," "Pans," etc.), see *LSS* 95 with Sokolowski's references ad loc.

5. An apophthegm of F. G. Welcker, cited by L. Preller, "Das Zwölfgöttersystem der Griechen," *Verhandlungen der neunten Versammlung deutscher Philologen, Schulmänner und Orientalisten zu Jena* (Jena, 1846), 48–56, at 49: "Nicht sowohl einzelne Götter... als ganze Accorde von Göttern." Monotheism v. polytheism: see Konaris, "Greek Gods," 64–71, 90–96, 200–205.

6. Cf. John North, "Pagans, Polytheists and the Pendulum," in *The Spread of Christianity in the First Four Centuries,* ed. W. V. Harris, 125–43 (Leiden, 2005). As North points out, it would not have occurred to Greek or Roman polytheists to define themselves as polytheists when no monotheist alternative was being promoted. In the survey of philosophers' views about the divine in Lucian, *Ikaromenippos,* 9, the monotheist position is in fact mentioned (this is already unusual),

for, though "god" could substitute for "the gods," the reverse also applies. But there was always a sense in which the gods were not a collectivity of individuals with individual wills, but rather the uncontrollable and inevitable element shaping and constraining human life and human lives.[7] This element could be spoken of indifferently as "the gods," "god," "the god," "the divine," "the godlike" (*daimonion*), "Zeus," and "fate."

In this sense, the Apollo of the Olympia pediment represents, within a spectrum of ways of envisaging deity, an extreme point of individualization and precision. But in another sense he is less precise than the gods of cult. In cult, gods were normally addressed under a specific epithet such as Athena Hippia or Apollo Delphinios or Artemis Brauronia. The claim sometimes made that the application of such epithets was invariable is wrong, but certainly the "cultic double name" (which could occasionally grow into a triple or even quadruple name) was the norm; a god with three sanctuaries in a given city would normally bear a different epithet in each. The cult epithet system was thus a central element in that emphasis on the particular sanctuary, the cult as practiced in a particular place, so characteristic of Greek religion; similarly, a god with three major sanctuaries would also normally have three priests.[8]

This greater particularity does not in itself make the god of cult an intrinsically different being from the god known by name alone; Athena Hippia, of horses, is one aspect of Athena seen in close-up, not the expression of a different conception of deity. But the system created de facto a certain fragmentation of the divine figure. It was common in oaths for a single god to be several times invoked under different epithets; oracles would very regularly advise cities to add a cult of a god under a new epithet to their existing set of cults of that god; and in a famous episode Xenophon, regular worshipper of Zeus Basileus, was told by a seer that his financial problems were caused by his neglect of Zeus Meilichios.[9] Even if in one perspective Zeus Meilichios was simply one aspect of Zeus, in another he had to be treated as an independent figure. He was often portrayed differently too, as a gigantic snake.[10]

---

but as one possibility among many. Even within Christianity, monotheism was merely, according to Paul Veyne, a "laborieux point d'honneur de théologiens" (*Quand notre monde est devenu Chrétien (312–394)* [Paris, 2007], 39); he also notes that "Platon, les stoïciens et Plotin sont polythéistes et monistes" (39 n. 2).

7. Cf. H. S. Versnel in *Sacrifice dans l'antiquité,* 171–79.

8. On all this see R. Parker, "The Problem of the Greek Cult Epithet," in *OpAth* 28 (2003): 173–83.

9. Xen. *Anab.* 7.8.1–6, to be contrasted with Xen. *Symp.* 8.9, "Zeus is believed to be one figure yet has many epithets."

10. See A. B. Cook, *Zeus: A Study in Ancient Religion* 2.2 (Cambridge 1925), 1160–78 (also citing snake representations of Zeus Philios).

Figure 1. Zeus Meilichios as a snake, approached by worshippers. Votive relief, fourth century, Piraeus. Berlin, Staatliche Museen K 91 (inv. SK 723). Photo © bpk / Antikensammlung, SMB / Ingrid Geske.

Some other applications of the system of the cultic double name may seem to stretch the unity of the god almost to breaking point. Herodotus (and other Greeks too) worked on the assumption that the difference between, say, "Zeus" and "Amoun" was no different from that between the Greek and

Egyptian words for "bread"; the god, like the bread, is the same everywhere, and Amoun is not a different god from Zeus but simply the Egyptian word for him. At the level of cult practice these assimilations were commonly accomplished via the cultic double name: the two names could be juxtaposed, as with the Carian Zeus Osogo, or the foreign god could simply be given a Greek name plus an epithet, whether local as with Zeus Thebaieus (Zeus of Egyptian Thebes, the god we call Amun-Re), or descriptive as with "Heavenly" Aphrodite (generally supposed to represent eastern goddesses such as Astarte).[11] At this point, the cultic double name has ceased, as viewed from outside, to be a way of picking out particular aspects of a single god, and has become an umbrella under which different gods shelter. Extreme cases exist even among figures we commonly think of as Greek. Zeus Meilichios is commonly represented on votive reliefs as an enormous snake (though depictions with the standard iconography of Zeus also exist) and received sacrifice of distinctive form;[12] it was probably this singularity that encouraged Xenophon's seer in the incident mentioned above to treat him as a wholly distinct figure. Ephesian Artemis too had the distinctive iconography that has made her famous (wrongly—the objects shown lack nipples) as "many-breasted."

The cultic double name allowed juxtapositions not just between a Greek and a non-Greek god's name but also between a major Greek god and a lesser: Apollo Paion, Artemis Eileithyia, Athena Nike. How the Greeks understood such compounds is not always clear, but it is plausible that in many cases the second element was taken as an epithet of the first: Artemis Eileithyia is Artemis in her relation to childbirth as Athena Hippia is Athena in her relation to horses. Yet in some parts of the Greek world Eileithyia is certainly treated as a freestanding goddess.[13] In literature from the fifth century onward the idea occasionally surfaces that the dividing lines between gods apparently drawn by distinct names may not reflect reality: in *Prometheus Vinctus* (209–10) the hero speaks of his mother as "Gaia and Themis, one form with many names (πολλῶν ὀνομάτων μορφὴ μία)," and in poetry

---

11. Zeus Thebaieus: Hdt. 1.182.2, and often; for a sixth-century Greek dedication to Zeus Thebaieus from Memphis, see L. H. Jeffery, *The Local Scripts of Archaic Greece*[2] (Oxford, 1990), 358, no. 49. Aphrodite Ourania: Pirenne-Delforge, *L'Aphrodite Grecque,* 437–39; Parker, *Athenian Religion,* 196 n. 158. Gods of all nations the same: Plut. *De Is. et Os.* 67, 377E–378A (but foreign religious cults might nonetheless appall: P. Borgeaud in *Norme réligieuse,* 73–75). Why some gods resisted assimilation (as, e.g., Bendis failed to become Artemis Bendis or Thracian Artemis) is a good question.

12. Iconography: A. B. Cook, *Zeus* (Cambridge, 1925), 2:1108–10; sacrifice: Xen. *Anab.* 7.8.5.

13. Cf. Parker, "Artemis Ilithye et autres: Le problème du nom divin utilisé comme épiclèse," in *Nommer les dieux: Theonymes, épithètes, épiclèses dans l'antiquité,* ed. N. Belayche et al. (Rennes, 2005), 219–26.

it is quite common to find, say, the myths and attributes of Demeter and Mother[14] or of Dionysus and Iacchus conflated. Cases such as Artemis Eileithyia show that such uncertainty about the boundaries of divine figures could also affect cult.

A parallel case in a slightly different way is that of Zeus Chthonios, Zeus of the earth and of the underworld. Is Zeus Chthonios to be understood as "Zeus in his aspect as god of the earth and the underworld," or is he rather "the underworld equivalent to Zeus"? In itself, the use of the epithet suggests the former, but in Aeschylus we hear of "another Zeus" (Ζεὺς ἄλλος) who judges human offenses under the earth.[15] Even to pose the question is perhaps to seek a precision that the Greeks knew to be unattainable. In Pausanias we sometimes encounter the phenomenon of cult addressed to a power whose identity is uncertain even to those who honor it. He registers no fewer than seven opinions as to who or what the Horse-Disturber, Taraxippos, honored at Olympia might be; he notes uncertainty among the Phigaleians whether Eurynome, possessor of a venerable shrine in their territory, is an epithet of Artemis or a daughter of Ocean.[16] The uncertainty can extend to the class of divine being (major god? minor god? hero?) to which the honorand belonged. But Taraxippos and Eurynome continued to receive cult whoever they were.

The Limited Diversity of Local Pantheons

There is, then, the argument thus far has shown, something illusory about the stability of a cultic calendar with its listing of clearly distinct gods. But at the level of cult practice Greeks accepted that illusion, and doubtless did not worry overmuch about the reality lying behind every name. It is to the world of civic pantheons as revealed in such cult calendars that I now turn. It is a commonplace that no two Greek political communities worshipped exactly the same gods: every city and tribe had its own set of figures that it worshipped collectively, and further differences arose at the level of the subdivisions of cities and tribes and of the private cults carried on within them.

---

14. The classic case is Eur. *Hel.* 1301–52, where the "Mother of the Gods" is described hunting for her lost daughter like Demeter; see too Pind. *Isth.* 7.3–4, where Demeter receives Mother's cymbals. Dionysus and Iacchus: see the works cited in Parker, *Polytheism,* 349 n. 95. The author of the probably fifth-century Derveni papyrus identifies (inter alia) Earth, Mother, Rhea, Hera, and Deo: T. Kouremenos et al., eds., *The Derveni Papyrus* (Florence, 2006), col. 22, 7–16.

15. Aesch. *Supp.* 231; on the issue see M. L. West's good note on Hes. *Op.* 465.

16. Paus. 6.20.15–19; 8.41.4–5; cf., e.g., Plut. *Cleom.* 9.2–3 on Pasiphae.

How deep these differences went is an open question; we know a certain amount about the cult systems of a large number of Greek communities, but a great deal only about very few, and everything about none at all. The Greeks themselves took local variation for granted, but never thought to suggest that the variations amounted to really radical differences; Herodotus mentions festivals confined to particular regions of the Greek world, but not gods.[17]

Listings of gods make dull reading, but a rough outline sketch is needed, to give a sense of the issue. As a working hypothesis it can be proposed (but not uncontroversially,[18] and certainly not demonstrably) that almost all Greek communities from about 700 onward, and in most cases very likely from much earlier, honored Zeus, Hera, Poseidon, Apollo, Artemis, Dionysus, Hermes, Aphrodite, Demeter (probably associated with Persephone/Kore), Heracles, and at a domestic level Hestia. But their prominence, titles, and functions will have varied notably from place to place. The groupings and family relationships among these gods that appear in Panhellenic myth will probably also have been widely accepted. The pairing of Zeus at his oracle at Dodona with Dione, not Hera, is striking, but unusual; what account a Dodonaean would have given of Zeus's relationship with the two goddesses is not known. From the late sixth century, cults dedicated to "the twelve gods" as a group begin to be attested.[19] Such cults had no broader effect on the religious calendar of cities or sacred sites that had them; they continued to worship other gods outside the twelve (an arbitrary number doubtless suggested by the twelve months). And listings of the twelve varied from city to city and even within a single city. But the concept confirms that the Greeks had an implicit notion of a distinction between major and minor gods (not their terms however—they spoke just of "the twelve gods"), and reached a tally of major gods roughly comparable to one that we might operate with.

---

17. 1.147.2, Apatouria as an Ionian festival; 2.171.3, disappearance of the Thesmophoria from the Peloponnese outside Arcadia.

18. H. A. Shapiro, for instance, suggests, *Art and Cult under the Tyrants in Athens* (Mainz, 1989), 13, that "many cults were probably introduced in Athens only in the course of the sixth century," and such arguments based on the absence of prior attestation are quite common. Total absence of a major figure seems unlikely to me; I would allow, however, that, say, in Sparta Ortheia may have stood in for Artemis if she was originally distinct from her (but such a "standing in" would inevitably have quickly led to assimilation). Irene Polinskaya in her forthcoming work on cults of Aegina will argue for a small pantheon.

19. First attested by the altar set up in the agora at Athens by the younger Pisistratus, Thuc. 6.54.6, and also probably going back to the sixth century at Olympia (*Hymn. Hom. Merc.* 128; Pind. *Ol.* 10.49; Herodorus of Herakleia *FGrH* 31 F 34a): see C. R. Long, *The Twelve Gods of Greece and Rome* (Leiden, 1987), or in brief K. Dowden in *Companion,* 43–45. Dione: see H. W. Parke, *The Oracles of Zeus* (Oxford, 1967), 69–70; E. Simon in *LIMC* s.v. Dione.

At a slightly lower level we can set, as figures by the fifth century very widely though perhaps not universally honored, the Dioscuri, Eileithyia, Hecate, and Mother; many regions too, perhaps all regions, paid cult to their local rivers, nymphs, and heroes. Asclepius and Pan rise in the fifth and fourth centuries from very humble beginnings to become honored in most of Greece. Some gods well-known from mythology, by contrast (Leto, Hephaestus, Kronos, Ares, Rhea), receive cult only here and there (Ares probably most widely, but always on a small scale). In a few localities, figures unknown to myth have, in the early period, an importance in cult normally only available to major gods: Aphaia, and Mnia and Auxesia, on Aegina; Ortheia at Sparta (if we assume that it is as a secondary development that she becomes "Artemis Ortheia"); Damie and Auxesie in Epidaurus; Alea in Tegea (if originally distinct from "Athena Alea"); Enodia in Thessaly; the Hyperborean Maidens on Delos. But with the exception of Aphaia (and Ortheia), they struggle to survive as independent figures beyond the fifth century. Some figures on the god/hero borderline too (Erechtheus at Athens; Hyacinthus, and Helen and Menelaus, at Sparta) are major powers locally. The gods of Mysteries, finally, are often distinctive and localized: the Kabeiroi of Thebes, the "Great Gods" of Samothrace, "Despoina" of Lycosura in Arcadia, the "Great Gods" or "Great Goddesses" of Andania in Messenia.

Important regional differences therefore there were. But we should not conclude that radically divergent local pantheons have been brought into partial and superficial conformity by the superimposition of Panhellenic gods and heroes; or, if they have, the superimposition has been extraordinarily successful. As far as we can tell, in every community (with the possible exception of Aegina) the Panhellenic figures prevail over the local. The distinctive character of each pantheon lies more in the specific weightings and roles assigned to the Panhellenic figures than in exclusively local figures. The story of how the local pantheons emerged would have been a highly instructive one, could it be told. (The attempt to tell it was a false trail much trodden in the early nineteenth century.) But it would certainly not have been a simple story of the particular yielding to the general. Widely shared elements, the great gods of myth, were evidently a part of it from a very early time.

But a doubt arises. The names of the Panhellenic deities, it can be agreed, were widely diffused from an early time, but it need not follow that the essence underlying the name was the same in every case. The skeptical position has two forms. According to one, the "same" god, that is, one bearing the same name, may have developed in notably different ways in different localities in response to the differing needs of the local worshipping group; in the Dark Ages, in particular, there were no Panhellenic sanctuaries and perhaps no universally circulating epic poetry to create a pressure toward conformity.[20] According to the other, the familiar names will sometimes have been imposed on unfamiliar natures, natures which will not, however, have surrendered their individuality, or not totally, merely through acquiring a new name. The unfamiliar nature might be that of an indigenous deity (in the colonial situation), of a foreign god whose worship entered the Greek world, of a perhaps anonymous local deity, or of an archaic type of deity (typically, the goddess of very wide powers) not recognized within the standard Panhellenic model.[21] We can call these the "local divergence" and the "foreign/archaic substrate" positions.

The question with local divergences is not whether they occurred, as they certainly did, but how often and on what scale; that issue will recur in chapter 7. As for the foreign/archaic substrate, it has doubtless been too often appealed to in colonial situations where no independent evidence exists for the indigenous cults that would supposedly have exerted pressure on the Greek.[22] We will see below that the archaic goddess of comprehensive powers is a figure to be viewed with suspicion. Nonetheless, it is a recognized truth that Greeks imposed familiar names on unfamiliar gods: Artemis Ephesia and Zeus Thebaieus were mentioned above, and innumerable Zeuses and Apollos and Areses of the interior of Asia Minor in the Hellenistic and Roman period are shown by their iconography to differ from the ordinary Olympians. Every postulate of a substrate must be assessed with great skepticism, but the possibility cannot be imperiously denied.

Natural Forces and Deified Abstractions

The differences not just in power but in nature between different gods have already been hinted at. The comparative mythologists of the second half of the nineteenth century expended extraordinary energy and learning on the attempt to reduce, or, as they thought, elevate, the Greek gods to natural forces or phenomena: Zeus was the sky, Hermes the winds, Athena

---

20. So C. Sourvinou-Inwood, *JHS* 98 (1978): 101–3 (= *"Reading" Greek Culture,* 147–51).

21. For the last see, e.g., M. Giangiulio, *Richerche su Crotona arcaica* (Pisa, 1989), 54–79, who sees a common template underlying certain cults of Hera and certain cults of Artemis, Athena, and Aphrodite; Hinz, *Demeter auf Sizilien,* 206, 215, 234; M. B. Hatzopoulos, "Artémis Digaia Blaganitis en Macédoine," *BCH* 111 (1987): 397–412 (with further references in *Leukopétra,* 29 n. 9), who postulates a pre-Hellenic Great Mother underlying a great variety of goddess cults in western Macedonia (ancient territory of the Brygian/Phrygians).

22. See the critics adduced by Sourvinou-Inwood, *"Reading" Greek Culture,* 181 n. 2; cf. the cautious formulations of Chiekova, *Pont gauche,* 289–93, and p. 244 below on the Euxine Achilles.

the rosy bloom of the sky before dawn, and so on. Early man worshipped nature, they thought, because the majesty of nature brought him closer than anything else to an experience of the absolute. We smile now at their efforts, and have done ever since L. R. Farnell observed that they reduced Greek mythology to "highly figurative conversation about the weather."[23] But it is in fact the case that Greeks paid cult to such natural forces as rivers and winds, not heavily disguised as mythological deities but under their own names.

The easier case is that of the winds. Aristophanes mentions sacrificing a black lamb when a typhoon is brewing. Pausanias expresses his amazement at the method used by the men of Methana against the wind Lips when it blows from the Saronic Gulf and withers their vines. Two men cut in half an all-white cock and, holding one half each, run in opposite directions around the vines; when they get back to their starting point, they bury the remains. (Similar methods were employed against hail at Kleonai in the Argolid.) The Athenians built a shrine to the North Wind because in 480 he answered their prayer and wrecked the Persian fleet when anchored off Thermopylae. Regular annual rites, where attested, are likely to have been performed at times of year when destructive winds were a particular threat (or in commemoration of a saving intervention such as that of 480).[24] The cult of the winds represents a rare case of religion operating in the way that J. G. Frazer supposed primitive religion always to operate, as a mechanism intended to control the environment. One sacrificed or prayed to the winds to stop them blowing, or occasionally, in a military context, to cause them to blow destructively against an enemy. (Or where they had contributed to a great military victory, one used them as a peg on which to hang a celebratory cult.) When there was no need to calm the winds or raise them, one ignored them. In the main, it does indeed seem to have been as simple as that.[25]

---

23. *Cults of the Greek States* (Oxford, 1896), 1:9; cf. Konaris, "Greek Gods," 104–30.

24. Ar. *Ran.* 847–48 (cf. Xen. *Anab.* 4.5.4); Paus. 2.34.2; Hdt. 7.189; cf. Stengel, *Opferbräuche,* 146–53; Parker, *Athenian Religion,* 156 n. 14. Kleonai: "When the hail-wardens signaled the approach of hail, each man on his account would sacrifice one a lamb, one a hen . . . anyone who had no lamb or hen pierced his finger with a stylus and performed the rite with this blood" (Seneca *QNat* 4.6). Annual rites: Paus. 2.12.1 (Sikyon, explicitly said to be intended to calm the winds); Paus. 8.29.2 (offerings to "thunder, lightning, and gales"); *LSCG* 52.19–20; commemorative cults: Hdt. 7.178, 189, Delphi and Athens; Paus. 8.27.14, 8.36.6, Megalopolis; Ael. *VH* 12.61, Thurii.

25. A mild complication (discussed by Stengel, *Opferbräuche*) is that of the forms of offering. The ad hoc sacrifices to winds were non-participatory slaughter-sacrifices; commemorative sacrifices are likely to have been participatory; annual non-commemorative sacrifices perhaps varied between the two forms.

Rivers are quite different. It may be that no river received a major state cult,[26] but lesser honors are quite widely attested, and Zeus's oracle at Dodona often advised consultants to make offerings to Achelous, the great stream of northwest Greece that came to be treated as the river and river god par excellence. Some rivers had precincts with altars and even small temples, but offerings could also be thrown direct into their waters; in a single rite on Mykonos Acheloos received three lambs on the altar and three "in the stream."[27]

> I do not know much about gods; but I think that the river
> Is a strong brown god—sullen, untamed and intractable,
> ....
>
> Keeping his seasons and rages, destroyer, reminder
> Of what men choose to forget. Unhonoured, unpropitiated
> By worshippers of the machine, but waiting, watching and waiting.

So writes T. S. Eliot in *Four Quartets*. The standard depiction of rivers as a bull or a man-headed bull or a horned man is doubtless a recognition of their strength. But they were not for the Greeks, unlike winds, the grim and dangerous powers that Eliot imagines. The many votive reliefs to Pan and the Nymphs that contain a head of Achelous do indeed associate him with the powers of wild nature, but wild nature in its cheerful, sportive aspect.[28] And what rivers embodied for the Greeks in cultic terms was the fructifying power of moisture, the source of life itself. In myth rivers often sired human offspring; in cult, one prayed to rivers for offspring and named the child born in answer to the prayer as a "gift" of the river in question, Cephisodotus as it might be. Cephisus had a sanctuary at Phaleron in which he was accompanied by a string of further deities all associated with childbirth and child rearing in some way; one dedication there was made by a Cephisodotus.

---

26. Depictions of river gods on the coins of various cities of Magna Graecia are sometimes taken to show that they had a "city-protecting" role in these cities (so, e.g., C. Weiss, *Griechische Flussgottheiten in vorhellenistischer Zeit* [Würzburg, 1984], 21–22). But a river could symbolize a city on coins, particularly, as was regularly the case in Sicily (Strabo 6.1.12, C 262; Douris *FGrH* 76 F 59), when the city was named from the river (so, e.g., Gela, Akragas, Selinus), without necessarily enjoying like prominence in cult. On river gods, see Nilsson, *Geschichte,* 236–40. Dodona: Ephorus *FGrH* 70 F 20; on the cult of Achelous see especially Σ T Hom. *Il.* 24.616b, mentioning cult performed by Athenians, "Didymaioi," Sikeliots, and Rhodians (games are also attested in Metapontum by a stater, *LIMC* s.v. Acheloos no. 75, N. K. Rutter, *Historia Numorum* [Italy], London 2001, no. 1491).

27. *LSCG* 96.34–37; cf. p. 146 n. 85.

28. See C. Edwards, "Greek Votive Reliefs to Pan and the Nymphs" (PhD diss., New York University, 1985). Ael. *VH* 2.33 gives a useful overview of the various iconographic possibilities for depicting river gods.

As the child grew up it retained an association with its patronal river, and might consecrate to it a lock of adolescent hair; the river Pamisos in Messenia cured children's diseases. Other cultic roles of rivers seem minor by comparison.[29]

Earth, too, was worshipped, on a modest scale, as the place of growth (she typically received pregnant victims as sacrificial offerings) and as a "nurturer of children" (*kourotrophos*).[30] Nymphs straddle the natural and the social. They are regularly intimately associated with features of the natural world, springs above all, and with particular places; they populate the landscape, one might say. Three illustrations from cult: a sacred law from Attica publishes the rule, endorsed by the oracle of Delphi itself, that anyone drinking from the spring Halykos should pay an annual fee of an obol (a very modest sum) to the nymphs "for rites"; another such law from the Asklepieion at Cos requires offerings for the nymphs to be sacrificed on the altars and forbids, what was evidently a temptation, the throwing of cakes into "the springs in the shrine"; one of the points at which the sacred Milesian college of the Molpoi stop to sing a paean during their procession to Didyma is "at (the) meadow (at Meadow?) on the height by the nymphs."[31] The very frequent "caves of the nymphs" are a different aspect of their embeddedness in the natural world. But a single spring is often inhabited not just by one nymph but by a cluster, so that a simple equivalence between natural phenomenon and deity such as is found with rivers does not apply. Such nymphs are depicted simply as young women, with nothing liquid about them, and "nymph" (νύμφη) is the ordinary Greek word for "bride"; a shrine of "Nymph" (singular—a rarity) below the acropolis in Athens has yielded a richer collection of offerings associated with marriage than has any other.[32] There is, it is true, a symbolic link between springs and marriage through the much-stressed ritual of the bridal bath, as also through the fructifying and child-nurturing force of water mentioned earlier. But nymphs escape narrow confinement within particular physical spheres in many other ways, in their regular association in cult with "Apollo leader of the Nymphs," for instance.

---

29. Fructifying moisture: e.g., Σ Pind. *Pyth.* 4.145. Shrine at Phaleron: Parker, *Polytheism,* 430–31. Pamisos: Paus. 4.31.4, confirmed by excavated votives: N. Valmin, *The Swedish Messenia Expedition* (Lund, 1938), 419–65. Hair: Hom. *Il.* 23.141–49 (where vows to a river on behalf of a son also appear); Aesch. *Cho.* 6. Other cultic roles: e.g., armies might make offerings to rivers that they encountered.

30. See, e.g., Parker, *Polytheism,* 416, 427.

31. *LSCG* 178; ibid. 152; *LSA* 50.29. On nymphs see H. Herter, *RE* s.v. Nymphai; J. Larson, *Greek Nymphs* (Oxford, 2001).

32. J. Travlos, *Pictorial Dictionary of Ancient Athens* (London, 1971), 361–64; C. Papadopoulou-Kanellopoulou, *Iero tis Numphis: Melanomorfés loutrophoroi* (Athens, 1997).

Like the nymphs, many major gods could be manifested through and as natural forces, though not as them alone. "Zeus rains," "the god rains," and "it rains" are interchangeable forms of expression, and Zeus both hurls and is the thunderbolt, "Thundering Zeus" or "Zeus Thunderbolt" or "Zeus who comes down" (Zeus Kataibates)[33] (and many other such titles); as "the cloud-gatherer" he perches on the peak of most major Greek mountains. The line between the god as the cause of a natural phenomenon and as the natural phenomenon itself is a fine one doubtless not worth agonizing over. Poseidon, strictly speaking, is perhaps the cause of storms at sea, not the storm itself, but, were there a single physical manifestation of the storm analogous to the lightning bolt, Poseidon would also be that (just as St. Elmo's fire, the electrical manifestation taken as a good omen by storm-pressed sailors, was a form of the Dioscuri); he also caused earthquakes.

Other gods have a non-personal substratum of different type: when the sophist Prodicus announced that Demeter was grain and Dionysus wine,[34] he was only giving one-sided expression to a general perception (but Demeter was also identified with earth), while several terms in common use for sexual intercourse derive directly from the name Aphrodite. On the other hand, the association of Apollo and Artemis with natural phenomena is secondary (if we disallow their early roles as senders of, respectively, plague and death in childbed), and Hermes, Athena, and Hera have none. The identifications of Apollo with the sun and Artemis with the moon that begin in the fifth century can be taken, at most, as indicating a potentiality inherent in the Greek conception of deity, a shape into which a god could be molded. Conversely, sun and moon received no significant worship in early Greece.[35]

So much for the divine as manifested in the world of nature. But these physically based gods consorted cheerfully with others whom we would describe—it is, however, important that the description is ours, not theirs—as personifications of abstract qualities or ideas. Greek art and literature (starting

---

33. Cf. p. 4 n. 5. On mountain Zeuses, see M. Langdon, *A Sanctuary of Zeus on Mount Hymettos* (*Hesperia* suppl. 16, Princeton, 1976).

34. DK 84 B 5. The reduction of gods to physical substances or phenomena is criticized as impious in Plut. *De Is. et Os.* 66–7, 377D–F, to "experiences and capacities and powers" (πάθη καὶ δυνάμεις καὶ ἀρεταί) in Plut. *Amat.* 13–14, 757B–C. I merely note the occasional instances where objects are said to be worshipped: Plut. *Quaest. Graec.* 13, 294C (a stone, among the Aenianes); Paus. 9.40.11–12 (the scepter, called Spear, of Agamemnon, at Chaironeia: Schachter, *Cults,* 1:199); cf. Nock, *Essays,* 242.

35. See in brief the articles Helios and Selene in *OCD*³. The cult of winds and rivers was certainly already strong in Homeric times (*Il.* 23.141–49, 193–95), and that of winds in Linear B (tablets KN 200 and 202). So no simple pattern reveals itself. And on one island, Rhodes, Helios was already prominent by the fifth century (*SEG* 27.481), and perhaps much earlier. A full study would need to consider much else, e.g., gods of the sea.

with Hesiod's *Theogony*) is full, not just of rivers and sea nymphs and so on, but also of groups such as Graces and Seasons and Destinies and individuals such as Love (Eros), Persuasion, Fair Fame, Peace, Strife, Fear, Blind Madness, Rumor, and many others. Substantial numbers of these figures acquired some role in cult, if usually in a small way, and though positive (Health, Peace, Concord) or neutral (Persuasion) qualities were normally chosen, the admiral of Philip V who established altars to Impiety and Lawlessness wherever he landed was working within the idiom; the list of such cults that can be established for Sparta, apparently a special case, includes Death, Laughter, and Hunger.[36]

A few quotations may help to illuminate the world of thought. Hesiod writes that "no rumor ever perishes that many men speak; she too is a goddess"; Themistocles sought to extort money from the Andrians, backed by what he called "two great gods, Persuasion and Compulsion," but was told that, since two useless gods never left their island, Poverty and Helplessness, they could not pay; while expressions such as "to recognize one's friends is a god" or "[if you are moved by shame], you will achieve nothing: that goddess is ineffectual" are quite common in tragedy. All the forces that are powerful within human life are in a sense divine; in Wilamowitz's famous formula, "god" is a predicate, a special power recognized in certain phenomena.[37]

In cult, the personifications tend to be tucked in with major deities, Persuasion, for instance, with Aphrodite or Health with Asclepius or Virtue (Arete) with Heracles, just as in poetry and genealogy they are often born of a major god or appear in his or her train. They thus extend or clarify the scope of a major divine figure, in a way somewhat comparable to the cult epithet system; sometimes they become epithets, as in Athena Victory or Aphrodite Persuasion. But figures such as the Graces and Eros can stand on their own; they are indeed such familiar components of Greek cult that we tend to forget that they are abstractions no less than is, say, the goddess Democracy. And the cult of Nemesis at Rhamnus in Attica is a remarkable example of a major freestanding cult of an abstract quality, "Righteous Anger/Indignation"; Themis, "Divinely Sanctioned Order," may have had

---

36. Admiral: Polyb. 18.54.10; Sparta: N. Richer in *Companion*, 248.

37. Hes. *Op.* 763–64; Hdt. 8.111.2; Eur. *Hel.* 560 (cf. R. Kannicht's note ad loc.); Eur. *Ion* 337. Wilamowitz's formula: *Glaube*, 1, 17; cf. S. R. F. Price, *JHS* 104 (1984): 79–95; P. Veyne, *Annales* (2000): 30: "Tout ce qui rompait avec la quotidienneté, tout ce qui était marquant, y compris les sources, les monts et les rois, prenait une forme religieuse. Car le sacré n'est pas une essence, mais une forme."

similar prominence in Thessaly. The goddesses known as "Reverend Ones" (Semnai) or "Kindly Ones" (Eumenides) are familiar as guardians of the moral order; to worship Nemesis or Themis was probably somewhat like worshipping them.[38]

Nobody denies that Greeks paid cult to rivers, winds, and Love. The tendency, however, is to acknowledge such phenomena rather briefly, and pass on to the major Olympians. But any attempt to analyze Greek conceptions of deity must take serious account of them. Their role in cult may be modest, but for analytical purposes what matters is that they can receive cult at all. Also relevant is the cult paid to living mortals, a phenomenon first attested in the fifth century though becoming much commoner in the time of the Hellenistic monarchs, its typical beneficiaries. Three positions are here available: that the phenomenon is a symptom of change/decline/a new "épistème," or however one chooses to describe it, and can thus be set aside; that the "godlike" honors paid to mortals were always perceived as distinct from the honors paid to actual gods, and can again be bracketed off for that reason; and finally that an extension to include living mortals was a potentiality present in the Greek conception of deity and must be reckoned with in any attempt to describe that conception.

I postpone discussion of the complicated problem to an appendix;[39] but in brief it can be said that, whereas position one (change and decline) is today largely discredited, the other two both capture aspects of the phenomenon. On the one hand, nobody was unaware that monarchs were doomed to death and thus radically different in nature from the immortal gods; when they received godlike honors, the traditional association between deity and immortality was bracketed off, not forgotten. On the other hand, the benefits in virtue of which they received those honors, such as the rescue of a city in time of acute danger, were exactly those for which gods also were traditionally thanked and honored. The relevant criterion is what the "god" does, not what he is. So ruler cult reveals the crucial importance of effective power within the Greek understanding of deity. A king is treated as a god not because of what he is (he is in fact a mortal) but because of what he can do.

---

38. On the worship of "abstractions," see Parker, *Athenian Religion,* 228–37 [+]; E. Stafford, *Worshipping Virtues: Personification and the Divine in Ancient Greece* (London, 2000); on Nemesis, Parker, *Polytheism,* 406–7; on Themis, Stafford, 2000, chap. 2; Rudhardt, *Thémis.* Heracles and Arete: *IErythrai* 207 (*LSA* 26) 9.

39. See appendix 3.

Olympians and Chthonians

We are almost ready to tackle the individual Olympians. But first the controversial topic of "chthonian gods" must be broached.[40] What is at issue is the whole shape of the divine world as seen by the Greeks. On one view the distinction between Olympians, gods of the bright sky, and chthonians, gods of the earth, constitutes a central division within the pantheon, expressed and made vivid above all by the different sacrificial rituals applied to the two groups. Individual gods straddle the divide, it is allowed, without diminishing its importance. On the other view, the distinction is simply one among several that Greeks draw from time to time within the pantheon, and the various divergences from standard sacrificial procedure that exist should not be brought together within a single class of "chthonian sacrifice." (On either view, the division is an unequal one, Olympians far outnumbering chthonians.)

The orator Isocrates draws a distinction between "the gods called Olympian," whom we approach in search of blessings, and "gods who bear less attractive names," who are honored only in order to turn them away.[41] Isocrates, no one denies, exaggerates to make a particular rhetorical point that has nothing to do with religion (he is urging mildness on King Philip); Greek religion was not dualist, and all gods were potentially sources of harm as well as of benefit, of benefit as well as of harm. The question is how gross is his distortion. Some categories of divine being were certainly treated with more elaborate displays of nervous respect than others. The chorus in Sophocles' *Oedipus at Colonus* speak of the Eumenides as the goddesses whom "we tremble to name and we pass by without looking, without utterance, without words." That is very different from the chorus in Euripides' *Ion* hailing Athena as "my goddess."[42] But are the Eumenides as represented by Sophocles representative of a broader class of "chthonians"?

First some points that are not in dispute. The adjective *chthonios,* of the earth, or closely comparable expressions, are from time to time applied to the

---

40. Pro the importance of the Olympian/chthonian distinction, see above all Scullion, "Olympian and Chthonian"; contra, R. Schlesier, article "Chthonian Gods," in *Brills New Pauly* [+] (note especially Nock, *Essays,* 592, 595). See too now A. Henrichs in *Greek Sacrificial Ritual,* 47–60.

41. Isoc. 5 (*Philippos*) 117: "In the case of gods too I observe that those who bring men blessings are called Olympian, while those responsible for calamities and punishment have less pleasant names; private individuals and cities have founded temples and altars of the one group, while the other is honored neither in sacrifices nor in prayers, but we perform rites of expulsion (ἀποπομπαί) against them"; cf. Sourvinou-Inwood, *Hylas,* 163–64. Note too Hippoc. *Vict.* 4.89 Jones, last sentence: after well-omened dreams, pray to Sun, Zeus of the Heavens, Zeus of Property (Ktesios), Athena of Property, Hermes, Apollo; after ill-omened dreams, to "the gods of aversion, Earth, and heroes." But in 4.90 (line 63 Jones) one should pray after dreaming of the earth to Earth, Hermes, and heroes.

42. Soph. *OC* 129–31; Eur. *Ion* 211.

following classes of being, and sometimes to more than one simultaneously: (1) the ordinary dead; (2) the powerful dead, the heroes;[43] (3) gods associated with the underworld such as Persephone, Hades/Plouton, Hecate, Hermes, and groups such as the Erinyes/Eumenides/Semnai; (4) the gods of agriculture, Earth, Demeter, and (in one of his aspects) Zeus. When applied to Demeter and Zeus, the epithet "earthy" may primarily indicate not a place of residence but a sphere of activity, agriculture. Even so, the fact that, Olympians though they are (so too is Hermes), they can receive the chthonian epithet, proves that the division between the two classes is not an absolute one. Even on a strong view of the importance of the divide, the divine world does not fall apart into two unconnected halves; Persephone, queen of the underworld, is daughter of the king of heaven (her husband is his brother), and according to the myth she commutes between the two spheres.

One context where certain chthonians come vividly into view is that of curse tablets.[44] Such tablets are deposited in graves or other points of access to the underworld and call on underworld powers to "bind" their targets. The powers invoked (often explicitly addressed as "chthonians") are broadly those of group (3) above, Hermes and Persephone above all; those of group (4) are absent, with the unsurprising exception of Earth herself. In this context, then, groups (3) and (4) split apart from one another. There is nonetheless a conceptual link between groups (1) to (3) and group (4) in that the dead and the underworld powers have influence over agricultural growth. Persephone, goddess of the underworld, is daughter of Demeter, goddess of corn, and Zeus Chthonios, the farmer's friend, can scarcely be dissociated from that Zeus Katachthonios whom Homer represents as ruling alongside Persephone. Even if the conception of plants coming "from the dead" is only attested once, the dead are regularly invoked to "send up good things"; Plouton bestows wealth, agricultural wealth above all; powers such as the Semnai, when duly appeased, promote the growth of plants or at least refrain from blighting it; and a powerful if vague symbolic association surely existed between the periodic return of Persephone from the underworld and the emergence of the corn.[45] (But the connection is not invariable: Hecate and Hermes have close links with the underworld but none with agriculture.)

---

43. See Scullion, "Olympian and Chthonian," 93 n. 43.

44. For an introduction, see D. Ogden in *Witchcraft and Magic in Europe: Ancient Greece and Rome,* ed. V. Flint et al., 1–90 (London, 1999); cf. pp. 259–61.

45. Zeus Chthonios agricultural: Hes. *Op.* 465; *LSCG* 96.25. Zeus Katachthonios: Hom. *Il.* 9.457. "From the dead": Hippoc. *Vict.* 4.92; "send up good things": Ar. fr. 504.14 with K/A's note ad loc.; Persephone and the corn: Burkert, *Homo Necans,* 259–61.

FIGURE 2. Enclosure of a "chthonian," probably a hero, in the Athenian agora: offerings—small pots, lamps, loom weights—were placed on the ground around an outcrop of living rock. Photo American School of Classical Studies at Athens: Agora Excavations.

Thus far we have been on firm ground. The classes of chthonians that we have looked at are so spoken of by good sources; and the double aspect of earth, as home of the dead and the source of growth, is well established; so too that those two aspects to some extent blend into one another. We can note too the practice sometimes found of simply depositing offerings for Demeter and Persephone in the earth.[46] The controversial question is partly whether Zeus under the title Meilichios (say) is a chthonian though not so described; partly whether the mixed status of Zeus, Hermes, Demeter, and Persephone, as powers part Olympian, part chthonian, is shared by further gods too. The older literature is so full of claims that this or that god "has a chthonian aspect" that one is left with few if any pure Olympians.[47] What the vague concept of a "chthonian aspect" may amount to can be focused as the proposition that a given god who is Olympian when worshipped under

---

46. Hinz, *Demeter auf Sizilien,* 53.
47. As was complained by A. Fairbanks in a pioneering critique, *AJP* 21 (1900): 241–59.

cult titles A, B, and C, is chthonian under titles Y and Z. What is at issue, or what should be, is not labeling for labeling's sake but a hypothesis about the perceived powers of the god in question as worshipped under a particular epithet: the claim that Zeus Meilichios, say, or Zeus Polieus is a chthonian is a claim that Greeks worshipped him under those titles with a view to securing his aid in making the crops grow (or some related goal).

The case for applying the chthonian label to deities not explicitly so described can occasionally seek iconographic support: Zeus, for instance, under certain aspects can be depicted as a snake, creature of the earth.[48] But it is based primarily on sacrificial ritual. It used to be believed, on the basis of certain schematic claims in late sources, that there existed a distinctive form of sacrifice, systematically different from that made to the gods above and universally employed, with a few rare exceptions, for offerings to the chthonians; this distinctive mode of chthonian sacrifice was the chief guarantee that the chthonians did indeed possess significant unity as a class, and a deity that received the distinctive form was thereby shown to be a chthonian even if not so described. Epigraphic discoveries have refuted that conception and it need be discussed no further.[49] It is also now agreed that no Greek word or group of words exists meaning "to sacrifice to the chthonians." Instead we are faced with a series of divergences from the standard type of sacrifice, which may occur singly or in combination; we learn more of these divergences, the ground shifts, whenever a calendar that gives more than a minimum of ritual detail is published.[50] More meat may be burnt than the portion traditionally assigned to the gods, whether the whole animal (holocaust) or, much more rarely, a fraction (e.g., a ninth part) (moirocaust). Libations of mixed wine may be forbidden, in favor of unmixed wine or "sober" wineless libations (an exquisite variant is "sober as far as the entrails," i.e., the character of the libations was altered during the ceremony). The blood of the victim may be poured not onto the altar but into the earth. A victim of particular type (black, or pregnant) may be required. There may be an explicit rule that the meat of the animal must be consumed "on the spot," not carried away to be eaten at leisure in the house. Other variations (type of altar used; time of day; direction in which the sacrificer faces) are attested in late sources but are

---

48. See n. 10 above.

49. See Ekroth, *Sacrificial Rituals,* passim, building on the classic study of A. D. Nock, "The Cult of Heroes," in *Essays* 575–602 (from *HThR* 37 [1944]: 141–74). On the linguistic point, Ekroth shows that ἐναγίζειν is never used of sacrifice to a god (but only to the dead or to heroes), and so cannot cover a field of "chthonian sacrifice."

50. A text from Aixone in Attica first published in 2004 brought important new evidence, for instance: see p. 144 n. 81.

usually not of a nature to find confirmation, or refutation, in the epigraphic record.[51]

Chthonian sacrifice as a single type has vanished. A spirited case has, however, been made for replacing it with a cluster of types of chthonian sacrifice. The issues involved are complex and technical, and I postpone discussion of them too to an appendix.[52] My conclusion is that there is little profit in applying the label "chthonian" where the ancients did not. The divergences from standard sacrificial forms will always have had a meaning, even if one we are often unable to recover. But those divergences obey a more complicated or more fragmented logic than even a sophisticated elaboration of the chthonian/Olympian opposition can capture.

The Different "Honors" of Gods: The Structuralist Approach

I revert to the great gods. How is one to analyze a major Greek god? One or two ancient theories that still, undetected as such, occasionally exercise an influence must first be pulled out into the light of day to give an account of themselves. K. O. Müller early in the nineteenth century argued the case for "tribal gods," and E. Curtius near its end introduced the still influential concept of "total goddesses."[53] In Müller's conception the Greek pantheon that we know emerged by combination of the gods of the different Greek tribes; they became, therefore, true polytheists only by chance, since originally the great god of an individual tribe, such as the Apollo of the Dorians, would have exercised almost universal powers. Curtius argued that

---

51. On all this, see pp. 144–150 below.

52. See appendix 4.

53. See Konaris, "Greek Gods," 133–34, 136–37 (K. O. Müller); 178–79 (Curtius). Lucian's Zeus claims to have been a "total god" until rivals eroded his powers (*Ikaromenippos,* 24). We do not, of course, need to believe him. In the panegyric to Hecate contained in Hesiod's *Theogony,* comprehensive powers are claimed for the goddess (411–52)—she grants wealth, and assists in judicial affairs, politics, war, sport, horsemanship, seafaring, stock rearing, and child nurture. But the poet stresses that some of these functions are shared with the more obvious patrons (stock rearing with Hermes, aid at sea with Poseidon) and that she is much esteemed by Zeus and all the gods; her activities are known and accepted, therefore. No other evidence suggests such a panoply of powers for Hecate, and the panegyric remains an intriguing and unexplained anomaly (one that illustrates, one must concede, a thought experiment that was possible within polytheism). The speech of Teiresias in Euripides' *Bacchae* (298–313) in which, for promotional purposes, he seeks to broaden the scope of Dionysus's powers works very differently: he explains the two extensions (into the spheres of prophecy and warfare) in terms of Dionysus's core mode of activity, "madness." So too claims for the universal power of Aphrodite (*Hymn. Hom. Ven.* 1–6; Eur. *Hipp.* 447–50) all relate to the ubiquity of sexual desire.

the Greek goddesses emerged by differentiation, a differentiation, however, only imperfectly accomplished, within a single universal goddess, that oriental "Great Mother" still so prominent in New Age, and in some branches of feminist, mythology.[54] Curtius, it should be noted, was not a spinner of orientalist fantasies but an archaeologist faced with the difficulty of distinguishing one goddess from another amid the figurines emerging in such abundance from excavations both in Greece and the Near East; and it is to his credit that he was willing to envisage Athena and the rest emerging from "Semitic" models. The details of the positions here crudely sketched need not concern us. What matters is the implication common to both that many Greek gods may still retain traces of an original almost universal competence; anything is possible, and even Athena, say, may be a "mother" or be able to promote the fertility of the fields.

Such assumptions run absolutely contrary to all that the Greeks say about their own pantheon. From Homer down to the *Hymns* of Callimachus and beyond, innumerable texts attest the idea of a division between the gods, and in the *Theogony* and the Homeric Hymns we are often shown such divisions taking place; in the *Homeric Hymn to Hermes* we see a division that is explicitly differential, as the functions of Hermes and Apollo are clearly demarcated one from another. What is divided is not quite constant. In Homer we find divisions of space—Zeus has heaven as his portion, Poseidon the sea, Hades the underworld, while earth is shared—and also of function—Aphrodite, for instance, is told that "the works of war" have not been granted to her—but in texts in general the dominant idiom is the imprecise one of "honors."[55] Perhaps there was also a sense in which any god was additionally an undifferentiated fragment of "the divine" and could in extremis be appealed to in any human need. But regular cult should have respected the notion of a division of functions (not necessarily the same in every community). As for heroes, they fall outside this frame of reference; they had no share in the division but certainly had powers, which were not, however, seen as in competition with those of gods. The working assumption ought to be that all Greeks had some notion of the divine world being structured by a division of "honors" between the gods. Exceptions, supposed manifestations

---

54. For a critique, see L. Goodison and C. Morris, eds., *Ancient Goddesses: The Myths and the Evidence* (London, 1998).

55. Hom. *Il.* 15.187–93; 5.428. "Honors": e.g., Hes. *Theog.* 74, 112, 203–6, 885; Hdt. 2.53 "honors and skills" (τιμαὶ καὶ τέχναι); there is minute division of functions still, e.g., in Plut. *Amat.* 14–16, 757D–758D. Cf. Rudhardt, *Mythe, religion,* 227–33, "La repartition des τίμαι, articulation centrale des systèmes mythiques grecs."

of the power of total gods or goddesses, need to be demonstrated rigorously, not allowed by default on the basis of ambiguous evidence.[56]

In the Greek conception, therefore, individual gods had a portfolio of exclusive functions. But the texts do not state or imply that the functions within such a portfolio have any organizing center; they are presented as a series of separate competences. There is therefore no objection from texts to what one might call the snowball theory of the Greek gods, the idea that as a god rolls down through history it picks up new functions and powers that need not cohere with its original nature or with one another: rather like a multinational company that starts out selling records and ends up running an airline. This assumption is occasionally stated explicitly within scholarship, more often (like so many others in the study of Greek deity) merely acted on. On the other hand, standard handbooks often try in greater or lesser degree to give a unifying account of a particular god's functions: the question of the unity of the divine remains a central and open one.[57]

One complication to what has been said about division of honors must be allowed. Though this was one way in which Greeks regularly spoke about the interrelationships of their gods, they also often spoke in terms of the especial love of particular gods for particular cities. The correlate was that a particular god (or more usually goddess) often had a prominence in the cults of a particular city apparently out of scale with its place in an ordered division of honors. Greeks did not attempt to reconcile the two ways of speaking about the gods; they deployed them separately in different contexts. The role of "chief god" or "special god" was not acknowledged explicitly, other than through the language of a god's love for a place, and there is no epithet that indicates it; chief gods are often called "of the city" (Polias) or "protector of

---

56. What do I say, it may be asked, about the pregnant animals twice offered (p. 286 n. 9 below) to Athena? They constitute, I concede, good evidence for Athena exercising a quite unfamiliar function. I can merely plead that they are too exceptional to be treated as vestiges of an original much broader competence.

57. W. F. Otto was responsible for some notable unifying analyses in *Die Götter Griechenlands* (Bonn, 1929; trans. M. Hadas as *The Homeric Gods,* New York, 1954). On the other side, see, e.g., C. J. Herington, *JHS* 89 (1969): 168–70 (criticizing the opposite approach of L. Séchan and P. Lévêque, *Les grandes divinités de la Grèce* [Paris, 1966]); Mikalson, *Athenian Popular Religion,* 72; F. Graf, *Apollo* (London, 2009), 5: "In mapping the provinces of Apollo's activities, I will not even try to find a unity that would underlie the different roles: the Aristotelian enterprise to reduce multiplicity to one single origin never convinced me when dealing with Greek gods." Cf. U. von Wilamowitz-Moellendorff, *Greek Historical Writing and Apollo* (Oxford, 1908), 45: "For too long a time Science was seeking for a formula which should express the whole being of the god.... The gods, too, have their history. Inasmuch as they live only in men's emotions, with those emotions they shift and change.... We have to understand not one Apollo, but many and diverse Apollos, living and changing in the ritual and belief of diverse places and periods."

the city" (Poliouchos), but not invariably, and those epithets are not confined to chief gods. But in many cities the phenomenon is undeniable: the roles of Athena at Athens and of Hera in Argos, Samos, and in many places in Magna Graecia are the model cases. Pausanias often identifies the god whom a community honors "most of all."[58]

It is because, say, Athena of Athens and Hera of Argos or Croton so resemble one another in this role that they have often been seen as late avatars of the "total goddess" or of a goddess who, if not total, possessed a bundle of attributes distinct from those of either Hera or Athena as described in Panhellenic myth (this is the "archaic substrate" theory mentioned above). But a chief god is not a "total god" in the sense of replacing all others; not, at any rate, in the one case that is open to really detailed observation, that of Athena at Athens. Specialized gods retain specialized functions even where a chief god exists. Even trespasses by chief gods on the domain of other gods are probably rare and restricted; that Tenos's leading god Poseidon was honored as "doctor" is unusual.[59]

The special goddess (to take the normal case) achieves her prominence, it can be argued, in two ways. On the one hand, every major god is a concertina that can be expanded or contracted. As we will see later, central human preoccupations, such as child rearing or warfare, potentially involved many different gods, if in different ways. Where a goddess is chief god of a city, all her potential involvements become actual: the concertina is stretched to its fullest extent (with consequent contraction, but not suppression, in other cases). On the other hand, many appeals, many expressions of hope or gratitude, do not clearly relate to the recognized powers of a particular god; they are therefore addressed, by individuals and by the city, to their chief god. We saw earlier that the divine world was normally perceived in terms of an undifferentiated "the gods." An individual who wished, as Greeks often did, to vow a dedication should the next year prove successful for him evidently needed the favor of the gods in general. But offerings were made to particular gods, not to the gods as a collectivity. So in such cases the beneficiary was the chief local god. Spoils, sacred fines, and so on similarly went to enrich the central cult.

I revert from the special god to the division of functions. The "native model" of gods with differentiated honors fits rather closely with the structuralist tenet that meaning in a closed system is created by differentiation:

---

58. Cf. Pirenne-Delforge, *Pausanias,* 262–63; cf., e.g., *LSA* 15.48–51, 33.16–19. On the "special god," see Parker, *Polytheism,* 395–97, 443–45 [+].

59. Philochorus *FGrH* 328 F 175: confirmed by sanctuary layout though not by votives, according to R. Etienne and J. P. Braun, *Ténos I: Le sanctuaire de Poseidon et Amphitrite* (Paris, 1986), 185–86.

as the signal amber in a traffic light is meaningless in itself but meaningful in opposition to red and green, so Artemis is defined by opposition (say) to Aphrodite and Hera. Whether the comparison between a pantheon and a very restricted sign system such as a traffic light may not conceal important differences is a question that can be asked. However that may be, the best model to think with or against in analyzing the gods is that offered by structuralism. I extract here from the best applications of this model a series of overlapping propositions that fill out the central claim that the organization of functions in a pantheon is, in Marcel Detienne's phrase, "differential and classificatory."[60]

1. Any major god is active in a variety of spheres that we would naturally class as distinct, as, for instance, domestic, political, agricultural, military.[61]
2. The god is not an arbitrary conglomerate of functions but has a central defining core, because—
3. The god brings to the distinct spheres in which it is involved a mode of activity or cluster of such modes that is peculiar to that god.
4. Gods are not therefore differentiated by spheres of activity, because spheres of activity such as the agricultural or political are common to many. They are differentiated by the mode or modes of activity[62] that they bring to the various spheres in which they are involved.
5. That differentiation is absolute; where two gods apparently share a function, investigation will reveal that they exercise it in different ways.
6. The defining core of a god is not a personality; it is rather a power/ cluster of powers or modes of activity.
   One must also add, as an unstated premise underlying most of what precedes—

---

60. Some key items out of many are J. P. Vernant, "Hestia-Hermes," in his *Myth and Thought among the Greeks* (London, 1983; French original, 1965), 127–75; Vernant, "The Society of the Gods," in his *Myth and Society in Ancient Greece* (Harvester, 1980; French original, 1974), 92–109; M. Detienne, *The Gardens of Adonis* (Harvester, 1977; French original 1972); Detienne and Vernant, *Cunning Intelligence* (the translator of all four books is Janet Lloyd). Since I am trying to use the model constructively, I omit an element that seems to me mistaken, the emphasis on specifically binary opposition as the vehicle of differentiation and meaning (as found, for instance, in Vernant's article "Hestia-Hermes"). As a heuristic device a binary comparison has often proved useful, but at a theoretical level I see no reason to contrast one god systematically with a single other: each letter of an alphabet contrasts with all the others, and so do gods.

61. Vernant, "Society of the Gods," 94.

62. A concept owed to G. Dumezil, e.g., *La religion romaine archaïque* (Paris, 1966), 179–80, 229.

7. It is legitimate to treat "Apollo," say, as an object of analysis; one is not reduced to analyzing, on the one side, "Apollo as represented in Panhellenic myth," and on the other a whole series of potentially divergent local Apollos.[63]

Proposition 1 is in many cases enlightening. To take an easy example, Aphrodite is not just the patroness of sexuality but also, as "Aphrodite of All the People," a source of civic harmony, and, as "Aphrodite Fair Voyage," a friend to sailors. As wife/cult-partner of Ares, she even has a certain relation, which is apparently not merely one of antithesis, with the world of war: in 480 BC, for instance, the women of Corinth are said to have prayed to the goddess to inspire in their menfolk "desire [n.b.] for battle against the barbarians."[64] Zeus is ruler of the world, controller of the climate, and also, as Zeus Ktesios ("of property"), steward of the domestic storeroom. But not all gods are so multidimensional. Demeter's explicit concerns relate merely to two closely related areas, fair crops and "fair birth" (not in the gynecological aspect, which belongs to Artemis and Eileithyia, but in terms of the woman's duty to produce healthy offspring). Hera too, as revealed by myths and epithets, is rather limited; she "holds the keys of marriage" and can consequently acquire a connection with childbirth, and she is the city-protecting special goddess in many places, but she seems to have no other regular spheres of activity.[65]

Proposition 2 on the list, as is clear from what was said above about the unity of the divine figure, is a strong taking of position on one side on a traditionally disputed topic. What is distinctive about structuralism is the kind of unifying principle that it offers (proposition 3), and its drastic refusal to allow for exceptions—occasional mutations or nonorganic developments—indeed to acknowledge the role of history at all.

---

63. As C. Sourvinou-Inwood recommends, *JHS* 98 (1978): 101–3 (= *"Reading" Greek Culture*, 147–51).

64. Plut. *De malignitate Herodoti* 39, 871A–B: cf. Pironti, *Figures d'Aphrodite*, 248–56: that Aphrodite had a significant relation to war is a central thesis of the monograph.

65. I speak of Demeter's "explicit concerns" and of Hera "as revealed by myths and epithets" to bracket off in the one case the important but implicit function of cults of Demeter as the context where citizen women's role in the polis was ceremonially recognized (p. 241 below), and in the other the extended vision of Hera that archaeology, colonial archaeology in particular, may offer. I have not forgotten the association between Hera and bovines revealed by her Homeric epithet "cow-eyed," the herds attached to her cult in Argos and at Croton, and the myths connecting her with the animal in various ways. But is there evidence that herders in fact prayed to her for increase of their herds? On Hera see now V. Pirenne-Delforge and G. Pironti in *La religion des femmes en Grèce ancienne*, ed. L. Bodiou and V. Mehl, 95–109 (Rennes, 2009).

The idea of "mode of activity" in proposition 3 raises some of the hardest questions. Whereas "spheres of activity" correspond quite closely with the indigenous concept of the "honors" assigned to each god, the Greeks did not ascribe distinctive modes of activity to their gods in the same way. But the concept might nonetheless catch an easily recognizable characteristic of the god. The most helpful illustration is again perhaps that of Aphrodite. Her role as "of all the people" is presumably to bring the citizens together in affection, as she brings together lovers;[66] and at sea she does not cause storms (as does Poseidon) but calms them, once again the charming and conciliatory power. She is therefore, it can be argued, the same smiling and persuasive goddess in each case; and the link between her activities in the different spheres is one that would have been easily perceived by a Greek.

The same can be said of the mode of activity ascribed to Athena in structuralist analysis, one that can even be expressed in a single Greek word often associated with the goddess, μῆτις, or "cunning intelligence." Again, Zeus's quality of sovereignty or mastery is made explicit in one of his commonest epithets, Zeus the King; and "madness" is an effective if crude summation of Dionysus's style.[67] The *Homeric Hymn to Poseidon* (22) associates that god with horses, the sea, and earthquakes, and a shared element can easily be identified in the power and dangerous violence of all three. Perhaps turbulence, and the power to overcome it, could be named as his mode of activity.[68] In the first application of structuralism to the Greek pantheon, Vernant built a systematic comparison between Hermes and Hestia around the mobility of Hermes and the fixity of Hestia.

Sometimes the unifying principle identified within a god's activities is harder to capture in simple words. Vernant has offered a superbly subtle and

---

66. On all this see Pirenne-Delforge in *Companion*, 311–23 [+]. On Aphrodite and the sea, note a neglected testimonium, Dionysius Byzantius *Anaplus Bospori* (ed. R. Güngerich [Berlin, 1927]), 36, recording annual sacrifices by the inhabitants of Byzantium to "gentle Aphrodite," who is believed to moderate the force of winds (τέμενος Ἀρτέμιδος Φωσφόρου καὶ Ἀφροδίτης Πραείας, ἧ κατ' ἔτος θύουσι Βυζάντιοι· δοκεῖ γὰρ δὴ ταμιεύειν τῶν ἀνέμων τὴν εὐκαιρίαν, πραΰνουσα <καὶ> καθισταμένη τὴν ἐπὶ πλέον αὐτῶν ταραχήν). On Aphrodite Pandemos I accept the traditional interpretation despite the lack of rigorous evidence, and despite the interesting reservations in relation to Aphrodite of Magistrates of J. Wallensten, *ΑΦΡΟΔΙΤΗΙ ΑΝΕΘΗΚΕΝ ΑΡΞΑΣ: A Study of Dedications to Aphrodite from Greek Magistrates* (Lund, 2003): Wallensten shows that Aphrodite has no special relation in cult to Homonoia, civic harmony. Pironti, *Figures d'Aphrodite,* stresses the less eirenic aspects of the goddess, which are incontestable; but worshippers who approach her obviously hope to see her smiling face.

67. Note how Teiresias builds on it when making extended claims for the god's spheres of activity: n. 53 above. It is not, however, through madness that Dionysus makes the vine and other plants grow. "Zeus of diseases" (Nosios), a doubtful reading in the archaic calendar *Milet* 1.3.31 a 8 (*LSA* 41), would, if verified, be hard to relate to Zeus's general persona.

68. "An embodiment of elemental force": Burkert, *Greek Religion,* 139.

comprehensive panorama of Artemis's powers whereby she is not, as has been often supposed, the "goddess of the outside" or "of the wild" but rather the goddess who presides over those contexts in human life where the civilized and the wild, culture and nature or culture and the human potential for bestiality, come into contact. The hunt is an obvious point of encounter between the two spheres; so too in a different way is childbirth, a violent and dangerous irruption of the merely physical within the human world; so too are those rituals of transition by which Artemis "acculturates" the young. As for warfare, Artemis is no warrior, but she receives offerings immediately before battle begins, the point at which violence, controlled or bestial, is about to break out. She also intervenes in battles as a savior at moments when the annihilation of one side, the destruction of a city and thus the negation of order, are in danger of occurring. "The hunt, the care of the young, child-birth, war, and battle—Artemis always operates as a divinity of the margins with the twofold power of managing the necessary passages between savagery and civilization and of strictly maintaining the boundaries at the very moment they have been crossed."[69] As a mode of action, "managing the necessary passages between savagery and civilization and . . . strictly maintaining the boundaries at the very moment they have been crossed" lacks the simplicity of Athena's cunning intelligence or Poseidon's turbulence or Aphrodite's persuasive charm. Indeed it is not strictly a mode of action comparable to them at all. But perhaps one should accept that unifying principles of different types could exist, and not fuss about words. As for the objection that ordinary Greeks did not think in terms of "the necessary passages between savagery and civilization," the answer might be that they nonetheless perceived them at a level below that of explicit consciousness; one role of Artemis was precisely, it can be argued, to give this fuzzy awareness a shape and name.

A comparable analysis of Hera has been presented by de Polignac.[70] He starts from two forms of votive offering that are distinctively characteristic of her early cult, though not exclusive to it, model houses and model ships; he notes that worshippers constantly bring her non-local objects as gifts, even in sanctuaries that are not obvious centers of international exchange: he

---

69. See "The Figure and Functions of Artemis in Myth and Cult," in Vernant's *Mortals and Immortals,* 195–206; the citation is from p. 204. The cults of Artemis within the city and with civic functions (particularly conspicuous in Achaea: Osanna, *Acaia,* 306–7) are a problem for this model, which Vernant seeks to address, *Mortals and Immortals,* 204–5.

70. F. de Polignac, "Héra, le navire et la demeure," in *Héra: Images, especes, cultes,* ed. J. de La Genière, 113–22 (Naples, 1997). On the different relations of Hera and Artemis to the outside, ibid., 118. The argument depends on treating the models as houses, not, as they are often seen, as temples.

suggests therefore that the interplay between home (house models) and away (foreign votives; the ship) was an important principle within her cult. Such an inside/outside dynamic would be an extension of Hera's core relation to the human institution that is above all concerned with the safe integration within the house of something coming from outside it, marriage. One can only wish that, to confirm this dazzling hypothesis, ships had some role in marriage imagery, or Hera were demonstrably involved in the precise rites by which the new bride was incorporated into the household...

Neither of these analyses operates with a "mode of activity" reducible to a simple phrase. The attempt to reduce a god to a single mode of activity has in fact been subject to auto-criticism within structuralism, as a misguided perpetuation of the static and lazy old vision of a "god naturally individuated who can be identified through a small number of traits without striking a blow."[71] Rather, attentive to Levi-Strauss's "logic of the concrete," we should "approach them via concrete details and segments of situations: through objects, gestures and situations." Like experimental scientists, we should investigate the different ways in which different gods "react" (almost in the chemical sense) to different entities (horses, as it might be), or the importance that apparently indifferent objects may assume in certain cults (such as stones and doors in the cult of Apollo). But this is perhaps a refined redescription of earlier structuralist practice rather than a wholly new approach; for, as Marcel Detienne, author of these programmatic statements, points out, his earlier study (with Vernant) of Athena's "cunning intelligence" had looked for its operations in concrete situations and in relation to concrete objects such as horse, bridle, ship, rudder; and the idea of modes of activity has not completely vanished from his later large-scale analysis of Apollo. He sees Apollo's essential mode as one of tracing paths, cutting, delimiting, and thereby founding (sanctuaries, temples).[72] What is radical is the gap that he creates, no doubt knowingly, between the god's modes of activity and the

---

71. Detienne, *Apollon,* 15, summarizing his "Experimenting in the Field of Polytheisms," *Arion* (1999): 127–49 (first in French in *Kernos* 10 [1997]: 57–72 = his *Comparer l'incomparable* [Paris, 2000], 81–104), whence, p. 140, the following quote and paraphrase. Pironti, *Figures d'Aphrodite,* in the spirit of Detienne's program, stresses the diversity of Aphrodite's modes of activity in the last paragraph of her book (285); but great stress has been laid throughout on *mixis,* "bringing together," as a core mode.

72. Detienne, *Apollon,* 232: "Il s'agit essentiellement, nous l'avons vu, de découper des chemins, de circonscrire des autels, de délimiter des sanctuaires, de poser les fondations de temples, aussi bien que de découper le territoire de cités et d'entourer les villes de murailles." P. Monbrun, *Les voix d'Apollon: L'arc, la lyre et les oracles* (Rennes, 2007), by contrast, sees the figure of the bowman shooting from afar as the symbolic node of Apollo. Incompatible Apollos proliferate (cf. Parker, *Polytheism,* 393 n. 28)!

kind of "honors" or spheres of activity the Greeks themselves ascribed to him. That gap, one may feel, is too large to allow adequate purchase on the facts of cult.[73]

Even when the single mode of activity is rejected, the presumption is that there exists a "profound coherence"[74] within the divine figure. It is, however, not difficult, by juxtaposing extremes of a god's activities, to make that assumption seem problematic. Why does Zeus, if his characteristic mode is sovereignty, watch over the household stores, in the form of a jar, as Zeus Ktesios? What has Zeus Meilichios, the great snake, to do with the master of Olympus? Why is Athena, the embodiment of "cunning intelligence," also a mistress of the battle cry? Why does Hermes, so involved with movement, communication, and exchange, also take such an interest in the increase of herd animals and (it seems) the maturation of the young?[75] One can, to be sure, devise answers to these questions. It can be said that the domestic correlate of the king is the master of the house, and control over the store cupboard is a symbol of such mastery; thus Zeus Ktesios remains an emblem of sovereign authority, at the household level. One can argue that Athena in her military aspect stands for rational and controlled violence, in opposition to the mad bloodlust of Ares. Perhaps Hermes, whose concern with spatial transitions is well-known, was involved also with status transitions, and so a fit patron of rites of maturation for young men. (But his interest in herd animals will need a different explanation.) These answers, or some of them, may well be correct. But they are, inevitably, our answers, not theirs, and to be treated with reserve for that reason. To test their validity, we would need to be able, for instance, to visit a selection of Greek households and see how Zeus Ktesios was spoken of and treated on a day-to-day basis. The workings of polytheism, it is said, must be studied by microanalysis.[76] But microanalysis of that kind is often impossible for us.

Propositions four and five together are those that give the approach real bite. The study of modes of action is a new and often productive way

73. Cf. Parker, *Polytheism,* 393. The book takes its start not from attested cults but from the narrative account of Apollo's coming to Delphi in *Hymn Hom. Ap.* Of course many aspects of cult are discussed on the way. But one important supporting argument drawn from cult is fallacious: ἄγυιαι are roads within a settlement (Macrob. *Sat.* 1.9.6) not between settlements, and so the title Apollo Aguieus cannot be associated with his travels in the hymn to make him a pathfinder. D. Jaillard, *Configurations d'Hermès: Une "théogonie hermaïque"* (Liège, 2007), is, like Detienne's book, a reading of a Homeric Hymn (that to Hermes).

74. Pironti, *Figures d'Aphrodite,* 285.

75. For the important evidence from Kato Symi in Crete linking Hermes (and Aphrodite) with maturation rites, see chap. 7, p. 233, and the interpretation by N. Marinatos there cited.

76. Detienne, "Experimenting" (n. 71 above).

of tackling an old issue; the attempt to distinguish one god from another rigorously and systematically is completely new. The paradigm case is the epithet "of horses" borne by both Athena and Poseidon. Poseidon embodies the power of the horse, the power needed to tame horses, and the potential of horses to resist control. Athena comes to the horse via skill and technology; she is associated with the driving of chariots and, above all, with the bit and bridle. In relation to seafaring, where Athena is a patroness of steersmen, their powers divide in similar ways.[77] These distinctions are well-grounded in evidence; and it can often be shown that, in spheres of life where many gods cluster (as, for instance, childbirth and child care; marriage; warfare; seafaring), they approach these crossroads down different paths.[78]

Two reservations can be made, however. First, it is not clear that there is any sphere of horsemanship or maritime life from which Poseidon is absolutely excluded; there is even an ode of Sophocles in which the invention of the bridle is ascribed to him and not, as elsewhere, to Athena.[79] It may be that Poseidon should be seen as the true and potentially omnicompetent master of these domains, Athena as a specialist who enters them via sharply defined functions. In that event we would be back, in the case of Poseidon, with distinctive spheres of activity as well as modes. Second, would these ideal distinctions, grounded in myths not necessarily widely known, be observed in the rough-and-tumble of cult practice? Structuralism postulates a large database of theological knowledge in the mind of every Greek, and a willingness to be bound by its implicit rules. A horseman told that Athena bore the title "of horses" might be forgiven for supposing her able to help him in any of his concerns.

Proposition six is one not confined to structuralism. Much can be said in its support. Rivers, winds, and abstractions such as Victory were gods; gods were manifested in physical phenomena such as lightning; all Greeks knew that Aphrodite was a power within themselves as well as a goddess on Olympus; the allegorists who identified Athena with "mind" or "reason" were only picking up on a very manifest trait of the goddess in myth. (On the other hand, Demeter became corn, a substance, not a power.) It is only to a limited extent that gods are divine equivalents of human statuses or professions: Hermes the herald, Hephaestus the smith, Zeus the king. Often they embody combinations impossible on earth: the hunter-god is a woman,

77. See Detienne and Vernant, *Cunning Intelligence,* chaps. 7 and 8.
78. Cf. P. Schmitt Pantel and L. Bruit Zaidman, *Religion in the Ancient Greek City,* trans. P. Cartledge (Cambridge, 1992), 186–91.
79. Soph. *OC* 707–19.

but an impossible woman who never marries, while Athena is supreme both in the masculine arts of war and in the feminine arts of weaving[80] (though, again, shunning marriage).

The opposite case, however, is pleaded by the whole mythological, poetic, and iconographic tradition, which so vividly presents the gods as beings of human form swayed by emotions, and embedded in family relationships, very like those of men. It is scarcely plausible to dismiss this, the main source of Greek imaginings of the divine world, as a delusive facade. Prayers and hymns constantly alluded to the family relationships among the gods, and it was surely relevant to the roles of Athena and Hera as preeminent protectresses of cities that the one was daughter, the other wife, of mighty Zeus; age and gender relationships are relevant too, if in complicated ways.[81] Above all, gods were approached in cult as beings with whom interaction in the human terms of reciprocity and gift exchange was possible. (Such at any rate was the norm. We never hear the kinds of supplication that might be addressed, say, to a threatening wind.) Gods, we might say, were powers who were treated as if they were persons.[82]

The issues raised by proposition seven (one Apollo or a host of local Apollos?) were touched on above (in discussing "local divergence" and "archaic/foreign substrates"); they are relevant to any approach to Greek deity, not the structuralist alone. The justification a structuralist might give would be empirical: it does in fact prove possible to interpret both the Panhellenic and the local figures within the same framework, by reference to the same cluster of modes of activities. And that claim is often enough persuasive (as in the contrasting analyses of Athena and Poseidon, which often use evidence from local cult) to have force. But this partial empirical confirmation does not

---

80. "Meanwhile Athena at her father's door/let fall the robe her own hands had embroidered. . . . /Armor of grievous war she buckled on": Hom. *Il.* 8.384–86, 388 (trans. R. Fitzgerald). Whence N. Loraux's argument in a well-known essay that goddesses are more deities than women: "What Is a Goddess?" in *A History of Women in the West,* ed. P. Schmitt Pantel, trans. A. Goldhammer, 1:11–45 (Cambridge, Mass., 1992).

81. The relation between young Apollo and young men is an obvious illustration in respect of age. Women have few occasions to turn to male gods except for healing. Men by contrast have much need of goddesses. The argument of P. Friedrich (*The Meaning of Aphrodite* [Chicago, 1978], 82–85) that these male-female interactions track those within human families is interesting, if anachronistic in the types of family stereotypes it postulates. He takes, for instance, Athena the helper of warriors as a projection of the supportive elder sister; but the elder sisters of warriors would tend to be married. It is plausible, however, that Athena's role as helper is a feminine one: for Heracles, say, to need help from another man would detract from his own manliness.

82. Similar compromises are recommended by Bremmer, *Greek Religion,* 23, and K. Dowden in *Companion,* 55. Reciprocity: cf. the essays of J. M. Bremer and R. Parker in C. Gill et al., eds., *Reciprocity in Ancient Greece* (Oxford, 1998).

establish a general principle. The possibility that a local cult has gone its own way can never be excluded.

I conclude the discussion of the structuralist model with some important limitations to its power. That model seeks to show how, within the spheres in which it is involved, each deity is active in a way distinctive to itself. But it has no way of predicting in what spheres the deity will be active. The power that Aphrodite exercises at sea is one of calming and conciliation, appropriate to herself. But there was no necessity that she should exercise her powers at sea at all; she does not calm storms on land. Zeus's control of the thunderbolt is a symbol of his general sovereignty, we can allow. But power over the sea or over earthquakes could equally have been a symbol of cosmic control. Conversely, why could not turbulent Poseidon have wreaked atmospheric havoc on land? The explanation for these distributions of activity seems partly to lie in history (an ancient division of what we will have to call spheres of activity between Zeus and Poseidon, for instance), partly in market demand: numerous gods become involved, each in their own way, with seafaring, child care, and marriage, for instance, because of the complicated human anxieties associated with these crucial activities and experiences.[83]

There is also the matter raised above of the concertina character of gods. Structuralism describes the gods as, so to speak, Platonic forms, not as embodied in the cult practice of any particular place. But the different degrees of expansion and contraction of different gods in different cities, to say nothing of the varying supporting cast of lesser deities, meant that different local pantheons bore strikingly different aspects. The question of why, say, Athena's powers are so extensive in Athens and those of Hera so limited is not one that structuralism can answer.

Another issue not addressed by structuralism is the open character of the pantheon, and the place of new gods. Structuralism was a reaction, and an appropriate one, to treatments that saw the fundamental question about a pantheon as being "What god came from where?" But gods did from time to time rise to prominence in Greece, or enter Greece from abroad, who had no place in the distribution of functions as described in Hesiod and the *Homeric Hymns*: Mother and her attendants, Asclepius, and later Isis are very successful instances, Sabazius and Bendis rather less so. The classic objection brought against functionalism—if society is such a well-functioning machine, how does change ever occur?—also strikes structuralism if it fails to explain through what cracks and crevices new gods were able to enter. Even when gods did not actually enter Greece from abroad, neighboring

---

83. Cf. my comments in *Kykeon*, 151–52.

pantheons are surely likely to have had an influence. We noted above that foreign gods were treated as variants of Greek gods and could be assimilated via the cult-epithet system in such forms as Zeus Ammon or Zeus Thebaieus. In these circumstances it would be very odd if "Greek" and "foreign" gods (but seen by their worshippers as different forms of the same god) never passed traits one to another. One may wonder finally whether, and if so how, the structural relations between the gods of archaic and classical Greece persisted unchanged in the Hellenistic period. Questions about the character of the Hellenistic pantheon remain in fact very largely still to pose.

This chapter has sought to show how hard it is to answer the question "What is a Greek god?" from which it started. Familiar gods such as Zeus rub shoulders with winds and rivers (and goat-faced Pan) and deified abstractions and, in the Hellenistic period, deified mortals. Zeus himself is both a personality with a history and, in some respects, a force of nature; in cult he is divided into almost as many pieces as there are sanctuaries dedicated to him (so, too, the other great gods), and is often treated de facto as if he were a consortium of gods rather than a single god with many facets. Structuralism traces, often with great success, the lines of demarcation that keep the great gods from spilling over into one another. But the Greeks often did not know whether a figure such as Eileithyia was a minor independent goddess or an aspect of a greater power.

Outside the context of cult, where every god had a name (uncertain though it might be what that name designated), the individual gods coalesced into "the gods," "god," "the divine." Carneades in the second century BC ridiculed Stoic attempts to rationalize traditional cult practice with a series of arguments of "little-by-little" or "soritic" form: "If Zeus is a god, Poseidon as his brother will be a god. But if Poseidon is a god, Achelous too will be a god. And if Achelous, the Nile too. If the Nile, every river. If every river, torrents too must be gods, and if torrents, then watercourses too. But watercourses are not. So Zeus is not a god either. But if gods had existed, Zeus too would have been a god. So gods do not exist." Some fourteen further arguments of like form are preserved.[84] Carneades' aim was not, Cicero's speaker explains, "to abolish the gods—for what could less befit a

---

84. In Sext. Emp. *Math*. 9.182–90 and Cic. *Nat. D*. 3.43–52; cf. P. Couissin, "Les sorites de Carnéade contre le polythéisme," *REG* 54 (1941): 43–57. They differ from the classic type of sorites argument ("if two grains are not a heap, nor are three; if three are not, nor are four," and so on ad infinitum) in that "the successive conditionals do not derive from a single general principle but from justificatory grounds which Carneades has to supply, and the justification stated or suggested varies with the argument" (and even within a single argument): M. F. Burnyeat, "Gods and Heaps," in *Language and Logos*, ed. M. Schofield and M. Nussbaum, 315–38 (Cambridge, 1982), at 328.

philosopher?—but to prove that the Stoics failed to offer any explanation of the gods."[85] "Godness" is a predicate that no definition can circumscribe.[86] The attempt to confer logical coherence on polytheism is a hopeless enterprise. But the incoherence made it all the more flexible a tool for coping with the diversity of experience.

Coda: A Greek Pantheon

After so many words of synthesis, let us turn to a concrete document. It is not merely through the accidents of survival of evidence that we cannot list "the gods" of a Greek city. No such lists ever existed. If all the civic bodies of a given city (the city itself, tribes, phratries, demes, and so on) had ever all simultaneously prepared calendars of their sacrifices and these had all survived, one could in principle repair the ancients' omission and create a list of all the gods and heroes honored at public expense in that city. For some subgroups, the Attic demes above all, a complete list or something close to it does survive; and the size of those subgroup lists shows that a total list would be a very long document. But such a procedure would still not capture the gods of private associations and private foundations, tolerated but not financed by the city. Nor would it include figures whose divinity the Greeks of a particular city might well concede even if no cult of them happened to exist there (Kronos, for instance, in cities that had no cult of him, and many personifications.) The divine world as perceived by a Greek was never limited to the gods actually worshipped.

These limitations aside, such simultaneous calendar making by all relevant bodies doubtless never occurred, and has certainly not left a product available for our use. What are occasionally at our disposal are documents that, for chance administrative reasons, present an extensive selection of public cults. The fragmentary records of the "Treasurers of the Other Gods" ("other" than Athena, the city's patron goddess) issued in Attica in the 420s reveal over forty heroes and "gods" (for these purposes Poseidon Hippios and Poseidon Kalaureates, say, count as two separate gods) important enough to have funds at their disposal.[87] The other such partial panorama comes from Erythrae in Asia Minor, from where we have a record of the sales tax

---

85. *Nat. D.* 3.44. Cicero's authority for this interpretation is not clear.

86. "On ne peut donner du dieu une définition qui convienne à tout le défini et au seul défini," P. Couissin, 1941, 46; cf. Burnyeat, 1982, 330–33; S. R. F. Price, *JHS* 104 (1984): 80.

87. *IG* 1³.369 and 383.

levied on the sale of public priesthoods over a period of thirty to forty years (c. 300–260 BC). The record covers only priesthoods of the city that were assigned by sale (others may have been transmitted in other ways), and only those that came up for sale in the relevant period; and breaks of the stone have removed the record for some years. The total is nonetheless impressive. The prices realized by the sales are also recorded; as different types of sale are involved, these are not all comparable one with another, but in a very broad way it is safe to conclude that the cult of Hermes Agoraios (sale price 4,610 drachmas) or Aphrodite in Daphneion (2,040 dr.) was much more popular than that of Earth (10 dr.). As it happens, a long though incomplete sacrificial calendar from about a century later also survives from Erythrae, and reveals several further cults.[88] The table that follows combines the evidence of the two documents (see table 1).

The priesthood sales record gives the prices in drachmas realized for each priesthood, in two main forms, a standard sale (here in bold) and a form of (probably) secondary selling that normally realized less. Where two figures linked by "and'" are given, the priesthood was sold more than once in the period covered. Fully preserved entries list both the actual sale price and the sales tax paid. Sale prices were divided into six bands for tax purposes: 5 dr., for instance, was levied on any sale between 100 and 199 dr., 10 on sales between 200 and 999, and so on. Sometimes the actual price is not preserved on the stone but must be estimated from the sales tax, which is. Figures given in a form such as 1,000–1,999 are of this type.

Some broad observations will be in place here, not a detailed commentary. In almost all documents of this type, there are in fact elements that defy commentary: cults located in places of which we know nothing, epithets we cannot explain, heroes or even gods otherwise unattested. The local particularism that creates the partial illegibility of such texts is a crucial datum. In Hellenistic Erythrae, however, the Olympians clearly predominate, if sometimes in unfamiliar form. This text is one of many that comprehensively refute many familiar clichés about Hellenistic religion: one looks in vain for the irruption of Fortune, Asclepius, and "oriental gods"; and "King Alexander," and in the later text Antiochus, though prominent, take their place amid a vast array of traditional cults. The high prices of the priesthoods of Hermes and Aphrodite imply a high volume of what must surely be private traffic: personal religion flourishes, but within an Olympian conduit. Alongside the great Olympians there is the usual scatter of lesser gods: that such a scatter

---

88. Respectively *IErythrai* 201 (*LSA* 25 + a new frag.) and *IErythrai* 207 (*LSA* 26) + *SEG* 30.1327.

Table 1.   Gods with Public Priesthoods and Recipients of Public Sacrifices in Erythrae
from Two Key Documents, Third to Second Century BC

SALES-TAX RECORD OF PRIESTHOODS (c. 300–260 BC)		SACRIFICIAL CALENDAR OF GODS WHO RECEIVED OFFER-INGS (SECOND CENTURY BC)
God	*Sale price (drachmas)*	
Major gods		
Aphrodite in Daphneion (?)	**2,000+** and *2,040*	
Aphrodite Pandemos	**200**	
Aphrodite Pythochrestos	**300** and **130**	
		Aphrodite Strateia
		Apollo Apotropaios
Apollo Enagonios	230	
		Apollo Hebdomaios Pythios
Apollo in K[..]elleia	Not preserved	
Apollo in Koiloi	**810**	
Apollo in Saberidai	150	
Apollo Kaukaseus, Artemis Kaukasis, Apollo Lykeios, Apollo Delios, and the river Aleon	*270*	the river Aleon
		Apollo Pythios Epikomios
		Apollo, Artemis, Leto
		Apollo at the Gate
Ares	**1,070**	
Artemis Aithopia	**2,000–2,999**	
		Artemis Apobateria
		Artemis at the Gate
Artemis Phosphoros	50–99	
		Artemis (?) Soteira
Athena Nike	120	
Athena [ ]	70	
		Athena Polias
Demeter Chloe	60 and 101	
		Demeter Eleusinia
Demeter in Kolonai	600 and **1,300**	
Demeter and Kore Demetros	**190**	
Demeter and Kore Pythochrestos	**210**	
Dionysus	**80**	
Dionysus Baccheus	100	
		Dionysus Phleus
Dionysus Pythochrestos	105	
Hera Teleia	**500–999** and 251	

SALES-TAX RECORD OF PRIESTHOODS (c. 300–260 BC)		SACRIFICIAL CALENDAR OF GODS WHO RECEIVED OFFERINGS (SECOND CENTURY BC)
Hermes Agoraios	4,610 and 4,600	Hermes Agoraios
		Hermes Hippios
Hermes Pylios Harmateus	270	
		Hermes
Kore Soteire	**302**	
		Poseidon Asphaleios at the Gate
		Poseidon Hippios
Poseidon Phytalmios	**136**	
Zeus Apotropaios and Athena Apotropaia	181 and **52** and 150	
Zeus Basileus	**230**	
		Zeus Boulaios
Zeus Eleutherios	300 and 1,000–1,999	
Zeus Hypatos	200–999	
Zeus Olympios	Not preserved	
Zeus Phemios and Athena Phemia	140	
Zeus Philios	1,300	
		Zeus Soter
Other gods		
Ablabiai	**400**	
Corybantes Euphronieioi and Thaleioi (?)	Female section **610**	
	Male section **180** and 171	
Earth	10	
Enyo and Enyalios	70	
		Great Gods
Great Mother	**480**	Great Mother
		Hekate
		Helios
Hestie Boulaie	**830**	
Hestia Temenia		200–999 and 105
		Leto
		Sibyl
Theoi Prokuklioi	**400** and 105	
Personifications		
Agathe Tyche	200–999 and **100**	Agathe Tyche
		Arete

(continued)

Table 1 Continued.

SALES-TAX RECORD OF PRIESTHOODS (c. 300–260 BC)		SACRIFICIAL CALENDAR OF GODS WHO RECEIVED OFFERINGS (SECOND CENTURY BC)
Personifications (cont.)		
Eirene	500	Eirene
		Homonoia
		Nike
Heroes		
Achilles, Thetis, the Nereids	Not preserved and 80	
		Anchianax
		Athamas
Dioscuri	**500** and 200–999	
		Erythros
Heracles	**1,921**	Heracles
		Heracles Kallinikos
		Heracles Kallinikos at the Gate
		[ ] hero
Heroes	**440**	
		Phanagoras
Monarchs and such		
King Alexander	**1,000–1,999**	King Alexander
		King Antiochos
		The Kings
		Rome
		Queen (Stratonike)
Unidentified, unclear		
[ ] Epimachos	200	Epimachos
		[ ] Epiteichea
		[ ] at Leuke
		[ ] to Mimas
[ ]	**820** and 710	

Note: Bold indicates a standard sale, nonbold a secondary sale, and underlining indicates a form of sale known as *diasystasis*. On the types of sale, see Dignas, *Economy of the Sacred,* 252–55.

will exist in any given city is predictable, though not its detailed contents. Personifications have a certain place, while natural forces are represented directly only by the river Aleon and by Helios; but the Erythraeans may well have honored nymphs and performed rites of aversion to winds without having instituted public priesthoods of either. The chthonians are represented by the Ablabiai, the "Harmlessnesses," a unique and surely euphemistically named group. Few heroes appear, apart from the ubiquitous Heracles and the Dioscuri; but throughout the Greek world there were many more heroes than there were priests of heroes.

❧ CHAPTER 4

The Power and Nature of Heroes

Few religions, it has been noted, get by with a cast consisting simply of major gods and mortals. In Greece, Titans, Giants, Satyrs, Silens, Corybantes, Kouretes, Telchines, Daktyls, Hours, Graces, and nymphs complicate the picture, to say nothing of other abstract qualities discussed in the previous chapter.[1] Some of these figures of difficult classification exist primarily in myth (Titans, Giants) or representation (Satyrs), while others are recipients of cult. Among these last much the most important are the heroes.

The Nature of Heroes

I shall approach them with some generalizations about the heroes of the classical age that come close to being uncontroversial, though they do not quite achieve it. Heroes were dead mortals believed by Greeks to have retained

---

1. See Brelich, *Eroi*, 325–35. For an excellent introduction to Greek heroes, see Ekroth in *Companion*, 100–14; note too A. Seiffert in *ThesCRA* 4:24–38, on hero shrines. I steer clear of the fascinating issues attaching to postclassical hero cult, now well treated by C. P. Jones, *New Heroes in Antiquity: From Achilles to Antinoos* (Cambridge, Mass., 2010). I sketch the problem of the early history of hero cult in appendix 5, below p. 287.

after death the power to influence human affairs, or at least to deserve continuing honor on a scale not accorded to the ordinary dead; they therefore received cult not from their kin alone. Though most heroes about whom anything was known—some were anonymous—were believed to have belonged to the so-called age of heroes, the class was not closed and there could be added to it, typically by a decision of the assembly (either directly, or through a consultation of Delphi), both further figures from the mythological period and even historical individuals.[2] (Occasional instances even appear to be recorded of individuals heroized during their lifetimes; but such cases are aberrant if they occurred at all.) They were tied to particular territories more closely than were gods: both gods and heroes could be said to "possess" a particular land, but only heroes were actually "of the territory" (ἐγχώριοι) or "inhabitants."[3]

As dead mortals who retain power they resemble Christian saints, but they differ from them also in crucial ways. Unlike the saints, their role is not to intercede on behalf of mortals with a higher power; they hear and answer prayers in their own right.[4] And piety and moral virtues do not normally make a hero; star quality, exceptionality, newsworthiness are the relevant criteria in a majority of cases. Doubtless the deranged mass-murdering athlete Cleomedes of Astypalaia has received too much attention and should not be allowed to overshadow founders of colonies, for instance, or the chaste Hippolytus entirely; but it is important that such a figure could be

---

2. Direct: e.g., Diod. 16.90, Plut. *Tim.* 39.5. This seems to have been the commonest way with popular leaders, despite Plato's stipulation that oracular authorization should be sought (*Resp.* 540B–C). In the case of Aratus, an oracle was consulted about the legitimacy of burying him *intra muros*, not about the heroic cult he was to receive (Plut. *Arat.* 53). Not surprisingly, the assembly vote might have been preceded by informal displays of popular enthusiasm: Currie, *Cult of Heroes,* 194, citing Thuc. 4.121.1 (Brasidas) and Plut. *Dion* 29.2 with Diod. Sic. 16.20.6. Through Delphi: either in response to a general question about welfare (Foucart, *Culte des héros,* 49–50) or a specific question about strange occurrences (Paus. 1.32.5, the phantom who appeared at Marathon; ibid. 6.9.6–9, the homicidal Cleomedes of Astypalaia; for Herodotean instances see p. 117 below). How often the heroes created on private or small group initiative (below, n. 49) acquired public acceptance is an interesting question. In *CEG* 854 a Cypriot from Salamis claims to have established Naulochus (eponym of Naulochon, the city's harbor) as a protecting hero of Priene, but the site—a niche in a tower of one of the city gates (*ThesCRA* 4:37 no. 41)—shows he must have had authorization; perhaps he just paid for a statue. How Kindly Hero/Drimakos, honored by both runaway slaves and slave owners on Chios (see p. 238), came to be recognized is a tantalizing and unanswerable question.

3. Hdt. 8.39.1; Thuc. 2.74.2, 4.87.2; Xen. *Cyrop.* 3.3.21; cf. Pirenne-Delforge, *Pausanias,* 244. Heroic cult of living? Currie, *Cult of Heroes,* 160–63.

4. Foucart, *Culte des héros,* 77–78. But one of my copyeditors pointed out from her own Roman Catholic upbringing that what I say about saints represents doctrine, not practice: "God was presented to me as rather corporate and distracted, compared with the saints, and the angels, for that matter, who were the ones you turned to, to get things done."

believed to have become a hero even if it is an exaggeration to take him as the ideal type.[5]

The controversial element in those generalizations must now be addressed. An influential view is that Greeks used the term "hero" both of dead mortals who received cult and also of certain minor supernatural figures, what A. D. Nock charmingly described as "gods in a small way."[6] In terms of their functions it is certainly helpful to think of almost all heroes as "gods in a small way," local gods. And many heroes have speaking names that seem to identify them as powers that do certain things rather than ex-mortals with a biography. A classic example here is Taraxippos, "horse-disturber," a name linked to a mound of earth in the shape of a round altar beside the racecourse at Olympia; horses unaccountably went out of control when they passed Horse-Disturber unless the charioteers propitiated him by sacrifices. Another is "fly-catcher," Muiagros, to whom preliminary sacrifices were made at a certain festival at Alipheira, after which "the flies caused no more trouble." At Larissa in Thessaly a dedication was made in the third century "to the hero City Warden, (dedicated by) Nikolaos son of Eupolis, and his fellow City Wardens." The hero sounds like transparent divinization of a function, not an individual. One can also quote the well-known facts that not all hero cults took place at tombs, and that the modes of sacrifice to heroes often differed little if at all from those to gods.

Taraxippos and Muiagros sound to us very much like instances of what Usener called "special function gods" (Sondergötter) or even "momentary gods" (Augenblicksgötter). But it does not follow that the Greeks too understood them so, and Pausanias in fact has a long discussion of Taraxippos that is very instructive. "The Greeks have varying views about Taraxippos," he begins, and goes on to list five different current theories about mortals who might be buried under the mound or whom it might commemorate as a cenotaph. A different possibility had been put to Pausanias by an Egyptian: there was no body under the mound, but something buried by Pelops, presumably a magical object of some kind. Pausanias himself, however, favors the view that Taraxippos is an epithet of Poseidon of Horses; rather inconsistently, he goes on to say that "at Isthmos too there is a Taraxippos, Glaukos son of Sisyphus."[7] What the case shows is that Greeks might pay cult to a

---

5. For Hippolytus honored for chastity (σωφροσύνη), see Eur. fr. 446. Cleomedes: Paus. 6.9.6–8.

6. Nock, *Essays,* 593 (from *HTR* 37 (1944): 162).

7. Taraxippos: Paus. 6.20.15–19. Muiagros: Paus. 8.26.7. City Warden: *SEG* 27.205 (similar are dedications by generals to "Aphrodite of Generals" and the like: J. Wallensten, *Kernos* 21 [2008]: 92). Muiagros obviously resembles the Zeus Apomuios of Elis (Paus. 5.14.1: at Cape Leucas the flies

power designated by a name without knowing what kind of being—hero, god, or magical force—underlay the name. But it shows also that, in Pausanias's day at least, if Taraxippos was a hero, then he was not a minor god but a mortal who had acquired that title after death. Pausanias is for these purposes a late witness, but no instance to my knowledge has been quoted of an individual whom a Greek clearly regarded as being both a hero and not a quondam mortal.[8] Heroes were sometimes loosely spoken of as gods, as we will see, but gods (one enigmatic fragment of a hymn to Dionysus aside) were not spoken of as heroes.

The case is perhaps different with heroines. Some heroines are single, identifiable figures from myth entirely parallel to heroes, and in those cults where every hero is paired with a heroine they are clearly precisely analogous; but we also find heroines, in contrast to heroes, receiving offerings as a group, like nymphs. And a group such as "the heroines of Thorikos" (Thorikos being a deme in southeast Attica) can be conceived, again like nymphs, as the supernatural guardians of a region. Are they then in effect Nymphs under a different name, and thus small gods rather than deceased mortals? The conclusion is not inescapable: heroines could no doubt serve as guardians of a region while also being envisaged as women of past ages, consigned to collective anonymity by the general destiny of women in a society in which the best woman is the one least spoken of. On the other hand, Apollonius Rhodius seems simply to identify the nymphs and the heroines of Libya. Some interaction seems to have occurred between the classes of nymph and heroine, a reminder of the fluidity of all these classifications. But there was no parallel class of male nymphs to affect the understanding of heroes. The argument can still stand, therefore, that, in contrast perhaps to heroines, heroes were never interpreted as minor gods.[9]

---

themselves supposedly received the sacrifice, Ael. *NA* 11.8), but, as with Taraxippos, the uncertainty whether a Muiagros/Apomuios was a divine epithet or a hero does not imply uncertainty as to what a hero was. Cf. Sosipolis, a hero in Mesambria (*IGBulg.* 5.5103), an epithet of Zeus in Magnesia on the Maeander (*LSA* 32), a δαίμων ἐπιχώριος in Elis (Paus. 6.20.2).

8. After discussing the evidence for heroines as minor goddesses, Nock, *Essays,* 596 n. 81, enigmatically writes, "Cf. the hero Ptoios (P. Perdrizet, *BCH* XXII, 1898, 244)." But the hero Ptoios has human genealogies. In the transmitted text of the hymn of the women of Elis in Plut. *Quaest. Graec.* 36, 299B, they summon "hero Dionysus" (for the many conjectures see Schlesier in *Kykeon,* 165 n. 20); even if the text is sound, it is little to build a case on.

9. On heroines see Larson, *Heroine Cults;* E. Kearns, "The Nature of Heroines," in *Sacred and the Feminine,* 96–110. Hero-heroine pairs (Larson, 28–29): above all in the Marathon calendar (p. 112 below), but also, e.g., in Elis (Paus. 5.15.12) and implied by the couples of standard "hero reliefs" (p. 114 below). Heroines as group (the instances are all Attic): Ar. *Nub.* 315; *LSCG* 18 A 19, E 3–4 (Erchia); several cases in the Thorikos calendar (below, p. 112), *LSS* 20.14–16. The argument is that nymphs and heroines were partially assimilated, not that they were identified (they occur separately

Functionally, however, minor gods is what in effect they were; and the best way to think of the heroes is not as a bipartite class consisting both of minor gods and of dead mortals, but as a single class of figures who were understood as dead mortals but exercised the powers of small-scale gods.[10] The question obviously arises of why such powers should be ascribed to the ancient dead; and an easy answer may seem to lie in the idea often expressed in Homer that men of past ages could accomplish "easily" feats that even ten "mortals such as men are now" would struggle to achieve. Many men of that time had a divine parent and so were literally ἡμίθεοι, "half-gods," by birth, and others slip in loosely under the same rubric even though both their parents were mortal; Hesiod can speak generically of the warriors who fought at Thebes and Troy as "the godlike race of heroes, who are called ἡμίθεοι," and prose authors of the classical period treat "heroes" and ἡμίθεοι as synonymous.[11] The "easy answer" is, however, widely rejected on the grounds that (1) many heroes who received cult were anonymous and so cannot have been identified by their worshippers with figures from that greater and more glorious time; and (2) some of the greatest heroes of the mythological period never received cult, or only tardily.

In answer to the second objection, the claim is not that the Greeks made a systematic effort to ensure that all the great names known from poetry were also worshipped; it is, more modestly, that where cult occurred it was understood by reference to the idea of an age of ἡμίθεοι. The first objection too can be readily met. Pausanias tells of a hero shrine at Tronis in Phocis of an anonymous "hero Archegete" that received daily offerings: some said that the hero was the warrior Xanthippos; others Phokos, grandson of Sisyphus. He tells also of an altar at Phaleron inscribed merely "of the hero,"

---

in *LSCG* 18). Libyan heroines: Ap. Rhod. *Argon.* 4.1322–23, cf. 2.504–5; Nicaenetus I Gow-Page *HE* (*Anth. Pal.* 6.225); Callim. fr. 602.1; Larson, 23, treats them as a special case, reasonably denying that Callim. *Hymn.* 3.184–85 provides a mainland identification of nymphs and heroines (she accepts Callim. fr. 66.1, but the context is too fragmentary for the case to be wholly clear). I hesitate to build on Wilamowitz's supplement in *IG* 12.3 *suppl.* 1340, which would show that Artemidorus of Perge thought that heroines fostered crops.

10. Cf. Kearns, *Heroes of Attica,* 134: "What tends to differentiate the hero from the god…is the addition of a historical perspective, the hero as man of a specific time in history.…We have in the hero the convergence of cult paid to a sort of intermediate being with narrative traditions and popular history."

11. Hes. *Op.* 159–60; cf. the very important Hom. *Il.* 12.23 (for the same generic usage in archaic poetry, see J. Bremmer, "Hero Cult," 24); for prose usage, see, e.g., Xen. *Symp.* 8.28 with 31 (where note that several of the "demigods" lack a divine parent); Pl. *Crat.* 398c ἡμίθεοι οἱ ἥρωες. Prose authors of the fourth century quite often speak of demigods with reference to recipients of cult whom we would term heroes (e.g., Isoc. 4.84, 9.70), and also use the term as a general designation for men of the mythological period (e.g., Pl. *Apol.* 28C, 41A); Isocrates has the series θνητός- ἡμίθεος- ἀθάνατος (9.39, cf. 3.42).

whom, however, "those who take trouble to know more than others about local traditions know to be Androgeos" (son of Minos). Pausanias was told by an old man that a curious tomb in the agora of Elis that most locals could not identify in fact belonged to Oxylus. The Attic "hero doctor" seems to have been variously identified as Amphiaraus or Aristomachus.[12] The working assumption was always, therefore, that an anonymous hero was indeed a figure from the age of ἡμίθεοι. Probably it was the existence of a manifestly ancient tomb that caused the presence of a hero, whose identity could only be guessed at, to be suspected.

The prose authors mentioned earlier in whom we find an identification, implicit or explicit, between "heroes" and ἡμίθεοι (i.e., figures from the mythological age) are Attic: Xenophon, Plato, and Isocrates. From their experience of Attic deme life they will have been familiar with the same mix that we find in the calendars of famous heroes, heroes who are little more than names, and heroes who are not even that. They were happy nonetheless to equate heroes, without exception, with ἡμίθεοι. Their evidence amounts to formal refutation, for the classical period, of the objections mentioned above. In the understanding of their worshippers in the fourth century, cult heroes were ἡμίθεοι: it is as simple as that. Historical individuals could be heroized when they displayed, exceptionally, the same extraordinary qualities as were inherent in the ἡμίθεοι by their very nature. Some god, Isocrates outrageously suggests, caused the Persian wars in order to allow the Athenians of that time to display their excellence "and not die ingloriously, but receive the same rewards as those descended from the gods and called ἡμίθεοι."[13]

No doubt to the eye of logic this understanding of the nature of heroes has its difficulties. Not all, perhaps not even a majority, of the heroes of cult could boast a divine parent even when they unambiguously belonged to the mythological age. It could not then be said, in explanation of the special powers that they exercised in life and retained after death, that they were, in Aeschylus's words, "those close in stock to the gods...those in whom the divine blood is not yet extinct." ἡμίθεοι in the strict sense could only emerge through sexual contact between god and mortal, a form of contact that Herodotus, for instance, seems to have thought could not occur. But there are still heroes for Herodotus even if he doubts the premise on which

---

12. Paus. 10.4.10; 1.1.5; 6.24.9. Hero doctor: see Kearns, *Heroes of Attica,* 172 (and for Aristomachus *SEG* 50 168 A 2 19–20).

13. Isoc. 4.84.

the conception of a special age of heroes/ἡμίθεοι was based.[14] The graves of men of the mythological era are still powerful, a worshipper might have insisted, however that power is to be explained.

Heroic mythology, the vision of an age of ἡμίθεοι, is always the conceptual underpinning of hero cult, but the interdependence is more evident in some cases than in others. Often the hero is active after death in the same spheres in which he operated in life, "since they are unwilling completely to abandon the nature they had when they were on earth."[15] Amphiaraus and Asclepius were, respectively, prophet and healer both as men and as heroes; Agamemnon's herald Talthybius avenged wrongs done to heralds even from the grave. Sometimes distinctive features of the cult have their origin in experiences of the hero during life: women may not partake of the sacrifices to the descendants of wife-murdered Agamemnon at Taras; heralds are banned from the cult of Okridion, women from that of Eunostos, because of bad experiences of these two heroes with, respectively, a herald and a woman. Aeschylus and Sophocles are operating within this idiom when they make Orestes and Oedipus promise to show favor to Athens after death in gratitude for the generous treatment that we see them receiving onstage.[16] The heroes whose biography no one now knows are obviously at the opposite extreme. But they earn cult because of the presumption that, but for the ravages of time, there would have been tales to tell about them.

The past justifies the cult; yet the cult is not rooted in antiquarianism or nostalgia. Even the innocent-seeming claim that hero cult represents a "use of the past," or an attempt to establish continuities with previous generations, needs to be treated with some caution. Doubtless the Spartan argument that as Agamemnon's heirs they should lead the Greek coalition against Persia could have been supported by the cult that they accorded him. But such was not the concern of the many faithful who left more than ten thousand objects in the sanctuary at Amyclae that he shared with "Alexandra" (a figure identified in literary texts with Cassandra). For them he was, we presume,

14. No sexual contact: Harrison, *Divinity and History,* 88–89; heroes: e.g., Hdt. 2.45.3. Aeschylus: fr. 162 from *Niobe;* Radt in his edition collects much interesting evidence for the continuing resonance of the concept.

15. Max. Tyr. 9.7 p. 109 Hobein (speaking of *daimones,* his word for souls departed from the body, but giving as his examples heroes such as Asclepius).

16. Aesch. *Eum.* 764–71; Soph. *OC* 576–82, 621–23, 1518–34; cf. Kearns, *Heroes of Attica,* 48–53, with other tragic examples. The Attic cult of the Herakleidai (on which see chap. 1 n. 59) will have been in part based on similar ideas. Talthybius: p. 7 above; Agamemnon at Taras: chap. 1 n. 59 above; Eunostos: Plut. *Quaest. Graec.* 40, 300D–301A; Okridion: ibid. 27, 297C–D.

a powerful local helper. Heroes, like gods, were worshipped for the benefits that they could provide in the present.[17]

It is this similarity of function that explains the blurring that often occurs on the borderline between hero and god. It is not just that a small number of major figures—Heracles, the Dioscuri, Asclepius, Amphiaraus, around the Black Sea Achilles—burst the heroic mold to become as powerful as gods. Such cases normally receive some form of explicit mythological justification, as in the myth of Heracles' reception on Olympus; Pindar too recognized the anomaly when he applied to Heracles the unique description "hero god," as did Herodotus when he postulated two Heracleses: one mortal, one divine.[18] But even quite minor figures are sometimes inadvertently described as gods: an Athenian decree regulating the cult of "the hero doctor" twice speaks of him, despite his name, as "the god," and in the epigram that records how Naulochus was established as a "city guardian" of Priene he changes from hero to god within two lines.[19] If a hero provides the same service as a god, a worshipper can slip into speaking of him as one.

Heroes are biographically dead mortals, functionally minor gods.[20] That formulation helps to explain the chief anomalies or inconsistencies in their cults. Sacrifice is sometimes made to them in a way that assimilates them to the dead, sometimes not (or at least not clearly so). The site of their cult is sometimes a grave, real or supposed, sometimes not. Contact with them is sometimes polluting, sometimes not. The variations in cult are oscillations on the line between dead mortal and minor god. But no hero is one or the other exclusively.

Some heroes, it may be objected, seem more like symbols than powers. The founders of cities were routinely accorded hero cult after their death,

---

17. Cf. Burkert, *Greek Religion,* 204: hero cult's "concern is with effective presence, not with the chain of blood across generations." "Use of the past": J. Whitley, *The Archaeology of Ancient Greece* (Cambridge, 2001), 150–56; cf., e.g., A. Mazarakis Ainian, in *Thesera* 2:133. Agamemnon: Hdt. 7.159; G. Salapata, "Myth into Cult: Alexandra/Kassandra in Lakonia," in *Oikistes: Studies … A. J. Graham,* ed. V. B. Gorman and E. W. Robinson, 131–59 (Leiden, 2002).

18. Pind. *Nem.* 3.22, where Maas's normalizing conjecture θοός has not been generally accepted: other considerations aside, speed is appropriate neither to the hero nor the context; Hdt. 2.44.5. On "immortalized mortals," see Sourvinou-Inwood, *Hylas,* 326–45.

19. *IG* 2².839 (*LSCG* 41); *CEG* 854; the Attic orgeonic hero Hypodektes too is a "god" in *IG* 2².2501; cf. Kearns, *Heroes of Attica,* 125, who also mentions Soph. *OC* 65, where Colonus the *archēgos* of the deme is a "god"; for Herodotean examples, see Harrison, *Divinity and History,* 160; note too J. Bremmer, "Hero Cult," 20.

20. I derive this position essentially from Kearns, *Heroes of Attica,* esp. 1–2, 125–29. Inconsistencies: Ekroth in *Companion,* 100–14.

yet only one private dedication to a founder-hero has ever been discovered;[21] private dedications to the ten Attic heroes after whom the Clisthenic tribes were named are also very rare. And were not the honors paid to the war dead just that, honors, rather than part of the exchange of benefits that Greeks sought to establish in their dealings with gods? But even if there were some heroes whom individuals did not approach with particular, personal requests, public cult still ensured their general benevolence. And Pericles supposedly said that the war dead, like the gods, not only "received honors" but also "conferred benefits."

The argument thus far has sought to bring out the sense in which the heroes can be seen as a unified category. There has by contrast, in the wake of L. R. Farnell's division of them into seven types, been a tendency to stress their diversity.[22] Certainly there were greater and lesser heroes, and different heroes to some extent had different capabilities (one would doubtless not turn to Taraxippos in time of sickness), even if the extreme specialization familiar from popular Catholicism did not exist: the doughty rustic Echetlaios, "he of the plowshare," supposedly fought at Marathon alongside more obviously military heroes. There was no standardized form of cult, even though there were practices that recurred regularly; even within Attica, it has been noticed, we find in different demes (a) individual heroes linked with a single heroine, (b) individual heroes linked with a cluster of heroines, and (c) clusters of heroines worshipped on their own apart from heroes.[23] And the biographies of heroes, mythical, and still more noticeably historical, read very differently. One can imagine a Lucian or a Menippus having merry fun juxtaposing figures from the extremes—Matton, for instance, Kneader, honored among cooks in

---

21. It is reproduced as the frontispiece to Malkin, *Religion and Colonization.* Clisthenic tribal heroes: Kearns, *Heroes of Attica,* 85–86. Pericles: Stesimbrotos *FGrH* 107 F 9 ap. Plut. *Per.* 8.9.

22. L. R. Farnell, *Greek Hero Cults and Ideas of Immortality* (Oxford, 1921). Farnell's seven categories were in part designed to find a compromise between previous more monolithic theories, which made all heroes faded great gods, or "special gods" in Usener's sense, or heroized mortals: cf. Brelich, *Eroi,* 15–16. Brelich rightly stresses that if one takes this view, one needs also to explain how such diverse beings came to be lumped together. Brelich's book is a notable but ultimately overschematic attempt to show how the heroes of both myth and cult derive from a single heroic template: the "ideal" hero is associated with nine interrelated spheres of human experience or activity (death, warfare, athletics, prophecy, healing, mysteries, rituals of growing up, city foundation, kinship groups); but he is also marked by traits of excess and monstrosity that differentiate him from current mortals. Brelich assumed both heroic myth and cult to have very ancient origins, and one would like to know how he might have modified his views in light of the discontinuities in hero cult apparently revealed by archaeology (p. 287 below).

23. Larson, *Heroine Cults,* 26–34. Echetlaios: Paus. 1.32.5. Specialization in popular Catholicism: see, for instance, the guidebook by H. Gancel, *Les saints qui guérissent en Bretagne* (Editions Ouest-France, 2000).

Sparta, with Brasidas, the great Spartan general, or the maiden-deflowering hero of Temesa and the chaste Hippolytus.

But a category can be capacious and flexible without being conceptually incoherent. The most important documents for the study of hero cults are surely the Attic cult calendars: they allow us to see the full set of sacrifices made to heroes and heroines over a year by a particular worshipping group in a particular place, in relation sometimes to a landscape. I present here the relevant extracts from the calendars of three demes and one *genos;* the first is probably to be dated c. 430, the others in the first half of the fourth century. (Names of heroes are in italics.)

Deme of Thorikos (*SEG* 33.147 = *NGSL* 1)

> For *Kephalos* a chosen sheep, for *Prokris* a table.
> For *Thorikos* a chosen sheep, for the *heroines of Thorikos* a table.
> For *Young Man* a full-grown victim.
> For *Thorikos* a bovine costing 40–50 dr., for the *heroines of Thorikos* a table.
> For the *Herakleidai* a full-grown victim, for *Alkmene* a full-grown victim.
> For the *"Lords"* [*Kastor and Polydeukes*] a full-grown victim, for *Helen* a
> full-grown victim.
> For *Philonis* a table.
> For *Above-the-Plain* ('Υπερπέδιος) a sheep, for the *heroines of Above-the-Plain*
> a table, for *Nisos* a sheep, for *Thras[]* a sheep, for *Save-Ship* (Σωσίνεως)
> a sheep, for *Rhogios* a sheep, for *Gate-Holder* (Πυλόχος) a piglet, for the
> *Gate-Holding* heroines a table.
> For *Aglauros* a sheep [*this offering is made along with one to Athena at the
> Plynteria*].
> For *Kephalos* a bovine for not less than 40 and up to 50 dr., for *P[rokris]*
> a sheep.

Deme of Marathon (*SEG* 50.168 A col. 2)[24]

> For the *hero* [-—-] a piglet, 3 dr.; table for the *hero* [-—-].
> For *[-—-]* a bovine, 150 dr., a sheep, 12 dr.; for the *heroine* [a sheep,
> 11 dr.?].
> For *Ioleos* a sheep, 12 dr. [*this offering forms part of a group with others to
> Earth, Zeus Hypatos and Korotrophos*].

---

24. I omit the offerings "before the Skira" to Hyttenios and (alternate years) Galios (lines 30, 51): they are unknown, and not certainly heroes.

For the *hero Pheraios* [*Pheraian hero?*] [a sheep, 12 dr.?]; for the *heroine* a sheep, 11 dr.

For *Aristomachus* a bovine, 90 dr., a sheep, 12 dr.; for the *heroine* a sheep, 11 dr.

For *Young Man* a bovine, 90 dr., a sheep, 12 dr., a piglet [3 dr.]; for the *heroine* a sheep, 11 dr.

For the *hero at Drasileia* a sheep, 12 dr., a table, 1 dr.; for the *heroine* a sheep, 11 dr.

For the *hero beside the Hellotion,* a sheep, 12 dr., a table, 1 dr.; for the *heroine* a sheep, 11 dr.

Deme of Erchia (*SEG* 21.541 = *LSCG* 18)

For the *heroines,* at Schoinos in Erchia, a sheep, no carrying away, skin to the priestess, 10 dr.

For *Basile,* at Erchia, a white lamb, burnt whole, wineless, 7 dr.

For *Epops,* at Erchia, a piglet, burnt whole, wineless, 3 dr.

For *Alochos* ("*Wife*"), on the hill at Erchia, a sheep, 10 dr.

For the *heroines,* at Pylon at Erchia, a sheep, no carrying away, skin to the priestess, 10 dr.

For *Semele,* on the same altar (*as an offering to Dionysus on the same day*) a goat, to be handed over to women, skin to the priestess, no carrying away, 10 dr.

For the *Herakleidai* a sheep, at Erchia, no carrying away,[25] 12 dr.

For *Leukaspis,* at Erchia, a sheep, wineless, no carrying away, 12 dr.

For the *"Lords"* [*Kastor and Polydeukes*], at Erchia, a sheep, 12 dr.

For *Menedeios,* at Erchia, a sheep, no carrying out, 12 dr.

For *Aglauros,* on the citadel at Erchia, a sheep, no carrying away, 10 dr. [*in association with several sacrifices to gods*].

Genos of Salaminioi (*ZPE* 119 [1997]: 86–88)[26]

For *Ioleos* a sheep, burned whole, 15 dr.; for *Alkmene* a sheep, 12 dr.; for *Maia* (*Nurse?*), a sheep, 12 dr.; for *Heracles,* a bovine, 70 dr.; for the *hero at the Salt Flat,* a sheep, 15 dr.; for the *hero at Antisara,* a piglet,

---

25. For the addition of this specification to the stone here and in B 59, see Scullion, "Olympian and Chthonian," 105 n. 85.

26. Older texts, e.g., in G. V. Lalonde et al., *The Athenian Agora,* vol. 19, *Inscriptions* (Princeton, 1991), L 4a; *LSS* 19.

3½ dr.; for the *hero at the Tower,* a piglet, 3½ dr.; in alternate years, for
Ion, a sheep.

For *Eurysakes* a pig, 40 dr.

For *hero Phaiax [Phaeacian hero?]* a piglet, 3½ dr.; for *hero Teucer* a piglet,
3½ dr.; for *hero Nauseiros* a piglet, 3½ dr. [*these offerings accompany a
large offering to Poseidon*].

For *Theseus* a pig, 40 dr.

For *Skiros* a sheep, 15 dr. [*this offering accompanies one to Athena Skiras*].

The details are not of importance here, but several general points emerge. A
first, very obvious, is the quite unexpected abundance of heroes and heroines honored by each of these relatively small groups. A second, revealed at
Thorikos in particular, is the landscape-mapping role of heroes and their
women: heroines of Thorikos, Above the Plain, Gate-Holder. A third is the
tendency of many heroes and heroines to operate as minor partners in association with gods: they receive lesser offerings when gods receive greater, just
as they often share their precincts and, in myth, are cast as their servants.[27] A
fourth, the one most relevant to the present argument, is the easy mingling
of heroes of what might seem to be diverse types. There are anonymous heroes (the heroes "at Drasileia" and "beside the Hellotion" at Marathon; "at
the salt flat," "at Antisara," "at the Tower" of the Salaminioi); heroes with a
name but no surviving legend (e.g., Pheraios and Aristomachus at Marathon;
Thorikos, Thras-, and Rhogios at Thorikos); heroes with apparently functional or speaking names (e.g., "Save-Ship," "Gate-Keeper," at Thorikos);
and a good admixture of heroes known and often well-known from myth.[28]
But there is no reason to think that in sorting them thus into classes one is
tracking divisions perceived by the ancients. All are just (as it might be) the
heroes of Erchia.

Another class of evidence can be called in support, one which has received strangely little attention in this regard. The "banqueting hero" relief
is a characteristic form of dedication; it typically shows a male reclining on
a couch with a table of foodstuffs in front of him, a female seated beside
him, and a standing youth waiting on him. Confusion long prevailed and

---

27. Aglauros at Thorikos; Ioleos at Marathon; Semele, and Aglauros, at Erchia; the heroes Phaiax,
Teucer, and Nauseiros among the Salaminioi. Cf. E. Kearns, "Between God and Man: Status
and Function of Heroes and their Sanctuaries," in *Sanctuaire grec,* 65–99, at 77–93; A. Seiffert in
ThesCRA 4:26.

28. At Thorikos Kephalos and Prokris, Herakleidai, Alkmene, "Lords," Helen, Philonis, Nisos,
Aglauros; at Marathon Ioleos; at Erchia Epops, Semele, Herakleidai, "Lords," Aglauros; among the
Salaminioi Alkmene, Heracles, Ion, Eurysakes, Teucer, Theseus, Skiros.

FIGURE 3. A banqueting-hero relief, Attica, late fourth century. Athens, National Archaeological Museum, Sculpture 3873. © Hellenic Ministry of Culture/Archaeological Receipts Fund.

has yet to be completely dispelled about this iconography, because it is found both on votive reliefs dedicated to heroes (occasionally also gods) and, with increasing frequency, on tombstones; accordingly the type used normally to be referred to as a *Totenmahlrelief,* "banquet of the dead relief," and attempts were made to bridge the gap between heroes and dead persons by the hypothesis that the recipients were recently dead persons treated as heroes. But in 1965 it was clearly established that the heroes were the original honorands of such reliefs and the transfer of the iconography to the dead was a secondary development, not occurring before the fourth century.[29] Weapons may

---

29. By R. N. Thönges-Stringaris, "Das griechische Totenmahl," *AM* 80 (1965): 1–99, confirmed in the monumental study of Dentzer, *Banquet couché;* on the later development see J. Fabricius,

be shown on the wall behind the banqueter, and a horse's head often appears anti-naturalistically in a frame in a corner: both are symbols of heroic status. Smaller figures of worshippers, perhaps leading a sacrificial animal, often approach the heroic couple from the left. The many specimens found in the precinct of Agamemnon and Alexandra at Amyclae near Sparta disprove all idea that the heroes so honored were necessarily recently dead. When Aeneas Tacticus in the fourth century alludes casually to a "heroic (votive) tablet" (πινάκιον ἡρωικόν), a banqueting hero relief is surely what he has in mind. That passing reference shows that this was a generic form of offering; it follows that heroes had enough in common for a generic offering to be appropriate. (Somewhat less common, but still probably generic, is the "riding hero" type.) In a papyrus fragment probably from Aristophanes' *Heroes,* the Heroes duly speak as a body; they declare themselves guardians of human morality who punish transgressions.[30]

The Power of Heroes

The question thus far has been that of what the ancients believed heroes to be. There follows that of the motives for the worship of heroes, the benefits that worship of heroes brought. Moderns have often tended of late to answer that question in broadly political terms: hero cults are used to legitimate territorial claims or claims to hegemony or the power of a ruling elite or the prestige of individual groups, or simply as a way of forging group identity. Ancients would have given a very different kind of answer: for them what mattered was not the hero as an idea but the hero as a power genuinely effective for good or ill. It would doubtless be crude to use the pious ancient understanding as a stick with which to chastise the unimaginatively secular assumptions of modern scholarship; even actions strongly motivated by belief can scarcely escape having a political dimension. But it is certainly worth beginning from the evidence of Herodotus, a privileged witness because of the quantity of testimony that he offers to fifth-century understandings of the effectiveness of heroes. Several long-established heroes show powers of diverse kinds. Two "local heroes" of Delphi (ἐπιχώριοι ἥρωες), Phylakos and Autonoos, drive

---

Die hellenistischen Totenmahlreliefs (Munich, 1999). These works are abundantly illustrated; for a few specimens see *ThesCRA* 2, pl. 22, nos. 100, 107; pl. 26, no. 184; pl. 46, no. 46.

30. Fr. 322 K/A. Aeneas Tacticus: 31.15. Agamemnon: see n. 17 above; for another remarkable heroic votive assemblage (from Messene), see P. G. Themelis in R. Hägg, ed., *Ancient Greek Cult Practice from the Archaeological Evidence* (Stockholm, 1998), 157–86. Riding hero: e.g., *ThesCRA* 1, pl. 70, nos. 60, 61; 2, pl. 22, no. 108.

the Persian invaders away from the sanctuary (8.39.1); Astrabakos leaves his hero shrine in Sparta and, disguised as King Ariston, visits Ariston's wife around the corner and engenders Demaratus (6.69);[31] Helen (but perhaps she should count rather as a goddess) transforms an ugly child into a great beauty (6.61.2–5); Protesilaus brings dead fish back to life as a warning to Artyactes that, though dead, he will avenge the wrongs done to him (9.120.1–2). Images of the Aeacids are fetched from Salamis or Aegina to serve as battle helpers, even if the Thebans after a defeat send them back and ask for men instead (5.80–81.1; 8.64, cf. 8.83.2).

Herodotus also recounts the circumstances leading to the establishment of several new hero cults. Onesilos, younger brother of the king of Salamis in Cyprus, was killed while seeking to force Amathous to join the Ionian revolt; the Amathousians cut off his head and positioned it above the city gates; a swarm of bees settled in the head, and an unspecified oracle, consulted about the portent, instructed the Amathousians to sacrifice to Onesilos as a hero (5.113.2–114). Philippos of Croton in the late sixth century was an Olympic victor and the most beautiful Greek of his day. When he joined Dorieus's assault on Egesta and was killed, he "got from [the Egestaians], because of his beauty, what no one else did": they put a hero shrine on his tomb and still propitiate him with sacrifices (5.47). The Agyllaeans stoned Phocaean survivors from a sea battle; all living creatures that passed the site of the stoning became twisted or mad, and on Delphi's advice they established large-scale offerings and athletic competitions for the victims (1.167.1–2).

In these three cases the peoples who set up the cults were, as it happens, non-Greek or only partly Greek, but there is no hint from Herodotus that their behavior, sanctioned in one case by Delphi, was anything other than very natural (the Egyptians, by contrast, are explicitly said not to honor heroes, 2.50.3). And he records a closely comparable case of the Akanthians: when Xerxes' honored officer Artachaies, the tallest of Persians and the loudest-voiced of all mankind, died of disease at Akanthos, the whole Persian army built a mound for him; and now on oracular advice the Akanthians sacrifice to him as a hero, invoking him by name (7.117).[32] On Delphic advice, the Spartans brought home the bones of Orestes and thus established a new cult (though of an old hero), as a talisman to improve their fortunes in their

31. On "neighboring heroes" such as Astrabakos, see J. S. Rusten, *HSCP* 87 (1983): 289–97.

32. Artachaies' fame is underlined if E. K. Borthwick's brilliant conjecture, which introduces him to Ar. *Ach.* 709 (*BICS* 17 [1970]: 107–10), is accepted. On the mourning for another giant Persian, Masistios (Hdt. 9.20–25.1), see A. Petropoulou in *Ancient Greece and Ancient Iran*, ed. S. M. R. Darbaudi and A. Zounatzi, 9–30 (Athens, 2008).

wars with Tegea (Hdt. 1.67–68). Again on Delphic advice, the Athenians set up a precinct of the Aeginetan hero Aiakos in the agora to help them in their Aeginetan wars (5.89.2–3). Herodotus also mentions the heroic honors customarily paid to founders of colonies (1.168; 6.38.1), and a case of colonists who on Delphic advice "establish" a mythical hero in their new foundation (1.167.4).

Onesilos, Philippos, Artachaies, and the Agyllaeans all received cult from their erstwhile enemies, in accord with a pattern attested in several other cases.[33] The Agyllaeans and, arguably, Onesilos had been treated in ways that violated civilized norms, and portents signaled the need for reparation; but the only motive given for the honors accorded Philippos and Artachaies is their exceptional physical characteristics. We should also note, however, that Onesilos was a king's brother and a military leader, Philippos an Olympic victor, and Artachaies a high-ranking Persian whom his compatriots buried in a huge mound: it was a blend of social prominence and remarkable attributes or fortunes that made them into heroes. None of this supports a view of hero cult as a device of legitimation or identity politics; one does not acquire legitimacy or group solidarity by worshipping an enemy.

There is very little at all in Herodotus to justify such an approach. The bringing home of the bones of Orestes by the Spartans (1.67–68) has long, it is true, been interpreted in these terms, as a signal sent by the Spartans to the Peloponnese, since Orestes was an Achaean, that Sparta was an Achaean and not a Dorian state; but, even if correct,[34] this is a rationalizing reinterpretation and not what Herodotus says. Better support comes from Clisthenes of Sicyon's attempt, when at war with Argos, to expel the Argive hero Adrastus from his hero shrine in the agora of Sicyon. At one level Clisthenes is certainly playing with symbols to foster anti-Argive feeling. But even here Herodotus's understanding is different. He goes on to tell how, forbidden to expel Adrastus by Delphi, Clisthenes sought to induce Adrastus to leave of his own accord, by establishing in the prytaneum of Sicyon a cult of his worst enemy Melanippus (5.67). Adrastus is a real presence, therefore, who retains the affections and antipathies of his mortal existence.

What needs to be done is to seek bridges between the kinds of explanation for hero cult offered by Herodotus on the one hand, and by politically minded modern historians on the other. Only where no bridge can

---

33. M. Visser, "Worship Your Enemies," *HTR* 75 (1982): 403–28; cf. Kearns, *Heroes of Attica*, 50.

34. For a powerful denial, see D. Boedeker, "Hero Cult and Politics in Herodotus: The Bones of Orestes," in *Cultural Poetics*, 164–77.

THE POWER AND NATURE OF HEROES

be found will a choice have to be made. The role of the cults in creating a sense of identity and reinforcing group solidarity is easy. In colonies, the cult of the founder could evidently provide a focus of loyalty for settlers recruited perhaps from different parts of the Greek world without shared traditions; so could other hero cults[35] established at the time of foundation. This functional explanation fits easily, like the two halves of an indenture, with the more pious account whereby the colonists honor the colonist for his achievements and the protection he continues to bring them.

When Messenia was liberated from Spartan domination in 369, Messenian heroes were ceremoniously called home; the Messenians would not have been a free people, equal citizens in the commonwealth of cities, without their own protecting heroes. Messenia is the one region of Greece in which the bringing of offerings to Mycenaean graves, elsewhere a phenomenon largely confined to the archaic and early classical period, resumes in the fifth century and increases greatly in intensity in the fourth. The post-369 boom probably reflects a repopulation of the territory with heroes, in parallel with the turn to much more intensive cultivation of the liberated region; the cults beginning in the fifth century were perhaps already symbols and focuses of a Messenian nationalism growing stronger (or for the first time emerging) after the great helot revolt of the midcentury.[36] Further examples of the social utility of such cults of broadly patriotic stamp, such as that of war heroes, could very easily be amassed. On a miniature scale, the devotion of the city wardens of Priene to City Warden can count as another example of the same phenomenon.[37] The particularity of heroes made them an ideal focus for group loyalty, the rennet around which social groups coagulated. (But let it be noted in passing that many heroes were not particularly suitable for such purposes, the "enemy-heroes" mentioned above, for instance.)

But could individuals or restricted groups exploit hero cults to their advantage in any sense other than this? Doubtless it was of advantage over a long period to the Battiad monarchy in Cyrene that their ancestor, founder of the colony, was honored as a hero, much as the kings of France profited from the veneration paid to their predecessor St. Louis. The same possibility was available, though never exploited for very long, where a founder-hero passed on power dynastically (like Miltiades in the Chersonese or several

---

35. Delphi helped colonists discover "secret burial places of heroes": Plut. *Pyth. Or.* 27, 407F; cf. Malkin, *Religion and Colonization,* 5; heroes could also be imported to colonies (Hdt. 1. 167. 4).

36. See Boehringer, *Heroenkulte,* 243–371, esp. 340, 367–69; Luraghi, *Ancient Messenians,* 239–45. Calling home in 369: Paus. 4.27.5–6.

37. See n. 7 above.

Sicilian tyrants). But such instances were unusual; and it has been acutely argued that, in the normal case, the hero cult accorded to the founder marked the end of the phase in a colony's life when altogether extraordinary powers were permitted to an individual.[38]

Families sought cachet by claiming descent from heroes, and it is sometimes suggested that the reopening of Bronze Age tombs to bring offerings is the work of groups concerned to equip themselves with prestigious ancestors.[39] Yet it is a commonplace of scholarship that hero cult, in contrast, say, to the worship of ancestors, transcends individual families and belongs to the collectivity. The commonplace needs to be nuanced to acknowledge that in Attica, the one region where the evidence is available for inspection in detail, many hero cults were administered by pseudo-kinship groups (*gene,* or groups of *orgeōnes*), not by the city or by one of its formal subdivisions. But since 1976 it has been widely accepted that actual families and the pseudo-kinship groups were different entities with different interests.[40] The appeal by families was normally to genealogical legend, not specifically to tombs, and the possibility of a powerful family exploiting a hero cult to its lasting benefit remains purely hypothetical. (So too does that of similar exploitation by a *genos* or society of *orgeōnes*.) Cimon's success in "bringing home the bones of Theseus" from Skyros in the 470s brought him, according to Plutarch's credible report, enormous popularity; there are some indications that Cimon's family claimed descent from the hero.[41] But the precondition for Cimon's coup de théâtre was Theseus's abrupt rise to celebrity in the preceding years. Cimon did not make the hero great, nor could he appropriate him, but merely exploited his celebrity at a particular moment.

The persons to whom a hero really mattered, it should be remembered, were those who visited his shrine, prayed to him, brought votives when their prayers were fulfilled, participated in his sacrificial banquets. Hero cults

---

38. F. de Polignac, *Cults, Territory, and the Origins of the Greek City-State* (Chicago, 1995), 132–33. Boedeker similarly argues that Orestes was a good hero for the Spartans to bring home in the sixth century because he had no descendants ("Hero Cult," n. 34 above). Battiads: Pind. *Pyth.* 5.95; Miltiades: Hdt. 6.34–41; cf. Currie, *Cult of Heroes,* 5, who speaks of the cults of Gelon in Syracuse, Theron in Acragas, Hieron in Aitna.

39. So S. Alcock, *AJA* 95 (1991): 456–58, sees hero cult being exploited by powerful families in the Hellenistic period to lay claim to distinguished ancestors; D. Damaskos in *ThesCRA* 2:142, speaks of "legitimations—bzw. Durchsetzungsversuch von politischen Parteien."

40. On the work of F. Bourriot and D. Roussel, see in brief Parker, *Athenian Religion,* 61. On the heroes of *gene* and of *orgeōnes,* see Kearns, *Heroes of Attica,* 64–79. Commonplace: Nilsson, *Geschichte,* 715; Burkert, *Greek Religion,* 204; W. Schuller in *ThesCRA* 2:130; most emphatically R. Seaford, *Reciprocity and Ritual* (Oxford, 1994), e.g., 109–14.

41. Plut. *Cim.* 8.5–7; cf. *Thes.* 36.1–4; Parker, *Athenian Religion,* 168–70 (ibid., 168 n. 54 for the family connection).

united groups because groups participated in them together. The bringing home of a hero's bones, that common practice, is often interpreted, by contrast, as a way for a state to send out messages to other states; so too the establishment of a cult for a figure of high mythological profile. The Seven against Thebes, it has been noted, were not all Argive even though the expedition set out from Argos; by establishing a shrine to them in the sixth century, therefore, the Argives were staking a claim to a role of leadership in the Peloponnese.[42] But the message would have been effective only if other Peloponnesian states had participated in the cult; as it was, the only people to whom the Argives were sending the message was themselves, and they doubtless needed no convincing. The same objection applies to most interpretations that have been offered of the bringing home of a hero's bones. When such an event occurred, the response that we need to consider is that of the receiving state. The context of the most famous instance, that of the bones of Orestes, was a prolonged and unsuccessful war. A recent study urges us to "set aside the obvious morale boost that the successful fulfilment of the oracle brought to the Spartans."[43] We should, rather, restore the morale boost to its rightful place.

A decision to heroize the newly dead was, it is true, often almost inevitably politically charged. The tyrannicides Harmodius and Aristogeiton received "honors equal to those of gods and heroes" at Athens (even if the word "heroes" is never applied to them), probably from quite soon after the overthrow of the tyranny: both those nostalgic for the old order and those who knew the tyrannicides' role in its overthrow to have been exaggerated must have looked askance when the decree was passed. The assassin of the Sicyonian populist leader Euphron was acclaimed at Thebes as another tyrant slayer, but Euphron's fellow citizens "brought him home as being a good man, buried him in the agora, and revere him as leader (*archēgetēs*) of the city." "To such an extent, it seems, do most people regard those who bring them benefits as being good men," comments Xenophon sourly.[44]

But even when the recently dead were heroized, the title to the honor was not always "for political services." Sophocles was supposedly given cult under the new name Dexion, "receiver," for his role in the reception of the new god Asclepius in Athens; the late tradition to that effect received unexpected support when fourth-century epigraphic evidence emerged

---

42. J. M. Hall, "Beyond the Polis: The Multilocality of Heroes," in *Hero Cult,* 49–59.

43. B. McCauley, "Heroes and Power: The Politics of Bone Transfer," in *Hero Cult,* 85–98 (a useful survey), at 88; cf. n. 34 on the case of Orestes.

44. Xen. *Hell.* 7.3.12. Tyrannicides: Dem. 19.280; cf. Parker, *Athenian Religion,* 136 n. 55.

for a hero Dexion associated with the cult of Asclepius. If the tradition is indeed historical,[45] Sophocles' standing as the grand old man of tragedy surely contributed to the wish to pay him cult, even if the explicit justification was religious. We are also told that several great athletes of the fifth century were heroized. Unfortunately the sources are all late: they record extraordinary legends that are profoundly revealing for one side of the image of the hero (the hero as uncontrollable force, in the case of the mass killer Cleomedes), but quite fail to set the decision to heroize in a specific, credible context. To fill the vacuum, political interpretations have been attempted in these cases too.[46] But no aspect of late archaic and early classical Greek culture is better established than the idolization of successful athletes; the evidence is abundant, that from the history of statuary for instance, but none perhaps more telling than a short phrase in Thucydides: he is describing the reception of the Spartan general Brasidas by the people of Scione in 423, and says that they "garlanded him and approached him as if he had been an athlete." The greatest general of his day in Greece raised to the level of a sportsman! Whatever political interests may have been at play in particular cases, the core phenomenon that permitted such exploitation was the charisma of sporting success.[47]

Into the play of interests surrounding hero cult a new interest has been introduced of late: that of the potential hero himself. Hieron, Diodorus claims (but how could he know?), founded Aetna "desiring to have heroic honors" there. And why should not athletes have nourished similar aspirations, and

---

45. It is doubted by A. Connolly in a careful study, "Was Sophocles Heroised as Dexion?," *JHS* 118 (1998): 1–21 (where see the testimonia). He argues that a Hellenistic or later biographer brought the tradition of Sophocles' role in receiving Asclepius into association with the minor and obscure cult of a Dexion who had nothing to do with the poet; this seems to me harder (Connolly's 20 n. 104 notes the difficulty) than the problems he detects (heroization of a poet in the fifth century; heroization under a new name). The sources speak of "the Athenians" honoring Sophocles, and Istros even has annual sacrifice decreed by the assembly (*FGrH* 334 F 38). But Dexion's altar is in a precinct owned by the *orgeōnes* of Amynos and Asclepios. Do the sources speak loosely? Or was the public cult in charge of the *orgeōnes*? In the latter case, did they establish it and the city adopt it? Or did they establish it on request from the assembly?

46. F. Bohringer, "Cultes d'athlètes en Grèce classique: Propos politiques, discours mythiques," *REA* 81 (1979): 5–18: good comments in Currie, *Cult of Heroes*, 126–29, 152–57 (with many further references). We know too little to build much on the interesting lack, which Bohringer stresses, of attested cult for the greatest of all athletes, Milon of Croton. J. Pouilloux, "Théogénes de Thasos...quarante ans après," *BCH* 118 (1994): 199–206, withdraws his own earlier political interpretation of the heroization of Theagenes of Thasos; even the fifth-century date of the heroization is now in doubt.

47. Thuc. 4.121.1. Being tied to class interests, athletic charisma was, I do not deny, contested and problematic in various ways; it was given more scope in some cities than in others. But it existed. Statuary: see R. R. R. Smith, "Pindar, Athletes, and the Early Greek Statue Habit," in *Pindar's Poetry,* 83–139.

worked while still alive to realize them, when they knew of other athletes who had escaped ordinary death in this way?[48] In the third century one Artemidorus, a man from Perge who settled in Thera and earned citizenship by building various sanctuaries, was eventually able to announce:

> The prophetess of the god at Delphi sent an oracle [ ] proclaiming Artemidorus a [divine? new?] immortal hero.

He seems to be claiming a status as hero that is not private only but generally recognized; and we can scarcely doubt that he pressed for his own consecration. The new perspective, through the eyes of an individual confronting his own mortality, is intriguing; but the individual's power to realize his hopes, since the decision to heroize was collective, will normally have been very limited. Prosperous citizens of the Hellenistic period endowed foundations to finance sacrifices to be made to themselves and their family members, as heroes, after their death; one secured the approval of an oracle before doing so. But these were private affairs; such individuals were normally heroes for their relatives alone.[49] It is important too not to exaggerate the place of recently heroized persons among the great ranks of heroes. If one lists all attested cases, their numbers may appear impressive.[50] But the numbers for any single city are very small, whereas even individual demes of Attica could offer ten or so heroes from the age of demigods.

Scholars in the main explain divine cults in terms of the benefits the gods are believed to have in their gift. The point of the preceding discussion has been to argue that hero cults should be viewed in the same way: the argument continues the earlier argument that functionally heroes were minor gods. And no political explanation of a hero cult will have much power that does not start from the experience of the worshipper who visited the shrine and, where it was not consumed in the flames, ate the sacrificial meat.

---

48. The central thesis of Currie, *Cult of Heroes*. Hieron: Diod. Sic. 11.49.2.

49. Artemidorus: *IG* 12.3.863, with IG 12.3 *Suppl.* 1349 and *IG* 12 *Suppl.* p. 90 (where Hiller compares a story about Heraclides of Pontus's attempt to get himself declared a hero, Heraclides Ponticus frs. 14–15 Wehrli): χρησμὸν ἔπεμψε θεοῦ Δελφοῖσι [προφ]ῆτις ε- - - /φράζουσ' ἀθάνατον [θε]ιὸν ἥρων ['Αρτ]εμίδω[ρον]. Hellenistic foundations: see, e.g., Nilsson, *Geschichte*, 2:115–17; oracular approval *LSA* 72 (*Syll.*³ 1044). It had always been possible for private individuals to set up hero shrines for whom they pleased (Theophr. *Char.* 16.4; cf. the shrine of his teacher supposedly set up by Parmenides, Sotion fr. 27 Wehrli ap. DL 9.21, and the famous passage of Plato quoted on p. 59), but there was no pressure on third parties to acknowledge such heroes.

50. Cf. A. Connolly's list, *JHS* 118 (1998): 21, with Currie's addenda, *Cult of Heroes*, 87 n. 2; Eudamos and Lydiadas of Megalopolis are important new Hellenistic cases, *SEG* 52.447–49. Boehringer, *Heroenkulte*, 36, notes the rarity, and rightly points to the depersonalization that a heroized individual underwent: he became a narrative pattern, a type.

❧ CHAPTER 5

Killing, Dining, Communicating

> It must, however, be remembered that in ancient
> religion there was no authoritative interpretation of
> ritual.
>
> — Robertson Smith, *Religion of the Semites,* 399

I turn now to the central ritual of Greek religion. Seeking to refute the charge that Socrates did not "worship/believe in the same gods as the city," Xenophon begins with an uncomplicated argument. "First of all, what evidence did they bring that he did not believe in the same gods as the city? For he could often be seen sacrificing at home, and often on the public altars of the city." The master must have been orthodox in religion because he regularly performed the ritual that, more than any other, achieved communication with the gods. When Plato speaks of the processes of socialization that instill piety into the young, the scene he envisages is that of children watching their parents perform sacrifice. In the comic fantasy of Aristophanes, the Birds seek to replace the gods as rulers of the universe; so they instruct mankind to make sacrifice henceforth first to them and only after that to the gods.[1] Sacrifice was, and was seen to be, the heart of the matter.

Sacrifice was also central to the late nineteenth- and early twentieth-century debate about the origins and essence of religion.[2] A phenomenon describable by that name was so common among the so-called primitive religions that it could scarcely fail to attract attention; an extra stimulus was

---

1. Xen. *Mem.* 1.1.2; Pl. *Leg.* 887d (above p. 11); Arist. *Av.* 561–63.
2. Cf. J. Carter, *Understanding Religious Sacrifice: A Reader* (London, 2003).

the transformation of blood sacrifice into the "pure and perfect sacrifice" of Christ that rescued mankind. This modern debate was not or was only marginally an inheritance from the ancients. Sacrifice is our problem, not (or not prior to Neoplatonism)[3] theirs.

Insofar as they worried about the point, early Greeks seem to have explained participatory sacrifice, the kind where men ate the flesh of an animal offered to the gods, as an inheritance from the time when men and gods dined together; at a certain point, it would appear, men and gods resolved to dine apart while still sharing the same animal, and the unequal division of meat between men and gods had its origin in the trick played by Prometheus on Zeus on that occasion.[4] Sacrifice as still practiced was therefore a product of the post–golden age world in which we now live, but a self-evident and unproblematic one. They also had myths that explained how particular animals came first to be sacrificed or why particular sacrificial rites were conducted as they were;[5] but the need to sacrifice to the gods was too self-evident to require an explanation. When certain unorthodox thinkers declared this most central of ritual acts to be, in fact, a form of impiety, their starting point was hostility to meat eating; had they accepted meat eating, the role of sacrifice would have remained self-explanatory. The vegetarian Porphyry even tolerates the idea that tradition may sometimes require animal sacrifice, but not consumption of the flesh.[6]

Paul Veyne in 2000 issued the robust but not unsubtle announcement that any attempt to offer a general theory of sacrifice was misguided:

> Sacrifice is a good example of a particular category of sociological objects: those that, by the chance of their constitution, can combine

---

3. For Neoplatonist explanations of the rationale and efficacy of sacrifice, see briefly Sallustius *De Mundo* 16, and at length Iambl. *De Myst.* books 5–6. Cf. L. Gernet in Gernet and A. Boulanger, *Le génie grec dans la religion* (Paris, 1932; repr., 1970), 234: "Il n' y a pas non plus en Grèce, faute d' organisation sacerdotale, ce qu' il y a eu par exemple dans l'Inde: une speculation religieuse sur les forces que le sacrifice met en jeu." There was, it is true, a strand in pagan philosophical thought that declared sacrifice to be inappropriate to a philosophically conceived deity (Varro fr. 22 Cardauns ap. Arn. *Adv. nat.* 7.1; Seneca fr. 123 Haase ap Lactant. *Div. inst.* 6.25.3, asking, *quae extrucidatione innocentium voluptas est?*); we learn of it primarily through its endorsement by Christian critics of pagan sacrifice, among which Arn. *Adv. nat.* 7.1–37 is the most extensive.

4. Hes. *Theog.* 535–61 with fr. 1.6–7 (cf. pp. 139–40 below). J. Rudhardt, "Les myths grecs relatifs à l'instauration du sacrifice," in his *Mythe, religion,* 209–26, is right that what Prometheus conducts at Mekone is not a sacrifice, but in making the sacrifice later performed by Prometheus's son Deucalion to Zeus Phyxios (Apollod. *Bibl.* 1.7.2) the true origin of the rite, he gives it a founding significance not present in the sources.

5. For the former see Porph. *Abst.* 2.9–10; works on aitia (Callim. *Aet.;* Plut. *Quaest. Graec.*) are full of the latter.

6. Porph. *Abst.* 2.2.1, 2.4.1.

in themselves a great number of possible meanings (even if these are mutually contradictory) and provide a great number of diverse satisfactions: this richness makes them popular and assures them an almost universal success, while obscuring for the conscious mind their raison d'être (so they seem to emerge from mysterious human depths). It is like this with sacrifices, with pilgrimages, or, in the profane sphere, with the importance of sitting at the same table, of eating together. These "black holes" are a kind of social trap: the most varied individuals fall into them, have fallen into them, or will fall into them, because all or almost all the reasons for falling are good; therefore learned discussions on "the" true meaning of sacrifice will continue without an end and without a purpose. Its misleading impression of profundity will lead to the temptation of finding ethological or even "abyssal" explanations. The riddle is, however, easy to solve: sacrifice is widely distributed across centuries and across societies because this practice is sufficiently ambiguous for everyone to find in it their own particular satisfaction.[7]

It would seem that his ban extends not just to transcultural theories of sacrifice, already declared impossible by others,[8] but to any attempt to generalize about sacrifice within a given culture, and even beyond that to any attempt to explain any particular form of sacrifice, such as "killing followed by banquet," within a given culture.

Veyne's warning is altogether salutary. Any form of sacrifice may well derive its power from responsiveness to a complex mix of human desires, fears, interests, pleasures, and imaginings. Greek sacrifice was entirely unaccompanied by the kind of learned or authoritative exegesis, even in the form of myth, that could have steered understanding in a specific direction. A popular approach has been to distinguish a set of original or ideal types, different in essence even if, as we now observe them, somewhat contaminated one with another.[9] But no Greek ever encountered these ideal types. Growing up within the Greek sacrificial culture meant on the one hand acquiring a familiarity with many differing but overlapping forms of ritual killing, on the other experiencing a single sacrificial form deployed in a variety of different contexts; one was not taught in school the different theological presuppositions underlying the different forms, or what was the most proper

---

7. "Inviter les dieux," 21–22; my translation.
8. See, e.g., M. Detienne's introduction to *Cuisine of Sacrifice.*
9. So, e.g., Nilsson, *Geschichte,* 132; and see below on Meuli and *Cuisine of Sacrifice.*

application of a form that was variously applied. The chapter that follows will be an attempt to apply Veyne's insight to Greek sacrifice. To analyze one must separate to some degree, but the separation is the observer's, not the participant's.

The Double Face of Sacrifice: Sacrifice as Feast, Sacrifice as Communication

We can begin with the association between sacrifice and banquet. Polemicists for vegetarianism in antiquity attacked meat eating and animal sacrifice with little distinction, because they regarded them as coextensive. Greek sacrifice is driven by gluttony, they argued: nobody sacrifices inedible species such as elephant or camel or snake, and if Greeks were forced to sacrifice like Semites, by burning the whole offering, leaving no edible remnant, they would abandon the practice.[10] The idea of sacrifice as a necessary preliminary to meat eating was central, if in a less moralizing vein, to some of the most influential theories of Greek sacrifice in the second half of the twentieth century. The great Swiss comparativist Karl Meuli saw Greek sacrifice in origin (an origin that he put far back among Paleolithic hunters) as a form of ritual slaughter preparatory to a feast.[11] The division of meat between gods and men as typically (if not wholly accurately) conceived by the Greeks themselves was scandalously unequal: the gods received on the altar little more than the tail, the thighbones wrapped in fat, and (in Homer, and occasionally later) small pieces of meat cut "from all the limbs" placed on them. For Meuli, these facts showed that the logic of the sacrifice leading to a feast (what it will be convenient to call alimentary sacrifice) was not that of providing a gift of food to the gods at all. He compared rather the practice of hunting peoples of giving symbolic special treatment to the bones of the animals they kill, burning being one attested form of such special treatment. What is at issue is the perpetuation of a supply of game. For hunting cultures, it has been brilliantly said, bones are like seeds, from which, if properly

---

10. Theophrastus ap. Porph. *Abst.* 2.25–26.

11. "Ein Tier wird nach herkömmlichen Ritual geschlachtet, damit es die Menshen essen": "Opferbräuche," 282. On what exactly the gods received on the altar (on the separate issue of table offerings, see n. 70), see van Straten, *Hierà Kalá,* 118–31, 143–44; for osteological evidence, see Ekroth, "Meat, Man and God," 262–64; "Thighs or Tails?" (where, p. 144, the possibility that pigs were treated differently from other animals is mentioned). The post-Homeric evidence for "small pieces" is *SEG* 36.206 (= *NGSL* 3) 16–17.

handled, next year's animals will spring;[12] the pieces of meat "from all the limbs" suggest the restoration of the whole animal.

Few today would regard such an appeal to Paleolithic hunters as a legitimate way to explain the sacrificial practices of the Greeks, agriculturalists and pastoralists of the first millennium BC.[13] Even if Meuli's highly seductive analogies illuminate the remote prehistory of Greek treatment of sacrificial bones, for the Greeks, bones were not seeds; the burning of the gods' portion was a way of bringing a food offering to them—an odd way and an odd offering, to be sure, but such is the nature of humans' traffic with immortals. Stripped of its Paleolithic dimension, however, the argument that a chief function of Greek sacrifice was to prepare for the feast reappears in the highly influential collective volume edited by J. P. Vernant and M. Detienne in 1979. The approach (further developed by these scholars and their collaborators in several places)[14] is summed up in the volume's title, *The Cuisine of Sacrifice:* this is sacrifice seen as a prelude to a collective meal, and the distribution of meat at that meal, between gods and men and among men, becomes the dominant theme.

Vernant writes that "the ceremony of sacrifice could be defined as the complex of procedures permitting an animal to be slaughtered in such conditions that violence appears to be excluded and the killing unequivocally has a character which distinguishes it clearly from murder." And, as he put it in explicit dialogue with Walter Burkert, who in *Homo Necans* (1972) had transposed Meuli into a quite different key, "To sacrifice is fundamentally to kill in order to eat. But, within this formulation, you put the accent on the killing, I put it on the eating."[15] For Meuli, sacrifice ensured that the killing

---

12. J. Z. Smith, "The Bare Facts of Ritual," in his *Imagining Religion* (Chicago, 1982), 53–65, at 60.

13. "Animal sacrifice appears to be, universally, the ritual killing of a domesticated animal by agrarian or pastoralist societies" (and so quite distinct from hunting): J. Z. Smith, "The Domestication of Sacrifice," in *Violent Origins: Walter Burkert, René Girard and Jonathan Z. Smith on Ritual Killing and Cultural Formation,* ed. R. G. Hamerton-Kelly, 191–205 (Stanford, 1986), at 197. A mundane alternative to Meuli's theory about the original motive for bone burning has recently been offered: they burn well, and could serve as fuel for cooking edible meat: Ekroth, "Thighs or Tails?" 146, with refs.

14. See, e.g., J. L. Durand and A. Schnapp, in *City of Images,* 53–70; J. L. Durand, *Sacrifice et labour en grèce ancienne* (Paris, 1986).

15. "Théorie générale du sacrifice et mise à mort dans la thysia grecque," in *Sacrifice dans l'antiquité,* 1–21, with discussion 22–39, at 7 and 26 (English version without the discussion in Vernant, *Mortals and Immortals,* 290–302). Professor G. Flood refers me to the exegesis by Hindu Mīmāṃsaka philosophers of how Vedic animal sacrifice (which in fact avoided bloodshed) was compatible with nonviolence: see W. Halbfass, "Vedic Apologetics, Ritual Killing, and the Foundations of Ethics," chap. 4 of his *Tradition and Reflection* (New York, 1991); see too McClymond, *Beyond Sacred Violence,* 51–52, with references.

required by hunting would not terminate the food supply. For Vernant, it licensed killing by ritualizing it. For both theories, as for the ancient vegetarians, it was inextricably bound up with meat eating.

Both theories take up an idea already found in ancient texts that the culpable violence inherent in sacrifice was ritually disguised: the fatal knife was hidden beneath the barley grains in the sacrificial basket, water was sprinkled on the victim's head to induce it to nod assent to its killing (and there were many stories of animals presenting themselves spontaneously for the slaughter). At the Attic festival of Dipolieia,[16] the killing of an ox led to a mock trial: the outcome was the condemnation not of a human but of the knife or ax that did the deed, and the ox's corpse was even stuffed with straw, set on its feet, and yoked to a plow, as though it were not dead at all. For this complex of ritual evasions Karl Meuli coined the term "comedy of innocence." He compared it with the many and varied fictions whereby (in particular) Siberian hunting peoples have excused and exculpated themselves before their prey. A hunter says to a dead bear, "Let us clasp paws in handshake. . . . It was not I that threw you down, nor my companion over there. You, yourself, slipped and burst your belly." Or, "Not by me was the knife fashioned, nor by any of my countrymen. It was made in Estonia from iron bought in Stockholm."[17] Artistic depictions too tended not to depict the moment of killing, except in the abnormal case of mythical human sacrifices. Though one can scarcely speak about sacrifice without using the English word borrowed from Latin *victima,* there were no "victims" in Greek sacrifice:[18] the Greek equivalent ἱερεῖον indicates merely that it is an object on which a priest, ἱερεύς, does his work, ἱερεύω.

Every link in this chain of argument has come under effective attack of late. The main sources that speak of the supposed need to hide the knife and seek the victim's assent are ancient commentaries of uncertain date on Aristophanes and (in the second case) Apollonius Rhodius:[19] the actual passages

---

16. See Parker, *Polytheism,* 187–91.

17. I borrow these quotations from Smith, "Bare Facts" (n. 12 above), 59–60. Smith shows how fictitious these exculpations are, or, better, how they represent an ideal known to be unrealizable.

18. Noted by P. Brulé and R. Touzé, in *Sacrifice antique,* 111. Killing seldom shown: see most recently A. Henrichs, "Blutvergiessen am Altar," in *Gewalt und Ästhetik,* ed. B. Seidensticker and M. Vöhler, 59–87 (Berlin, 2006), at 81–82; van Straten in *Cuisine et autel,* 20–21; *ThesCRA* 1:116–18;. For scenes (still not numerous) relating more broadly to the kill, see van Straten, *Hierà Kalá,* 103–13; Gebauer, *Pompe und Thysia,* 254–89 (on knives, ibid., 513–14, and good comments 256, 289). The differential treatment in art of human and animal victims: Durand, *Cuisine of Sacrifice,* 91 (138 in the Fr. orig.); on the iconography of the former, Durand and F. Lissarague, *Archiv für Religionsgeschichte* 1 (1999): 83–106.

19. Knife: Σ RV Ar. *Pax* 948b. Shake: Σ RV Ar. *Pax* 960, similarly Σ Ap. Rhod. 1.425.

that they are discussing do not speak in these terms, and the order given in Aristophanes to the sheep on whose head water is sprinkled is not "nod" but "shake yourself," a sign of vitality rather than of agreement.[20] The only sources apart from the commentaries that speak of the animal's assent have, certainly or probably, been influenced by Pythagorean opposition to animal sacrifice.[21] When in stories animals offer themselves spontaneously for sacrifice, this can be seen as a remarkably good omen, a sign perhaps that the god has chosen that animal as its preferred offering, rather than a proof that every ordinary sacrificial victim was required to agree to its death.[22] There was no artistic taboo on showing animals vigorously resisting being led to the altar, as of course they often did; men with knives and axes are occasionally shown near animals, and depictions of altars smeared with blood are commonplace, even if the actual coup de grâce is mostly avoided. The "comedy of innocence" at the Dipolieia is therefore a special case, an unusual development at a particular festival, not a general key to the ideology of Greek sacrifice. On this account, sacrifice did not create a horrified fascination with violence, nor go out of its way to preempt the same; violence was simply not an issue.[23]

Has the reaction gone too far? It is not a strong argument against the "comedy of innocence" that the comedy was not played out very consistently and that reality often peeked through; all those involved are aware that ritual fictions are just that, fictions.[24] The question is whether a comedy of innocence was enacted at all, other than at the Dipolieia, whether, that is, such sources as speak in these terms can be dismissed en bloc as contaminated by Pythagorean ideology even when (as in the scholia on Aristophanes and Apollonius) there is no sign of such influence. That question is, and will probably remain, unanswerable.[25]

---

20. Cf. Plut. *De def. or.* 46, 435B–C with 49, 437A–B; cf. Serv. ad *Aen.* 4.61: *hostiae exploratio, utrum apta sit.*

21. The oracle ap. Porph. *Abst.* 2.9.3; Plut. *Quaest. conv.* 8.8.3, 729F.

22. Cf. Macrob. *Sat.* 3.5.8.

23. On all this see S. Peirce, "Death, Revelry and Thusia," *ClAnt* 12 (1993): 219–66 (in particular on the artistic evidence); van Straten, *Hierà Kalá,* 100–102 ("The Assenting Animal?"); P. Bonnechère, "'La machaira était dissimulée dans le kanoun': Quelques interrogations," *REA* 101 (1999): 21–35; S. Georgoudi, "'L'occultation de la violence' dans le sacrifice grec: Données anciennes, discours modernes," in *Cuisine et autel,* 115–47; "Le consentement de la victime sacrificielle: Une question ouverte," in *Sacrifice antique,* 139–53; A. Henrichs, "Blutvergiessen" (n. 18); F. S. Naiden, "The Fallacy of the Willing Victim," *JHS* 127 (2007): 61–73.

24. See n. 17.

25. I do not find the argument from Ar. *Pax* 960 decisive. An animal sprinkled with water is much more likely to shake itself than to nod, and ritual had to work with that datum; but a shake could have been interpreted in this context as a mark of assent. Perhaps both interpretations coexisted in earlier times as they do in Plutarch (contrast *De def. or.* 49, 437A–B with *Quaest. conv.* 8.8.3, 729F) and, it seems, ethnographically (Meuli, "Opferbräuche," 266).

The link between sacrifice and banquet, however, is not based on the reality of the "comedy of innocence" alone. There is also the issue of the eating of unsacrificed meat. The authors of *The Cuisine of Sacrifice* argue that sacrifice was the ritual that rendered legitimate the killing of animals (domesticated animals, in their more careful formulations), and that meat from them was not normally eaten by Greeks unless it had first been sacrificed. (This argument too goes back to Karl Meuli.) One even occasionally encounters the suggestion (though not in *The Cuisine of Sacrifice*) that sacrifice was a Greek equivalent to kosher or halal butchery. That extreme claim is refuted by the obvious point that Greeks ate game animals killed in no special way,[26] whereas (for instance) in Orthodox Judaism wild animals must be trapped in nets and killed according to the normal kosher rules if they are to be eaten. There is also considerable evidence that meat from species that were sacrificed only exceptionally, such as dog, donkey, and horse, quite often found its way onto Greek tables, even if usually processed into a sausage or pie. (Subtle osteological analysis may even show that their meat was sometimes added, unsacrificed, to fill out the portions at a sacrificial banquet in a sanctuary.)[27] Some Greeks even apparently ate meat from animals that had died naturally, though others shunned it as impure.[28]

The claim therefore has probably to be reformulated as "Greeks ate the meat of the typical sacrificial species only after sacrifice." It now acquires considerable prima facie plausibility; for there are many references to animals being "sacrificed" where the point is merely to kill them, whether for a feast or for other reasons: Themistocles in Herodotus, for instance, advises the Greek forces to "sacrifice" as many of the herds kept in Euboea as they wish, to keep them from falling into the hands of the enemy.[29] Even if some difficulties and possible countercases remain, the normative pattern seems to have been that a feast required a sacrifice; and a few obscure references occur to "eating unsacrificed things" as a disgusting form of behavior that might

---

26. Pious hunters offered the god a portion of their catch (Xen. *Cyn.* 6.13) and hung up skin and horns in sanctuaries (Meuli, "Opferbräuche," 263 n. 5), but that is a different matter.

27. See Ekroth, "Meat, Man and God," 275–76; Ekroth, "Meat in Ancient Greece: Sacrificial, Sacred or Secular?" *Food and History* 5 no. 1 (2007): 249–72, at 260–72. On foods actually eaten in Greece, see esp. Hipp. *Vict.* 2.46 and the texts from Galen quoted by P. Garnsey, *Food and Society in Classical Antiquity* (Cambridge, 1999), 83–85.

28. Ar. *Av.* 538 and fr. 714; cf. my article "Eating Unsacrificed Meat," forthcoming in *Paysage et religion. Mélanges offerts à Madeleine Jost, ed. P. Carlier and C. Lerouge-Cohen (Travaux de la Maison René Ginouves* 6, 2010), 139–47.

29. 8.19.2; cf., e.g., 6.129.1, Hom. *Il.* 6.174, and numerous other uses of ἱερεύω in Homer (Casabona, *Vocabulaire des sacrifices,* 23), Hom. *Od.* 9.231, Xen. *Anab.* 4.4.9.

offend the gods.[30] It would be interesting to inquire how general in societies that perform sacrifice the ban on eating meat non-sacrificially may be; it is certainly common.[31]

The vegetarian critique is well-founded up to a point, therefore: the motive for sacrificing was very often that it was socially impossible to eat the most attractive forms of meat without sacrificing. Yet the proposition that "to sacrifice is fundamentally to kill in order to eat" is wholly inadequate as a general theory even to explain those sacrifices that left edible meat behind them. The objection is not just that the meat from sacrifices of this type was occasionally not eaten but sold.[32] In other cases too the rationale for conducting such a sacrifice was manifestly not to provide religious legitimation for human sociability. Odysseus in *Iliad* 1 (430–74) takes a hecatomb to appease Apollo. The sacrifice ends in a feast, but it starts from the urgent need to propitiate an angry god. And cases of this type can be multiplied almost indefinitely. Sacrifices that have a purpose (propitiation, thanksgiving, fulfillment of a vow, or whatever) are commonplace. The sacrifices carefully listed in a group's sacrificial calendar have a purpose too, the systematic cultivation of the deities judged responsible for the particular group's welfare. In some cases participants were probably few, and the fact that the sacrifice produced meat almost incidental.[33]

Sacrifice opened the channel of communication between man and god. It enabled prayers to be made for a return of blessings; it required such prayers indeed, since there were no sacrifices without prayers. Fixed formulas seem not to have been used: the essential was to address the god, make a request ("grant health and prosperity"), and identify the recipients of the benefit that was sought. As recipients, "all of us present" would be the simplest form, but absentees such as wives and children could be added; in the fifth century the grateful Athenians included the Plataeans in their prayers.[34] Sacrificial divination too is very relevant. At every public sacrifice in the classical period, omens were taken; many sacrifices were performed primarily for divinatory purposes, most obviously in the military sphere but also in private life. It is not coincidence that the will of the gods was revealed so regularly by

---

30. Semonides fr. 7.56 West; G. Petzl, *Die Beichtinschriften Westkleinasiens* (= *Epigraphica Anatolica* 22, Bonn, 1994), nos. 1 and 123; *LSA* 84.11.

31. For Rome, see J. Scheid in *Cuisine et autel,* 273–88; cf., e.g., Gibson, *Sacrifice and Sharing,* 185.

32. Lupu, *NGSL,* 71–72; cf. Ekroth, "Meat, Man and God," 271 n. 65.

33. See Jameson, "The Spectacular and the Obscure."

34. Hdt. 6.111.2; cf. Pulleyn, *Prayer,* 7–15. Prayer essential: Plin. *HN* 28.10; for prayer gestures accompanying sacrifice, see *ThesCRA* 3, plates 18–19.

the tails and livers of sacrificial animals.[35] Sacrifice was a time of close contact between the two worlds. "May he not be able to sacrifice" was a curse one could invoke on a wrongdoer. It was through bad omens at sacrifices that flawed relations between men and gods were typically exposed.[36]

The mediator of that contact was the animal. Sacrifice, it has rightly been said, turns an animal into a symbol.[37] The hopes of a community rest on the back of the victim, which becomes a literal embodiment of its piety. Hubert and Mauss, in their celebrated *Essai sur la nature et la fonction du sacrifice,* wrote that: "[The victim] is the means of concentration of religious feeling; it expresses it, it incarnates it, it carries it along. By acting upon the victim one acts upon religious feeling, directs it either by attracting and absorbing it, or by expelling and eliminating it."[38] The animals offered in public rites were often specified as "selected" (κριτός) victims, and might be subject to an "examination," δοκιμασία, the same word used for the testing of the qualifications of a human candidate for a magistracy.[39] The process of choice could itself be turned into a spectacle. For the sacrifice to Zeus Polieus on Cos, wave upon wave of cattle bred up by the various city segments were driven successively into the agora until finally one designated itself as the appropriate victim by (probably) "kneeling to Hestia"; at Bargylia, responsibility for rearing cattle for Artemis Kindyas was distributed among various magistrates and even metics, and the finest specimens were to be chosen by the same judges as judged the human competition in "manliness." A serious issue, therefore, selecting an animal for a god: the fairest pig for Demeter was chosen on Mykonos by the boule.

In Magnesia on the Maeander, the bull that was to be sacrificed to Zeus Sosipolis was "shown" to him months in advance "at the beginning of the sowing"; it was fed during the intervening months by voluntary contributions from the populace. At the great Coan civic festival mentioned above, the ox for Zeus Polieus once selected was "commenced" (that is,

35. On the tail, see now Ekroth, "Thighs or Tails?" [+]; *ThesCRA* 3:7; Ekroth notes that the first literary evidence for the tail as part of the god's portion is Aesch. *PV* 496–97. On livers, van Straten, *Hierà Kalá,* 156–57; Flower, *Seer,* index s.v. divination, sacrificial.

36. H. S. Versnel, *ZPE* 58 (1985): 247–69 (the curse); Hdt. 7.134.2; Ant. 5.82, cf. *LSA* 16.25–27, with Sokolowski's note (bad omens).

37. J.H.M. Beattie, "On Understanding Sacrifice," in *Sacrifice,* ed. M.F.C. Bourdillon and M. Fortes, 29–44 (London, 1980), at 29–30; cf. de Heusch, *Sacrifice in Africa,* 95: "Sacrifice is a symbolic labour on living matter."

38. Hubert and Mauss, *Sacrifice,* 60.

39. Cf. *ThesCRA* 1:95–97; Lupu, *NGSL,* 99–100, 355–57; C. Feyel, *RPhil* 80 (2006): 33–55; F. S. Naiden, *JHS* 127 (2007): 70–73 (who, however, runs together the preliminary selection with the sprinkling of water just prior to sacrifice).

the preliminary rites were performed) "with olive branch and laurel" the day before the sacrifice. At a sacrifice to Athena in Hellenistic Ilion, each tribe was required to provide a cow and a sheep; the tribesmen processed behind "their" animals, which were branded with marks identifying them as offered by the particular tribe. A beautifully adorned sacrificial animal is once described in the *Odyssey* as an ἄγαλμα, an "object of delight (to a god)," the term normally applied to dedicated statues.[40] Some resemblance could be sought between the animal and the divine recipient. At a minimum, gods usually received male animals (if female, never pregnant), goddesses female; the symbolic connection went further when, for instance, earth was given black or pregnant victims. All victims had to be "whole" and "perfect," like the gods.[41]

Mauss and Hubert saw sacrifice as a ritual that opened communication with the gods through consecration of a victim; through that consecration the human participants too were temporarily brought into the divine sphere.[42] In relation to the Greek material, their schema errs perhaps only in trying to define too precisely the steps and modalities of consecration, both of the animal and of the human participants. Little was normally required of humans by way of preparation beyond washing and clean clothes.[43] As for the animal, we cannot identify a precise moment when it became the god's. "Beginning" a sacrifice is a function often referred to. In the case just mentioned from Cos it was done by sprinkling with water from a bough; more often, hair was cut from the victim's brow and burned on the altar. After the kill, blood was splattered on the altar (or poured directly into a river, if the river was the recipient), and the officiant in a vitally important

---

40. Cos: RO 62 (*LSCG* 151) A 1–19 (selection); ibid. 31–32 (beginning). Bargylia: *SEG* 45.1508; *SEG* 50.1101 (the latter decree alters the judging arrangements mentioned in my text). Mykonos: *LSCG* 96.13. Magnesia: *LSA* 32, cf. p. 198. Ilion: *LSA* 9.20–24; for other examples of such branding, see L. Robert, *Hellenica* 11–12, 120 (Paris, 1960). ἄγαλμα: Hom. *Od*. 3. 438. On the beautification of sacrificial animals, see van Straten, *Hierà Kalá*, 43–46; Gebauer, *Pompe und Thysia*, 186–89.

41. See C. Feyel, *RPhil* 80 (2006): 36–42 (but Spartans and Eretrians supposedly tolerated maimed victims, Plat. *Alc. II* 149A, Ael. *NA* 12.34). On pregnant victims, J. N. Bremmer in *Greek Sacrificial Ritual*, 155–65. Despite many exceptions, the sex of animal/sex of deity correlation applies in far more than 50 percent of cases: see *ThesCRA* 1:97–99 and, e.g., Hom. *Il*. 3.103–6; *LSA* 32.46–59. On the species preferred by individual gods, see *ThesCRA* 1:68–95 (with osteological evidence).

42. Hubert and Mauss, *Sacrifice*, 97, "This procedure consists in establishing a means of communication between the sacred and profane worlds through the mediation of a victim, that is, of a thing that in the course of the ceremony is destroyed." The commonest Homeric verb for sacrifice, ἱερεύω, apparently acquires that sense not directly from the idea of consecration but as "do the work of a priest" (Casabona, *Vocabulaire des sacrifices*, 19).

43. The requirement of sexual purity in RO 62 (*LSCG* 151) A 40–44 (n. 145 below) is unusual.

act placed the god's portion on the altar for burning along with vegetable offerings.[44] As we have noted, a simple but indispensable accompaniment to the gift was the officiant's prayer. But the animal had started to belong to the god even before the "beginning," through the process of selection. And the procession to the altar, where one occurred, enacted quite literally the approach of all concerned to the divine. A law from Astypalaia stipulates that all animals that are led in the procession for Dionysus be branded, to ensure that they are indeed sacrificed in due course to the god to whom they have been led.[45] The religious charge built up cumulatively through all these procedures, partly through the spectacle that they presented: even quite a modest procession at a private sacrifice, with the burning of incense and the piping of an aulos player, could become a multisensory experience.[46]

One cannot reduce sacrifice to the ritualized preparation for a banquet, therefore; the gods have to be given their place. The point is reinforced if one remembers an aspect that is obscured by the best-known literary descriptions of sacrifice, which make no mention of it. It is from inscriptions that we learn that public alimentary sacrifices were normally and perhaps invariably accompanied by offerings of wheat or barley cakes.[47] In some contexts such vegetarian offerings replaced blood sacrifice; and the verb used for bringing them was that used also for animal sacrifice, θύειν.[48] These side offerings in one sense reinforce the association of alimentary sacrifice with food and eating. But they have nothing to do with the legitimation of killing through ritualization; nor are they, like the thighbones burned for the gods, a token portion set aside from a larger whole that falls to men. They are a food offering to the gods, pure and simple.[49] Exactly the same considerations apply to the libations, vinous or "sober," which also accompany sacrifice. They

---

44. Beginning: n. 143 below. God's portion: n. 144 below. Blood splattered: van Straten, *Hierà Kalá*, 104; G. Ekroth, 'Blood on the altars?', *Antike Kunst* 48 (2005), 9–29; cf. the exceptional Ar. *Pax* 1019. Rivers: *LSCG* 96.34–37, cf. Hom. *Il.* 23.147–48, and R. Koch Piettre in *Cuisine et autel*, 87–89.

45. *LSS* 83, Astypalaia, second/first century BC. On branding see C. Feyel, *RPhil* 80 (2006): 49–54.

46. On incense see V. Mehl in *Sacrifice antique*, 167–86; on music, Gebauer, *Pompe und Thysia*, 173, 481–82, 488 [+]; *ThesCRA* 2:371–75. Sacrifices unaccompanied by music were unusual enough to be remarked on: F. Graf in *Kykeon*, 117.

47. See especially now *SEG* 54.214, where priests are systematically reimbursed for the raw materials; also, e.g., *LSCG* 63, RO 62 (*LSCG* 151) A 36–37, 47–48; *LSA* 37.10–12. *LSCG* 134 (Thera, fourth century BC) is a good illustration from what is apparently a private foundation: "They shall sacrifice an ox, wheat of a *medimnos*, barley of two *medimnoi*, a *metrētēs* of wine, and seasonal fruits"; cf., e.g., *LSA* 39.14–16. See E. Kearns in *Ancient Greek Cult Practice*, 65–70; van Straten, *Hierà Kalá*, 139–43; L. Bruit-Zaidman in *Cuisine et autel*, 31–46.

48. See, e.g., *LSS* 21; 30; *LSA* 24 A 21–23; Casabona, *Vocabulaire des sacrifices*, 73.

49. McClymond, *Beyond Sacred Violence*, stresses the role of vegetarian offerings in Hebrew and Vedic sacrifice in order to move the theory of sacrifice in the direction indicated by her title.

round out the association of sacrifice with eating and drinking, but gods not men are the recipients. Incense too is "sacrificed"[50] (the original application, as it seems, of the verb θύειν, and one it never loses): the sweet smoke goes up, like the savor of sacrifices, to please the nostrils of the gods. θύειν, we note, relates to what is burned for the gods (whether incense, cake, or bones), not what is eaten by men.

The argument thus far has been intended to bring out the double aspect of Greek alimentary sacrifice, a double aspect of which one side or the other regularly seems in some measure redundant. Even where the primary motivation was propitiation, there normally followed a banquet; even where the primary motivation was meat eating, there preceded a sacrifice. From case to case more emphasis was placed on one aspect or the other, but both were always present. It cannot readily be said that one function is more basic than the other: a means of honoring the gods, and the most basic form of human sociability, are combined in an indissoluble new unity. The contexts in which sacrifices of this type were performed are too numerous to be worth listing; it was all but omni-functional.[51]

If asked about the purpose of sacrifice, a Greek would probably have answered roughly in the terms of a much-quoted phrase of Plato, that it was a "giving to the gods."[52] Two objections can be made to that explanation. In ordinary gift giving, no part of the gift is retained by the giver, whereas in sacrifice the human givers keep the best meat for themselves; many jokes in comedy show how aware the Greeks were of that anomaly. Second, it is not clear why, if an animal is to be given to a god, it must be killed in the first place and not, for instance, kept in a sacred herd.[53] (Neoplatonists met the second objection by explaining that the gift was not the animal but the life of the animal.)[54] But, once one has recognized the double aspect of Greek alimentary sacrifice, one sees why this particular form of giving necessarily could not conform to the principles generally governing that practice. The gift had to be killed and eaten. Nonetheless, Greeks saw it as

---

50. See, e.g., *LSCG* 87.10, with Sokolowski's parallels; Casabona, *Vocabulaire des sacrifices,* 69–75.

51. Cf. P. Stengel, *Die griechischen Kultusaltertümer,* 3rd ed. (Munich, 1920), 107–8. In Theophrastus's well-known formula (ap. Porph. *Abst.* 2.14.1), sacrifice was made ἢ διὰ τιμὴν ἢ διὰ χάριν ἢ διὰ χρείαν τῶν ἀγαθῶν.

52. Pl. *Euthyphr.* 14C τὸ θύειν δωρεῖσθαί ἐστι τοῖς θεοῖς; cf. Pl. *Plt.* 290C. Critics accordingly, taking a lead from Plato (e.g., *Resp.* 365E), could see sacrifice as a form of attempted bribery: Theophr. (?) ap. Porph. *Abst.* 2.60.1, and Christian apologists (e.g., Arn. *Adv. nat.* 7.12).

53. Cf. de Heusch, *Sacrifice in Africa,* 55–57, 96. Jokes in comedy: see, e.g., Men. *Dysk.* 447–53, with E. W. Handley's note ad loc.

54. Cf. n. 3 above.

a gift, strictly comparable to that more conventional form of giving to the gods that was dedication. We noted above the description in the *Odyssey* of a beautifully adorned sacrificial animal as an ἄγαλμα, like a dedicated statue. The whole Greek conceptualization of the relation between gods and men becomes incomprehensible if one denies that a sacrifice was a gift that would ideally call forth a countergift.[55]

There is anyway a sense in which sacrifice was indeed a gift. The use of wild animals such as deer and of fish, even if osteology is extending the evidence in interesting ways, remains rare enough to count as an exceptional extension inviting special explanation.[56] Among domesticated animals dogs, donkeys, and horses are used only in special circumstances; some gods welcome doves, cocks, and geese, but the central sacrificial breeds are cattle, sheep, pigs, and (rather less common) goats. What these breeds represented, at least in the Homeric world, was productive wealth in its most concrete form.[57] There is therefore in sacrificial killing an element of surrender of wealth.

The presence in Greek sacrifice of "sacrifice" in the sense the word often bears in English is, to be sure, a delicate topic where alien assumptions are always in danger of insinuating themselves: one cannot translate "that was a great sacrifice for him" into Greek by dipping into any part of the vocabulary of Greek ritual sacrifice. The myths that speak of the requirement to "sacrifice the fairest product of the year"[58] or something similar (in the event usually a highborn child) are not a reliable guide to the everyday ideology of sacrifice. In such myths, the community is forced without explanation to surrender an object of great value, like Polycrates throwing his ring into

---

55. Countergift: cf. p. x. In two Arcadian inscriptions, ὀναθύειν was used, remarkably, for "dedicate" (Casabona, *Vocabulaire des sacrifices*, 94). ἄγαλμα: Hom. *Od.* 3.438.

56. See, e.g., *ThesCRA* 1:75 (Artemis, at Kalapodi; cf. Ekroth, "Meat, Man and God," 276; Ekroth, "Thighs or Tails?" 141, 144); cf. the votive from Aegina showing a deer brought to Artemis, Athens NM 1950 (*ThesCRA* 1, pl. 3, no. 91), and the "deer" cakes brought to her in Athens during Elaphebolion (Parker, *Polytheism,* 468); on the important iconographic evidence, not of completely clear interpretation, from the sanctuary of Hermes and Aphrodite at Kato Symi, see Lebessi, Τὸ Ἱερὸ τοῦ Ἑρμῆ, 1:113–36; Prent, *Cretan Sanctuaries,* 345, 587, 647 (wild goat); note too the boar shown on a lost Campanian vase (the Rainore vase: D. Gill, *Greek Cult Tables* [New York, 1991], 83–84, with fig. 29). On fish see *ThesCRA* 1:81, 95 (the whole article is a valuable archaeological vade mecum); Gebauer, *Pompe und Thysia,* 744–45; B. Kowalzig in *Animal Sacrifice in the Greek World,* ed. S. Hitch and I. Rutherford (Cambridge, 2011). For ancient lists of animals used in sacrifice, see Stengel, *Opferbräuche,* 222–33; for literary evidence on wild animals and fish, ibid., 197–202.

57. On sacrifice and wealth, cf. de Heusch, *Sacrifice in Africa,* 203.

58. Eur. *IT* 20–21; cf. S. Georgoudi, "À propos du sacrifice human en Grèce ancienne: Remarques critiques," *Archiv für Religionsgeschichte* 1 (1999): 62–82, at 71. On (mostly mythical) self-maiming, see the brilliant study of H. S. Versnel, "Self-Sacrifice, Compensation and the Anonymous Gods," in *Sacrifice dans l'antiquité,* 135–85; W. Burkert, *The Creation of the Sacred* (Cambridge, Mass., 1996), 34–40.

the sea. This is self-maiming pure and simple. But few Greek sacrifices are at all like that. The nearest approach perhaps lies in the very rare practice of throwing victims, horses especially, live into rivers or the sea, for Poseidon or the river in question.[59] It represents an intense and extreme way of achieving communication with the deity; the communication comes through the symbolic link of horses with rivers and the sea, the extremity from the waste of a highly valuable animal. Normal Greek sacrifice, however, is not understood as pointless and self-punishing renunciation, but as the renunciation for another's benefit known as a gift.

All the same, the wealth you give away, with whatever hope of return, you no longer have; the wealth embodied in the sacrificed animal has been used, not stored, and is not available to use again. If one made sacrifice at a public shrine, one was obliged to surrender perquisites of substantial value, which, though ultimately benefiting the priest, were sometimes presented first to the god or said to belong to him; the sacrificer lost the use of them, in favor of god/priest.[60] J. Z. Smith has pointed out that globally sacrifice is characteristic not of hunters but of pastoralists; with poised irony he suggests that, were it good method to seek an "origin of sacrifice," the best place to look might be the ambiguous emotions (but not guilt) of the stock raiser—perhaps we should rather say, since sacrifice is a collective activity, the "stock-raising society"—who must both increase and selectively cull his herd.[61]

---

59. Hom. *Il.* 21.132 (the Trojans, to Spercheios; possibly envisaged as non-Greek); Paus. 8.7.2 (Argos, in the past); Diod. Sic. 5.4.2 (individuals sink smaller victims, the city sinks bulls, into the lake beside the well Kyane in Syracuse); Harp. κ 7 κάθετος· ὁ καθιέμενος εἰς τὸ πέλαγος ἀμνός (citing Lysias fr. 281 Carey, Meliton *FGrH* 345 F 1); *Anecd. Bekk.* 1.270.8 κάθετον· βοῦν τινα καθιέμενον εἰς τὴν θάλατταν τῷ Ποσειδῶνι θυσίαν; cf. R. Koch Piettre, "Précipitations sacrificielles en Grèce ancienne," in *Cuisine et autel*, 77–100 (esp. 87 on the element of conspicuous waste). That the animals are alive when thrown in is explicit in Hom. *Il.* 21.132 (and in a myth in Plut. *Conv. sept. sap.* 20, 163B), probable in the other cases. A very spectacular rite is attested for Rhodes by Festus s.v. October Equus: *Rhodii…quotannis quadrigas Soli consecratas in mare iaciunt, quod is tali curriculo fertur circumvehi mundum.* Despite the difference in addressee and periodicity, scholars associate this rite with the Rhodian festival Hippokathesia (*LSS* 94.8–14, which, however, refers to ordinary sacrifice; *ILindos* 490.11), celebrated every eight years (*ASAtene* 30–32 [1952–54]: 256–59, no. 5), which they take to honor Poseidon: D. Morelli, *I culti in Rodi* (Pisa, 1959), 65–66, 98–99, 169. Non-Greek parallels in Nilsson, *Geschichte*, 237 n. 1; Festus (s.v. Hippius) knows of an eight-yearly throwing of four horses into the sea among the Illyrians. On a much humbler level, the throwing of cakes into springs is forbidden in *LSCG* 152.

60. See below nn. 70–71 on table offerings and "entrails on hands and knees." For priestly perquisites said to belong "to the god," see, e.g., *SEG* 28.750 (*NGSL* 24), *LSCG* 55.9–11; Stengel, *Opferbräuche*, 170–71.

61. Smith, "Domestication of Sacrifice," n. 13 above. There are some signs that the timing of sacrifices in Greece was determined by the logic of the stock-rearing year, with sacrifices being most frequent when there was an abundance of surplus young animals: M. Jameson, "Sacrifice and Animal

Sacrifice is a gift to the gods that permits communication between god and man; it is also the indispensable prerequisite for human feasting. Can this double aspect be explained? This may belong to the order of questions that Veyne's warning should discourage one from posing. But it is worth recalling one of the classic theories of sacrifice, the "communion" theory of Robertson Smith.[62] Robertson Smith saw the rite as a coming together of man and god through the basic form of human sociability, the feast. The sacred banquet forges bonds both between men and between man and god; the emphasis can shift in either direction, toward sociability or toward communication with a god, as the situation dictates. In Plato's *Symposium* too, sacrifice and divination are spoken of as aspects of "the mutual association of gods and mortals" (ἡ περὶ θεούς τε καὶ ἀνθρώπους πρὸς ἀλλήλους κοινωνία).[63] As presented by Robertson Smith, the theory contained the further proposition that what was eaten at the sacred banquet was in a sense the god himself. This disastrous addition, an amalgam of the Christian Eucharist with nineteenth-century theories of the totemic animal, inevitably bred resistance to the whole approach. Stripped of that excess, the theory has considerable appeal.[64] God is present because, on the rare occasion of a meat feast, men as a group feel themselves supremely well and at peace. As a device for approaching a god, the sacrificial feast represents, therefore, the polar antithesis of asceticism.

There is, however, controversy about the kind of table fellowship, if any, that Greek sacrifice established between man and god, the question whether the rite brought together the two kinds or by contrast confirmed their separation. There had once been a time when "feasts were shared, seats were shared, between immortal gods and mortal men."[65] Several myths revolve around such table fellowship: those of Lycaon and Tantalus show the abuse of it by wicked mortals that rendered it unsustainable; Pindar poignantly contrasts the brief but extraordinary felicity of Peleus and Cadmus, at whose wedding feasts "gods dined, and they saw the royal children of Kronos on golden seats, and received wedding gifts," with the sufferings that inevitably awaited them later, mortals as they were.[66] Later Greeks doubtless understood alimentary sacrifice

Husbandry in Classical Greece," in *Pastoral Economies in Classical Antiquity,* ed. C. R. Whittaker, 87–119 (*PCPS* supp. 14, Cambridge, 1988).

62. The theory is developed gradually through the later chapters of Robertson Smith, *Religion of the Semites,* and summarized on the penultimate page, 439: "The fundamental idea of ancient sacrifice is sacramental communion."

63. Pl. *Symp.* 188B–C.

64. Cf. Gibson, *Sacrifice and Sharing,* 182–85.

65. Hes. fr. 1.6–7 M/W; cf. Hom. *Od.* 7.201–3 (the Phaeacians); Paus. 8.2.4.

66. Pind. *Pyth.* 3.93–95. Tantalus and Lycaon: cf. Ekroth, "Burnt, Cooked or Raw?" 95–97.

as an altered memorial of the primeval time of actual table fellowship. Hesiod may associate the origin of sacrifice in its present form precisely with the ending of that lost age. He tells how it was at the time when gods and men "disputed," or "were separated" (the Greek verb ἐκρίνοντο is maddeningly unclear), at Mekone that Prometheus tricked Zeus into taking bones wrapped in fat as his portion; Zeus's subsequent revenge on Prometheus locked us into the imperfect world in which we now live.[67]

J. P. Vernant has built on this myth to give what one might call a world-ordering view of Greek participatory sacrifice. Sacrifice is an expression and re-creation of the separation between gods and men. The immortal gods above receive smoke and incense, incorruptible substances, only; mortals feed on putrescent flesh. The third species, that of animals, is confirmed in its separate role as a means of communication between gods and men. Each sacrifice puts the different species of the world in their place. And this symbolic re-creation of the world is a large part of what gives Greek participatory sacrifice its religious charge.[68] But it seems necessary to charge an interpreter for once not with Christianizing but with Vedianizing assumptions. According to the Brâhmaṇas, every sacrifice is a repetition of the original cosmogonic act, which was itself a sacrifice.[69] Vernant distinguishes, it is true, his understanding of Greek sacrifice from Vedic, which is not merely world ordering but cosmogonic. But he still ascribes to it a foundational role in Greek understanding of the order of things.

Yet the Greek situation was entirely different from the learned Brâhmaṇas tradition. The myth told by Hesiod was not repeated at every Greek sacrifice; strangely enough, it is not even alluded to by any author of the classical period. Greek sacrifice was entirely unaccompanied by exegesis; there is no reason to think that it was perceived as repeating a world-ordering act. And, as several scholars have observed, actual sacrificial practices conflict with the

---

67. Hes. *Theog.* 535–36.

68. See, e.g., *Religion grecque, religions antiques* (Paris, 1976), 31 (Englished in *Mortals and Immortals,* 280–81); cf. J. L. Durand in *Cuisine of Sacrifice,* 104 (155 in the Fr. orig.), "Un moment où le monde se met en place sous le regard des dieux"; Durand, *City of Images,* 53, "Eating meat means re-enacting around the smoking and bloody altar the very order of the universe" ("Manger la viande équivaut chaque fois à remettre en place autour de l'autel fumant et ensanglanté l'ordre même de l'univers.") For comparable claims about sacrifice in Indo-European ideology, see B. Lincoln, *Death, War, and Sacrifice* (Chicago, 1991), 167–75.

69. S. Lévi, *La doctrine du sacrifice dans les Brâhmaṇas* (1898; 2nd ed., Paris, 1966), 82: "Le lieu où converge l'univers"; cf. M. Biardeau and C. Malamoud, *Le sacrifice dans l'Inde ancienne* (Paris, 1976), 14–23: "Le sacrifice comme principe cosmogonique"; in brief McClymond, *Beyond Sacred Violence,* 141–42. On the character of the Brâhmaṇas, Lévi, 77: "Le sacrifice est une combinaison savante et compliquée d'actes rituels et de paroles sacrées." It is noteworthy to Herodotus that every Persian sacrifice required the presence of a *magos,* who recited a theogony (Hdt. 1.132.3).

notion, so familiar from literature, that the gods' share of sacrifice comes to them only in the form of smoke.[70] In addition to the portion burned for them on the altar, it was a common practice to set out further offerings, of raw meat and other foodstuffs, on a table for the gods. These table offerings commonly went in the end to priests as perquisites, but this characteristic piece of religious double accounting does not affect the point that at an ideal level this raw meat was given to the gods. Cooked entrails too could be placed on the hands or knees of divine images before passing to the priest.[71] Sacrifices as actually performed, therefore, were not based on an ontological distinction between flesh-eating men and gods content with smoke alone.

That point aside, is it true that sacrifice affirms the gap between gods and mortals? Two perspectives on the issue are possible. On a very large view, participatory sacrifice as the Greeks knew it was indeed a product of the great divide. Men still share an animal with the gods because they once shared a table with them too; now, however, the two breeds live and eat apart. But this cosmogonic perspective was one that Greeks seldom had reason to adopt. That gods were gods, men men, and that a radical divide existed between the two species was a basic datum of experience, a thing taken for granted. In an everyday perspective the issue was to communicate with the gods across the great divide, and in that perspective the point of sacrifice was precisely to create a bridge.

Anthropologists distinguish between conjunctive sacrifices, those designed to bring men into beneficial contact with supernatural powers, and disjunctive sacrifices, those that separate them from malevolent or polluting powers and other sources of danger.[72] In those terms Greek participatory sacrifice is unquestionably to be seen as conjunctive. Gods were urged in prayers to "come" and to "receive" their offerings; describing a sacrifice in *Odyssey* book 3, Homer mentions the human participants and adds, "And Athena came to receive her offerings";[73] in doing so, she behaves just like the deities shown on votive reliefs standing behind altars to which worshippers are leading a victim. At the ideal level, gods attend their sacrifices, and the gap

---

70. See, e.g., L. Bruit Zaidman in *Cuisine et autel,* 31; G. Berthiaume, ibid., 241–50 (who, however, probably consigns too much real meat to the gods: Ekroth, "Thighs or Tails?" 127–29). On table offerings, see D. Gill, *Greek Cult Tables* (New York, 1991) (the essential already in his article in *HTR* 1974); Ekroth, *Sacrificial Rituals,* 136–40; Ekroth, "Meat, Man and God," 267–68.

71. See Graf, *Nordionische Kulte,* 40–41, on, e.g., *LSS* 129.4–6, Ar. *Av.* 518–19, *Eccl.* 780–83.

72. See, e.g., Beattie (n. 37 above), 38, adducing de Heusch. Similarly, E. E. Evans-Pritchard, *Nuer Religion* (Oxford, 1956), 275, cites Georges Gusdorf for the idea that sacrifice "is made not only to the gods but against the gods."

73. Hom. *Od.* 3.435–36; a speaker in Ath. 8, 363D–F draws the correct conclusion from this passage. On the deity awaiting worshippers at the altar in art, see Gebauer, *Pompe und Thysia,* 489–90.

between the two worlds is bridged; this point is central. The two conceptions, of the god as invisibly present and as enjoying the scented smoke from on high, coexist in unresolved but unproblematic tension.

There also existed a rite of theoxenia, "god entertaining."[74] A table of foodstuffs was prepared and a couch with a coverlet was set beside it, on which an image of the god might be placed. As a word, heroxenia, "hero entertaining," is much less common, but the practice of setting out a table for heroes and heroines is very well known from Attic calendars.[75] Strictly perhaps theoxenia should be distinguished from sacrifice, since the foods served to the gods were predominantly vegetarian, as at ordinary human meals, and were placed on a table, not burned. But there is evident continuity between entertaining a god with table plus couch and the simpler practice of providing table offerings alongside sacrifice; theoxenia goes a step further in make-believe assimilation of the god to a human guest. And we have recently learned that at Selinus, and in the cult of the Corybantes in Erythrai, the procedures of sacrifice and of theoxenia were thoroughly intertwined.[76]

A fragment of Bacchylides invites the Dioscuri (the commonest recipients of theoxenia) to the entertainment prepared for them: "We have here no bodies of oxen, no gold, no purple coverlets; but friendly hearts, a sweet Muse, and delicious wine in Boeotian cups." Greek poets of the Roman period and their Roman followers imitated this style of invitation in poems inviting powerful human patrons to dine: a difference in status and wealth is acknowledged but the attempt still made to achieve a temporary intimacy.[77] Neither at sacrifice nor even at theoxenia rituals, it is true, did the Greeks claim to be recovering the primeval table fellowship of man with god: in theoxenia, mortals might dine under the same roof as the god, but the god

---

74. M. H. Jameson, "Theoxenia," in *Ancient Greek Cult Practice,* 35–57; Veyne, "Inviter les dieux"; L. Bruit Zaidman in *ThesCRA* II, 225–29. For theoxenies as based on "Dinge, wie sie eben auch die Menschen essen," see Meuli, "Opferbräuche," 194–95; Ekroth, *Sacrificial Rituals,* 282.

75. See especially the Marathon calendar, *SEG* 50.168, face A col. 2. The relation of such tables to those shown in the very frequent type of the "banqueting hero" relief is disputed (Dentzer, *Banquet couché,* 513–27), but some connection is hard to doubt.

76. In Jameson, Jordan, and Kotansky, *Selinous (NGSL* 27), A 13–16, a sacrifice is followed by preparation of table, couch, and coverlet; meat, presumably from the sacrifice, is placed on the table, and a portion of offerings from the table is burned. In A 18–20 a table is again placed after a sacrifice, and the instruction follows to "burn a thigh and the offerings from the table and the bones" (trans. the editors): cf. G. Ekroth, "Bare Bones," in *Animal Sacrifice* (n. 56). Erythrai: *SEG* 47.1628.5–7, fees payable if anyone "entertains the gods" (the Corybantes) on the public altars. But Ekroth's argument, "Burnt, Cooked or Raw?" 102, from a supplemented text (*IGLSM* 3.47 [new text of *LSCG* 90]) for the use of roasted meat in theoxeny is insecure.

77. Bacch. fr. 21 ap Ath. 11.101, 500A–B; cf. Hor. *Od.* 1.20, with Nisbet/Hubbard's introductory note.

FIGURE 4. Theoxenia: the Dioscuri arrive on horseback at a table spread for them. Clay votive relief, Taranto, Museo Nazionale, 4118; photo museum, reproduced by permission of the Ministero per i Beni e le Attività Culturali-Direzione Regionale per i Beni Culturali e Paesaggistici della Puglia-Soprintendenza per i Beni Archeologici della Puglia.

had his own table,[78] and there was no attempt to localize precisely the where-abouts of the god who "came" to "receive" sacrifices. The difference in na-ture between man and god was irreducible; these rituals, however, did what

---

78. So Veyne, "Inviter les dieux," 4, 10–11, 20, 24; L. Bruit Zaidman in *Cuisine et autel,* 40–42. In some Greek families, stories were told of a forebear who had entertained the Dioscuri (Hdt. 6.127.3; Pind. *Nem.* 10.49–51), presumably in person; but these were stories of an earlier time. No goddess, Veyne notes, 20, receives theoxeny.

they could. (Note, however, that a ritual formally very similar to theoxenia could also be applied to polluting spirits with whom intimacy was certainly not desired.[79] Here the gesture of hospitality was aimed to appease the recipient and thus end a relationship.)

A Labyrinth of Variations: Nonstandard Forms of Alimentary Sacrifice

Not all ritual killings led to human dining, even apart from those such as purifications and oath sacrifices that were not cast in the idiom of foodstuffs at all. Animals and accompanying vegetable offerings could be burned whole, or (for water deities) thrown into water, or (in the cult of the dead) simply abandoned. The word "destruction" is often used in this context, though it has been pointed out that "removal" was really the result sought. An intermediate form has been identified and termed a "moirocaust," "partial burning":[80] here more meat was burned for the recipient than usual but the majority was still left for human consumption. An inscription first published in 2004 suggests that the valuable pelt was sometimes, and perhaps regularly, taken off before an animal was burned whole; in another form the meat might be eaten but the pelt added to the flames.[81]

Karl Meuli assigned such practices an origin quite different from that of ordinary participatory sacrifices: he saw the holocaust as deriving from the cult of the dead, and explained it by the kind of destructive rage displayed by Achilles after the death of Patroclus in the *Iliad*: my friend is dead, let

---

79. See *LSS* 115 B 29–39 (RO 97.111–21), with the commentary in RO; also Jameson, Jordan, and Kotansky, *Selinous* (*NGSL* 27) B 3–7 as supplemented in 4 by the editors (for other views see *NGSL* ad loc.). Cf. p. 147 below on "disjunctive sacrifice."

80. Removal: J. Svenbro in *Cuisine et autel,* 217–24. Moirocaust: S. Scullion, *ZPE* 132 (2000): 163–71; cf. Ekroth, *Sacrificial Rituals,* 313–18; Ekroth, "Burnt, Cooked or Raw?" 89–93. Where extra meat was burned, the recipients were either the kinds of god who might be given holocausts (Zeus Meilichios, at Selinous), heroes/heroines (Heracles, on Thasos and perhaps at Miletus; Semele on Mykonos), or hero-like figures (the ancestral Tritopatores at Selinous). Different types of figure seem to be involved when the skin is destroyed: Artemis at Erchia, the Graces on Cos (for references see Ekroth, *Sacrificial Rituals,* 217–25). The position is complicated further if J. Prott is right (*Leges Graecorum sacrae* [Leipzig, 1896], 1:15–16), that the back (plus, in the first case, shoulder blade) "cut out" from several offerings on Mykonos (*LSCG* 96.7, 12–13, 30–31: for Poseidon Temenites, Demeter Chloe, Apollo Hekatombios) was burned; as he observes, the specification "a libation is poured over the shoulder-blade" points strongly that way.

81. Skin saved: S. Scullion, "Sacrificial Norms, Greek and Semitic: Holocausts and Hides in a Sacred Law of Aixone," in *Norme religieuse,* 153–69, commenting on *SEG* 54.214. Skin burned: see previous note.

everything else die too.[82] But, many other difficulties aside, there is no reason to think that the holocaust sacrifices occasionally listed in sacrificial calendars, amid those of the other kind, were conducted with the savage passion of the greatest of epic heroes. The calendars list holocausts, moirocausts, and ordinary participatory sacrifices indiscriminately. This last consideration invalidates the sharp distinction implicitly drawn in *The Cuisine of Sacrifice* between sacrifices followed by a banquet, sole subject of the book, and all other kinds. This distinction is particularly surprising given the strong structuralist imprint on *The Cuisine of Sacrifice*. Sacrifices that do and do not end in a feast are listed in the same sacrificial calendars; the terms applied to them (θύειν, ἐναγίζειν) and the practices associated with them (libations with and without wine) are often contrasting pairs defined by mutual opposition: they look like components in the same structure or system that ought not to be analyzed in isolation one from the other.

It may seem that the holocaust confronts us with a choice: either we must make the absolute but illegitimate separation made in *The Cuisine of Sacrifice* between the majority of sacrifices that were followed by a feast and the minority that were not; or we must abandon the tie between sacrifice and feast altogether. But the dichotomy is too extreme. In its commonest form, an alimentary sacrifice is a combination of food offering to a deity and feast. Sometimes the element of "food offering" is nominal only, and what predominates is the feast. Occasionally the feast (among humans) is suppressed completely, and only the recipient dines. But sacrifice plus feast (accompanied by libations of wine) is certainly the dominant and normative form. Discrepancies are explicitly signaled in the sacrificial calendars: a sheep for x, burned whole, sober. They are variations on a theme.

Such variation on a theme is a characteristic mechanism of ritual, and one that sacrifice invites in particular, because at its center is a body, a ready object of symbolic manipulation. When sacrifices to expiate incest were performed by the Nuer and Dinka, the animal was cut longitudinally down the middle in such a way as to cut the sexual organs into two halves.[83] At funerary sacrifices among the Uduk, another Sudanese people, the animal was suffocated without blood being shed, to keep it intact to serve the dead in the other world. A pun in Aristophanes seems to be based on a Greek sacrificial

---

82. "Opferbräuche," 201–9. Plut. *Pyrrh.* 31.1 speaks of the enemies killed by Pyrrhus in revenge for the death of his son as "so to speak an *enagismos.*"

83. G. Lienhardt, *Divinity and Experience: The Religion of the Dinka* (Oxford, 1961), 285; E. E. Evans-Pritchard describes the same longitudinal cutting (*Nuer Religion,* 184, 216, 298), but interestingly his informants failed to make explicit the point about the genitals; W. James, *The Listening Ebony,* 2nd ed. (Oxford, 1999), 128–29.

practice of "cutting the tongue [the organ of speech] for the herald."[84] The blood of an animal sacrificed to a river could be poured directly into it, not as usual onto an altar.[85] In such cases (which could be multiplied many times), the whole rite has not been invented as a vehicle for the transparent symbolism; these are adaptations for particular purposes of a dominant form, "special functions" to which the general schema is turned in the phraseology of Hubert and Mauss. Holocausts and moirocausts and other sacrifices without a full feast can be seen as similar adaptations, though with symbolism often, alas, much less transparent.

The rare practice of throwing victims live into rivers or the sea was discussed above. As for offerings burned whole, in the cult of the gods the practice was rare, and the victim was usually a small one such as a piglet. These at least are the conclusions to be drawn from the epigraphical evidence. The picture changes if we admit the testimony of Pausanias, but there is reason to doubt whether "potlatch holocausts" such as he occasionally describes occurred earlier.[86] The "rise of the holocaust" between the fourth century BC and the second century AD (but where in that period?) becomes therefore a theme for investigation: but not in this place.[87] The small victim of the classical period often served as a preliminary or subsidiary offering within a longer ritual sequence; a distinctive verb "to pre-burn" (προκαυτεῖν), which acknowledges this preliminary function, occurs once.[88] A pig burned whole as a preparation for the ordinary sacrifice of an ox can be seen as an intensified version of the burning of a portion for the gods in ordinary sacrifice.

There remains a small but obstinate group of holocausts that do not prepare for a subsequent rite. It is tempting to apply here the distinction between "conjunctive" and "disjunctive" sacrifices: the holocaust or quasi holocaust would be a disjunctive sacrifice that created a separation from a power whom

---

84. Ar. *Pax* 1110. In surviving sacred laws the tongue goes rather to the priest (Stengel, *Opferbräuche,* 172–77); but note the lovely ad hoc rule at Erchia (*LSCG* 18 E 49–58) where the sacrifice to Hermes is performed by the herald.

85. *LSCG* 96.34–37; cf. Hom. *Il.* 23.146–48. R. Koch Piettre in *Cuisine et autel,* 87–89, supposes that the bodies were then burned, but I see no reason why they could not have been eaten.

86. See below, pp. 167–69.

87. The issue is not just the mass holocausts discussed below. Holocausts for heroes are far more frequent in Pausanias than in earlier evidence (see G. Ekroth in *Hero Cult,* 145–58; cf. Ekroth, *Sacrificial Rituals,* 307–8); in a well-excavated case, though the hero cult for Palaimon/Melikertes at the Isthmus goes back on literary evidence to the archaic period (E. R. Gebhard and M. W. Dickie in *Hero Cult,* 159–65), the regular holocausts of bovines begin c. AD 50 (E. R. Gebhard and D. S. Reese in *Greek Sacrificial Ritual,* 125–53) and doubtless attest a Roman-period reconstruction (M. Piérart, *Kernos* 11 (1998): 85–109).

88. RO 62 (*LSCG* 151) B 12–13. Heracles on Cos receives on the same day both a burned offering and an ordinary sacrifice, but apparently in different places: ibid. C 8–15.

the worshippers wished to accord the necessary honor only from a safe distance. When in Smyrna a black ox was cut in pieces and burned for "ravening hunger" (literally "ox hunger," βούβρωστις), it is easy to identify the rite as one of separation; one may suspect that the black bull was seen as embodying βούβρωστις. A holocaust to the Eumenides, figures whose grove prudent persons passed by silently with eyes down, is not a surprise either. The same explanation might fit holocausts to heroes, in the minority of heroic sacrifices that had this form. The practice of depositing "meals for Hecate," the dangerous goddess, at the crossroads is a model example of a somewhat different form of disjunctive offering.[89]

But there are many contexts where separation might seem desirable yet the sacrifice was not a holocaust. One might think that a plague was an occasion calling for a disjunctive offering if ever one did. Yet, in Homer's depiction at least, the Greeks ate of the hecatomb that they brought to Apollo at the end of *Iliad* book one (430–74). No holocaust for Apollo, the sender of plague, is to my knowledge ever attested. The most astonishing prescription in the altogether astonishing Lex Sacra from Selinous is the last: "When (someone) wishes to sacrifice to the *elastēros,* sacrifice as to the immortals, but let him slaughter (so that the blood flows) into the ground." An *elastēros* is in all seeming a polluting spirit, yet it receives sacrifice as to the gods, with the single exception that the blood is directed toward the underworld. There is no sign that sacrifices to "gods who avert evil" or that those involved in the process known as "sacrificing out" (an ill omen, a crime, a pollution) could not be eaten.[90]

Conversely, holocausts occur in contexts where there is no obvious need for disjunction. Why should the men of the Attic deme of Erchia, say, seek separation from "Zeus Overseer (Epopetes)" to whom they made an annual holocaust sacrifice of a piglet on their "hill"? Why was it Xenophon's ancestral custom to make holocausts of pigs to Zeus Meilichios?[91] Much

89. Boubrostis: Metrodorus *FGrH* 43 F 3 ap. Plut. *Quaest. conv.* 6.8.1, 694 A–B. Eumenides: Σ Soph. *OC* 42, Paus. 8.34.3 (holocausts sacrificed by Orestes in the Peloponnese); Soph. *OC* 125–33. But participatory sacrifices to them were also possible, Jameson, Jordan, and Kotansky, *Selinous* (*NGSL* 27) A 8–9, Σ Soph. *OC* 489, ? Paus. 2.11.4, Paus. 8.34.3 (Orestes' second sacrifice). Meals for Hecate: A. Zografou in *ThesCRA* 2:229–31; cf. n. 79 on "disjunctive'" theoxeny.

90. Jameson, Jordan, and Kotansky, *Selinous* (*NGSL* 27) B 12–13. "Gods who avert evil": see Parker, *Polytheism,* 413–14; that they receive normal sacrifice is noted by Burkert in *Sacrifice dans l'antiquité,* 123. The killing of a red he-goat to avert "disease or [] or death" for Apollo the Averter outside the gates of Cyrene (RO 97 [*LSS* 115] A 4–7) sounds like a classic "destroying the embodiment of evil" offering; but the verb used is θύειν. "Sacrificing out": see LSJ s.v. ἐκθύω; Arist. *Ath. Pol.* 54.6; J. Gibert, *HSCP* 101 (2003): 167–71.

91. *LSCG* 18 γ 19–25; Xen. *Anab.* 7.8.4. On these problems see Scullion, "Olympian and Chthonian," 111 (and the reservation p. 285 n. 7 below); Ekroth, *Sacrificial Rituals,* 240–41; on

here remains thoroughly uncertain. Only a limited range of gods appear to receive holocausts whether self-standing or preliminary. The observation (if it is sound!—these things are not so easy to control) that Zeus quite often receives holocausts whereas Artemis, say, and Apollo never do is important. It supports the view that the issue is not one of situation (the need for separation) but the character of the god.

A context where, by contrast, the idea of disjunctive sacrifice is clearly helpful is the cult of the dead. The two verbs θύειν and ἐναγίζειν are sometimes explicitly contrasted;[92] when they are, θύειν denotes sacrifices followed by dining, ἐναγίζειν destruction or removal sacrifices. The primary reference of ἐναγίζειν is to offerings made to the dead. It looks as if the practice of killing an animal as a προσφάγιον, "preliminary slaughter offering," at funerals went out of use between the fifth and fourth centuries;[93] thereafter the offerings (whether at the funeral, or commemorative) removed from human use by the rite of ἐναγίζειν will have consisted of such things as cakes, seasonal fruits, flowers, and libations. But ἐναγίζειν could also be used of animal victims burned whole for heroes;[94] for one ritual idiom through which heroes could be treated was as dead mortals, if still receiving rather grander offerings than did ordinary men. Such a heroic holocaust might be accompanied by a "blood glutting" (αἱμακουρία), whereby the blood of the animal victim was poured onto the ground to seep down to those below. (There also existed a compromise form in which the blood was poured into the earth but the animal still eaten.)[95] There is an obvious possibility of

---

the possible influence of the hero Epops, who receives a holocaust in the same calendar, on Zeus Epopetes, Burkert, *Homo Necans,* 183; cf. A. Hollis, *ZPE* 93 (1992): 11–13. Ekroth, *Sacrificial Rituals,* 307, 326, suggests that a distinction made by some anthropologists between low- and high-intensity rites (i.e., routine rites versus those responding to a crisis) might bear some relation to the *thysia/* holocaust distinction, but notes that regular, calendrically regulated holocausts do not fit the model; even an advocate of it concedes that it is an observer's distinction that fails to track the distinctions in actual sacrificial practice with precision (J. van Baal, "Offering, Sacrifice and Gift," *Numen* 23 [1976]: 161–78).

92. Hdt. 2.44; F. Pfister, *Der Reliquienkult im Altertum* (Berlin, 1909), 468.

93. See the endnote to this chapter.

94. Holocausts for gods were never so designated, even if the meat received objectively exactly the same treatment in the two cases. Confusingly, burned offerings to heroes could be designated either with the ἐναγίζειν or with the "burn" vocabulary. The burned offerings to heroes in the Erchia calendar (*LSCG* 18) are examples of the latter: they sound exactly like burned offerings to gods. The verb καρποῦν is in sacral usage synonymous with καίειν, burn; how it acquired that sense is a mystery (Stengel, *Opferbräuche,* 166–68; a different view in P. Chantraine, *Dictionnaire étymologique de la langue grecque* [Paris, 1968–80], s.v. καρποῦν).

95. See, e.g., Jameson, Jordan, and Kotansky, *Selinous* (*NGSL* 27) B 12–13; Paus. 10.4.10; R. Parker in *Greek Sacrificial Ritual,* 41–42. On blood glutting, Ekroth, *Sacrificial Rituals,* 171–77; on the mixed form, which she associates especially with military heroes, ibid., 257–68.

aligning the θύειν/ ἐναγίζειν distinction with that between conjunctive
and disjunctive sacrifices: the gods live apart from us and contact with them
needs to be established; the dead must be first separated from mortals and
then kept separate. ἐναγίζειν is generally supposed to contain in it the root
ἄγος / *ἄγος denoting the sacred in its most dangerous and unapproach-
able form: ἐναγίζειν is to give something over to that sacredness and put
it beyond the human sphere.[96] An offering made to the dead or to heroes
assimilated to them might be described as a "feast," but one in which no
human would care to participate.[97]

Variation in the use of meat and skin and blood was only one of the
variations that occurred in sacrifice. Others included the choice of victims
(species, age, sex, color), the manner of killing, the types of altar that were
used, the accompanying libations, whether "carrying away" of the meat was
permitted; also perhaps, if less often, the time of day at which the rite was
performed, the direction in which participants faced, and so on. The inventory of differences here is enormous and every new sacrificial regulation
that is published adds to it, one might almost say. Patterns certainly exist
among these variations, but they refuse to align with one another in any
completely systematic way.[98] There is, for instance, a close but not an invariable relationship between holocausts and "sober" libations, those consisting
of honey mixed with water or milk (*melikraton*)[99] and not (as at most sacrifices) of wine. All the holocausts listed in the calendar of the Attic deme of
Erchia were "sober," but not all sober offerings were holocausts; even the
sober non-holocausts, however, were made to figures who in other contexts
received holocausts or might have done so. Remarkably, the offering to Zeus
Meilichios (who received holocausts elsewhere, though not here) was "sober

---

96. Cf. Parker, *Miasma*, 5–7, 328–29.

97. "Feast and blood glutting" for the war dead of Plataea: Plut. *Aristid.* 21.5–6; for Achilles:
Philostr. *Her.* 53.11–13; Odysseus revives dead souls with blood: Hom. *Od.* 10.504–40, 11.23–50;
"banquets" for underworld powers also Aesch. *Eum.* 108–9. Possibly the idea that the dead need
sustenance (Meuli, "Opferbräuche," 189–95) lurks in the background and partly explains the "feasting" language.

98. "Non seulement le Grec possède des mots nombreux pour désigner les rites sacrificiels, non
seulement les êtres en l'honneur desquels ces rites semblent accomplis appartiennent à des catégories
inégales, non seulement on consacre tantôt des offrandes végétales tantôt des victimes animales,
selon des modes divers d'immolation, de crémation ou de partage, mais surtout il n'y a aucune correspondence systématique entre toutes ces variations": J. Rudhardt, *Notions fondamentales de la pensée
religieuse et actes constitutifs du culte dans la Grèce classique* (Geneva, 1958), 253. On "no carry out" rules,
see p. 284.

99. See Graf, "Milch, Honig und Wein," 212. For the evidence on recipients of sober libations,
see A. Henrichs, *HSCP* 87 (1983): 96–98; add now the epithet 'sober' applied to Zeus Epopetes in
IG 2² 2616 as read by N. Papazarkadas, *Horos* 17–21 (2004-9), 99–101

up to the entrails," that is, the libations switched from sober (or none) to vinous during the ceremony, once the entrails had been roasted and eaten: the god oscillates between types of sacrifice and types of libation alike.[100] But no ready explanation presents itself for the provision in the new sacred law from Selinous that the impure Tritopatores should receive libations of wine, while their pure equivalents are given "honey mix"; the best we can say is that the Tritopatores, like Zeus Meilichios, were on the margin between the two types.[101]

It is instructive if discouraging to read a passage such as the following, from one of the rare texts that give step-by-step instructions for performance of a ritual:

> The [heralds] burn the piglet and the entrails on the altar, making libations of milk and honey over them; they wash the intestines and burn them beside the altar. When they have been burned without libations, let him make libation of honey and milk over them. . . . Let [the priest] sacrifice over the intestines (τοῖς ἐντέροις ἐπιθύετω) incense [or a type of cake: θύη] and the cakes and libations of [unmixed] and mixed [wine] and a woollen fillet.[102]

So even in a holocaust sacrifice, the animal was not necessarily placed whole on the flames.[103] The inner organs could be cut out and receive elaborate differentiated treatment; and we even seem to find a progression from "honey mix" via unmixed wine to mixed wine.[104] We fumble in interpreting these variations, and it is very plausible that different Greek communities deployed the repertory of symbols in different ways. The basic components, however—foodstuffs—are always the same.

---

100. Recipients of sober holocausts at Erchia (*LSCG* 18): α 14–20, Basile (probably a heroine); γ 19–25, Zeus Epopetes (cf. previous note); δ 18–23 and ε 9–15, Epops; sober non-holocausts α 37–43, Zeus Meilichios ("up to the entrails"); γ 48–53, Leukaspis (hero); δ 43–6, Tritopatreis; ε 59–64, Zeus Epakrios. For holocausts to Zeus Meilichios, see Xen. *Anab.* 7.8.4; a holocaust to a hero is always a possibility; for the Tritopatreis/ores as recipients of moirocausts, see n. 80; for Zeus Epakrios, Zeus Epopetes in this same text is a parallel.

101. Jameson, Jordan, and Kotansky, *Selinous (NGSL* 27) A 9–16, with their agnostic comment p. 72.

102. RO 62 (*LSCG* 151) A 32–38.

103. See Scullion, in *Norme religieuse,* 158.

104. It is strongly stressed by Graf, "Milch, Honig und Wein," who argues that both sober offerings and those of unmixed wine are marks of abnormality, since normal adult Greek males drank mixed wine with their meals and saw this as the norm of civilized existence. But it is implausible to combine such different forms as sober and unmixed libations in a single category of abnormality; the unmixed wine accompanying an oath is surely not abnormal wine but concentrated wine.

Sacrifice and the Group

We have wandered, in the last few paragraphs, in the sacrificial maze. Details are hard to interpret; and the coherence of a practice that is so intimately related to eating has been challenged by sacrifices that are followed by no human meal. But our starting point was Veyne's warning that the institution is one that is pushed and pulled and reshaped by conflicting imaginings and interests and needs. "Feasting in communication with the gods" is certainly the description that would cover most cases, but the balance shifts between "feasting" and "communication"; and adaptations are possible that eliminate the feast in order to establish the different forms of communication appropriate to different gods (or to heroes and the dead). Another variable ought now to be introduced. It is both conventional and surely correct to think of sacrifice as a preeminently communal activity, one that is performed by groups and also helps form them.[105] Only gluttonous Heracles sacrifices on his own. In the canonical literary descriptions, sacrifice is marked by elaborate preliminaries, many of which involve a group. The participants lead the animal to the altar in procession, form a circle, purify themselves with lustral water, and throw a handful of barley grains at the victim; these practices are consistently alluded to in a wide variety of texts, and their unifying function was so strongly felt that "sharing lustral water" was a way of referring to membership of a group.[106]

As for the events that followed the kill, the great contribution of *The Cuisine of Sacrifice* was to stress the sociopolitical importance of the sacrificial feast. The feast had two parts, the immediate roasting and eating near the altar of the unsalted entrails; the more leisurely consumption, at a distance from the altar or even at home, of the animal's flesh, boiled with salt in cauldrons (or distributed raw). The religious power of the sacrifice inhered in its most concentrated form in the entrails, the vital organs (in their conception as well as ours) of the animals.[107] Privileged participants received a portion of the roasted entrails (which could not be distributed to all), or an especially honorable cut or a double share of the remaining meat; the right to at least

---

105. See the texts cited in Parker, *Polytheism,* 43, esp. n. 21.

106. Aesch. *Eum.* 656; Ar. *Lys.* 1129–30; Eur. *El.* 791–92. For the Homeric descriptions of sacrifice, see G. S. Kirk in *Sacrifice dans l'antiquité,* 41–80 (who stresses variations); the main Attic descriptions are Eur. *El.* 783–843; *HF* 921–30; Ar. *Pax* 937–1043. The collective aspect is almost always present in visual depictions (van Straten, *Hierà Kalá,* passim).

107. See excellent pages of M. Detienne, *Dionysos Slain* (trans. M. Muellner and L. Muellner, Baltimore, 1979, of *Dionysos mis à mort,* Paris, 1977), 74–77 (174–79 of the Fr. orig.); also J. L. Durand in *Cuisine of Sacrifice,* 92, 99 (140, 148 in the Fr. orig.); van Straten, *Hierà Kalá,* 190 and in *Cuisine et autel,* 23–24. On salt see Athenio fr. 1.9–26 K/A.

a single "share" was synonymous with full membership of whatever socio-political group was celebrating the rite. Outsiders could be incorporated by being granted the right to a "share," which could even in extreme cases be dispatched overseas; more modestly, private sacrificers distributed portions to absent friends, like slices of wedding cake.[108]

The importance of all this in the lived reality of ancient Greece can scarcely be overestimated. The unequal distribution of meat could reinforce hierarchies, equal distribution could negate them, a mixed mode of distribution could allow compromise between different political models. Lienhardt in his study of Dinka religion published a diagram of the cuts of meat on a cow much like those that one sees in a butcher's shop, with the exception that the parts are identified not by their names but by the typical recipients of them: for "brisket" read "people of the sacrificer's cattle camp," for "shank" read "girls of the sacrificer's lineage," and so on.[109] An individual's social relations are mapped out on the body of a cow. *The Cuisine of Sacrifice* encourages us mutatis mutandis to think about the social role of Greek sacrifice in similar terms.

These are manifest truths; and yet some complication is needed even here. It may not be very important that, as Greek societies grew in scale, many sacrifices may have ended not in a group feast but in the "carrying away" (mentioned above) of portions to the participants' separate homes. The practice is sometimes explicitly forbidden, likely therefore often to have occurred.[110] Despite the carry-out option, true sacrificial feasts surely remained commonplace. They did not occur, obviously, when the meat of the victim was burned whole. And it is doubtful both in this and in some other contexts whether the collective preliminaries with lustral water and barley grains were actually performed. Philostratus in his *Heroikos* states explicitly that "beginning with the basket and the entrails" did not take place in an ἐνάγισμα, a destruction sacrifice, for Achilles as a hero (in contrast to a subsequent θυσία to him as a god).[111] Much of the religion of the *Heroikos* (written in the late second century AD) is fantasy, but we can hope that this ritual detail is based on sound antiquarian knowledge. The basket probably takes with it the associated rite with lustral water. An ἐνάγισμα, as we saw, is a good candidate

108. On all this see Ekroth, "Meat, Man and God." Dispatch: see A. Jacquemin, "La participation *in absentia* au sacrifice," in *Sacrifice antique,* 225–34, with my comment ibid., vi.

109. Lienhardt, *Divinity and Experience* (in n. 83 above), 24.

110. For a homely example see Herod. 4.92–93.

111. Philostr. *Her.* 53.11–13; on the work see C. P. Jones, *JHS* 121 (2001): 141–49.

for a ritual of separation, being reserved either for the dead or for heroes in their aspect as dead mortals. Perhaps then it is natural that the communal aspect of the event should have been drastically reduced. What preliminaries introduced holocausts to gods is unknown.

The doubts do not concern cases such as these alone. One may wonder how much collective involvement there was, say, in a divinatory sacrifice performed by a seer on campaign.[112] Such rituals could certainly attract an attentive audience, but perhaps not one that was invited to participate. The prominence of the seer on such occasions is itself a reminder of the difference between them and ordinary civic sacrifices, presided over by a priest or magistrate. The animal was killed to answer a specific question put to its liver, not to inaugurate a meal; probably its meat was eventually eaten, but as a matter of good housekeeping rather than of religion. This is a different way in which the aspect "communication with the gods" could come to prevail over the aspect "collective feast."

Where Killing Matters: Slaughter-Sacrifices, and the Problem of the Unity of "Sacrifice"

The sacrifices discussed thus far have been what we might call "gift and foodstuff" sacrifices. These divide into those, the majority, that are part eaten by humans and a minority of holocausts that are burned whole for the gods. Even the latter are gifts to identifiable recipients and normally include vegetable offerings alongside the animal victim; they are cast in the idiom of food. The barley grains mixed with salt held by participants in most forms of the rite,[113] and the libations, emphasize the association with nutrition. But the Greeks also practiced various forms of ritual killing that were not food offerings; even their status as offerings to a defined god can be uncertain. Here

---

112. Or in one conducted in a private house and intended primarily to provide meat for a meal. Eumaeus in Hom. *Od.* 14.419–36 kills a pig for, but not with, a group (no sacrificial word is used, but the rite should probably be accounted a sacrifice: see my "Eating Unsacrificed Meat," above n. 28, 141–42). For a seer performing slaughter-sacrifice alone, see Plut. *De gen.* 27, 594E. Audience: Xen. *Lac.* 13.3–5. Omens were reported from all public sacrifices and this may imply the presence of a seer, but the presiding role always fell to a magistrate or priest; on campaign the seer is in sole charge of the prebattle σφάγια (Thuc. 6.69.2) and has a very prominent role at all sacrifices.

113. Σ vet. Ar. *Eq.* 1167, Stengel, *Opferbräuche,* 13–16; on what was done with them, van Straten, *Hierà Kalá,* 38–39, 66; on their significance, F. Graf in *Kykeon,* 121. The Boeotians used them for their eel sacrifices, *FGrH* 86 F 5.

for the first time must be confronted the issue of definition that bedevils all discussion of sacrifice in every culture.[114]

The difficulty is not precisely or not merely that sacrifice is a class the members of which are held together not by any universally shared characteristics but (in Wittgenstein's famous phrase) by a family resemblance; in a different metaphor Wittgenstein spoke of a rope that "consists of fibres, but it does not get its strength from any fibre that runs through it from one end to another, but from the fact that there is a vast number of fibres overlapping."[115] The problem is rather that we are not dealing with an indigenous concept—as it might be αἰδώς, shame—the logic of which we are trying to establish. "Sacrifice" is an observer's category bringing together phenomena that the Greeks described by a variety of terms, a variety that also changed over time; and though those terms often overlap, they do not intertwine so densely as to give the concept the firmness of a rope. As we have already seen, the Greek vocabulary extends out to include practices that we might wish to exclude. The closest multipurpose verb in classical Greek for "to sacrifice," for instance, θύω, is used in Homer for the burning of offerings of any kind for the gods (the related noun refers to incense); it continues to be applied to the burning of vegetable offerings even when, after Homer, it has come to be applied also to the ritual killing of animals (for which Homer has a different vocabulary). Again, we might want to distinguish between sacrifice conceived as a food offering, normally followed by a banquet, and ritual killings performed for other purposes such as to ensure safe passage over a river. And indeed Greeks tend to make such a distinction linguistically, calling the one rite θυσία and the other σφάγιον, slaughter offering. But we find Herodotus blithely applying the verb θύω to a σφάγιον offering.[116]

---

114. Cf. J van Baal, "Offering, Sacrifice and Gift," *Numen* 23 (1976): 161–78; van Baal wishes to distinguish sacrifice *stricto sensu* from ritual killing, 161.

115. Preliminary studies for the *Philosophical Investigations,* generally known as the *Blue and Brown Books* (Oxford, 1958), 87; I take the citation from R. Needham, "Polythetic Classification: Convergence and Consequences," *Man* n.s. 10 (1975): 349–69, which leads into the bibliography on these issues.

116. Hdt. 9.62.1; cf. Casabona, *Vocabulaire des sacrifices,* 83–84, and on the noun, 129–30. Traditional doctrine is that θύειν has both a "marked" use in which it indicates specifically sacrifices from which mortals ate and an "unmarked" use for a wider range of killings. Ekroth, *Sacrificial Rituals,* 295–96, notes that no unmarked use can be demonstrated in relation to classical hero cult, but has to concede that θύω/θυσία are also used quite often of human sacrifices, which functionally are σφάγια. An author-by-author study is needed: for the unmarked use in Pausanias, see Pirenne-Delforge, *Pausanias,* 227. "'Sacrifice' is a word, a lexical illusion. What exists is the *thusia,*" writes Durand, *Cuisine of Sacrifice,* 89 (136 in the Fr. orig.). But *thusia* is also a word, of complicated application. Note, for instance, θυσία ἄπυρος παγκαρπείας of Eur. fr. 912.4. "Unburned sacrifices" violate the requirement of destruction that Hubert and Mauss, *Sacrifice,* 11–12, took as the dividing line between sacrifice and offering.

There is then real doubt as to what is to count as a sacrifice and what not; and a sampling of the anthropological literature reveals that similar problems of vocabulary, and similar uncertainties, occur very widely. Was it a sacrifice when a piglet was slain before a meeting of the assembly at Athens and its body carried round the meeting place? The act is normally described as a purification and no divine addressee is ever named. But the piglet rather similarly used to purify a murderer could be spoken of as one element among the sacrifices made in such a case to Zeus of Purification. And when the sanctuary of Aphrodite Pandemos at Athens was purified, the usual piglet was replaced with a dove, the goddess's preferred sacrificial victim.[117] (The overlap here is not one of language but of practice.) Thus a chain of a kind extends from the actions universally recognized as sacrifice to the purificatory slaughter of a piglet.

We are faced with an array of practices that resemble one another in varying degrees and, again in varying degrees, are described in similar terms.[118] The answer to a question such as "Is the slaughter of an animal before crossing a river a sacrifice?" is that there is no answer. Such a killing differs in obvious and important respects from alimentary sacrifices. But in this and other such cases the resemblances were also great enough for crossovers in vocabulary to occur. In our inability to answer the question we follow (but with anxiety, whereas they felt no need to know) the Greeks. Does that inability matter? I will revert to that question; but first the slaughter-sacrifices must be briefly described.

Before a battle, both sides commonly killed a goat or a ram as a "slaughter-victim" (σφάγιον). For the Spartans it was an offering to Artemis Agrotera; in the other attested cases (mostly Attic) no recipient is named.[119] *Sphagion* killings could also be made to deal with meteorological crises such as a sudden and violent storm. "Slaves, quickly, bring a black she-lamb. A typhoon's on the way!" exclaims a character in Aristophanes. A seer in Xenophon's *Anabasis* advises the ten thousand to "make a slaughter to the wind," the wind being treated as recipient.[120] A form sometimes found in offerings to

---

117. Murder: Ap. Rhod. *Argon.* 4. 700–709; θυηπολίη, 702. Dove: *LSCG* 39.23–24.

118. "A continuous field of overlapping shades of meaning or potential meaning": van Straten in *Cuisine et autel,* 26.

119. See M. H. Jameson, "Sacrifice before Battle," in *Hoplites: The Classical Greek Battle Experience,* ed. V. D. Hanson, 197–227 (London, 1991). Young she-goat at Sparta: Xen. *Hell.* 4.2.20 (which gives the recipient); Xen. *Lac.* 13.8 (whence Plut. *Lyc.* 22.4); ram: two vases and a relief, Jameson, 217–18; see too his "Athena Nike Parapet" (n. 146 below) at 320–24.

120. Ar. *Frogs* 847–48; cf. Xen. *Anab.* 4.5.4 σφαγιάσασθαι τῷ ἀνέμῳ. But "lightning, storms, and thunder" could also receive what Pausanias describes as *thysiai,* Paus. 8.29.1 (Bathos, in Arcadia); so too could hail (ibid. 2.34.3: θυσίαι καὶ ἐπῳδαί).

rivers or sea deities was to "cut the throat into the water/river/springs," so that the blood poured out there, water replacing earth as a recipient of the blood. The corpse could then be thrown into the sea. This rite resembles both the killing of a *sphagion* to stay a storm and also the holocaust, hurling replacing burning as a means of removal from the human sphere.[121] At Methana in the eastern Argolid the two halves of a white cock were carried in opposite directions around the vines, then buried, to keep off the destructive wind known as Lips; the Spartans apparently killed horses on Taygetus for similar purposes;[122] and no doubt many such practices have eluded our sources.

A very widely established practice in the cult of Demeter was the throwing of piglets, apparently still live, into underground pits along with cakes; in Attica at least, the rotten remains were later retrieved and mixed with the seed corn.[123]

Important oaths were almost always sanctified by a killing. Practices varied in detail. Of one Greek people we read that "when the Molossians swear an oath, they provide oxen and bowls full of wine. They cut the oxen into small pieces and pray that those who transgress the oath be cut likewise. And emptying the bowls, they pray that the blood of transgressors be poured out likewise."[124] The Molossian rite is characteristic in emphasizing the idea of

---

121. Cutting into the sea plus hurling: Ap. Rhod. *Argon.* 4.1595–1602; Arr. *Anab.* 6.19.5; probably Theophr. fr. 709 Fortenbaugh ap. Ath. 6.79, 261D–E. Note too Cleomenes' two *sphagion* offerings, one to the river Erasinus, one to the sea, in Hdt. 6.76: the former, relating to the crossing of a river, differs in form from the crossing offerings standardly made by Spartans on leaving Spartan territory, of which θύω is always used (Thuc. 5.54.1; Xen. *Hell.* 4.7.2; Xen. *Lac.* 13.2–3). Speaking of a similar rite performed by the *magoi* at the Strymon, Herodotus uses the extraordinary verb φαρμακεύω, 7.114.1. But Arrian has θύω for Alexander's river-crossing sacrifices (e.g., *Anab.* 4.4.3). There are clear overlaps between these ad hoc *sphagia* to watery powers and regular cult to them, where blood could also be poured into water but the meat (probably) eaten: nn. 59 and 85 above.

122. Paus. 2.34.2; Festus s.v. October Equus.

123. See, e.g., Σ Lucian p. 275.23–276.28 Rabe with Parker, *Polytheism,* 273; Paus. 9.8.1; U. Kron, "Frauenfeste in Demeterheiligtümern: Das Thesmophorion von Bitalemi," *AA* (1992): 611–50. For deposition in the earth in the cult of Demeter, see Hinz, *Demeter auf Sizilien,* 53; on Demeter and pigs, Ekroth, "Thighs or Tails?," 137.

124. T. Gaisford, *Paroemiographi Graeci* (Oxford, 1836), 126 no. 57 (from Codex Coislinianus 177), also printed in the app. crit. to Diogenianus 3.60 Leutsch-Schneidewin. The treaty formula of the *pater patratus* in Livy 1.24.8 is an excellent Roman parallel (I ignore minor textual difficulties): *si prior defexit [populus Romanus] publico consilio dolo malo, tum illo die Juppiter populum Romanum sic ferito, ut ego hunc porcum hic hodie feriam.* On "as...so" in oaths (cf., e.g., Hom. *Il.* 3.300), see C. A. Faraone, *JHS* 103 (1993): 72–76; on Homeric oaths, M. Kitts, *Sanctified Violence in Homeric Society: Oath-Making Rituals and Narratives* (Cambridge, 2005), chap. 3; on oath rituals in general, Bickerman, "Cutting a Covenant"; I. Berti, "Greek Oath-Rituals," in *Ritual and Communication,* 181–209. Whether the "as...so" relation between animal and swearer still applies in post-Homeric oaths (that of the Molossians aside) is uncertain: possibly the killing merely strengthens the affirmation (for these distinctions see Bickerman, "Cutting a Covenant," 15–21).

"cutting"—to "cut an oath" was a regular expression, and swearers were often required to hold or stand on "cut pieces"[125]—and probably in suggesting an analogy between the fate of the animal and a perjured swearer. Oaths are thus one of the few forms of Greek ritual killing in which there may occur that symbolic identification between animal and human that in anthropological literature is often seen as intrinsic to sacrifice.[126] In descriptions of oath-sacrifices in the *Iliad,* the animal victims are "for" the gods by whom an oath is sworn, though in fact they receive no portion of them, and several details of the ritual follow or vary sacrificial forms: those who are to swear wash their hands, and hair is cut from the victim's brow and put in the swearers' hands (in ordinary sacrifice it goes on the altar, and participants receive barley grains).[127]

Later texts contain numerous allusions to oaths but (the Molossian case aside) no detailed descriptions; oaths, however, continue to be sworn "over full-grown sacred things" or "over burning sacred things" or "over new-burned sacred things." (The vagueness of "sacred things" reproduces that of the Greek, and it is not clear whether this is a different mechanism from that with "cut pieces," or the same differently viewed.) These "sacred things" must have derived from sacrifices that had recipients; and oaths were always taken by particular gods who were invoked as witnesses: once we are told that entrails taken from an animal sacrificed to Zeus were employed to administer an oath.[128] A change is identified by Pausanias when he says that it was only "of old" that, as in *Iliad* 19.266–68, the animals by which oaths

---

125. What these "cut pieces" were is never made explicit and may have varied; the picturesque theory that they were the animal's testicles has fallen out of favor (Berti, "Greek Oath-Rituals" [n. 124 above], 194). One swears while "cutting the *tomia*" (Aeschin. 2.87, cf. Eur. *Suppl.* 1196), or standing on a rock where *tomia* have been placed (Arist. *Ath. Pol.* 55.5), or holding the entrails (Hdt. 6.68.1) or "the *sphagia*" (Ant. 5.12), or, in an extreme case, "standing on the *tomia* of boar, ram, and bull" (Dem. 23.68). A recent archaeological discovery from Thasos is said to confirm that the procedure of walking between the halves of a slaughtered animal (διὰ τομίων πορεύεσθαι), better known as a purification, could also be used to ratify an oath (D. Mulliez, *BCH,* forthcoming): cf. Pl. *Leg.* 753D, and several passages in Dictys of Crete: Bickerman, "Cutting a Covenant," 13; Faraone (n. 124 above), 71. In a military variant animals were slaughtered to make the blood run into an upturned shield, into which hand or spear was then dipped (Aesch. *Sept.* 43–44, Xen. *Anab.* 2.2.9).

126. Cf. my "Substitution in Greek Sacrifice," forthcoming in *Le sacrifice humain: regards croisés sur sa représentation,* ed. P. Bonnechere (provisional title, Liège). Note, however, that the dire fate of the perjurer could be differently represented, as by the melting wax figurines of ML 5.44–51, or the poured wine of Hom. *Il.* 3.300.

127. *Il.* 3.103–20, 245–301; 19.250–68.

128. Hdt. 6.67.3–68.1. "Over full-grown sacred things (κατὰ ἱερῶν τελείων)": Thuc. 5.47.8 and often; "burning": *Syll.*³ 588.81, *LSCG* 65.2; "new-burned" *IC* 3.4.8.8–9, *OGIS* 229.48; cf., e.g., ἐπιτελεῖν ὁρκωμόσιον ἐπὶ τοῦ Διὸς τοῦ Σωτῆρος τῶι βωμῶι, *LSA* 13.28–29. A new Hellenistic treaty from Boubon gives an oath δι' ἐντόμ[ων]: N. P. Milner in C. Schuler, ed., *Griechische Epigraphik in Lykien* (Vienna, 2007), 157.

were sworn were not eaten.[129] In the classical period, it seems that when a father introduced his child to a phratry, for instance, he swore an oath to the child's legitimacy by the same animal that also served to feast the *phratores*.[130] So an original differentiation between oath-sacrifice and alimentary sacrifice seems to have vanished or become weakened over time.

Purification was performed with the blood of a small animal, a piglet, lamb, or puppy (or occasionally a bird). To purify a place such as a temple or the Athenian assembly, the bleeding corpse of a piglet was carried around it; to purify people, the blood was poured over their hands. An army was purified by dividing a dog's corpse in two and marching it between the two halves. Individuals suspecting bewitchment or other misfortune could have themselves "purified around with a puppy" or "puppied around"; we do not know the exact procedure, but it surely entailed the animal's death.[131] In the one elaborate literary account that we possess of the purification of a murderer, the blood rite was followed by offerings and invocations to Zeus of Purification and the Erinyes; the whole procedure is described by a word from the θυ- root (θυηπολίη), but the killing itself has no named addressee, is accompanied by no prayer, and is not described as a sacrifice.[132]

Of the species used in purifications, pig and sheep had a place in sacrifices of every kind. Dogs were apparently reserved for purifications and other slaughter-sacrifices: Spartan ephebes killed puppies for Enyalios immediately before a mock battle, and it was a widespread custom to "carry out [the corpses of] dogs for Hecate to the crossroads," as a way of keeping the dangerous

---

129. 5.24.10–11. Bickerman, "Cutting a Covenant," 17, takes the "sacred things" of the formulas quoted in the previous note as the entrails, and supposes that the force of the oath was focused on them, not as in Homer on the whole animal, for economic reasons, to allow consumption of the rest of the meat. The explanation is plausible but, in the phrase κατὰ ἱερῶν τελείων, ἱερά are clearly "sacrificial animals," not "entrails." I am not sure whether the use of the verb σφαγιάζω in σφαγιασθέντος ἱερείου ὠμόσαμεν καθ᾽ ἱερῶν, *Syll.*³ 685.27, or σφαγιασάμενοι κατάρας ἠνάγκασαν ἐπὶ τῶν ἐμπύρων ποιεῖσθαι, Polyb. 16.31.7, proves the old Homeric practice of destruction of the victim to have persisted in some cases.

130. See sources in Parker, *Athenian Religion,* 105. The eating of the meat by the *phratores* itself had ritual meaning; we are not dealing with meat from oath-sacrifices that merely ended up in the market, as is surely likely to have often occurred de facto to avoid waste (the triple offerings often used in oaths, Berti, "Greek Oath-Rituals"[n. 124 above], 194 n. 66, are not merely majestic but also very expensive). On oath and sacrifice, cf. Nilsson, *Geschichte,* 140–41; on the role of gods, Rudhardt, *Essai,* 148–49. A complication is that oaths were often sworn by multiple gods, whereas in sacrifice one animal went to one god.

131. Theophr. *Char.* 16.14, Plut. *Quaest. Rom.* 68, 280B–C.

132. Ap. Rhod. *Argon.* 4.698–717. On all this, see Parker, *Miasma,* 21–22, 30 n. 66, 229–30, 283 n. 11, 370–74. Note, however, the possibility (ibid., 283 n. 11; *FGrH* 356 F 1) that a sacrifice used for the purification of suppliants could be eaten.

goddess at a distance.[133] Why puppies were also killed for goddesses of birth is unclear,[134] but analogy with the other cases suggests that they will not have been eaten. In general, the animals used for pre-battle killings, control-of-the-weather killings, purifications, and (in Homer) oaths were as far as we can tell thrown away (if human scavengers chose to pick them up, that was their affair), not eaten.[135]

These various rites almost explain themselves. The power resides in the killing itself. Specific direction can be given by the manipulation of the body: it is carried around the area it is supposed to protect or purify, or it is cut in half and walked through; it is cut up to prefigure the fate of perjurers; it is thrown into an underground pit as a fertilizing agent; in murder purification, the blood is treated as a kind of washing agent, "purifying blood with blood." Whether, in the pre-battle sacrifice, invocations were employed to make the animal death represent a human one, and what form the representation took if so, is uncertain: Was it "As we kill this goat, so let us kill the enemy," or "Take this animal and spare us," or neither of these things?[136] All that is certain is that omens were taken from the flow of the blood. As has often been observed,[137] these are powerful actions more than they are offerings: one kills a black lamb to a typhoon in the hope of making it stop blowing, now. All those who swear an oath must come into contact with portions of the dead animal; but with that exception there is little emphasis on collective involvement in these rites. Before battle, the army looks on while the seer cuts the animal's throat.

---

133. Sparta: Paus. 3.14.9 (also mentioning a Colophonian sacrifice of a black female puppy to Hecate: both are conducted by night): his word is θύω, but Plut. Quaest. Rom. 111, 290D speaks of whelps "cut" (ἐντέμνειν) for Enyalios at Sparta (cf. Cornut. Theol. Graec. 21 on dog sphagia to Ares). An offering of boar, dog, and kid to Enyalios that appears in the fifth-century Lindian law LSS 85.28–30 may, however, to judge from the context, have been eaten; the verb is lost. "To the crossroads": Aristophanes fr. 209, Plut. Quaest. Rom. 68, 280B–C, and 111, 290D (where he remarks that dogs are consecrated to no Olympians but are used for aversion and purification); cf. n. 89 above; other puppy killings for Hecate: Sophron fr. 4.7 K/A, Orph. Arg. 959.

134. Σ Paus. 1.1.5 (Genetyllis); Socrates of Argos FGrH 310 F 4 ap. Plut. Quaest. Rom. 52, 277B (an Argive deity Eilioneia); Plutarch's comparison of Roman dog sacrifices to the birth goddess Genita Mana (on which see the extraordinary archaeological evidence discussed by R. Gordon, Revista de historiografía, 5, no. 3 [2/2006]: 4–14) with Greek to Hecate (ibid.) may belong in the same context. Hecate was often worshipped as a birth goddess, but it is not self-evident that the dog sacrifice should have come over to her (and to other birth goddesses) in that aspect from her other aspects.

135. For oaths and purifications, see n. 132 and p. 157. For the other cases there is no explicit evidence, to my knowledge, but analogy suggests it.

136. Cf. "Substitution in Greek Sacrifice (n. 126).

137. Nock, Essays, 590–91 (from HTR 37 [1944]: 158–59); M. H. Jameson, BCH 89 (1965): 162–63; cf. Ekroth, Sacrificial Rituals, 325–30.

"These rites almost explain themselves," I wrote. But they do so only if one accepts the premise that an inflicted death is charged with religious power. The religious force ascribed to killing is one of the mysteries at the heart of sacrifice. Perhaps it is best frankly to admit that we do not fully understand this force, even if we can obscurely feel it. J. Z. Smith's tentative appeal to the stock raiser's dilemma was mentioned above. The Neoplatonist Sallustius explains, not very helpfully, that one can communicate with the givers of "life," the gods, only by means of "life": they give life, and we take it, and that claims their attention and earns their favor! "What pleasure [is there for the gods] in the butchering of the innocent?" asks Seneca.[138] Two of the most influential writers on sacrifice of the late twentieth century, Walter Burkert and René Girard, built their theories on killing. I confine myself here to the Hellenist Burkert.[139] To summarize a complex argument briefly, Burkert saw sacrifice as a social ritual that dealt with the problem of human, more specifically male human, aggressiveness in two ways: on the one hand it discharged it harmlessly against an animal victim; on the other hand, even in regard to that discharge it created a sense of guilt which helped inhibit aggression against fellow humans. Burkert linked sacrifice to guilt by taking Meuli's "comedy of innocence" and turning it on its head. The comedy, he claimed, did not efface the moral ambiguity of sacrificial killing, but drew attention to it; and the ambiguity did not concern the killing of animals, but the male potential for violence. (Vernant, as we have seen, restored the comedy to its original way up.)

A plain man's objection to this thesis is that, as a general theory of Greek sacrifice, it is counterintuitive. If one reads the several stately descriptions of sacrifices in Homer, they seem to constitute almost the essence of steady, ordered human existence. To most ears, they do not speak of murderous violence with difficulty restrained and always threatening to burst out catastrophically. "They spent their days sacrificing and having a good time," says Herodotus of certain individuals in a characteristic phrase; Lysistrata reproaches the Greek states for fighting each other, they who also sacrifice together like kin.[140] Burkert would counter that "having a good time" began

---

138. See n. 3 above. "The meaning of this ritual murder—for that is what sacrifice is—is to appropriate for oneself the mystical strength of the victim's life in order to be able to apply this to one's own goals": Bickerman, "Cutting a Covenant," 8.

139. Above all in Burkert, *Homo Necans* (the German edition of 1997 contains an important retrospect): cf. *Violent Origins* (n. 13 above). Among anthropologists, M. Bloch, *Prey into Hunter* (Cambridge, 1992), chap. 3 (but cf. pp. 6–7), and Gibson, *Sacrifice and Sharing,* 156, both make something of the aggression/violence of sacrifice.

140. Hdt. 8.99.1; Ar. *Lys.* 1128–34; cf. S. Peirce, *ClAnt* 12 (1993): 219–66 and the texts assembled by Casabona, *Vocabulaire des sacrifices,* 131–33.

after the killing had been accomplished: it was the preceding tension that made the subsequent pleasure of meat eating so pleasurable, the release of aggression that made relaxed sociability possible. But was there in fact such tension and such a release? It does not emerge from the combined evidence of literary texts, art, and ritual rules that the act of killing was the central moment in the ritual. The only emphasis placed on it was a cry (of excitement, not distress) raised by such women as were present (an evasive formula, since it is unclear how regular the presence of women was); in the one precise reference,[141] they shouted when the animal was struck down with an ax, thus before the throat was cut and blood shed.

Treatment of the victim's blood was, it is true, almost always important; it was normally used to "bloody the altar" by sprinkling. This special treatment linked the victim's death to the gods, but did not underline the very act of killing. The knife entering or even held close to the flesh of an animal is, as was noted above,[142] seldom portrayed in art (the treatment of the human victims of myth, victims indeed, is significantly different); were it never shown, one might postulate a taboo reinforcing the "comedy of innocence," but occasional depiction argues mere indifference. Ritual rules show the main function of the officiant at a sacrifice to have lain in one of two acts: either "beginning the rite," probably by cutting some hair from the victim's brow to place in the altar fire,[143] or, more commonly, the deposition on the altar of the portions of the animal that were burned for the god.[144] Both seem to indicate that what was central was the giving of the animal to the deity. This

---

141. Hom. *Od.* 3.450–52, where the women in question are the kin of the sacrificer. The Ἑλληνικὸν νόμισμα θυστάδος βοῆς is still known and associated with women in the fifth century (Aesch. *Sept.* 269; *Ag.* 595; Hdt. 4.189.3; cf. Xen. *Anab.* 4.3.19: Nilsson's view, *Geschichte* 150, that flute music replaced it ignores this evidence), but the number of women who will have been available at public sacrifices to perform it (priestess, *kanēphoros, aulētris?*) is often uncertain; *LSA* 12.25–26 (Pergamum, second century BC) attests an ὀλολύκτρια. Cf. Gebauer, *Pompe und Thysia,* 482–86. On the positive character of the *ololygē,* see B. J. Collins, *GRBS* 39 (1995): 315–25; van Straten in *Cuisine et autel,* 19, who cites Hom. *Od.* 4.767, *Il.* 6.301, Xen. *Anab.* 4.3.19. The timing of the *ololugē* after a *sphagion* sacrifice could be different: n. 148 below.

142. See p. 129.

143. *LSS* 19.31, 61–62; Ma, *Antiochus III,* dossier 18.13; *SEG* 54.214.32–33; cf. Eur. *IT* 40 (with 56, 1154), where Iphigeneia says explicitly, κατάρχομαι μέν, σφάγια δ' ἄλλοισιν μέλει. Cutting the hair: Hom. *Od.* 3.446 with S. West's note ad loc.

144. B. C. Petrakos, Οἱ Ἐπιγραφὲς τοῦ Ὠρωποῦ (Athens, 1977), no. 27 (*LSCG* 69) 25–29 (along with "pray over the offering," κατεύχεσθαι τῶν ἱερῶν); Isaeus 8.16, Arrian *Anab.* 7.25.4; *Iscr. Cos* 145.10–11, 216 B 11–12 (by supplement also 3.9, 15.9, 177.14); *SEG* 55. 926.8-9, 928 A 13-14, B 14, 931. 17-18 (all from Cos); *LSS* 14.33; in *LSA* 24 A 33–34 this is the moment for the singing of the paean. Cf. van Straten, *Hierà Kalá,* 119, 170 (and on scenes showing an officiant pointing to the god's portion, ibid., 136); Gebauer, *Pompe und Thysia,* 441–43; Ekroth, "Thighs or Tails?," 132–34.

was the officiant's central duty or privilege. The question by contrast of who wielded the ax or knife was of peripheral importance. Only one sacred law (admittedly one referring to an important civic ritual on Cos) lays emphasis on the selection and obligations of the actual "slaughterer."[145] As for the comedy of innocence, the sustained recent attempts to drive it from the stage were discussed above.

These criticisms all strike Burkert's theory in its application to alimentary sacrifice. Slaughter-sacrifices and their like, on the other hand, as we have seen and as their name suggests, center on killing; and it is conspicuous that the rare artistic depictions of the knife actually piercing an animal's throat almost without exception show such *sphagia*. In Euripides' *Supplices,* the actual knife used in an oath-sacrifice is to be preserved as a guarantor of its efficacy. The iconographic type "Victory stabbing an animal" derives from the pre-battle *sphagia;* according to a persuasive interpretation it appeared on the parapet of the lovely Ionic temple of Athena Nike at the entrance to the Athenian acropolis.[146] But even in relation to the pre-battle *sphagion* the move from killing to violence can be questioned. The hypothesis speaks of the male sacrificial group unleashing its aggression against an animal victim. When at some festivals hearty young men lifted a young bull over the altar for the slaughter, this was certainly a display of domination over the animal.[147] But, as we have seen, the sacrifices with strong group participation such as these were those where the death of the animal received least emphasis. When a pre-battle slaughter-sacrifice was performed in sight of the enemy, the pipers played (in the Spartan army at least) and every man was garlanded. But they merely watched while a seer or seers performed the slaughter. The rite is an intense focus of communal attention but not of

---

145. RO 62 (*LSCG 151*) A 40–44: on the night before the sacrifice to Zeus Polieus, the priest and the heralds both choose a slaughterer and instruct him to remain sexually pure that night. The Homeric verb ἱερεύω, which is etymologically "act as a priest" but in usage "sacrifice," does not seem to me decisive counterevidence: it simply poses again for an earlier period (in this case insolubly) the question of which action of the priest constituted the essence of sacrifice. Nor does the iconographic use of the sacrificial knife to denote the priest (van Straten in *Cuisine et autel,* 19). For the θύτης as a fairly lowly functionary serving several cults, see *Syll.*[3] 589.18 with note 10 ad loc.

146. See M. H. Jameson, "The Ritual of the Athena Nike Parapet," in *Ritual, Finance, Politics,* 307–24, with the conspectus of such scenes at 320–24 (cf. *ThesCRA* 1:359–63). Almost without exception: for two other scenes that show the knife close to the throat, see the following note and van Straten, *Hierà Kalá,* 220 V147 (fig. 110), with his comments *Cuisine et autel,* 20–21. Knife: Eur. *Suppl.* 1205–9.

147. See van Straten, *Hierà Kalá,* 109–13. It is true that a black-figure amphora in Viterbo (ibid., fig. 115) shows a young man stabbing the throat of a bullock so lifted, contrary to the usual indifference to the moment of the kill. But is not the point stressed the prowess of the youths who have achieved enough elevation to permit this stabbing from below?

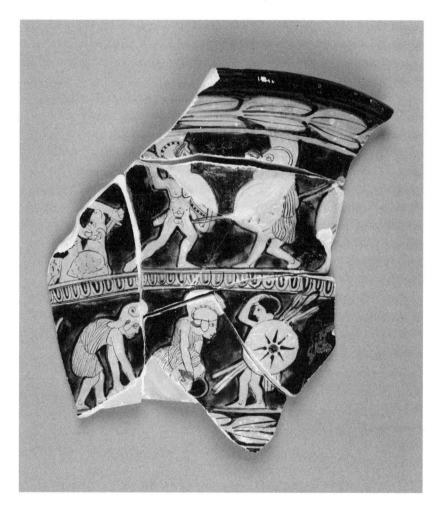

FIGURE 5. The kill explicitly depicted in a "slaughter-sacrifice" associated with conflict. Fragment of an Attic red-figure calyx krater, c. 430 BC, unknown maker (86.AE.213). The J. Paul Getty Museum, Villa Collection, Malibu, California.

communal aggression. In the one allusion to the timing of the "sacrificial cry" after a slaughter-sacrifice, it occurs not at the point of death but a little later when it is known that "the omens are good."[148]

Still, killing is unquestionably central to the slaughter-sacrifice. It is at this point that the question postponed above about the definition of sacrifice, which is also a question about the unity of a concept of sacrifice, becomes

---

148. Communal attention: Xen. *Lac.* 13.8. Sacrificial cry: Xen. *Anab.* 4.3.19, noted by van Straten, *Cuisine et autel,* 20.

important. As we have seen, the vocabulary used of alimentary sacrifice differs from that used of the other forms of ritual killing, but not without some overlapping. In just the same way, the rituals themselves diverge, but not absolutely. The element common to all the rituals is the killing of an animal; one of the most important overlaps in vocabulary lies in the verb σφάζειν, "to slaughter." (But it should be remembered that θύειν, "to sacrifice," is also applied to vegetarian offerings.) Killing receives little emphasis in alimentary sacrifice, at least in many interpretations of the ritual. But it is central to the slaughter-sacrifice. If killing is the one constant within a variety of forms of "sacrifice," it may seem necessary to assign it importance in all those forms; alimentary sacrifice will therefore need to be reinterpreted in a way that allows the kill positive religious force there too. Or should we accept that the kill is a mere necessary preliminary to alimentary sacrifice, an essential only in the rites of slaughter? This approach leaves us with "types of ritual killing" but no overarching concept of sacrifice.

The question is not easy to answer. There is no theological exegesis to guide us, there was no theological exegesis to guide them, as to what to make of these rites. Veyne teaches us that "sacrifice is widely distributed across centuries and across societies because this practice is sufficiently ambiguous for everyone to find in it their own particular satisfaction." Doubtless this ambiguity can inhere in individual forms of sacrifice as well as in the many different practices that can be brought together under the rubric "sacrifice." What satisfactions found in alimentary sacrifice ensured its popularity over so many centuries? It sanctioned and solemnized human feasting; it was also a gift to a god that the god was invited to come and enjoy along with mortals; it established closer contact with the divine, therefore, than did the other modality of gift, dedication. But did the killing that preceded it give it extra solemnity, an added potential to communicate with the divine? At least for some participants? It would be presumptuous to deny the possibility: On what basis could one do so? But this could have been only one "satisfaction" (or better, in this case, source of imaginative power) among several. The structure of the rite certainly did not allow the individual participant the sadistic sense of being one among a group converging on a victim for the kill. The dispatch of a scapegoat is a ritual of quite different type.

As for the theses of Burkert and Girard in their broadest scope, it does not seem possible to establish a relation of co-variability of any kind between animal sacrifice and human violence. One can claim neither that animal sacrifice inhibits violence against humans among societies that practice it (a "safety-valve" theory), nor that such violence diminishes when the practice is abandoned. (This second point strikes hard against theories that see a subterranean connection between sacrifice and male violence against women.)[149] The two things seem simply to follow their own, distinct trajectories.

"Raw Eating" and Other Wild Rites

Some very violent activities fall too far outside the normal run of sacrificial practices to affect the broad conclusion. But the topic cannot be finally signed off before they have been acknowledged. The "raw eating" associated in some way with Dionysus is famous, but fraught with problems. Sacrifice was often made to Dionysus as to any other god. But myth also ascribes to the female followers of Dionysus the tearing apart of animals by hand; there are also allusions to the "raw eating" of flesh. Who supposedly ate this raw flesh (in the mythical representation) is not clear, since the rite is not described in detail in any source. In Euripides' *Bacchae,* the messenger reports the capture and tearing, but not eating, of animals at some length (734–47), amid other manifestations of the women's extraordinary conduct and capacities when possessed by the god. The play elsewhere contains an allusion to "blood of a slain goat, raw-eating delight," but the surrounding context is difficult and interpreters do not agree whether the clause in question speaks of Dionysus or of his followers.[150] (A secondary complication is that on vases maenads are typically shown with the rent pieces of fawns in their hands,[151] whereas in *Bacchae* it is domestic animals that they attack.)

One view is that the raw flesh was envisaged as an offering to Dionysus, who bore more than one epithet involving the idea of the raw.[152] But the rite is never described as an offering or a sacrifice. In the most atrocious Dionysiac myth of all, the daughters of Minyas "driven mad, craved human flesh and cast lots" to determine which should offer her child for rending;

---

149. W. Beers, *Women and Sacrifice: Male Narcissism and the Psychology of Religion* (Detroit, 1992). Beers was influenced (through earlier work) by N. Jay, who in *Throughout Your Generations Forever: Sacrifice, Religion, and Paternity* (Chicago, 1992) sees sacrifice as men's way of asserting their ownership of children against the women who have actually brought them forth in blood. But sacrifice is far too multifunctional for such theories to be plausible.

150. See R. L. Fowler, "Euripides *Bacchae* 135–42," *ZPE* 158 (2006): 43–48.

151. T. H. Carpenter, *Dionysian Imagery in Fifth-Century Athens* (Oxford, 1997), 115.

152. A. Henrichs, *HSCP* 82 (1978): 150–52, with references; contrast P. Bonnechere, *Le sacrifice humain en Grèce ancienne* (Athens, 1995), 215, and Goff, *Citizen Bacchae,* 272. Epithets: ὠμάδιος, ὠμηστής.

the women of Argos too ate their children.[153] If that extreme version can be taken as a guide to what "normal" maenads (those who contented themselves with animal victims) were imagined to do, it follows that those who tore apart an animal victim also ate it raw. This would be not a sacrifice but an anti-sacrifice; for to the obvious inversions (multiple women officiants against single male priest; hands against knife; wild against tame animals; raw against cooked) would be added the fact of eating without offering. Or perhaps they both ate and offered.

So much for the mythical representation. As for reality, we know that in some Greek states (but how many?) bands of women reveled for Dionysus in the mountains in alternate winters;[154] we know too that the mythical practice of raw eating could be symbolically evoked in some way. But the character of that evocation depends on the doubtful interpretation of an enigmatic two-word phrase in an inscription of 276 BC from Miletus. It is defining the privileges of the public priestess of Dionysus, and prescribes, "It shall not be permitted for anyone to throw in an *ōmophagion,* 'a raw bite,' before the priestess throws one in on behalf of the city."[155] Interpretations of the crucial phrase "throw in an *ōmophagion*" have ranged from very drastic to very tame: at one extreme, an animal is hurled into the midst of a circle of worshippers, who then fall upon it (E. R. Dodds thought, unpersuasively, that the maenads were eating their god raw); at the other, a token piece of raw meat is placed in a sacrificial basket.[156] If the more drastic interpretations are correct, such rites must somehow have represented, for the female participants, an awesome extreme of experience. More probably the awesome extreme existed only in the imagination, and any evocation of the mythical practices in the ritual was just a gesture.

What is clear amid all this is that the raw eating (imagined or real) is of a piece with the other reversals of normality of Dionysiac cult. The eating of raw meat, whoever does it, is as bizarre as the dancing of matrons on a

153. Plut. *Quaest. Graec.* 38, 299E; Apollod. *Bibl.* 3.5.2. Ap. Rhod. *Argon.* 1.636 speaks (as do later authors) of μαινάδες ὠμοβόροι.

154. See J. N. Bremmer, "Greek Maenadism Re-Considered," *ZPE* 55 (1984): 267–86. Men may sometimes have joined them (S. Scullion, "Maenads and Men," forthcoming), but at the imaginative level it remained a distinctively female practice.

155. *LSA* 48.2. Dodds, *Greeks and the Irrational,* 281 n. 47 notes that Plut. *De def. or.* 14, 417C, speaking of "days of ill omen on which raw eatings and rendings occur," should also attest historical practice. The sacrifices to Semele and Dionysus in *LSCG* 18 A 44–51, D 33–40 are marked παραδόσιμος γυναιξί, which merely tantalizes, as does the sacrifice to Dionysus Anthius made without mention of fire in *SEG* 54.214.9–11 (cf. Parker, "Aixone," 204–6).

156. Drastic: Dodds, *Greeks and the Irrational,* 276, with a vivid modern parallel; tame: some views there rejected by Dodds, and A. J. Festugière, *ClassMed* 17 (1936): 31–34 (= *Études de religion grecque et hellenistique* [Paris, 1972], 110–13).

mountain. Whether one interprets the Dionysiac phenomenon as a whole as challenging norms or reinforcing them or simply extending somewhat the possibilities of women's existence,[157] the idea of raw meat eating and the associated violence are parts of that total phenomenon. What is at issue here is not fundamentally a modality of sacrifice; the dialectic is between the need for limits and control and the need for their absence.

Certain other extreme sacrifices are occasionally mentioned. The *non plus ultra* is the festival Laphria, celebrated annually by the people of Patrai for Artemis and mildly described by Pausanias as embodying a "local style of sacrifice" (τρόπος ἐπιχώριος θυσίας). According to Pausanias, a stockade of green logs is built around the altar, within which dry wood is piled. A magnificent procession provides a prelude; at its rear rides a virgin priestess on a chariot drawn by deer. On the next day

> great enthusiasm is shown for the festival by the city publicly and no less by individuals. For they throw onto the pyre, still alive, edible birds and sacrificial animals of all kinds, also wild boar and deer and roe; some bring wolf and bear cubs, some the full-grown animals. They also put the fruit of cultivated trees on the altar.

He goes on to tell how this great bonfire is kindled and the animals are driven back in as they try to escape the flames.[158]

With this we can compare a rite at the sanctuary of Despoina at Lycosura in Arcadia: "The Arcadians conduct a rite at which they bring victims to Despoina in great abundance. Each individual sacrifices what he has. They do not cut the throats of the victims as at other sacrifices, but each participant cuts off a chance limb from the victim." Unfortunately the ethnographer lets us down here, and does not explain what species were brought as victims nor what treatment they received after the cutting off of the limbs. He is a little vague also about a rite in Messene: "There is a megaron of the Kouretes, where they make burned offerings of every kind of animal. They begin by throwing cattle and goats into the fire and work down to birds."[159] "Every kind of animal" ought to include wild animals, but the examples are all from the familiar sacrificial species. They must have been killed before

---

157. See p. 243 below.
158. Paus. 7.18.11–13.
159. Paus. 8.37.8 (Lycosura); ibid. 4.3.9 (Messene).

being thrown on the pyre, though Pausanias is not explicit, or the birds would have escaped.

One or two further similarly extreme sacrifices are also recorded or postulated.[160] They have been taken as illustrations of one distinctive ancient modality of Greek sacrifice, that associated with a huge fire (sometimes identified as a "year-fire"); they have also been traced back, along winding paths, to the secret rituals of warrior bands.[161] But it has been pointed out of late that a ritual such as the Laphria attested at Patrais, a city that dissolved into villages in the third century and was refounded, initially as a Roman veteran colony, c. 14 BC, cannot present itself as an unproblematic witness to ancestral traditions of Greek sacrifice. All these extreme sacrifices are attested only in Pausanias or in sources of the same late date; and several were practiced by cities or organizations that demonstrably had undergone drastic historical change in the late classical or postclassical period.[162] The holocausts known from sacred calendars of the classical period are on an altogether more modest scale.

All the same, the argument from silence is scarcely infallible; we can say confidently that extreme sacrifices of this type were exceptional in the classical period (as indeed later), not that they never occurred. Hypothetical rites of the classical period, however, elude inspection; all we can analyze are the practices attested much later. The most fully described is the Laphria, and Pausanias's account well brings out its abnormality. In the classical holocaust the victim was a domestic animal that was killed and, at least in some cases, cut up before being put on the fire. Here wild and domestic animals alike are thrown onto the flames alive. There is none of the usual fussiness about the selection of victims, nor does there seem to be an officiant: everyone hurls on what they have brought. It is all about totality and the abolition of limits: everyone participates (but does this include women?), all species are involved, there is no selection, and the destruction too is total. Any invocations that may have accompanied the rites go unmentioned. In Pausanias's account it is

---

160. A festival of Isis at Tithorea (Paus. 10.32.14–17); the "Laphria" at Hyampolis, questionably reconstructed from an aition; the Daidala (Paus. 9.3.7–8; cf. p. 221); a festival on Mt. Oeta associated with the death of Heracles: see Nilsson, *Geschichte,* 130–32; Graf, *Nordionische Kulte,* 411–12, 416–17.

161. So respectively Nilsson and Graf, cited in previous note.

162. See V. Pirenne-Delforge, "Ritual Dynamics in Pausanias: The Laphria," in *Ritual and Communication,* 111–29; Pirenne-Delforge, *Pausanias,* 218–29. Messene was founded in 371; the Daidala (p. 221 below) was a restructured ritual; a festival of Isis cannot be ancient. Pirenne-Delforge explains the Laphria as "an Augustan reconstruction... perfectly in accordance with the violent Roman shows and the taste for presumed antiquity," *Ritual and Communication,* 126.

the killing that creates the communication. Mutatis mutandis, similar observations could be made about the other extreme rites that he describes.[163]

This, it seems, is a perfect expression of sacrifice as theorized by Burkert
and Girard, sacrifice as pure and comprehensive violence. The urgent next
question concerns the social context in which raw killing was credited with
such power. The Laphria was celebrated, Pausanias told us, "with great enthusiasm... by the city publicly and no less by individuals"; the city that
celebrated it, Patrai, was one put together from disparate elements, Greek
and Roman. A festival that also concluded with a bonfire holocaust, the
Great Daidala, was a Pamboeotian celebration of regional unity. These instances point, it has been suggested, to "the strong federal impact of this form
of spectacular and participatory ceremony." A grim device for reinforcing
group and federal solidarity, if so![164] The link between collective violence and
group formation rests, however, on too few cases to be wholly secure. What
is certain is that such rites were exceptional.

Endnote: Blood Sacrifice for the Dead

If we set aside as historically problematic the luxuriant slaughter (sheep, oxen,
horses, dogs, and prisoners of war) conducted by Achilles in Homer on Patroclus's pyre,[165] the best evidence relates to what is called a *prosphagion*. A
fifth-century inscription from Ioulis on Ceos regulating funerary practices
says that a "*prosphagion* should be employed in accord with tradition," but a
passage in Ps.-Plato that speaks of a *prosphagion* being performed "before
the carrying out" (a useful detail) consigns the practice to "former times."[166]

---

163. But Pirenne-Delforge, *Ritual and Communication*, 123–24, doubts whether the burning of
live animals should be generalized from the Laphria; she notes that Paus. 9.3.8 on victims at the
Daidala stuffed with wine and incense implies butchery and extraction of the entrails.

164. So Pirenne-Delforge, *Pausanias*, 229. But the bonfire holocaust at the Pamboeotian Great
Daidala may have been borrowed from the Plataian Lesser Daidala, which was not a federal festival
(see p. 222 below).

165. *Il.* 23.166–76. For archaeological parallels suggesting some basis in eighth-century reality,
see *ThesCRA* 1:108–9; cf. Lane Fox, *Travelling Heroes*, 55–58. The sheep and oxen provided fat that
Achilles wrapped around Patroclus's body; the role of the other victims is not explained, but one can
guess that the prisoners of war were killed in revenge, the dogs and horses to allow Patroclus to be
accompanied by what he loved in life.

166. *LSCG* 97 A 12; [Pl.] *Min.* 315C. L. Robert, *Études anatoliennes* (Paris, 1937), 306–8, however, plausibly reads προσφα[γ]ιάζοντες in a funerary context in an inscription from Amorium,
"basse époque impériale." The sacrifices to gods performed at or after the conclusion of mourning
(e.g., Plut. *Lyc.* 27.4; Plut. *Quaest Graec.* 24, 296F–297A; D. D. Hughes in *Greek Sacrificial Ritual*,
75–83) are different.

Several passages in tragedy also refer to it; in Euripides' Alcestis, Heracles ghoulishly supposes that he will be able to find Death "near [Alcestis's tomb], drinking the *prosphagmata*."[167] Possibly we can reconcile the evidence about where and when it took place by supposing that it happened at the grave but before the corpse had been brought thither. What became of the animal's body once its blood had been poured out is unclear; Ps.-Plato shows that the custom went out of use by the fourth century, but the archaeological evidence of animal bones at graves is slight even before that. A *prosphagion* is clearly an offering made to the dead person or possibly the underworld powers more generally (is Death, in Heracles' imagining, drinking it by right, or by usurpation?).[168] Beyond that general formulation, we do not know how a *prosphagion* worked, what rituals accompanied it, and what words of invocation.[169] At the commemorative rituals performed for the dead in subsequent years, they were urged to "send up good things," that is to say, like the gods they were urged to make a return for the gifts brought to them;[170] but the offerings burned, left, or (above all) poured for them on these occasions were apparently bloodless as a rule.

---

167. Eur. *Alc.* 845; cf., e.g., Eur. *Hel.* 1255, which stresses its preliminary quality, Eur. *Hec.* 41, where the location is clearly the tomb itself. Solon's ban on the funerary sacrifice of an ox (smaller victims were therefore still permitted) probably refers to the *prosphagion* rather than to subsequent commemorative rites (Plut. *Sol.* 21.5).

168. Ekroth, *Sacrificial Rituals,* 229–30 argues that it was addressed to the dead person rather than to a god; the evidence from tragedy confirms this view, insofar as a specific addressee was envisaged; the possibility that it was addressed more generally to the dead or to underworld powers, but certainly not the gods, is raised by Eur. *Hel.* 1255 (plans for the fictitious sea burial of Menelaus) προσφάζεται μὲν αἷμα πρῶτα νερτέροις; but ibid. 1564, the same sacrifice is σφάγια τῶι τεθνηκότι.

169. Unless we treat the killing of a human victim by Neoptolemus for his father Achilles in Eur. *Hec.* 521–82 as a model, which would be rash despite the application of *prosphagma* to it in 41 (for other allusions to the rite, see 126, 260–61, 391–93).

170. Ar. fr. 504.14 with Kassel/Austin's note. Bloodless: Ekroth, *Sacrificial Rituals,* 278; Parker, *Polytheism,* 29. On the content of libations to the dead, see Hom. *Od.* 10.518–20, Aesch. *Pers.* 611–17, Eur. *IT* 159–65; *Or.* 115; *LSCG* 97 A 8–10; Lucian *Luct.* 19.

❧ CHAPTER 6

The Experience of Festivals

A speaker in one of Plutarch's dialogues remarks at one point that "during a long stay in Crete I got to know of a strange festival they performed, at which they display an image of a headless man and explain that this was Molos the father of Meriones, and that after raping a young woman he was discovered headless."[1] Plutarch's puzzlement may be shared by us today in relation not just to the Cretan festival of the headless man but a great number of the details that are recorded about other ancient rituals. Much here appears bizarre, fragmentary, inconsequential. One reason is the character of two main sources, Plutarch's own *Greek Questions* and Callimachus's *Aitia,* which approach the Greek festivals in the spirit of Trivial Pursuits: it is the piquant and puzzling that constitutes a Question in Plutarch's terms, or that provides a starting point for Callimachus's witty and whimsical explanations.

Only rarely are other sources any more helpful. The very few accounts of ancient festivals that extend to more than a sentence or so were given for special purposes: Plutarch in a fragment of a lost work was concerned to allegorize the Boeotian festival Daidala, the source of two anonymous scholia on Lucian that discuss a cluster of Attic festivals had similar aims, and Theophrastus offered

---

1. *De def. or.* 14, 417E.

an account of the Attic Bouphonia as evidence that the ancients had shared his own repugnance for the sacrifice of living beings.[2] Lost books with titles such as "On the Sacrifices at Sparta" tantalize us, but it is likely (one good fragment of Polycrates on the Spartan Hyacinthia notwithstanding) that they concentrated on particularities and peculiarities and provided at best cursory summaries of what happened day by day. The one thing that made ritual worth describing in detail was extravagance: the account of Ptolemy's sumptuous procession for Dionysus covers many admiring pages in Athenaeus.[3] As for inscriptions, the norm there too is that the traditional procedures for the conduct of a festival are taken for granted. The few exceptions where extensive ritual detail is provided require special explanation.

The sources that ideally we would need never existed, therefore. To take another illustration, the Samian festival of Tonaia honoring Hera is one about which a certain amount is known.[4] The ancient image of Hera was taken to the beach, purified, and wrapped in withy branches; cakes were then set before it. Modern heortologists duly set to work comparing and contrasting in an effort to extract the meanings these acts may have had for those who conducted them. But it is again Athenaeus's interest in luxury that has preserved a fragment of an old epic poem by Asios that sets the Tonaia in a different perspective:

> And they [masculine] used to go down, once they had fine-combed
> their tresses,
> to the precinct of Hera, wrapped in fine robes;
> they swept the surface of the broad earth with their snowy tunics.
> There were golden clusters like grasshoppers on them,
> and their hair tossed in the wind, bound in gold,
> and there were elaborate bracelets on their arms.[5]

What mattered most about the Tonaia? Was it the ritual with the ancient image and the withy branches, or the opportunity it provided to

---

2. Plut. fr. 157.6–7 Sandbach = *FGrH* 388 F 1; Σ Lucian pp. 275.23–276.28 and 279.24–281.3 Rabe (Parker, *Polytheism,* 272, with references); Theophr. ap. Porph. *Abst.* 2.28.4–31.1 (Parker, *Polytheism,* 187–88).

3. 5, 196A–203B, quoting Callixenus of Rhodes (*FGrH* 627 F 2); so too on Antiochus Epiphanes' games at Daphne, Ath. 5, 194C–195F (= Polybius 30.25). Lost books: see A. Tresp, *Die Fragmente der griechischen Kultschriftsteller* (Giessen, 1914). Polycrates: p. 189 below.

4. Nilsson, *Griechische Feste,* 46–49.

5. Asios fr. 13 Davies ap. Ath. 12, 525F. Athenaeus's source Douris (*FGrH* 76 F 60) took the reference to be specifically to the Tonaia. On special festival clothes, see Xen. *Oec.* 9.6, Chaniotis, "Sich selbst feiern?" 148 n. 9.

the luxurious youth of the island to swagger in their pride? Both things mattered, no doubt; and an adequate ethnographic account of the festival would take trouble to do justice to both aspects.[6] "Thick description" in Geertz's term is what is needed; but the descriptions we can provide tend to be very thin indeed.

The ritual with the image and the withy branches was one of the things done at the Tonaia. But there will have been many others; and it is seldom guaranteed that the scraps of information that we have relate to activities that were perceived as central. Festivals lasting any number of days up to ten are often mentioned; a decree published in 2003 even attests a "sixteenth day" of the panēgyris for Athena Ilias in the Troad (evidently a blend of fair and festival such as often occurred).[7] Games played at festivals are occasionally attested,[8] and there will have been many more such than have been preserved in our sources. Ritual roles might be assigned on the basis of playful competitions; at Elis, for instance, a male beauty contest was held, with as first prize the right to carry Athena's armor, as second to lead the sacrificial cow, as third to place certain offerings on the altar.[9] There is no need to seek an origin in forgotten beliefs for unusual forms such as the "amphora race" on

---

6. One must remember too that "what might seem a mere group of worshippers to the modern researcher was in fact a polymorphous assemblage consisting of people having different needs and reasons to participate in a festival": M.-Z. Petropoulou, *Animal Sacrifice in Ancient Greek Religion, Judaism and Christianity, 100 BC to AD 200* (Oxford, 2008), 101.

7. Demeter in Sicily, probably at Syracuse, ten days (Diod. Sic. 5.4.7); Karneia at Sparta, nine days (Demetrius of Scepsis ap. Ath. 4, 141F); Demeter Mysia near Pellene, seven days (Paus. 7.27.9). Athena Ilias: *SEG* 53.1373.6; for long duration of later festivals, see Wörrle, *Stadt und Fest,* 245–48. Cf. C. Chandezon, "Foires et panégyries dans le monde grec classique et hellénistique," *REG* 113 (2000): 70–100 [+], who sees rural festival fairs as playing "un rôle d'irrigation économique des campagnes grecques." An abundance of goods for sale is the virtue of a market or *panēgyris*, not a polis, says Dem. 10.50. Tax exemptions at festival fairs are first attested in RO 73.32–35 (Artemisia at Eretria). Some revealing texts: Livy 33.32.1 (on the Isthmian games); Strabo 10.5.4, 486 on a Delian festival: ἥ τε πανήγυρις ἐμπορικόν τι πρᾶγμα ἐστι; Paus. 10.32.15–16 (a festival fair briefly described).

8. Karystios ap. Ath. 14, 639C: slaves play knucklebones with citizens on one day of a "many-day" festival in Troizen; for swinging and jumping on wineskins at certain Attic festivals, see Parker, *Polytheism,* 184; for telling of riddles at the Chaironeian Agrionia, Plut. *Quaest. conv.* 8.1.1, 717a.

9. Ath. 13, 565F, cf. 13, 609F–610A (Nilsson, *Griechische Feste,* 94). At Tanagra, the "ephebe judged fairest" carried a lamb around the walls on his shoulders at the festival of Hermes (Paus. 9.22.1). Female festival beauty contests are also attested: Lesbos, for Hera: Alcaeus fr. 130 b 17–20 in the ed. of E. M. Voigt (*Sappho et Alcaeus* [Amsterdam, 1971]; fr. 130.32–35 Lobel-Page), with Voigt's note ad loc.; Tenedos, unknown deity: Theophr. fr. 564 Fort. ap. Ath. 13, 610A; Basilis in Arcadia, for Demeter Eleusinia: Nikias *FGrH* 318 F 1 ap. Ath. 13, 609E–F (cf. Paus. 8.29.5); Anthelos, for Demeter Pylaia?: so L. Preller and C. Robert, *Griechische Mythologie,* 4th ed. (Berlin, 1894), 1:780 n. 1, from Hesych. π 4342 πυλαιΐδεες· αἱ ἐν κάλλει κρινόμεναι τῶν γυναικῶν καὶ νικῶσαι. That the winners in such contests acquired privileged ritual roles is not attested, though possible.

Aegina (the mythological model for which both Callimachus and Apollonius record): variety was the spice of festival life.[10]

An enormous amount of private sacrificing, entertaining, and other activities took place in the interstices of the more public program; Pindaric scholars nowadays believe that some Pindaric epinicia were performed during
public festivals; later they might host oratorical displays, lectures.[11] They were
a magnet that attracted to themselves every kind of social and holiday activity; also, the major festivals, tourists in large numbers. Martin Nilsson's still
unreplaced repertory was entitled (translated) "Greek Festivals of Religious
Meaning":[12] "of religious meaning" set aside the innumerable athletic and
musical competitions associated with or actually constituting festivals. That
setting aside is anachronistic and misleading: such competitions will play
little part in what follows, but let their centrality within what festival meant
to the Greeks be underlined at the outset. The counterpart to extension in
time is proliferation of participants. The more we hear about a particular
festival, the more social groups we tend to find involved. Sometimes different
roles for different groups, such as men and women,[13] married women and
maidens, are set in an expressive counterpoint; sometimes it is perhaps simply
that "everyone can play" (in different ways). "All-nighters" for women, for
instance, punctuate the daytime activities dominated by men at festivals in
both Sparta[14] and Athens.

Another cautionary tale: Plutarch reports that, "imitating" an incident
that occurred during the return of the Achaeans from Troy, the Aeginetans "conduct a sacrifice for Poseidon called *Thiasoi,* at which they dine
by themselves in silence for sixteen days, and no slave is present. Then they
conduct Aphrodisia and end the festival. From this they are called Lone-
Eaters (*Monophagoi*)." The extended austerity of that unsocial fortnight, only

10. Callim. *Ia* VIII (fr. 198 Pfeiffer); Ap. Rhod. *Argon.* 4.1765–72. No need: *pace* Nilsson,
Griechische Feste, 172–73. "Außerdem aber hatte die Göttervehrung alle Lebensfreude in den Dienst
ihrer Feste genommen": Burckhardt, *Kulturgeschichte,* 454 (cf. 462, 465).

11. Private sacrificing: see S. Georgoudi, *Ktema* 23 (1998): 325–34; Parker, *Polytheism,* 44, 163
n. 30, 268 n. 66; even at Sparta, Xen. *Mem.* 1.2.61 and p. 189 below (Hyacinthia). Epinicia: for a
cautious view see C. Carey in *Pindar's Poetry,* 200–202. Lectures: Chaniotis, "Sich selbst feiern?" 162;
Wörrle, *Stadt und Fest,* 249–50.

12. M. P. Nilsson, *Griechische Feste von religiöser Bedeutung* (Leipzig, 1906). Against the claim of
F. Bömer that a procession is "keine Kulthandlung," see A. Kavoulaki, "The Ritual Performance of
a *Pompê,*" in Δώρημα: *A Tribute to the A. G. Leventis Foundation on the Occasion of Its 20th Anniversary*
(Nicosia, 2000), 145–58, at 154.

13. See, e.g., Sourvinou-Inwood, *Hylas,* 76–77; Parker, *Polytheism,* 166–67; Paus. 2.11.3.

14. At the Hyacinthia: Eur. *Hel.* 1469–70; and the Karneia? (Eur. *Alc.* 445–51). At Athens: Parker,
Polytheism, 166. On the ideal of universal participation in Hellenistic festivals, Chaniotis, "Sich selbst
feiern?" 157. All ages involved: see, e.g., Paus. 2.35.5–7, on the Chthonia at Hermione.

briefly relieved by the concluding Aphrodisia, is unique, and unexplained. It is with amazement then that one learns from a different source that the Cyrenaean philosopher Aristippus dallied disgracefully with the courtesan Phryne for two months each year at the Poseidonia on Aegina (two months that included the Poseidonia, we should probably interpret: the festival can scarcely have lasted so long), and that once on this occasion she stripped and entered the sea "in sight of all the Panhellenes."[15] To attract this louche celebrity couple and "all the Panhellenes," there must have been more to the Poseidonia than quiet *en famille* dining by the Aeginetans without their servants.

The fact needs to be faced squarely: we know and will always know much less that is really useful about Greek festivals than about almost any other aspect of Greek religion. The fragments available to us were inadequate even in terms of an older tradition of religious history that thought that festivals had clearly definable purposes and meanings; they are much less adequate still if we understand them in the modern way not as a means to an end, but as a special form of social transaction and interaction, or as a performance.[16] From a fragment of a technological device one can hope to infer the function of the whole; but to catch the mood and nuances of, say, the abuse exchanged between men and women at various festivals one would need a transcript and video recording.

Perhaps then, to signal a necessary break with a long tradition, this chapter ought to end at this point, on its fifth page... But the festivals constrained the Greeks—it was supposedly the need to celebrate the Karneia that prevented the Spartans from marching out in full force to defend Thermopylae, and there are many similar incidents[17]—and they constrain us; they were too central a part of Greek religious experience to be neglected. One possibility is to stick to the small cluster of festivals for which enough snippets of information converge to form something of a detailed picture. But that entails (for the classical period) confining the account to the much-studied festivals of Athens. As a second-best approach to achieving a larger view, one can hope to sketch some broad outlines, trace common characteristics, identify possibilities. What is essential is not to mistake the outline for a full picture; nor to take festivals that share certain common characteristics as belonging to

---

15. Plut. *Quaest. Graec.* 44, 301 D–F; Ath. 13, 588E, 590F (which mentions similar exhibitionism by Phryne at another festival, the Attic Eleusinia).

16. Kowalzig, *Singing,* chap. 1, is a very useful introduction to recent thought from a Hellenist's perspective.

17. Hdt. 7.206.1; cf., e.g., Thuc. 8.91.1 and Parker, *Miasma,* 154 [+]. There were exceptions: C. Habicht, "Versäumter Götterdienst," *Historia* 55 (2006): 153–66.

a fixed type. Etiquetting and pigeonholing ossify a much more flexible and variable reality. Many festivals, for instance, disturb social norms in various ways, but it is a mistake to treat "festival of reversal" as an ideal type; reversal is just one among the many differing interwoven strands that make up the specificity of each festival.

A first approach might be through generalizations of the Greeks themselves about festivals, or metaphorical applications of the idea of festival. The dominant image that emerges is that they are a context of pleasure and well-being. For Pericles in Thucydides they are "relaxations from labor"; the Cynic tradition urged that to a good man "every day was a festival," since every day brings to the tranquil mind that "pleasure and refreshment" that unphilosophical man seeks from festivals;[18] and, in what is perhaps the most eloquent account of the comforts of religion that survives from the ancient world, Plutarch explains how the Epicureans by their godlessness deprive themselves of pleasures that are otherwise available to all mankind, even the humblest and most oppressed: "For no way of passing time delights us more than that in shrines, nor any occasions more than festivities, nor deeds or sights more than those we see or do ourselves in relation to the gods, conducting rites or dancing or attending sacrifices or ceremonies."[19] Strabo speaks of "festival relaxation," ἄνεσις ἑορταστική. Piety, pleasure, splendor, and utility for war are the criteria against which festivals are to be measured according to the fourth-century *Rhetoric for Alexander*. The worst one can hold against them—a few exceptional dismal occasions aside—is that they can be noisy and hectic.[20]

They are also a time of peace, when execution and violent legal procedures are suspended. In the Hellenistic period we hear of "truces" involving holidays for children and slaves and in some cases the release of prisoners from chains. The bonds of social division are loosened a little at these times: the delight taken in them by slaves is especially emphasized by Plutarch. Implicit

---

18. Thuc. 2.38.1 (cf. Pl. *Leg.* 653C–D). Cynic tradition: Plut. *De tranq. anim.* 20, 477C–F; cf. ibid. 4, 466E Κράτης δὲ πήραν ἔχων καὶ τριβώνιον παίζων καὶ γελῶν ὥσπερ ἐν ἑορτῇ τῷ βίῳ διετέλεσε. See in general J. D. Mikalson, "The Heorte of Heortology," *GRBS* 23 (1982): 213–21, and the passages quoted by Halliwell, *Greek Laughter*, 157 n. 5, 203 n. 138.

19. Plut. *Non posse* 21, 1101E; the whole chapter 21 is very notable. Cf. Plut. *De superst.* 9, 169D; Strabo 10.3.9, 467.

20. Strabo 10.3.9, 467; Arist. [*Rh. Al.*] 1423a 29–1424a 6. Noisy: Men. fr. 871 K/A (416 Koerte). Dismal: Plut. *De def. or.* 14, 417C ἑορτὰς δὲ καὶ θυσίας, ὥσπερ ἡμέρας ἀποφράδας καὶ σκυθρωπάς, ἐν αἷς ὠμοφαγίαι καὶ διασπασμοὶ νηστεῖαί τε καὶ κοπετοὶ πολλαχοῦ δὲ πάλιν αἰσχρολογίαι πρὸς ἱεροῖς 'μανίαι τ' ἀλαλαί τ' ὀρινομένων ῥιψαύχενι σὺν κλόνῳ' (Pind. *Dith.* 2.10–14 Snell/Maehler), θεῶν μὲν οὐδενὶ δαιμόνων δὲ φαύλων ἀποτροπῆς ἕνεκα φήσαιμ' ἂν τελεῖσθαι μειλίχια καὶ παραμύθια. His *De Is. et Os.* contains various examples.

in most of the references to the pleasure of festivals are the pleasures of eating and drinking: they were the occasion both for meat eating from sacrifices and also for preparation and consumption of the special festival foods that were as characteristic as the Thanksgiving turkey. It hardly needs to be said that drunkenness, even if especially characteristic of Dionysiac festivals, was not confined to them.[21]

A limited number of special categories within the broad class of festivals were recognized by the Greeks. There were mysteries; there were *orgia*, rites marked by excited dancing and loud music; there were "women's festivals." *Thalysia* designated the type of offerings brought after the harvest, a typical occasion for festivals according to Aristotle. A section in Athenaeus assembles instances of festivals at which masters waited on slaves or the like. Festivals involving lamentation are mentioned as exceptions to the general tone of good cheer, and there was an awareness that some festivals enjoined striking exceptions to the general religious rule of "fair speech." "Theoxeny," god hosting, was primarily a ritual form found in the cult of the Dioscuri, but was applied to other gods too. We will meet below the rather vague notions of advent and presence. But these concepts put together form only an outline sketch, with large blank spaces, of the Greek festival landscape.[22]

Moderns were keen, until recently, to explain the purposes for which festivals were performed. That was not in the main the Greek way. Post-harvest festivals could be seen as expressions of thanks for goods received. But more commonly festivals were seen in relation to much more distant past events, whether as expiation for offenses or as imitations (or remind-ers or commemorations or simple repetitions) of noteworthy occurrences.[23] The need for such unending commemoration was explained, if at all, by stories of divine anger when it did not occur; and in a general way the point of performing festivals was simply to keep the gods contented. We could perhaps identify more specific aspirations linked to particular festivals if we

---

21. Truces, etc.: see Chaniotis, "Sich selbst feiern?" 148 nn. 7–8; for release of prisoners, cf. Ath. 14, 640A (Thessalian Peloria). Slaves' enjoyment: Plut. *Non posse* 16, 1098B; 21, 1101F–1102A. Fes-tival food: Parker, *Polytheism,* 164–65, 184–86. For the link between abundant eating and "hymning the gods," see Plato's "city of pigs," *Resp.* 372A–D. Drunkenness: Dionysiac, e.g., Ar. *Ran.* 217–19, Pl. *Leg.* 637A–B; at a festival of Artemis, Polyb. 8.37.2.

22. On *orgia* see Strabo 10.3.7–18, 466–71. In 10.3.9 he distinguishes rites according to whether they include *enthousiasmos* or not, are accompanied by music or not, and are open or "mystical." Women's festivals: Ar. *Thesm.* 834–35; *IG* 2².1177 (*LSCG* 36) 8–12. Thalysia: Theoc. *Id.* 7.3 with A.S.F. Gow's note ad loc.; Arist. *Eth. Nic.* 1160a 25–28. Masters and slaves: Ath. 14, 639B–640A. Lamentations: above, n. 20 (cf. nn. 59–60). Rude speech: Halliwell, *Greek Laughter,* 159–60 and pp. 206–9 below. Theoxeny: p. 142. I exclude *teletai,* initiations, which are not exactly festivals.

23. Parker, *Miasma,* 272–75 (past offenses; cf. Plut. *Thes.* 18.2, for a continuing rite spoken of as a "propitiation"); Parker, *Polytheism,* 378 n. 32 (imitations, etc.).

could listen to the prayers that they certainly included. Callimachus's *Hymn to Demeter,* for instance, ends with a prayer for civic harmony, agricultural abundance (flourishing livestock as well as rich harvests), and peace ("that he who plowed may also reap"); earlier the women have uttered various "like to like" predictions that resemble prayers:

> Just as the four white-haired horses draw the basket, so the great goddess, the wide-ruler, will come bringing us a white spring, a white summer and winter and autumn, and will protect us till another year; as we go through the city without sandals and headbands, so shall we have feet and heads all unharmed forever; as the basket bearers carry winnowing baskets full of gold, so shall we get gold in abundance. (120–27)

On that evidence it sounds as if almost any festival could be exploited opportunistically in search of almost every blessing. The emphasis might perhaps lie on the specific competences of the god in question (prosperity with Demeter, flourishing of the young men with Apollo, safety of the city with Athena)[24], but it is not clear how a prayer to Demeter at one of her festivals would differ from one at another.

To say that festivals (in the main) lacked explicit purposes does not mean that all Greek ritual action did. The clearest countercases are rites performed in response to particular crises, and annually recurrent rites that reproduced their form. Greeks responded to drought and plague and extreme weather by ritual actions that had the clear intent of ending the affliction. Scapegoats were (supposedly) driven out in crises; ad hoc supplications for rain and the like are attested. The annual expulsion of scapegoats at the Thargelia in several Ionian cities continued to be understood as a way of "purifying the city"; and certain seasonally related annual rites were also assigned clear purposes.[25] The Hellenistic travel writer Herakleides writes that:

> On the top of the mountain [Pelion] there is a cave called Cheironion and a shrine of Zeus Akraios [Osann: Aktaios mss.], to which at the rising of the Dog Star in the intensest heat there go up conspicuous citizens in the prime of life chosen by [ὑπό Buttmann: ἐπί mss.] the

---

24. Cf. Callim. *Hymn* 2.12–15; *Hymn* 5.142. The prayer addressed to Artemis in *LSA* 33.45–48 (for health and wealth) could have been addressed to any deity.

25. On scapegoats see p. 216 below. On crisis rites see, e.g., pp. 3–4, 74 on weather rites; *LSS* 103, Rhodes, sacrifice to be made to Zeus of Rain "when necessary"; RO 97 (*LSS* 115) A 4–7, Cyrene, sacrifice to be made to avert "disease or [] or death."

priest, wearing new triple-thickness fleeces. Such is the cold on the mountain.[26]

With this have often been compared the reports of sacrifices performed by the *genos* of priests of Zeus Aristaios Ikmaios on Keos to "make gentle the rising Maira [Dog Star]" and bring on the cooling Etesian winds."[27] A scholion even reports that "the Keans" (perhaps rather just the relevant *genos*) "each year watched for the rising of the Dog *in arms* and sacrificed to it," in a kind of Star War.[28] The rites in question are routinizations of crisis rites, and retain at least apparently the goal-directedness of these. But one might wonder whether they are properly termed "festivals." The expulsion of a scapegoat was never the whole content of a festival; the Thargelia remained purposeless, even if one element within it had a clear aim. We do not know whether the rites on Mount Pelion and on Keos stood on their own or formed part of more-extended festivals. In the former case, they are perhaps to be classified with many other rites performed by a restricted group for the general welfare[29] rather than as festivals (with large general involvement). In the latter, the simple purpose of controlling the weather will no longer explain the whole. It is important that, as was noted earlier, festivals were magnets that drew everything toward them. There is no reason to suppose that all the activities at a festival narrowed in to a single point of meaning.

Festival Plots: The God Arrives

The attempt to approach the festivals through ancient concepts, categories, and statements takes us only a short way, therefore. I start again. A broad distinction that might be useful is that between things imagined, the role of the god in the festival, and things done, the actions of the celebrants. At the level of things imagined, some festivals have a plot: an event concerning gods is enacted or reenacted. Perhaps the commonest such plot was that of the god's "advent" to the city;[30] "advent" here is a useful cover term for phenomena

26. F. Pfister, *Die Reisebilder des Herakleides* (Vienna, 1951), 2:8 (same numeration in the edition of A. Arenz [Munich, 2006]).

27. Callim. *Aet.* fr. 75.32–37; Ap. Rhod. *Argon.* 2.516–28; for more sources see R. Pfeiffer's note on Callim. loc. cit., Nilsson, *Griechische Feste,* 6–8.

28. Σ Ap. Rhod. *Argon.* 2.498–527 (w).

29. See Jameson, "The Spectacular and the Obscure."

30. The following discussion of advent is largely based on W. Burkert, "Katagōgia-Anagōgia and the Goddess of Knossos," in *Early Greek Cult Practice,* 81–87, and Sourvinou-Inwood, *Hylas,* 151–62;

described in Greek by a variety of related words such as "visit" (ἐπιδημία—the same term as used for the visitation of a disease!), "bringing in" (κατ-αγωγή), "reception" (ὑποδοχή),[31] "appearance of gods" (θεοφάνια). There is a certain difficulty in circumscribing the type, in that the invocation to gods to "come" was a standard element in hymns, and votive reliefs regularly show the deity standing behind the altar to receive the offering brought in a sacrificial procession; every sacrifice, therefore, was ideally the occasion of an advent. Plutarch indeed treats a sense of the god's presence as the central element that makes any festival magical.[32] But we can accept the formulation that advent festivals are those that lay special emphasis on the idea of coming or presence by ritual enactment of some kind.[33]

One striking enactment of the idea of presence was the Athenian ritual by which the wife of the king-archon was "given as wife" to Dionysus. This probably occurred during the three-day festival Anthesteria, and it was perhaps at the same festival that a statue of Dionysus in a ship on wheels was led in procession, as a way of representing the god's arrival from the sea. The Anthesteria was also (amid much else) the festival at which the Athenians broached the new wine, and rituals relating to drinking occurred on at least two of its three days. So here the god's advent coincided with the annual new instalment of his great gift to mankind. Festivals of the "bringing in" or "sailing in" of Dionysus are attested in other places, without further details, as is a ship-cart procession; the rituals in a broad way run in parallel with the many myths that tell of Dionysus's first arrival in this or that place. The god's marriage to a living mortal at Athens, however, has no parallel,[34] and no obvious mythical original that it could be thought to have imitated. We cannot enter the god's bridal chamber, and so do not know how he consorted with his new wife (did she recline with a statue? did her husband impersonate the god?). But this was the real presence of the god enacted in the most drastic and dramatic way possible.

Dionysus was also "brought in" in statue form to attend the City Dionysia at Athens; he was then set up in the theater, perhaps after a ritual of

---

see too for Dionysus, M. Detienne, *Dionysos à ciel ouvert* (Paris, 1986: Engl. trans. by A. Goldhammer as *Dionysos at Large* [Cambridge, Mass., 1989]), chaps. 1–2.

31. Cf. Currie, *Cult of Heroes,* 182.

32. *Non posse* 21, 1102A–B. On summoning the god to join a chorus, see S. Scullion, *ClAnt* 17 (1998): 103–4 (who cites, e.g., Ar. *Eq.* 559, *Thesm.* 1137).

33. Sourvinou-Inwood, *Hylas,* 151, 157. The lyric fragment *PMG* 929 (b), which greets Dionysus after twelve months' absence, is noteworthy here (A. Henrichs, *HSCP* 82 [1978]: 146 n. 82). Note too, e.g., Paus. 6.26.1, the Eleans claim that Dionysus attends their festival Thuia (ἐπιφοιτᾶν ἐς τῶν Θυίων τὴν ἑορτήν).

34. For a skeptical Greek reaction to such unions, see Hdt. 1.182.

reception, to watch the plays. So he seems to have made at least two advents in Athens each year.[35]

In alternate years in midwinter, select groups of women from an uncertain number of Greek cities went "to the mountain," there to dance excitedly and roam, probably in a state of trance, until, in some cases, they collapsed in exhaustion.[36] They supposed that they were imitating the maenads of myth led to the mountain by Dionysus at the time of his first tumultuous arrival in the city;[37] perhaps also, the more imaginative, that the god was leading them in the present. This was, then, another kind of response to advent.

Just as Dionysus was a god who famously arrived in myth, Kore was one who came and went. Rituals of "the fetching of Kore" or the like may have had as their plot her seasonal returns, even if they do not in the form known to us refer to a "coming up" from the underworld. At the Koragia ("Kore fetching") at Mantinea a statue of Kore was, as it seems, removed from the temple, "received/entertained" by the priestess, and in due course brought back in procession; at some point it also received a new robe. At a festival of uncertain name in Lakonia, a statue of Kore was "brought up" from Helos by the sea to the Eleusinion just south of Sparta; the physical "bringing up" from the sea probably stood symbolically for Kore's mythological coming up from the underworld. Of the "bringing of Kore" in Sicily we know for sure only that it happened "when the fruit of the grain became ripe" (unfortunately we lack a date for the other two festivals), but it may be identical with a ritual at which sacrifices were made into the spring that emerged when Pluto split the earth to draw Kore down.[38] The sources fail to bring us closer than this, unfortunately, to the lived experience of any of these festivals. Nor can we do much with two rituals associated by ancient sources with the myth that Dionysus fetched up his mother, Semele, from the underworld: a "bringing up of Semele" at Delphi, and a summoning of Dionysus by trumpets from the waters of a lake at Lerna, preceded by offerings to "Gatekeeper" (the

---

35. On all this see Parker, *Polytheism*, 302–5, 318 [+]; G. Hedreen, *JHS* 124 (2004): 45–47; other Dionysiac bringings in: W. Burkert in *Early Greek Cult Practice*, 84 n. 22; the ship-cart at Smyrna: Nilsson, *Griechische Feste*, 268–69.

36. See J. Bremmer, "Greek Maenadism Reconsidered," *ZPE* 55 (1984): 267–86.

37. A. Henrichs, "Greek Maenadism from Olympias to Messalina," *HSCP* 82 (1978): 121–60, at 143, citing Diod. Sic. 4.3.2–3 (imitating the mythical maenads, the women celebrate the παρουσία and ἐπιφανεία of Dionysus).

38. Mantinea: *IG* 5.2.265; cf. Jost, *Arcadie*, 246–49 (who disputes any reference to Kore's underworld sojourn); Helos: Paus. 3.20.7; cf. *Early Greek Cult Practice*, 103; Sicily: Diod. Sic. 5.4.6 with 5.4.2; cf. Sourvinou-Inwood, *Hylas*, 161–62. An obscure Attic festival, the Procharisteria (Parker, *Polytheism*, 196–97), was celebrated in spring "because of the coming up of the goddess"; it may have mimicked the coming up in some way, but no details are known.

gatekeeper of Hades, that is). These were further advents, and, involving as they did a rescue/return from the underworld, of a very dramatic kind.[39] But again an adequate context is lacking.

Gods who periodically arrive must also in logic periodically depart, but perhaps understandably such departures seem not to have been ritually marked; indeed it has been argued that gods were never perceived by the faithful as being fully absent and inaccessible.[40] The "sending away" hymn (ἀποπεμπτικός) is the rarest of types according to Menander Rhetor, though he does claim to know some written by Bacchylides. Even the departure of Persephone, mythically famous though it was, did not generate "departure of Persephone" festivals symmetrical with those of her "fetching," whatever place laments or searches for her might play in her joint cult with Demeter. The scenes on a striking pithos urn of the ninth century from Knossos seem to provide, it is true, a significant exception.[41] A winged goddess on a wheeled platform is depicted on front and back: on the front she is flanked by richly growing foliage and has her arms up, wings down; on the rear the foliage is withered and she has arms down, wings up—as if ready to depart with the fading of the year. She seems to have stepped straight out of the pages of Frazer's *Golden Bough,* so close is she to the life of nature, so satisfactorily cyclical. The wheeled platform points to a ritual in which she was physically moved to and fro. But she dates from the Crete of the ninth century, and nothing much like her is known from the classical period.

In the cases discussed so far, the god's epiphany is through a statue, carried in by hand or on a wagon or chariot. At Stratonikeia in Caria the ten

---

39. Semele: Plutarch writes of the Delphic festival Herois, celebrated every eighth year, that "most of its elements have a mystic rationale known to the Thyiades, but from the acts performed openly one would conjecture it to be a 'bringing up of Semele'" (*Quaest. Graec.* 12, 293c). Lerna: Socrates of Argos (*FGrH* 310 F 2 ap. Plut. *Is. Os.* 35, 364F; cf. *Quaest. Conv.* 4.6.2, 671E): generally identified (but see Sourvinou-Inwood, *Hylas,* 194) with secret nocturnal rites performed annually for Dionysus at the Lake Alkyonia at Lerna known from Pausanias (2.37.5–6), who specifies that this was the lake through which Dionysus went down to fetch Semele. The myth that Perseus killed Dionysus by drowning him in the Lerna lake (Σ T Hom. *Il.* 14.319) is apparently a second aition for these rites; it is a drastic variation of the myth of Perseus's hostility to Dionysus that already appears on sixth-century vases. For discussion of these tantalizingly fragmentary traditions, see Sourvinou-Inwood, *Hylas,* 190–207 [+].

40. Sourvinou-Inwood, *Hylas,* 159.

41. See Burkert, "Katagōgia-Anagōgia and the Goddess of Knossos," (n. 30), commenting on J. N. Coldstream, "A Protogeometric Nature Goddess from Knossos," *BICS* 31 (1984): 93–104 (*ThesCRA* 2:482 no. 583). On the partial exception of the Katagogia-Anagogia of Aphrodite of Eryx (Ath. 9.394F–395A; cf. Ael. *VH* 1.15 and *NA* 4.2) Burkert notes that the cult is only "para-Greek" and the period of Aphrodite's absence, signaled by the absence of her doves, just ten days. Menander Rhetor: p. 12.5–23 in the ed. of D. A. Russell and N. G. Wilson (Oxford, 1981).

days during which Zeus Panamaros's statue was present, having been fetched from Panamara, were spoken of as "the god's visit" (ἐπιδημία).[42] Occasionally the deity was impersonated by a priestess or priest.[43] But a strong sense of presence could be created in other ways. Callimachus's *Hymn to Apollo* begins:

> How Apollo's laurel branch has trembled, and how the whole shrine! Away, away, sinners! Phoebus is surely kicking the door with his lovely foot. Can't you see? The Delian palm tree nodded sweetly suddenly, and the swan in the air is singing beautifully. Bolts of the gates, bars of the gates, pull back of your own accord! The god is no longer far off... the boys should not keep their lyres silent nor their feet noiseless now that Phoebus has arrived.

"Door-opening miracles" are widely attested, but what matters to us is not the mechanism but simply the possibility of the god's presence being dramatized not by an image but by clues and tokens.[44] At festivals of Dionysus, clusters of ripe grapes might be discovered out of season, bowls might fill up with wine spontaneously, a vine might sprout and fruit in a single day:[45] such abnormal events reveal the god's power at work and can plausibly be taken as having been, for the participants, tokens of his advent. "Those who lived near the Galaxion in Boeotia became aware of the god's presence (ἐπιφάνεια) through an abundance and surplus of milk," writes Plutarch; he goes on to quote lyric verses describing the miracle.[46] In the first lines of his *Hymn to*

---

42. *IStraton.* 242.16–17, cf. 222.8.

43. Polyaenus, *Strat.* 8.59, priestess of Athena in Pellene; Paus. 8.53.3, priestess of Artemis at Tegea; Paus. 8.15.3, Pheneai, the priest dons a mask of Demeter Kydaria and beats "those under the earth" with a staff; cf. Connelly, *Portrait of a Priestess,* 104–8. The ephebe who carries a lamb around Tanagra on his shoulders for Hermes is a kind of embodiment of Hermes Kriophoros (Paus. 9.22.1).

44. How Apollo's advent at Delphi was ritualized, if it was, is not clear. A specific reference to a festival celebrating his *epidēmia* first occurs to my knowledge in Procopius *Ep.* 20 in Hercher, *Epistolographi Graeci,* 540 (Nilsson, *Griechische Feste,* 158 n. 20); scholars connect this with Plutarch's mention of special cakes, implying a festival, baked on the seventh of the spring month Bysios, supposedly the one day on which the god originally gave oracles and also his birthday (*Quaest. Graec.* 9, 292E–F).

45. Paus. 3.22.2 (Mt. Larysion above Migonion in Laconia); Theopomp. *FGrH* 115 F 277, [Arist.] *Mir. ausc.* 123, Paus. 6.26.1–2 (cf. S. Scullion, *Philologus* 145 [2001]: 203–18) (Elis); Soph. fr. 255 and passages cited ad loc. by Radt (probably Aigai in Euboea, Sourvinou-Inwood, *Hylas,* 153–54). For other such Dionysiac wine miracles, see, e.g., Plin. *HN* 2.231, ibid. 31.16 (Andros); Diod. Sic. 3.66.2 (Teos). Cf. A. Henrichs, "Changing Dionysiac Identities," in *Jewish and Christian Self-Definition,* ed. B. F. Meyer and E. P. Sanders, 3:137–60 (London, 1982), at 148.

46. *De def. or.* 29, 409A–B: probably in fact an aition.

Demeter Callimachus speaks as master of ceremonies at a basket-carrying ritual for Demeter (perhaps one attested in Alexandria, though the poet's own role is fictional),[47] and urges the celebrants: "As the basket comes in, call in response, women, 'Demeter, warm greetings, nurturer of many, bringer of many bushels.'" So the carrying in of the basket was perhaps perceived as an advent. So too, no doubt, the "dancing" of the baskets at the festival of Koloene Artemis at the Gygaian lake near Sardis.[48]

The bringing in of a statue, to suggest advent,[49] was perhaps the commonest form of statue manipulation, but others occur. At Aigialeia a propitiation of Apollo and Artemis by "seven youths and seven maids" apparently required them to escort images of those two gods "back" to the temple of Apollo, via a shrine of Persuasion: this bringing "back" (not "in") will have indicated successful propitiation and "persuasion."[50] The ad hoc creation of a statue of Dionysus from a mask and column and clothes, as shown on the much-discussed Attic "Lenaea vases," was another way, it has been argued, of creating a presence of the god.[51] Karl Meuli left unfinished at his death the sketch of a theory of "chained gods": gods whose statue was symbolically bound throughout the year but released at a single "great festival," at which the ancestors returned and the living too were freed from the chains of social restraint and allowed to enjoy for a while the freedoms of the age of Kronos. A partial illustration is found at Patrai, where the chest containing a celebrated image of Dionysus was brought into the open once a year only during a festival. This image, according to myth, had driven mad Eurypylos son of Euhaimos, who had actually viewed it; the effect of the ritual was perhaps not one merely of presence, but of dangerous presence, of the god. Another sinister image, that of Artemis from the land of the Taurians, was held by the priestess of Artemis Orthia Lugodesma at Sparta during the notorious whipping of ephebes at Artemis's altar; the goddess's epithet

---

47. Cf. Burkert in *Early Greek Cult Practice,* 85.

48. φασὶ δ᾽ ἐνταῦθα χορεύειν τοὺς καλάθους κατὰ τὰς ἑορτάς: Strabo 13.4.5, 626 (cf. Nilsson, *Griechische Feste,* 253–54).

49. E.g., Paus. 7.20.8: Artemis Limnatis's image is brought in from the suburb of Patrai, Mesoa, whither it first arrived in mythical time, to the temple in the center for the goddess's annual festival; ibid. 2.7.5–6 (images of Dionysus Bakcheios and Lysios, in Sicyon).

50. Paus. 2.7.7–8. Not all the details are clear (Nilsson, *Griechische Feste,* 171): the young people go to the river Suthas, which is not a surprise in a puberty rite; whether they take the images with them or find them there is not stated.

51. Sourvinou-Inwood, *Hylas,* 211–40: she argues that the rite illustrated is the Delphic ἐγείρειν τὸν Λικνίτην (Plut. *Is. Os.* 35, 365A), to be understood as "arousing the Liknites," i.e., a mask of Dionysus initially placed in the form of basket known as *liknon,* not, as is usually supposed, the "awakening" of a reborn baby Dionysus (*liknon* as cradle).

"withy-bound" may show that the image was bound for the rest of the year.[52] But there is no trace of the ancestors in either case, nor of the age of Kronos. The only actual festival that fully fits Meuli's elegant theory is, unfortunately, the Roman Saturnalia.[53]

The plot "the ancestors return" (an inauspicious variant on the advent of the god) is attested only once, by an entry in the Byzantine encyclopedist Photius: "Unclean day: at the Choes at Athens [day two of the Anthesteria] in the month Anthesterion, in which the souls of dead are believed to come up, they used to chew buckthorn from morning and anoint their doors with pitch" (presumably as ways of protecting themselves from the dangerous presence of the dead).[54] The temples too were roped off on that day.

The God Dies or Disappears

In Athens and Argos statues of Athena were given annual baths, in the sea (probably) after a long procession at Athens, in the river Inachus at Argos. Revealingly, sources in both cases (inscriptions in the one, Callimachus in the other) speak of the goddess herself being taken out to bathe, not her image.[55] For Athens, we have the rare luxury of a text that illuminates the mood of the festival (the Plynteria). The disrobing of the statue prior to its carrying out received, it seems, ritual emphasis: the goddess's nakedness was hidden with a veil, and the statue was left thus veiled for a sufficient period of time to give the whole day an inauspicious character. No Athenian, Plutarch records,

52. Meuli, *Gesammelte Schriften*, 1035–81. Patrai: Paus. 7.20.1; on Eurypylos, 7.19.7 Sparta: Paus. 3.16.7–11. For these (and other) partial instantiations of Meuli's theory, see Graf, *Nordionische Kulte*, 81–96. Statuettes from the sanctuary of Artemis Ortheia at Messene show young female votaries holding a small *xoanon*, a ritual also mentioned in an inscription of (?) the first century AD, SEG 23.220 (b) 4–5: see P. G. Themelis in *Ancient Greek Cult Practice*, 116. No hint of danger here. About the "carrying round of the image" at the Dionysia of Methymna (*IG* 12.2.503.10) nothing certain is known, though it is very likely (Nilsson, *Griechische Feste*, 282) that the image involved was the well-known Dionysos Phallen (Paus. 10.19.3). Still less is known about the Dionysophoroi (Hesych. δ 1991: mss. Διονυσιοφόροι) at Syracuse and σιοφόροι(i.e. θεοφόροι) of Poseidon at Cape Taenarum (*IG* 5.1.210.55, 211.51, 212.5).

53. For the loosing of Saturn from woollen bands at the Saturnalia, see Apollodorus of Athens FGrH 244 F 118 = Macr. *Sat.* 1.8.5 (*Saturnum Apollodorus alligari ait per annum laneo vinculo et solvi ad diem sibi festum*) and Jacoby ad loc. The possibilities that Apollodorus there refers to the Greek Kronia (tentatively Graf, *Nordionische Kulte*, 92; contra Jacoby) or that the Roman custom comes from the Greek seem to me very slight.

54. Photius μ 439; for those who doubt the conclusion drawn here, see Parker, *Polytheism*, 294 n. 25; ibid., n. 24 for closing of temples.

55. E.g., *IG* 2².1011.11 (Parker, *Athenian Religion*, 307–8); Callim. *Hymn* 6 passim. Hera was said to recover her virginity annually by bathing in a spring at Nauplion (Paus. 2.38.2–3): this too was doubtless a statue-bath.

would embark on any serious enterprise on that day. It was therefore a very ill omen that Alcibiades happened to return to Athens from exile precisely then, when the veiled goddess seemed to spurn his presence.[56] The correlate, unattested, will have been a period of particularly auspicious time once the goddess was reinstalled in her temple, refreshed and re-robed. The example neatly illustrates the way in which simple manipulation of sacred objects could create a mood, a little drama. (Whether there were festivals that were unrelievedly bleak is uncertain. The Diasia, a festival of Zeus Meilichios at Athens, is said to have been conducted "with a certain grimness."[57] But that brief phrase need not cover the mood of the whole event.)

Worse things could happen within the festival fiction than the temporary veiling (a kind of absence) of a goddess. Disasters could occur, deaths, disappearances of deities. Festivals that included an element of mourning seem to have been recognized as a distinct type by the ancients. In a striking passage where he compares Roman cult with Greek, Dionysius of Halicarnassus accounts to the credit of the Romans that "there is no black-robed or mourning festival among them containing breast-beating and women's laments for the disappearance of gods, such as are conducted among the Greeks in relation to the rape of Persephone and the sufferings of Dionysus and other such things." Among the classes of rites that Plutarch supposes are designed "for the aversion of bad *daimones*" are those requiring "fasting and breast-beating'." Aristotle already knows a pointed rejoinder supposedly made by the philosopher Xenophanes to the Eleans when they asked him "if they should sacrifice to Leukothea and lament or not": if they considered her a god they should not lament, if a mortal, not sacrifice.[58]

The one lamentee whose rites we know in some detail is Adonis (who did not, however, receive a public cult in Athens). Much more briefly we hear that one of the cult acts performed by the maidens of Troizen for Hippolytus was lamentation; that, in obedience to an oracle, Achilles was lamented at sunset near the start of the Olympics by the women of Elis; that the women of Croton too lamented and wore mourning for Achilles at the Heraion on Cape Lacinium; that a Tegeate hero Skephros was lamented during the festival of Apollo Agyieus; that "Mysian women" (perhaps in

56. Xen. *Hell.* 1.4.12, Plut. *Alc.* 34.1–2; cf. Pollux 8.141 (temples closed). But in Argos no such mood emerges from Callimachus's *Hymn.*

57. Σ Lucian p. 107.15 Rabe; cf. Parker, *Polytheism,* 425.

58. Dion. Hal. *Ant. Rom.* 2.18.2; Plut. *De def. or.* 14, 417c; Arist. *Rhet.* 2.23, 1400b 6–8. Plutarch thrice has Xenophanes make the same remark to the Egyptians in respect of Osiris, and a Plutarchan work ascribes the remark to Lycurgus (in answer to the Thebans): for references see Xenophanes DK 21 A 13.

fact Greek women from Kios in Mysia) lamented Hylas.[59] In some further cases actual lamentations are not attested, but indications of mourning are: the Naxians maintained that they honored two separate Ariadnes, of whom they celebrated one with merriment, while the sacrifices for the other were "mixed with mourning and grimness"; the feasting on the first day of the Hyacinthia at Sparta was restrained and austere "because of grief for Hyacinthus"; the Corinthian children whose task it was to propitiate the dead children of Medea cut their hair and wore black.[60] Where actual lamentation is attested in a cult and its performers are identifiable, they are always women; the mimicked laments over ancient deaths at festivals follow the form of the laments over actual deaths in present time.

An obvious question to ask about ritual laments concerns the mythological career of the god or hero mourned for. Was the disaster lamented over by the participants temporary or permanent? The mourning of Good Friday would drastically change its character were it not believed that the victim of that day was to rise again in three days' time. A closely related question is that of the place of the laments within the whole festival: Easter would be different again were the Crucifixion an event in ritual but the Resurrection merely a belief, not also an event enacted within the same ritual sequence. In answer to the first question, the occurrence mourned over was a temporary affliction in some but not all the relevant mythical biographies. Persephone and Dionysus certainly recovered from their sufferings, and traditions that Achilles, Hyacinthus, and Leukothea became gods or something similar are attested early, even if they were not necessarily activated in the cults in question; Hylas too seems to have become a local god.[61] It can be argued that in such cases the mourning was conducted in order to stress the transformation subsequently undergone by the ex-mortal: the paradox underlined by Xenophanes in his

59. Eur. *Hipp.* 1426–27; Paus. 6.23.3 (Achilles at Elis); Paus. 8.53.3 (Skephros); Lyc. *Alex.* 859–65, with Σ (Achilles at Croton); Hesych. ε 4645 (Hylas: cf. Sourvinou-Inwood, *Hylas*, 75–76). According to Conon, the Linos song had its origin in laments for Linos and his mother, Psamathe, performed at an Argive festival (Conon *FGrH* 26 F 1 ¶ 19: cf. Paus. 1.43.7). But in its first attestations the Linos song is a lament performable on any occasion, not tied to a particular cult (Hom. *Il.* 18.570, Hes. fr. 305), and Nilsson is probably right that its association with the Argive cult, if real at all, is secondary (*Griechische Feste*, 435–38). The Lityersas song/lament too (Theocr. 10.41 with Gow's commentary) was not cultic. Whether the "tragic choruses" that honored Adrastus (Hdt. 5.67.5) were laments is unknowable.

60. Plut. *Thes.* 20.8–9 (Ariadne); Polycrates *FGrH* 588 F 1 ap Ath. 4, 139d (Hyacinthia); Paus. 2.3.7, cf. Parmeniskos in Σ Eur. *Med.* 264 and Σ ibid. 1379 (πένθιμος ἑορτή) (children of Medea). Philostr. *Her.* 53.4 p. 67 de Lannoy speaks of Corinthian laments for Melikertes and for the children of Medea: how reliably (cf. p. 152 n. 111)?

61. Achilles: e.g., *PMG* 894, and the Black Sea cult of Achilles (p. 244 below); Hyacinthus: see below; Leukothea: Hom. *Od.* 5.334–35; Hylas: Sourvinou-Inwood, *Hylas*, 329–45.

answer to the Eleans, that they were treating the same individual as both dead and divine, was precisely the point.[62] On the other hand, Skephros and the children of Medea were heroes at best, and, if Plutarch's report is trustworthy, the Naxians blocked off the thought of a happy future for the Ariadne they mourned by treating her as a separate figure from the one they celebrated. Most strikingly, the current consensus is that there was no ritually enacted resurrection of Adonis; the festival ended with the "gardens of Adonis" being disposed of, and the only comfort for the participants was the knowledge that the beautiful youth would somehow be available to die and be mourned for again next year.[63]

As for dramatization of the "death/apotheosis" or "loss/recovery" sequence within a festival, the cult of Demeter and Kore probably provided the nearest Greek equivalents to a Good Friday–Easter Sunday sequence: laments for Kore are likely to have led to her recovery, as certainly at her festival the Thesmophoria the grim middle day of "Fasting" prepared for what we may presume to be the joy of the final day, "Fair Birth." The ritual for Hylas too seems to have ended with a reassurance that he had become a god; in other cases of laments for future gods (Achilles, Leukothea) we know too few details to be able to judge.[64] The dramatizations of the "sufferings of Dionysus" that Dionysius of Halicarnassus mentions with such disapproval perhaps occurred in private mystery cults, not at public festivals at all.[65]

About the Spartan Hyacinthia we have a little more information. The day that was understood as one of mourning for Apollo's lovely young lover was the first. Pausanias tells us that on the altar that served as base for the great statue of Apollo of Amyclae were depicted various gods "escorting to heaven" Hyacinthus and his sister Polyboia.[66] The myth of the apotheosis was therefore visually presented to every visitor to the sanctuary from the sixth century onward. No source records that it was also evoked during the ritual of the subsequent days. But whether it was or not, one of the longest

---

62. Sourvinou-Inwood, *Hylas,* 125.

63. See J. L. Lightfoot, *Lucian: On the Syrian Goddess* (Oxford, 2003), 305–11. But for the suggestion that in late antiquity Adonis's annual return was interpreted as a resurrection to rival Christ's, see Lane Fox, *Travelling Heroes,* 253–54.

64. Hylas: Sourvinou-Inwood, *Hylas,* 352–55. Thesmophoria: for the day names see Σ Ar. *Thesm.* 80, with Parker, *Polytheism,* 272 n. 11.

65. See Sourvinou-Inwood, *Hylas,* 184–85, on Plut. *De Is. et Os.* 35, 364F. Alternatively, the allegorical interpretation (e.g., Cornutus *Theol. Graec.* 30, p. 62.10–16 Lang) of the myth (originating probably in Orphic poetry/rites) of the *sparagmos* of Dionysus may already in Dionysius's time have caused elements of the public ritual to be so understood: so, e.g., Σ Clem. Al. *Protrept.* 1.2 (cited by A. Pickard-Cambridge, *The Dramatic Festivals of Athens,* 2nd ed. [Oxford, 1968], 28) claims that a song on this subject was sung at the Lenaea.

66. Paus. 3.19.4.

descriptions that we possess of any Greek festival shows that the movement of the Hyacinthia was felt to be from a mood of inhibition to one of indulgence, celebration, affirmation of vitality. An otherwise unknown writer on Spartan customs, Polycrates, writes as follows:

The Laconians conduct the sacrifice of the Hyacinthia over three days and because of their mourning for Hyacinthus do not wear garlands at dinner nor do they bring in bread or serve cakes and other such things; they do not sing the paean to the god or introduce anything of the kind such as they do at their other sacrifices, but they dine in great good order and depart. [We must presume, though Polycrates does not make explicit, that these restrictions apply to the first day only.] But on the middle of the three days there is a varied spectacle and a remarkable great communal celebration (πανήγυρις). Boys in high-belted tunics play the lyre and, singing to the *aulos* while running over all the strings with their plectra, hymn the god in an anapestic rhythm with a high pitch. Others go through the theater on decorated horses. Numerous choruses of young men come in and sing some of the local poems, while dancers intermingled with them perform old-fashioned dance movements to the accompaniment of flute and song. As for the maidens, some ride on expensively decked-out *kannathra* [a kind of cart], while others compete (?) in procession on yoked chariots, and the whole city is absorbed in the movement and joy of the spectacle. On this day they sacrifice numerous animals and the citizens feast all their acquaintances and their own slaves. Nobody is absent from the sacrifice, but the whole city is emptied for the spectacle.[67]

A further description of the distinctive Spartan form of dinner known as a *kopis* probably concerns the Hyacinthia,[68] though we cannot be sure which of the three days it relates to; it is a lovely illustration of "festival food":

When they hold a *kopis,* first they set up tents beside the god, and in these ground covers made of wood, and on them they lay rugs, on

---

67. Ath. 4, 139D–F (Polycrates, *FGrH* 588 F 1 quoted via Didymus). The link of day one with mourning for Hyacinthus is secondary interpretation, according to Nilsson, *Griechische Feste,* 133, and A. Brelich, *Paides e parthenoi* (Rome, 1969), 144. But see the comments of Sourvinou-Inwood, *Hylas,* 122 n. 27. On the festival, see N. Richer, "The Hyacinthia of Sparta," in *Spartan Society,* ed. T. J. Figueira, 77–102 (Swansea, 2004); Ducat, *Spartan Education,* 262–67.

68. See Nilsson, *Griechische Feste,* 131–32, on Polemon ap. Ath. 4, 138F–139A; he supposes that it belongs to day one, but M. Pettersson, *Cults of Apollo at Sparta* (Stockholm, 1992), 14–17, puts it later.

which guests recline; they feast not just those who come from the territory but also foreigners who are present. At *kopides* they sacrifice goats and no other animal. They give portions of meat to everybody and the so-called *physikillos,* which is a small loaf resembling an oil-and-honey cake but rounder in shape. They give each of those assembled a green cheese and a slice of black sausage and as relishes dry figs and beans and green kidney beans.

Indulgence of this type was out of place where the story had no happy ending. The Adonia finished very differently: no feasting, no display of the skills and beauty of the rising generation. Its pleasures, at least if we can place reliance on the interpretation offered by Theocritus in his fifteenth *Idyll,* were of a different kind, the pleasures of lamentation itself.[69] Adonis was the young lover of Aphrodite who died, and the women who mourned him luxuriated self-indulgently in fantasies of a similar relationship and a similar bereavement. The pleasures of lamentation were especially intense in the case of Adonis because of the cult's strong erotic charge. But the fantasy of bereavement (or even the vicarious experience of bereavement) is as sweet as the real experience is sour, and perhaps the maidens who mourned for Hippolytus, the women who mourned for Achilles did so not without pleasure. We may presume that these festivals played tricks with time and treated the deaths in question not as events from the distant past but as recurring, like that of Adonis, each year. Plutarch is perhaps being psychologically naive in supposing that the experience of such rituals was a painful one appropriate only "for the aversion of bad *daimones.*"

A lament for a lost god could easily be associated with a search. The type is not common, but a few cases are known. The most important is Lactantius's statement that at the Eleusinian Mysteries, "Proserpina is sought with lighted torches, and when she is found the whole rite concludes with celebration and throwing of torches."[70] We also hear from several sources that the inhabitants of the Greek city of Kios in Mysia went to the mountains each year and hunted for Hylas, the young companion of Heracles whom the amorous nymphs had dragged into a spring. A different source tells of a sacrifice performed at the spring, of a threefold invocation of Hylas by the priest, and of the echo's threefold response; the triple echo has been

---

69. Cf. Parker, *Polytheism,* 283–88 [+].

70. *Div. Inst. Epit.* 18.7. Similarly, Paus. 1.43.2 speaks of a reenactment of the myth by the women of Megara.

interpreted as the auditory epiphany that in the ritual proved to the faithful that the lost youth lived on, transformed into a protecting spirit.[71]

More enigmatic is a characteristically inconsequential-seeming brief notice in Plutarch:

> Not unreasonably then among us [probably the Chaironeians] too at the Agrionia the women seek for Dionysus in the belief that he has run away. Then they stop and say that he has fled to the Muses and is hidden with them. A little later, at the end of the dinner, they set each other puzzles and riddles.[72]

Plutarch is impressed by this ritual because feasting and drinking are combined with exercise of the rational faculties, and the wildness of drunkenness is gently restrained by the Muses. But what of the events prior to the meal? Dionysus's flight to the Muses echoes the old myth whereby he took refuge with Thetis when Lycurgus pursued his nurses,[73] but in this case his need to flee is unexplained. Possibly this is an exception to the principle that a god's departure at the end of a festival is not dramatized; or perhaps, as so often, we simply know too little.

An enneateric (once in eight years) festival, or rather whole ritual sequence, at Delphi, the Septerion, was said by most ancients to have as its plot the killing of the dragon Pytho by Apollo and the god's subsequent exile to Tempe; he was purified there and returned in triumph bringing his beloved laurel. A speaker in one of Plutarch's Delphic dialogues, however, disagrees, while also giving us the fullest account of the ritual action.

> For the hut that is set up there around the threshing floor every eight years seems to be an imitation not of the snake's lair but of a tyrant's or king's residence. And the silent approach to it along the so-called Dolonia, along which the Labyadai [?] escort the boy with both parents still living and, throwing fire on the hut and overturning the table, flee through the gates of the shrine without turning back; and finally the wanderings and service of the boy and the purifications performed in Tempe suggest a great pollution and crime. For it's utterly absurd, my

---

71. See Sourvinou-Inwood, *Hylas,* 74–78, 352–55. Different source: Nicander ap Ant. Lib. *Met.* 26.

72. *Quaest. conv.* 8.1.1, 717a. Scraps of other evidence for Dionysus at Chaironeia do not help: Schachter, *Cults* 1:173–74.

73. Hom. *Il.* 6.130–37.

friend, that Apollo, after killing a wild beast, should flee to the limits of Greece seeking purification, and when there pour certain libations and perform the acts that men perform when expiating and appeasing the anger of powers (*daimones*) whom they call "drivers" (*alastores*) and "murderous spirits" (*palamnaioi*).[74]

Other sources reveal that the flight from Delphi to Thessaly was only the preliminary to a ritualized bringing of laurel from Thessaly to Delphi.[75] The "boy with both parents still living" was the leader of a "sacred expedition" that, after making "impressive" sacrifices in Thessaly, followed a formal route, the "sacred way" or Pythias, back to Delphi; the laurel that they brought served among other things to crown victors at the Pythian games. The festival was a diptych, therefore: destructive and polluting acts and, according to the ancient explanation, actual absence of the god prepared for an auspicious coming back. Was ordinary existence for the Delphians subjected to restrictions during the interval between the flight of the polluted god/youth and his return? This return was also a bringing in, and thus aligns the festival with others at which a valued substance (such as fire) was fetched from afar; the link between the festival and the games at which the laurel was used may have been a close one.[76] Such fetching establishes a linkage between a city or sanctuary and one or many others. Linkage of this type was often created by means of the dispatch of a "sacred expedition," *theōria,* from city A to attend a festival in a sanctuary controlled by city B. Here by contrast the *theōria* visits

---

74. *De def. or.* 15, 418A–B; for the speaker such myths and rites concern *daimones,* not gods: ibid. 417E–F, 418C–D, cf. 21, 421C–D. For the standard aition, cf. Ephorus *FGrH* 70 F 31b ap. Strabo 9.3.12, 422 (the rite commemorates the burning of the dragon's tent by the Delphians); Callim. *Aet.* fr. 86–89; Plut. *Quaest. Graec.* 12, 293C (which mentions flight along the sacred way); Σ Pind. *Pyth.* p. 4.9–14 Drachmann; Ael. *VH* 3.1 (seen by editors as a paraphrase of Theopompus, whence *FGrH* 115 F 80); probably already Pind. *Paean* 10. The *Paean* of Aristonous (Powell, *Coll. Alex.* 162–64) may have been written for the festival (Rutherford, *Paeans,* 29)—on which see Burkert, *Homo Necans,* 127–30; Rutherford, *Paeans,* 200–202 [both +].

75. Callim. *Ia.* fr. 194.34–36; Ael. *VH* 3.1 (with details of the route); Plut. [*De mus.*] 14, 1136A; Steph. Byz. s.v. Δειπνιάς; Σ Pind. *Pyth.* p. 4.9–14 Drachmann. For the possibility that the δαυχναφόροι found in several Thessalian and one Perrhaibian city making dedications to Apollo under various epithets (*IG* 9.2.1027, 1234, and two inedita) attest regional involvement in the rite, see B. Helly, *JSav* (1987): 140–42; M. Mili, "Studies in Thessalian Religion" (D. Phil. diss., Oxford University, 2005), 281–84.

76. On fire fetching from Delos and Delphi, see below, p. 213. Cf. the bringing of offerings to Delphi by the Athenian Pythaïdes (Parker, *Polytheism,* 83–87); a link between the Hyperborean offerings sent to Delos and a particular festival is highly plausible, but currently indemonstrable (J. Bruneau, *Recherches sur les cultes de Délos à l'époque hellénistique et à l'époque impériale* [Paris, 1970], 38–48). Festival and games: the games, like the festival, were supposedly originally held every eight years; but note the caution of Rutherford, *Paeans,* 202 n. 4.

a variety of sanctuaries outside its own territory while enacting the plot of a festival sequence of its own city. The Septerion is about a god's exile and the fetching of a valued substance and the links between Delphi and an outlying region; such multidimensionality is entirely normal.

The "lost god" motif is early attested in the Hittite myth of the angry withdrawal, leading to general infertility, of the god Telepinus. It apparently ends, once Telepinus is appeased, with an allusion to a ritual: "Telepinus cared for the king. A pole was erected before Telepinus; and from this pole the fleece of a sheep was suspended; in it lay the fat of sheep, grains of corn, wine, in it lay cattle and sheep, in it lay long life and progeny." The fleece symbolized general abundance, therefore. Burkert has suggested that "abundance returns with the recovery of the lost god" provided the plot of several Greek rituals.[77] No instance coincides exactly with the presumptive Hittite archetype, but each contains some of the motifs "lost god," "pole/plank image/ tree," "symbols of abundance," "feasting."

(a) The cave at Phigaleia in Arcadia to which Demeter once withdrew in wrath used to containe a rare wooden horse-headed image of the goddess. In lieu of animal sacrifice, worshippers still in Pausanias's day placed on the altar in front of the cave "the produce of cultivated trees, especially grapes, honeycombs, unworked wool still full of grease"; they then poured on olive oil.[78]

(b) We noted above the ritual of Hera on Samos at which foodstuffs were placed in front of the goddess's image on the beach; according to the etiological myth, the festival commemorated an occasion when pirates had tried unsuccessfully to steal the image but abandoned it (and propitiated it with food) on the shore, and the Samians had to hunt for their lost goddess. The image of Hera in question was, in its body, a plank decorated with a necklace of circular objects that were perhaps, by analogy with clearer cases, symbols of abundance.

(c) At Ephesus, an image of Artemis was brought out on a particular day into a field by boys and girls and "feasted" on salt; if the image resembled the famous Ephesian Artemis, it was girt with the mysterious "breasts," perhaps again symbols of abundance.[79]

---

77. *Structure and History*, 123–42; Telepinus's pole, ibid., 124.
78. Paus. 8.42.1–13.
79. *Etym. Magn.* 252.11–25 s.v. Daitis.

(d) In Magna Graecia and Sicily, statuettes of Demeter or Persephone with necklaces like those of Samian Hera ([b] above) are
commonplace,[80] though without associated rituals penetrating our
rare sources for the region.

(e) In the same area as (b) and (c), at Miletus, the city's founder, Neleus,
on oracular instruction made an image of Artemis Chitone from an
oak on which "all kinds of fruit" were hung.

(f) On the mainland we find, not plank images decorated (arguably) with symbols of abundance, but poles or branches hung with
them: such are the *eiresiōnai* carried by young boys in Attic rituals
of Apollo, such the decorated olive branch carried in the ritual of
Daphnephoria at Thebes.

(g) A Boeotian ritual for Hera centered on rough wooden images
known as *daidala*.[81]

(h) He could perhaps have added the Delphic Septerion ritual
discussed above.

Burkert concludes:

> To sum up: in various forms, the *eiresiōnē* or laurel branch, the *daid-
> alon,* the plank with garment and pectoral, and the Hittite *eia* tree, we
> have the same ritual activity of bringing in the tree adorned, which
> ultimately conveys a single message: the return of prosperity, the return
> of the god.[82]

For the worshipper, a sacrificial feast will have conveyed the experience of
"prosperity returned" in the most agreeable fashion. And he continues with
a drastic claim: "The gods may be quite different, Telepinus or Artemis,
Hera, Demeter, Persephone, Apollo, Dionysus, all different in name, sex and
spheres of influence; but after all, the gods are 'givers of good things' almost
by definition."

I have laid out his case thus fully to reveal both its allure and the difficulties it brings. About details one can certainly quibble. Are poles and
branches really equivalent to images, of however rudimentary a kind? Perhaps (f) should be bracketed off as a separate though still important type, one

80. See now Hinz, *Demeter auf Sizilien,* 38–39, and index s.v. Athena Lindia.
81. Miletus: Σ Callim. *Hymn* 1.77b, cf. Callim. *Aet.* fr. 80.17–18, *Hymn* 3.225–27. *Eiresiōnai:*
Parker, *Polytheism,* 204–6. Daphnephoria: n. 168 below. Daidala: p. 221 below.
82. *Structure and History,* 136.

not based on a myth, the bringing in of symbols of prosperity. Is a meal of salt (c) a good harbinger of abundance? Can a meal served to a deity symbolize the abundance brought by that deity? And so on. But fuller information might meet most of these difficulties. What is most puzzling is how the great, grand myth of the angry god's withdrawal has disappeared completely or has been replaced by trivial substitutes: Hera had not left her temple on Samos in cosmic rage, but pilfered by Carian pirates; the rite at Ephesus commemorated a picnic casually offered to the goddess one year that she then insisted should be repeated. Were the ritual acts in themselves strong enough to give to the participants the authentic "prosperity restored" experience, even when backed by such weak myths?

The God Weds?

"Sacred marriages" have been much talked about in the modern literature.[83] But as the plot of a festival the type seems seldom to occur; or, if it does, not in a context where we can make sense of its meaning for participants. Varro's statement that on Samos "the annual rites [of Juno] are celebrated in the form of a marriage" fails to find support in what else we know of Hera's festival Tonaia there; either he refers to a different festival of which we know nothing, or he errs.[84] The wedding of Zeus and Hera was briefly evoked during the complex Plataean festival of the Daidala, but did not provide a plot that can be traced right through the ritual sequence. The Cretans claimed that the union of Zeus and Hera occurred in the territory of Knossos near the river Theren, at the site of a sanctuary where now annual sacrifices are performed and "the marriage is imitated." How close that imitation was we have no way of judging; nor do we know anything beyond the name of the Sicilian festivals of the "Unveiling of Persephone" (sc. after marriage) or "Divine Marriage" (of Persephone again).[85] A union of Dionysus with a mortal woman did occur, as we have seen, during (probably) the Anthesteria at Athens. And a festival called precisely "Sacred Marriage"

---

83. See A. Avagianou, *Sacred Marriage in the Rituals of Greek Religion* (Bern, 1991); for a minimalist account, see I. Clark, "The Gamos of Hera: Myth and Ritual," in *Sacred and the Feminine,* 13–26.

84. *Simulacrum (sc. Iunonis) in habitu nubentis figuratum et sacra eius anniversaria nuptiarum ritu celebrantur:* Varro ap. Lactant. *Div. Inst.* 1.17.8; for other sources associating the mythical union of Zeus and Hera with Samos, see Nilsson, *Griechische Feste,* 47; on the Tonaia, pp. 172–73 above; for the possibility of a second festival Avagianou, Sacred Marriage (n. 83), 46–48.

85. Daidala: see p. 221. Crete: Diod. Sic. 5.72.4. Sicilian festivals: Pollux 1.37 (Theogamia); Σ rec. (to be found in A. Boeckh's edition of Pindar) Pind. *Ol.* 6.160 (Anakalypteria). I doubt in fact whether the latter festival name, attested only in one late scholion, has any authority.

was also held there, in the marriage month Gamelion; it honored the proto-
typical couple, that of Zeus and Hera. No ritual enactment is attested, but
married men were apparently expected to spend the evening of that day at
home; it may have been essentially a domestic event, a quiet celebration of
human marriage.[86]

"New Life," and the Seasons

A different kind of plot might be provided by the astronomical year. But it
does not seem that such "cosmic" plotting was very important. The timing
of many festivals was, it is true, tied to the motions of the sun and moon. In
all Greek poleis, as far as we know, the sequence of festivals was regulated by
a lunisolar calendar (often termed by moderns for that reason "the festival
calendar") whereby they were celebrated not more than once each solar
year. Within that calendar, the times of the new and full moon were especially favored, notionally at least, for festival activity.[87] Solar events (solstices,
equinoxes) were important in time reckoning, and the new year in the city
of Plato's *Laws* (767c) was to begin, probably in accord with actual practice
in Athens, at the first new moon after the summer solstice. If the rare and
late-attested eight-yearly (enneateric) festivals really go back to archaic times,
they are based on an eight-year cycle of intercalation (three extra months
each eight years); so too the much better-attested four-yearly festivals (pen-
teteric), if they are best viewed, as apparently by some ancients, as divided
enneaterides.[88] From early times, if so, the timing of certain festivals was tied
to elaborate calendrical calculations. But it is one thing for a festival to be
located in time by an astronomical calendar, another for its content to relate
to that calendar in any significant way. As far as we can tell, the solstices
and equinoxes were not more than useful time markers for the Greeks. The
entry of a new set of magistrates in annual office was accompanied by "entry
sacrifices" that could become elaborate, but only occasionally was this entry
described as the beginning of a "new year."[89]

86. See I. Clark, "The Gamos of Hera," 18–19, in n. 83 above; Parker, *Polytheism,* 42 (ibid.,
356–57 for a possible marriage during the Eleusinian Mysteries).

87. M. P. Nilsson, *Die Entstehung und religiöse Bedeutung der griechischen Kalender,* 2nd ed. (Lund,
1962), 35–44; C. Trümpy, *ZPE* 121 (1998): 109–15.

88. Nilsson, *Die Entstehung* (in n. 87 above), 46–48; R. Hannah, *Greek and Roman Calendars*
(London, 2005), 35–41. The Pythian Games had supposedly originally been enneateric (Censorinus,
DN 18.6; Σ Pind. Pyth. p. 4.14–16 Drachmann).

89. New year: so, e.g., Pl. *Leg.* 767C, cf. Lys. 26.6; *SEG* 38.1462.57. Entry sacrifices: Wörrle,
Stadt und Fest, 193–94. The importance of the new year is downplayed by Parker, *Polytheism,* 194

Even, however, if Greeks lacked new-year festivals, did the idea of renewal and fresh beginning sometimes provide a plot? The useful concept of "incision ceremonies" has been introduced here.[90] The possibility becomes explicit in Philostratus's statement that on Lemnos (in the third century AD) all fires were quenched on the island for nine days while rites were performed for secret chthonian gods; then new fire brought in a special ship from Delos was distributed, and "they began a new life from then on."[91] The bright new start is ritually emphasized there by a preceding period of gloom. Perhaps the gloom that descended on Athens at the Plynteria while Athena's ancient image was veiled was followed by a sense of cleansed renewal when the newly washed image was re-robed. We noted earlier the possibility that the sequence from Septerion to laurel bringing at Delphi, supposedly mimicking Apollo's flight-purification-return, worked similarly. Purity after pollution is an easy symbol of an incision. Athens was purified by the dispatch of scapegoats at the Thargelia, a festival that had some relation to the year's new corn (another potential symbol of a new start). There was also an impure day during the Anthesteria: at this festival the year's new wine was broached, and little children (newness again) were a focus of attention in some way. Several good candidates for festivals of incision can therefore be identified in one city alone, without it ever being possible to press the case home.[92]

Some of these cases already show how the agricultural year could contribute to the plotting of a festival. Diodorus claims that the Sicilians, by the timing of their festivals to Demeter and Kore, indicated the nature of the gifts they had received.

For they placed the bringing in [or bringing back—*katagōgē*] of Kore at about the time at which the corn crop reached maturity, and they celebrate this sacrifice and festival with all the strictness and zeal that is natural for men to show in repaying thanks who have been granted the best of all gifts in advance of the rest of mankind. And they preferred as time for the sacrifice of Demeter that at which the sowing of the corn is begun.[93]

(following Nilsson against Burkert); but for an argument for the importance of the new year in the Milesian calendar, see now A. Herda, *Der Apollon-Delphinios-Kult in Milet und die Neujahrsprozession nach Didyma: Ein neuer Kommentar der sog. Molpoi-Satzung* (*Milesische Forschungen* 4, Mainz, 2006); note too *LSA* 33.36. Paus. 6.20.1 speaks of a sacrifice at Elis tied to the spring equinox: that is unusual.

90. See Versnel, *Transition and Reversal,* 119 n. 101.
91. Philostr. *Heroic.* 53.5–7 (p. 67 de Lannoy).
92. On all this, see Parker, *Polytheism,* 210–11.
93. Diod. Sic. 5.4.6–7.

The men of Magnesia on the Maeander resolved in 197/6 BC to "show" a beautiful bull to Zeus Sosipolis "at the beginning of the sowing in the month Kronion at the new moon," which bull was then to be fed on charitably donated fodder ("May it go better for those who donate") until sacrificed, we assume at or near harvest time, on Artemision the twelfth; prayers were to be made for all the inhabitants of the land, for the recently concluded peace, "and for wealth and yield of corn and all other crops and the livestock."[94] At the Attic Thesmophoria, a kind of symbolic compost of the rotten remains of earlier offerings was brought up and placed on altars, and "they think that anyone who takes some of this and mixes it in when sowing will have good crops." (In such cases we come closer than usual to explicit statements about the purpose of festivals, or parts of them.) *Thalysia* were explicitly described, admittedly by a late source, as "first offerings, that is, those given to the god after the collection of the crops to ensure that the fields flourish in future too. Some orators call them 'bringing together' offerings."[95]

Festivals might signal a relation to the agricultural year in their name, as with the Attic "Pre-Plowing" (Proerosia) or the Laconian "Pre-Collection" (Prologia).[96] As for the symbolic deployment of seasonal produce, as by the Spartan "Grape-Bunch Runners" (Staphylodromoi) or the Athenian "Vine-Branch Bearers" (Oschophoroi), instances are too numerous to catalog; the special food eaten at festivals too, which might give the event its name (e.g., Thargelia), was often seasonal and reinforced the connection with the farmer's calendar. An older tradition of scholarship supposed, in the wake of Mannhardt and Frazer, that, once such seasonal relations had been established, all that was necessary had been said about the festival in question. It was one of the great achievements of the heortology of the last forty years of the twentieth century to break with that reductive paradigm. But evidently some awareness of a relation to the agricultural cycle must have been part of the experience of participants.[97] The question—and the answer may have

---

94. *Syll.*³ 589 (*LSAM* 32); Artemision unfortunately lacks a precise location (cf. Nilsson, *Griechische Feste*, 25–26; C. Trümpy, *Untersuchungen zu den altgriechischen Monatsnamen und Monatsfolgen* [Heidelberg, 1997], 110–11).

95. Eustath. ad *Il.* 9.534 p. 791 van der Valk: Θαλύσια δὲ αἱ ἀπαρχαὶ ἤγουν αἱ μετὰ συλλογὴν τῶν καρπῶν διδόμεναι θεῷ ὑπὲρ τοῦ καὶ εἰς ἔπειτα θάλλειν τὰς ἀρούρας. Τινὲς δὲ τῶν ῥητόρων καὶ συγκομιστήρια ταῦτα καλοῦσιν. Cf. *Etym. Magn.* 442.13–15 Θαλύσια· Τὰς ὑπὲρ εὐθαλίας καὶ εὐφορίας τῶν καρπῶν διδομένας θυσίας μετὰ τὴν συγκομιδὴν τῶν καρπῶν τοῖς τε ἄλλοις θεοῖς καὶ τῇ Δημήτρᾳ. Compost at the Thesmophoria: Σ Lucian p. 276.3–8 Rabe.

96. Proerosia: Parker, *Polytheism*, 429. Prologia: Hesych. π 3565 προλόγια· θυσία πρὸ τῶν καρπῶν τελουμένη, ὑπὸ Λακώνων.

97. Versnel's treatment of the Thesmophoria, *Transition and Reversal*, 235–60, is exemplary in its multifacetedness; see too now R. Chlup, *Kernos* 20 (2007): 69–96.

differed greatly from case to case—is of the extent to which that experience was reducible to anxious expectation of a forthcoming harvest or relaxed gratitude for a successful bringing in. Part of the symbolism of the Thesmophoria related, as we have seen, to abundant yields, but it was surely not in the fantasy of Aristophanes alone that the women at the Thesmophoria—the "women only" festival par excellence—had more on their minds than the well-being of the crops.

The Past in the Present: Etiology

In analyzing the "plots" of festivals, what is one to do with those provided by the ancients in the form of etiologies? We have already equipped the Attic Anthesteria with two plots, in the sense of divine events imagined to occur during the festival: the advent of the god Dionysus, culminating in his union with an Athenian woman; and the return of the ancestors. But at least two particular rites of the Anthesteria had plots of their own: the strange unsocial drinking customs of the Choes commemorated protective measures taken when the polluted Orestes was in Athens, and the "all seed offerings" of the last day perpetuated those made from surviving rations by survivors of Deucalion's flood. The rites of the first day too probably commemorated the first arrival of Dionysus in Attica in the time of King Amphictyon.[98] The last example is easy, since the ancient aition is merely a narrative version of the idea of advent that provides a main plot of the festival; when gods are involved in aitia, such coincidence is not rare. But the other two have nothing to do with any divine plot of the festival, nor directly with the gods at all. How much they mattered to participants is uncertain, but it would clearly be rash, in trying to understand the experience of festivals, to set them aside altogether. They introduce a different level of plot, one relating not to the god's involvement in the festival but to human activities during it.

No one in modern time has attempted to classify or even collect festival aitia en masse,[99] and this abstention is probably well judged; they are too diverse to allow sorting into a set of plots. But since they regularly present a festival or a part of one as an "imitation" or a "commemoration" of a past event (or simply performed "because of" it), they underline the element of

---

98. See Parker, *Polytheism,* 380.

99. But for remarks on etiology, see Kowalzig, *Singing,* 24–32; the best single source is Plutarch's *Theseus* (cf. C. Calame, *Thesée et l'imaginaire athénien* [Lausanne, 1990]).

acting or make-believe or distance from normality in festival activities. The participants in festivals oscillate between being themselves and acting a role. The element of acting, as in the case of the boy who supposedly represented Apollo at the Delphic Septerion, could be very considerable. A festival may be perceived as "imitation" of a specific event or, more generally, of a different manner of life: for one observer a Sicilian festival of Demeter was "imitation of the ancient way of life," for another the Spartan Karneia "an imitation of the military life."[100] There is, it seems, such a thing as a lifestyle festival. At the Attic Kronia, slaves and masters dined together: the social relations of the "time of Kronos," when there was no distinction between slave and free, were therefore briefly restored.[101]

Related to the question of acting a role is that of the time frame of festivals. In the Orthodox Church, the faithful announce to one another on Easter Day that "Christ is risen," which evokes the response "He is risen indeed." The past event of Christ's death and resurrection is treated as recurring at the festival each year: it is not so much that the festival acts as a time capsule to translate the faithful backward, as that it suspends temporal order altogether. Such a playing of tricks with time is a characteristic festival mechanism in many cultures. Not all Greek festival plots create such a suspension of time, but some do.[102] The ancestors can "come up," the gods can visit a city, in the present; but a lament for Achilles or a search for Kore is, we presume, a reenactment of a mythical event that pretends that it is not a reenactment but something actually happening in the present. The young people who sailed from Athens to Delos each year in a penteconter were described by an archaic term, ἤθεοι ("unwed young people"), that identified them with the ἤθεοι who sailed with Theseus, in a penteconter, as tribute to the Minotaur.[103] A covariant with these oscillations in time is, as already suggested, the extent to which participants in festivals stayed themselves or assumed a role. But we should not suppose that the distinction was one that they were very strongly aware of. The ease of slippage is part of the special character of festivals.

---

100. Diod. Sic. 5.4.7; Demetrius of Scepsis ap. Ath. 4, 141E–F.

101. See Versnel, "Kronos and the Kronia," in his *Transition and Reversal,* 89–135. R. Hunter and T. Führer write in *Callimaque* (*Entretiens Hardt* 48, Vandoeuvres, 2002), 154, that "the emphasis on performative re-enactment of an event in the immemorial past is typical of the Hellenistic historical sense": just Hellenistic?

102. Cf. Rutherford, *Paeans,* 412; Kowalzig, *Singing,* index s.v. "aetiology, mythical past and ritual present interacting in."

103. Arist. *Ath. Pol.* 56.3; cf., e.g., Plut. *Thes.* 23.1.

The City Celebrates Itself, and Its Young

I have discussed festival plots relating to the arrivals and disappearances of gods and the like, and the different kind of shaping given by a clear connection with the agricultural cycle. But by no means all festivals are obviously plotted in either of these ways, except in the weak sense that every festival ideally entailed some presence of the god. Though some have supposed that the Athenian Panathenaea, for instance, was a celebration of Athena's birthday, the connection is far from established. The victory of the gods over the giants was woven on the Panathenaic robe, probably with special emphasis on Athena's slaying of Enceladus (or Asterius), prototype of victories to be achieved by her citizens, but the festival was not a reenactment of the victory.[104] The Greater Panathenaea is a superbly elaborated form of something quite simple, the presentation to a god of gifts, in this case a new robe and sacrificial animals. The elaboration lies in the splendor of the gifts and the involvement, ideally, of the whole city in the procession that delivers them; the accompanying games are an added honor paid to the goddess.

A characteristic of Hellenistic religion, it has been argued, is the festival at which, under the guise of paying honor to the gods, the city celebrates itself: such festivals where all come together and participate and display themselves to one another are the supreme moments of self-awareness and, ideally, of pride and harmony as a group.[105] That festivals could function in this way is an observation of fundamental importance, but the Panathenaea shows that the phenomenon is not one confined to the Hellenistic period. And it is crucial to realize that "honoring the god" and "celebrating the community" were never perceived as goals in rivalry or tension: to make a procession "fair" or "splendid" was a constantly expressed aspiration, but a splendid performance that did the polis credit was an expression of piety, not a derogation from it. Another such festival was that at Eretria in honor of Artemis

---

104. See Parker, *Polytheism,* 256 (birthday); ibid., 255 for the etiological association with the killing of the giant Asterius. Decoration of the peplos: Eur. *Hec.* 466–74, *IT* 222–24.

105. Chaniotis, "Sich selbst feiern?" Chaniotis is well aware of the classical precedents, but argues nonetheless (162) for a decisive shift of emphasis. I agree that there probably was some shift, but the great preponderance of evidence both literary and epigraphic for festivals after 400 (and the inevitable bias of epigraphic evidence toward showy festivals requiring organization: P. Gauthier, *BÉ* [1996] no. 135) make a comparison difficult; many traits identified by Chaniotis are already strongly present in the pre-Hellenistic fourth century. See now A. S. Chankowski, "Processions et ceremonies d'accueil: Une image de la cité de la basse époque hellénistique," in *Citoyenneté et participation à la basse époque hellénistique,* ed. P. Fröhlich and C. Müller, 185–206 (Geneva, 2005), who argues that what was new was the increased need felt by cities to emphasize their festivals of civic unity and order by elaborate epigraphic publication. "Das große Fest der Stadtgottheit, in welcher die Polis sich eigentlich selber verehrte": Burckhardt, *Kulturgeschichte,* 421.

Amarysia: an inscription of uncertain date mentioned by Strabo prescribed that three thousand hoplites, six thousand cavalry and sixty chariots were to process in honor of the goddess; an extant inscription of c. 340 adds a musical competition with the stated aim that "we may conduct the Artemisia as finely as possible and as many persons as possible may sacrifice."[106] The procession attested by Strabo is a military one and finds parallels both in Sparta and in generalizations by the fourth-century author of *Rhetorica ad Alexandrum*.[107] Whether non-combatants also had an unattested role at these festivals or, in the archaic way, the fighting men were seen as in effect constituting the city by themselves, these too were occasions of civic self-display; so too very probably was the famous long procession from Argos to the Argive Heraion in which Cleobis and Biton pulled their mother's oxcart in lieu of the absent oxen, and expired on completion of the pious task.[108] There will have been many further cases.

A special form of self-celebration by the city at festivals is that involving young people. The instances are numerous and very varied. All the maidens of Argos have been summoned to dance at a sacrifice of Hera, according to a situation imagined in Euripides' *Electra* (171–74). A team of unmarried young men (fifteen) organized the Spartan Karneia, and supplied the important "grape-runners."[109] Maidens compete in racing for Hera at Olympia; at Athens, the many torch races are the special preserve of the ephebes.[110] At the festival of Apollo in Sicyon, seven youths and seven maidens go down to the river Suthas and fetch back the images of Apollo and Artemis (who in myth have taken fright and fled thither).[111] At the festival of Dionysus Aisymnetes in Patrai, "a certain number of children of the region go down to the river Meilichos garlanded on their heads with ears of corn. This is how of old they adorned those they led out to sacrifice to Artemis [according to an etiological myth Pausanias has just told]. In our time they deposit the garlands of corn ears with the goddess, and after washing in the river and putting on crowns

---

106. Strabo 10.1.10, 448, with D. Knoepfler in *The Polis as an Urban Centre and as a Political Community*, ed. M. H. Hansen (Copenhagen, 1997), 392; RO no. 73. "Fair" or "splendid" performance: Chaniotis, "Sich selbst feiern?" 158–59.

107. Polyb. 4.35.2, a procession under arms of all men of military age to the temple of Athena Chalkioikos; Arist. [*Rh. Al.*] 1423a 2–5; 1424a 4–5: military utility is one of the factors to be adduced by an orator in discussing the scale of processions.

108. Hdt. 1.31, cf. Σ Pind. *Ol.* 7. 152d ("great procession"): Nilsson, *Griechische Feste,* 42–45.

109. Hesych. κ 838 Καρνεᾶται and σ 1673 Σταφυλοδρόμοι.

110. Paus. 5.16.2–3; torch races: Xen. *Poroi* 4.52, Σ Patm. on Dem. 57.43 (*BCH* 1 [1877]: 11); cf. N. Sekunda, *ZPE* 83 (1990): 149–58.

111. Paus. 2.7.8

of ivy, they go to the shrine of Aisymnetes."[112] At a festival of Artemis on Samos, choruses of maidens and youths carried sesame-and-honey cakes, which other youngsters apparently sought to snatch from them.[113] In the fourth century, Spartan ephebes were likewise required to steal cheeses from the altar of Artemis Orthia, at the risk of a whipping if caught. Thence grew, apparently, the deadly "competition in endurance" below whips of the Roman period.[114] This is only a modest selection of the ritual roles assigned to young people of both sexes. As for choruses, particularly of girls, they are ubiquitous. The evidence on these topics can fill, indeed has filled, large books.[115]

The concept of initiation has often been introduced in this context, and it is certainly possible that festivals could have marked important stages in the process of culturally "growing" children into adulthood.[116] But clear cases are rather uncommon. One, in a sense, is the Ionian festival of Apatouria, which at Athens at least was the context in which male children were introduced to their fathers' phratries and thus made eligible for citizenship. The festival, however, was not an occasion for display by the new citizens-to-be; for them it was a registration more than a performance. Another is the Ekdysia, "taking off," known from Phaistos in Crete. There was a Cretan age-class of ἐκδυόμενοι, "takers off," and it looks as if the festival celebrated the moment at which they removed adolescent garb (or an assumed female garb) for the last time; the aition for the festival spoke drastically of a girl who actually changed into a boy Leucippus at this stage in her life.[117] Here then is a festival that took its name from a rite of passage; and we may assume that a young Phaistan who missed the Ekdysia failed to become a man. The festival Periblemata, "Putting On," of another Cretan city, Lyttos, may reflect the same transition viewed from the other side.

These rigorous criteria, however,—that the festival be built around a rite of passage undergone by all the members of an age-class—appear not to be

---

112. Paus. 7.20.1–2.

113. Hdt. 3.48.3; cf. Ducat, *Spartan Education*, 256–59.

114. Xen. *Lac.* 2.9; cf. Ducat, *Spartan Education*, 249–60.

115. H. Jeanmaire, *Couroi et courètes* (Lille, 1939); A. Brelich, *Paides e parthenoi* (Rome, 1969); C. Calame, *Les choeurs de jeunes filles en Grèce archaïque* (Rome, 1977).

116. See of late D. B. Dodd and C. A. Faraone, eds., *Initiation in Ancient Greek Narratives and Rituals* (London, 2003).

117. Nicander ap. Ant. Lib. *Met.* 17: for references on the Cretan festivals, see an admirable study by D. D. Leitao, "The Perils of Leukippos," *ClAnt* 14 (1995): 130–63, at 130–36; he compares the Argive Endymatia ([Plut.] *De mus.* 9, 1134C). In other Cretan cities the youths "graduate" at "Gods' Feast," Theodaisia, so at a more comprehensive polis festival (ibid., 136). Apatouria: Parker, *Polytheism*, 458–61.

met in any other case. The Attic Brauronia (and perhaps the ill-known Mou-nichia) come close, because they probably brought to a festive end the period of seclusion undergone by the little girls who served Artemis as "bears." At an ideal level, perhaps, all Athenian girls went through bearhood; but in reality probably only a modest proportion did. About many other festivals, such as the Attic Oschophoria or the Theban Daphnephoria or the Delphic Septerion, we can say with some confidence that the main ritual roles went to young people.[118] But not all young people underwent them, and not as a required transition. The main actors at the Oschophoria were, it is true, two youths dressed as maidens, and the detail seems to cry aloud that this rite, like the Ekdysia, had something to do with the growth of "boys with the look of a girl" into true men. But the most that can be said of such rites is that they dramatize crucial experiences of adolescence in the person of select individuals; the ages involved too are very various. They are not initiations; for, as has been well said, "I cannot be initiated for someone else any more than another can take a bath for me."[119]

Often the young were just one group of persons among many active at a festival. The description of the Spartan Hyacinthia quoted above stresses the prominent role of "boys in high-belted tunics" and "numerous choruses of young men." But from a different source we happen to hear of an occasion when King Agesilaus, a mature man, "took the place where the chorus leader put him" to sing the paean at the festival. Another great Spartan festival, the Gymnopaidiai, was similarly comprehensive. A festival mentioned above that the Magnesians established for Zeus Sosipolis in 197/6 BC is revealing.[120] They resolved that the prayers accompanying the "showing" of the bull should be uttered not just by a variety of sacred and civil officials, but also by nine boys with both parents living and nine girls with both parents living. The festival is being created before our eyes; this is no initiatory survival, even if groups of nine youths and maidens may well have had roles before this in Magnesian cult. The flourishing children are indispensable because they stand for hope, for the future of the city.

According to Dionysius of Halicarnassus, young men were given a promi-nent role in a great Roman procession derived (he believes) from a Greek original "in order that visitors might see how fine in numbers and beauty the

118. Oschophoria: see Parker, *Polytheism,* 211–17; bears: ibid., 232–48 (and general remarks on initiation, 209–10, 227–28). Daphnephoria: n. 168 below. Septerion: p. 192 above.

119. Redfield, *Locrian Maidens,* 91.

120. See above, n. 94. Spartan festivals: Ducat, *Spartan Education,* 262–74; Agesilaus: Xen. *Ages.* 2.17.

flower of the city growing to manhood was." When the city celebrates itself, it displays what it judges most valuable. Hoplites, chariots and cavalry matter, as do gold processional vessels; no less important are children. Their importance is far from decreasing with time, as the initiatory hypothesis might cause one to predict. It was in the Hellenistic period that the participation of the ephebes became an indispensable part of almost every Athenian festival; and pressure is applied on the young to participate in the festivals of other Hellenistic cities.[121] Such participation is a crucial part of their integration into the life and traditions of the city; but these are festivals, and traditions, that they share with other citizens, not exclusive to themselves.

Festivals Disorderly and Rude

An elaborate sacrificial procession was typically at the center of a festival of self-celebration. The importance of the sacrificial animals could be emphasized, as we saw in the chapter on sacrifice, by elaborate ritualization of the process of selection, by special arrangements for feeding of the chosen beasts, and by the attention directed toward them during the procession. Two festivals of Zeus in Caria had recurrent goat-miracles attached to them: at one the animal would detach itself from the herd and go spontaneously to the altar; at the other it would march steadily ahead of the priest through the pious crowds a distance of seventy stades to the sanctuary.[122] Such elaborations underlined the splendor of the sacrificial gift, or its acceptability to the deity, in an unproblematic way. But the effect must have been very different on those rare occasions when abnormal modes of sacrifice were adopted. Pausanias offers a detailed description of the annual festival Chthonia in the celebrated cult of Demeter Chthonia in Hermione. A succession of frisky cows were brought, roped and resisting, to the temple; they were then released to go inside spontaneously, where they were killed behind closed doors by four old women, cutting their throats from below with sickles;[123]

---

121. Chaniotis, "Sich selbst feiern?" 161. Dionysius: 7.72.1.

122. Apollonios *Mir.* c. 13 p. 107 Westermann; [Arist.] *Mir. ausc.* 137. Strabo reports another festival animal miracle from Caria, 14.1.44, 650: ephebes bring a bull to the Charonion cave; it advances a little, then falls lifeless.

123. Paus. 2.35.6–7. Aelian *NA* 11.4 and the poet Aristokles, whom he quotes, speak of "full-grown cows" (Aelian)/a bull (Aristokles) being led to the altar by a single priestess (Aelian)/old woman (Aristokles): they say nothing of the mode of sacrifice, laying all emphasis on the miraculous power of the woman over the animal. On the cult, see F. Ferrari and L. Prauscello, *ZPE* 162 (2007): 197–98 [+].

Pausanias reports as a "second marvel" that all the victims fell in death on the same side.

In terms of Greek sacrificial norms, everything here, except the brief hint of the well-omened "self-offering victim," is bizarre: killing indoors (no mention of an altar) by old women with a sickle.[124] One norm still observed at Hermione was that of the designated sacrificer. Even this was breached in wild events such as the Laphria (discussed in chap. 5), ruled by a horrible ethos of "everybody must kill." Very occasionally, the act of sacrifice was treated as a polluting killing. At Athens at the Bouphonia a trial was held to establish responsibility for the sacrifice of a plowing ox; on Lindos the sacrifice of a pair of plowing oxen was accompanied by curses against the sacrificer.[125] Why on these few occasions the normal protocols of sacrifice were so outrageously reversed, or sacrifice itself was treated as problematic, is very hard to discern. The cult at Hermione had a mystic tinge apparently relating both to agriculture and the underworld: women (in Greek ritual logic) and sickles perhaps evoke agriculture,[126] while the strange killing behind closed doors certainly has the strangeness of mystic experience even if it is not formally an unrevealable mystery. The Attic and Lindian rites dramatized not sacrificial killing *tout court* but the very special emotions evoked by the killing of a particular animal, the plowing ox: a killing that the rites nonetheless ended by justifying, in their own way. But beyond these vague generalities we cannot guess what sense the participants made of the particularities of the rites.

With a different set of divergences from the standard template we can do a little better. At festivals of self-celebration such as the Panathenaea, everything is decorous, ordered, hierarchical. But in other festival contexts very different forms of behavior were permitted or even de rigueur. The paradox, well known to the Greeks themselves,[127] is not simply that the normal religious requirement of "fair speech" was so drastically violated at certain festivals, but also that festivals were the privileged context for such violation. They were the natural home for gross obscenity. Attempting to ban "foul speech" and obscene images from the well-ordered society, Aristotle is obliged to make an exception, in the case of images, for "certain gods to whom custom also assigns ritual abuse (τωθασμός)," though even these gods

---

124. M. Detienne, in *Cuisine of Sacrifice,* 140–42 (203–6 in the Fr. ed.).

125. Laphria: see p. 167. Bouphonia: see p. 129. Lindos: Callim. *Aet.* frs. 22–23 Pfeiffer, with Pfeiffer's notes.

126. Pirenne-Delforge, *Pausanias,* 204.

127. Heraclitus fr. 15 DK; cf. Halliwell, *Greek Laughter,* 201–2. I rely heavily on Halliwell's thorough and acute discussion, ibid., 155–206.

are to be worshipped by none but mature males "on behalf of themselves, their children, and wives." He goes on to exclude boys below the age of participation in symposia from watching comedy and iamboi, thus implying a continuity between "ritual abuse" and these literary or protoliterary genres.[128] Where the lines are to be drawn between abuse and obscenity, where between rude words and rude gestures, where between these and carrying phalluses in procession, eating vagina-shaped cakes, and the like, is seldom clear; the various modalities of rudeness often flow into one another.

The phenomena Aristotle has in mind no doubt extend from the "jests from the carts" hurled by young men at Dionysiac festivals and the joshing (τωθασμός) of old by young before the Eleusinian Mysteries to phallic processions accompanied by song and abuse of spectators.[129] The "abusers" involved are therefore predominantly and perhaps exclusively young men. But the uttering of obscenities, and handling of lewd objects, by women on their own at festivals of Demeter (Thesmophoria and Stenia) is also well attested;[130] at a festival of Apollo (unexpectedly) on Anaphe and of Demeter Mysia near Pellene in Achaia we find reciprocal mockery between the sexes; and Herodotus speaks in a revealingly taken-for-granted way of formally orchestrated "abusive female choruses" in the cult of Damia and Auxesia on Aegina that "spoke ill of no man, but of the women of the country."[131] That "presentation by negation" of Herodotus may imply that one would have expected the women to abuse men, as at Anaphe and Pellene, not other women. Ritual abuse can often be seen (but with the Aeginetan case as an unexplained exception) as a playing out of the tensions between young men and their seniors, and between the sexes. During the seven-day festival of Demeter Mysia at Pellene, the day on which men and women abused each other was preceded by one on which all male creatures, even dogs, were excluded from the shrine.[132] Gender opposition was evidently a dominant theme.

It was a dominant theme also at the festival Hybristika in Argos (honorand uncertain, perhaps Ares), celebrated at the new moon of the month Hermaios, at which, we are told, "they dress women in male tunics and cloaks, and men in women's dresses and veils." The festival's name, "Outrageous

128. *Pol.* 1336b 2–23.
129. Phot. (and Suda) s.v. τὰ ἐκ τῶν ἁμαξῶν; Ar. *Vesp.* 1361–63; Semos of Delos in Ath. 14, 622A–D (items F6b, F1b, and F6c in Halliwell's catalog, *Greek Laughter,* 161–91).
130. Various sources: Halliwell, *Greek Laughter,* 174–77, F3 and F4.
131. Anaphe: Ap. Rhod. *Argon.* 4. 1719–30, Callim. *Aet.* fr. 21, etc. (Halliwell, *Greek Laughter,* 184 F 8); Pellene: Paus. 7.27.9–10 (Halliwell, 177 F5); Aegina: Hdt. 5.83.3: same rites in the same cult at Epidaurus, Herodotus notes, and adds that they (the Aeginetans? both?) also had secret rites.
132. Paus. 7.27.9–10.

Acts," suggests that, in this context where symmetrical cross-dressing so stressed, if paradoxically, the idea of sexual difference, rude words and perhaps rude deeds too may have been exchanged between the two groups.[133] The rite was explained etiologically by the supposed exploit of the women of Argos, led by the poetess Telesilla, in beating off a Spartan army from the city's walls when the male defenders had failed. In a wild spirit, one could guess that the Hybristika was a military festival at which women goaded men to valor by shame and insults: "Are you planning to go back in there?" said the Spartan woman, pointing to her vagina, to her cowardly sons. But it is not easy to envisage how such a festival could have arisen or been tolerated. Plutarch does, however, claim that, at certain unspecified festivals in Sparta, choruses of young women mocked young men in public for their inadequacies.[134] This is the negative side, only occasionally apparent, of the festival as society's showcase: the festival as a place of shaming, of social control.

To revert to a festival of assured obscenity: at the Thesmophoria, women were rude with no men present. But it is an attractive suggestion that even here the women will have directed much of their rudeness against the male outsider; that the mock phalluses and female genitalia so much manipulated encouraged a mood of uninhibited jesting about the absurdities of husbands and of sexuality; that shared indulgence in uninhibited dirty talk was a vehicle of bonding between citizen wives at festivals the "women-only" character of which was so strongly emphasized.[135] That explanation is not necessarily incompatible with the practice's mythic origin, whereby grieving, fasting Demeter was brought to laugh by Iambe's no doubt lewd jests or even by Baubo's indecent self-display.[136] Bringing the obsessively interesting but largely tabooed and highly embarrassing topic of sexuality into the open

---

133. Socrates of Argos *FGrH* 310 F 6 ap. Plut. *De mul. vir.* 4, 245C–E; cf.Pirenne-Delforge, *L'Aphrodite grecque,* 154–60 [+]. [Lucian] *Erotes* 30, stating that the incident caused Ares to be accounted a women's goddess in Argos, may give the honorand. The rudeness of the festival is not assured: Halliwell, *Greek Laughter,* 161 n. 14. But note that a similar myth of female valor explained the statue of "Ares Gynaikothoinas" ("feaster of women" or "feasted by women") in the agora of Tegea, and that in that myth the women were led by "Marpessa known as Choira" (Paus. 8.48.4–5), whose nickname irresistibly suggests *choiros,* the standard slang term for vagina (cf. "Perimeda known as Choira" in a related legend, Deinias of Argos *FGrH* 306 F 4; M. Moggi, "Marpessa detta Choira e Ares Gynaikothoinas," in *Ancient Arcadia,* ed. E. Østby, 139–50 [Athens, 2005]).

134. Plut. *Lyc.* 14.4–6. "Get back in there": Plut. *Apophthegmata Laconica* 241B; cf. Halliwell, *Greek Laughter,* 165 n. 26. Clearchus of Soli fr. 73 Wehrli ap. Ath. 13, 555C–D, claims that at an unspecified Spartan festival bachelors were dragged around an altar by women and whipped. On shaming practices in Greece, cf. Halliwell, *Greek Laughter,* 179 n. 83.

135. Winkler, "Laughter of the Oppressed"; A. C. Brumfield, *The Attic Festivals of Demeter and Their Relation to the Agricultural Year* (Salem, NH, 1981), 122–26.

136. E.g., *Hymn. Hom. Dem.* 198–205, "Orph." fr. 395 Bernabé; Halliwell, *Greek Laughter,* 160–66, with 204 on Iambe and Baubo as "life-affirming."

generates laughter, relieves tension, reaffirms life amid mourning. Even the discredited old theory that obscenity has to do with "fertility" (but fertility of what or whom?) can be reclaimed in some measure. The third day of the Thesmophoria was Kalligeneia, Fair Birth. Women at the Thesmophoria thought about procreation and so inevitably about sex. So in this context where sex was a serious matter it was also a sportive one; innuendo and ribaldry are guests at weddings, ancient and modern, for the same reason.[137]

Sexuality was fundamental to some aspects of Dionysiac cult too, though with the emphasis on potency or virility more than on procreation. The ever-lusty satyrs who accompany Dionysus prove that all the phalluses of Dionysiac cult do indeed have something to do with sexual desire and performance.[138] (I merely note the problem that rites of Aphrodite seem to be free from smut, though they might involve actual sexual indulgence.)

There existed also a whole world of dirty dancing—or rather of dancing judged by some observers, not necessarily native to the poleis in question, to be dirty. But it is a largely lost world: we glimpse it through sparse and often corrupt notices in lexicographers, and through the iconography of the two thousand or so vases and other artifacts (the largest group is Corinthian) that depict "padded dancers" or komasts.[139] These last are as vivid as one could wish and of manifest lewdness in some cases, but take for granted in the viewer a knowledge of the context of which we are deprived. It is debated whether the padded dancers are human or semidivine, or perhaps human imitating semidivine (like men dressed as satyrs); and, if they are human, whether they are performing in a private context or at a festival; and, if at a festival, of which god, and at what point on the spectrum from "ritual dance" to "protodramatic performance." A small number of instances that juxtapose padded dancers with ordinary, decorous male or female choruses may point to a festival context, and an intriguingly mixed one.[140] Some

---

137. Cf. P. Leigh Fermor, *Roumeli: Travels in Northern Greece* (London, 1966), 25: "The Sarakatsánissas, usually so silent in the presence of men, look forward to weddings as their only chances of fun. The talk, as though preordained, takes on a bawdy turn of hair-raising frankness. None of the exciting, comic or absurd aspects of sex are left unexplored.... All this goes on beyond male earshot, while, at a distance, their husbands and fathers and descendants smile indulgently at the seasonable ribaldry." On ribaldry at Greek weddings, Halliwell, *Greek Laughter,* 198 n. 125; updating of the fertility paradigm, ibid., 196–99.

138. Cf. above all E. Csapo, "Riding the Phallus for Dionysus," *Phoenix* 51 (1997): 253–95.

139. See above all the general introduction and the essays in part 1, "Komasts and Predramatic Ritual," in E. Csapo and M. C. Miller, eds., *The Origins of Theatre in Ancient Greece and Beyond* (Cambridge, 2007).

140. See especially Staatliche Museen zu Berlin, Antikensammlung Inv. 4856 (Csapo and Miller, *Origins of Theatre,* figs. 8–9, in n. 139 above), with the comments of Csapo and Miller, *Origins of Theatre,* 17.

connection with protocomedy and thus with the cult of Dionysus is very plausible, but the details refuse to come clear.

Of the dirty dances found in texts, least ill-known is the *kordax,* occasionally mentioned as a lewd dance by Aristophanes but also embedded in the cult of Artemis Kordaka in Elis; who danced it there, however, we do not know. We also hear, for instance, of a dance called *kallibas* or *kal(l)abis,* again associated with Artemis and involving an "indecorous" drawing apart of the thighs; of Brullichistai who wore "comically ugly female masks" and female clothes; of "Lombai: the women who initiate sacrifices to Artemis, so called from the equipment used in sport: for it *(lombai)* is a name for phalluses."[141] But what is one to do with dances of varying degrees of lewdness performed by dancers whose sex and age are often uncertain and whose social status is so always, in honor of often indeterminable gods at an unspecified point in usually unidentified festivals?

"Fertility" was the catchall explanation of the past (with startling implications, not rejected, for the nature of Artemis in whose Peloponnesian cult such practices seem to have been particularly common). Today we might be more inclined to think of conscious violation of decorous norms and the various implications such violation might have. In some contexts bawdy perhaps stands simply for festival relaxation, for a certain kind of holiday, like the lewd seaside postcard.[142] But there must be many other possibilities. We are told that the Spartiates used to humiliate their helots by forcing them to perform shameful dances when drunk. According to an elegant theory, young Spartiates at a certain stage in their training were required to perform similar dances, as an acknowledgment that they were not yet full equals, but also as a kind of inoculation against sharing the lumpish pleasures of their inferiors.[143] The theory is indemonstrable, but points up the possibility that social differentiation might be an issue in such a case. That approach lays stress on the comic/shameful side of such dances. But in lascivious dances can there not be also something, well, lascivious? To judge that possibility we

141. Artemis Kordaka: Paus. 6.22.1. *Kallibas:* Eupolis fr. 176 K/A with notes ad loc.; Brullichistai: Hesych. β 1245 and a chaos of other lexicographical notices (Nilsson, *Griechische Feste,* 186). Lombai: Hesych. λ 257. Cf. in general *ThesCRA* 2:325–27. W. R. Halliday, *BSA* 16 (1909–10): 218–19, detects symmetrical cross-dressing beneath these notices.

142. Leigh Fermor, *Roumeli,* in n. 137, 42–43, describes the carnival mumming, some of it transvestite and obscene, performed by the Sarakatsani of northern Greece, a people in daily life observing ferocious standards of decorum. "These goings on are said to drive away drought and guarantee an abundance of leaves and grass for the flock," he comments: he clearly detects a gap between the stated purpose and actual ethos of the "goings on."

143. Plut. *Lyc.* 28.8–9; J. P. Vernant, *L'individu, la mort, l'amour* (Paris, 1989), 181–90 (English in his *Mortals and Immortals,* 225–31).

would need to be able to observe the dances themselves and the reactions of spectators to them. (And what spectators? What dances by girls did men watch?) The deficiencies in our evidence cannot be overcome. The best that can be done is to emphasize how much is here missing in our picture of the festival world.

Social Reversal

Norms not of decorum but of social hierarchy were breached at other festivals. Athenaeus has two pages on festivals at which servants waited on masters; his aim, and perhaps that of his sources, is to show that there existed a Greek equivalent to the much more famous Roman Saturnalia.[144] He cites instances from Crete (the Hermaia), Troizen (an unnamed festival, perhaps, to judge from the month-name, a festival of Poseidon), and Thessaly (the Peloria, for Zeus Pelorios), as well as one from Babylon; less extreme was the Attic custom whereby at two festivals (Anthesteria, Kronia) masters dined or drank with slaves, a practice also found at the Spartan Hyacinthia.[145] Though the reversal is a different one, the Argive Hybristika (mentioned above), with symmetrical cross-dressing of the two sexes, perhaps belongs hereabouts too.[146] Explanations range from the commonsensical to the cosmic: at one pole, we are dealing with no more than the "authentic human need to loosen the reins from time to time," at the other with festivals of total renewal at which the order of the world is dissolved in order to be remade.[147]

The cosmic approach works best with the Thessalian Peloria; this was a major festival that supposedly had its origin in a feast that followed a crucial primeval event, the emergence of the Thessalian plain, without which the Thessaly known in historical times would not have existed. One can also note that the "white day for slaves" at the Attic Anthesteria was one of many reversals of normality occurring at that festival, and that the joint carousing of masters and slaves at the Kronia was doubtless seen as a reversion to the easy social relations of the time of Kronos. Both Kronia and Anthesteria occurred

---

144. 14, 639B–640A. A festival Eleutheria at Smyrna, at which maids and mistresses changed clothes, is known only, and doubtfully, from one of the invented authorities ("Dositheus" *Lydiaka: FGrH* 290 F 5) of [Plut.] *Parallela Minora* 30A, 312E–313A.

145. Parker, *Polytheism,* 202, 294; Hyacinthia: p. 189 above.

146. So W. R. Halliday, *BSA* 16 (1909–10), 212–19.

147. Commonsensical: e.g., Nilsson, *Griechische Feste,* 36, citing A. Lang; Halliday (in n. 146 above), 217 on "the sentiment of unity" at these festivals. Cosmic: see Versnel, *Transition and Reversal,* 119–21, on Eliade and Lanternari; Meuli's theory of "tied gods" (p. 184 above) is related.

at important incisions in the agricultural year (harvest and new wine), incisions that could easily be perceived as moments of transition or renewal. And one of the various aitia attached to practices of the Anthesteria related it to the aftermath of Deucalion's flood, a world-defining event.[148] But not just slaves but strangers too were entertained at the Thessalian Peloria, and we find the same pairing at the Spartan Hyacinthia (which has etiological associations of a different type); the emphasis placed by our sources in both cases is on "overflowing hospitality" more than on disruption of the normal social order. Like the Peloria and Hyacinthia, the Attic Anthesteria was perhaps the most popular festival of the community in question; at Hyacinthia and Anthesteria (as also at the nameless Troizenian festival) the feasting of slaves was just one element in a much more complex festival program. Certainly, no single template underlies these various festivals honoring various gods. The cosmic approach may over-mythologize, therefore, what was just a special application of the general ideal of festivals as a time of community. We noted earlier the Hellenistic festival truces that released slaves and schoolchildren from their tasks, and prisoners from their bonds.

One does not imagine that a master usually found the prospect of the Anthesteria very alarming. Did festivals ever reverse the established order in a genuinely disturbing way?[149] Maenadism in myth was as disruptive of masculine order as any behavior could possibly be, and it looks as if in some cases the maenads' disruptiveness could be reenacted and repressed within a festival.[150] But that was ritual, and it was priests who did the symbolic repressing; the doings of the historical maenads were viewed by the actual male civic authorities with complaisance. Dazzled by the largely mythical secessions of small numbers of women to the mountains in the cult of Dionysus, one should not forget the actual annual secession of potentially the entire married female population for three days at the Thesmophoria. This was the most drastic possible dissolution of the social order, and occurred in

---

148. Theopompus *FGrH* 115 F 347 (a) and (b); cf. Parker, *Polytheism,* 295–96. On the epoch-defining role of the flood in Meuli's thought, see, e.g., his *Gesammelte Schriften,* 1032–33; cf. G. A. Caduff, *Antike Sintflutsagen* (Göttingen, 1985). It might be pedantic to insist that the relation to primeval time is slightly different in Kronia (reversion to the "age of Kronos," before the present condition of the world) and Peloria and Anthesteria (immediate aftermath of the flood, i.e., emergence of the new world).

149. For an excellent discussion, and answer in the negative, see Versnel, *Transition and Reversal,* 115–21.

150. See below, p. 214. The *dendrophoroi* of Magnesia are a species of male bacchants (though serving Apollo Aulaites), men who in frenzy uprooted trees and ran with them amid precipices (Paus. 10.32.6, and much numismatic evidence: L. Robert, *Documents d'Asie Mineure* [Paris, 1987], 35–44, 237–39). But we know nothing of the social or festival context.

most Greek states. But it was expected and licensed and accepted without audible complaint.

The Thesmophoria aside, there are isolated cases. The fifteen-day austerities of the Aeginetan Poseidonia (dining at home without servants) were mentioned earlier, with some wonderment. We saw too that on Lemnos in the third century AD, if we trust Philostratus, all fires were quenched on the island for nine days in preparation for the arrival of new fire from Delos.[151] How often this happened unfortunately is obscured by textual corruption. Fireless life for nine days cannot have been very comfortable, and this may have been the context in which, according to a different source, "there is till now a certain day each year, on which the women [of Lemnos] keep away husbands and sons because of their [the women's] bad smell." No sex then as well as no hot meals, for one day at least. Myth and ritual stand, for once, in a significant relationship: in myth the Lemnian women murder their husbands, while the ritual too imposes an abnormal pattern of life for an extended period. This is an extreme case, however. New fire was ritually brought to Athens too, but without, to our knowledge, such a period of preparatory firelessness.[152] The isolated island, favored resort of the god of fire himself, nurtured rare traditions. Another rare tradition was that of "certain festivals at Kydonia [in Crete], at which free men do not enter the city, but the slaves control everything and have power to whip the free."[153] That case represents the *non plus ultra* of festivals of reversal, an extreme to which it is very surprising to learn that any Greek city went. Specific factors that might explain the rare case elude us, as usual.

Awe and Terror?

The "competition in endurance" in the festival of Artemis Orthia, at which ephebes allowed themselves to be whipped to death, "proudly and cheerfully competing for victory," was a popular spectacle in Roman Sparta. But this nostalgic recreation of an imagined ancient machismo, partly geared to the tourist trade, is no safe guide to the festival culture of the classical city. A similar caution applies to the competition in the same city in which

---

151. Philostr. *Her.* 53.5–7 (p. 67 de Lannoy).

152. See W. Burkert's celebrated article, "Jason, Hypsipyle and New Fire on Lemnos: A Study in Myth and Ritual," *CQ* 20 (1970): 1–16 (= *Oxford Readings,* 227–49). Bad smell: Myrsilos of Methymna, *FGrH* 477 F 1a. New fire at Athens: Parker, *Polytheism,* 84 n. 17 (the association with the Thargelia, accepted by Parker, *Miasma,* 26 n. 37, is wrong).

153. Ephorus *FGrH* 70 F 29 ap. Ath. 6, 263F.

Roman visitors watched teams of ephebes "fighting with unbelievable passion with punches, kicks, scratching, even biting, readier to be killed than admit defeat."[154] Predominantly, we have seen, festivals were fun, for participants as well as for spectators. Were there exceptions? Mock battles and ritual chases are occasionally mentioned in our sources, usually too briefly for their mood to be at all clear.[155] One of the few specific rites that we know within the long program of the great Dorian festival of Karneia was the pursuit of a heavily garlanded figure (perhaps called the "Garland-Man," Stemmatias) by the young "Grape-Cluster Runners"; if he was caught, this counted as a good omen for the coming year. This chase of the lone individual by a pack could no doubt have been experienced, at the imaginative level, as something grim and terrifying.[156] But the Garland-Man invoked blessings on the city as he ran: this was not the hunting down of an enemy to the city, and it is possible to imagine the event as quite cheerful.

The clear exception is Plutarch's remarkable report that in Boeotian Orchomenos "every other year at the Agrionia they [the supposed descendants of the murderous daughters of Minyas] flee and are chased by the priest with a sword. Anyone he catches he may kill, and in our time Zoilos the priest killed one."[157] But the event turned out badly, Plutarch continues; Zoilos fell ill and died, and the Orchomenians, subjected to public suits and fines, removed the priesthood from Zoilos's family and made it open instead. Zoilos was out of order, it is clear: the ritual license to kill does not mean that one may kill in fact. (It is interesting both that prosecutions were brought, and that they were, in a mysterious way, directed against the Orchomenians rather than against the killer himself.) It is suggested that the pursuit must have been motivated by an act on the part of the women, a symbolic reenactment perhaps of the child slaying perpetrated by their ancestors. The ritual was supposed to present a drama of women hurtling out of control but recalled

---

154. Orthia: Plut. *Apophthegmata Laconica* 40, 239C–D; for the context, see P. Cartledge and A. Spawforth, *Hellenistic and Roman Sparta,* 2nd ed. (London, 2002), 205–11. Biting, etc.: Cic. *Tusc. Disp.* 5.77; on the Platanistas competition referred to, see Paus. 3.14.8–10 and in brief Ducat, *Spartan Education,* 208. From Plato's allusion to "terrific endurance" at the Spartan Gymnopaidiai, as "they fight in (or against) the baking heat" (Pl. *Leg.* 633C), it has been concluded that Spartan festival culture already then set a premium on toughness; but Ducat, *Spartan Education,* 273–74, argues that the ordeal was an attendant circumstance, not design.

155. Battles: the Balletys at Eleusis (*Hymn. Hom. Dem.* 265–67, with N. J. Richardson's note ad loc.); the "stone throwing" at Troizen in the cult of Damia and Auxesia (Paus. 2.32.2). Chases: Hesych. δ 2036 with Suda χ 43 (Thesmophoria); Paus. 8.53.3 (the priestess of Artemis reenacts the mythical pursuit of Leimon by Artemis, which ended in death).

156. So Burkert, *Greek Religion,* 234–36, with the sources: most important is *Anecd. Bekk.* 1.305.25–30 s.v. σταφυλοδρόμοι.

157. Plut. *Quaest. Graec.* 38, 299F. On what follows, see Hughes, *Human Sacrifice,* 130–33 [+].

to order by a man with a sword; through zealotry or simple accident, the ritual drama became actuality. On either view, we must suppose that the play was acted with some intensity. At a biennial festival of Dionysus in Alea, "in accord with an oracle from Delphi women are whipped," Pausanias briefly and blandly records. A way of purifying them or rendering them fertile?[158] Or a further way of bringing them back to order?

Alongside the Orchomenian Agrionia we may set a rite at Halai Araphenides in Attica, as founded by Artemis in Euripides.[159] She instructs Orestes, just rescued from being sacrificed, to set up there the image he has stolen from the Taurian land, and goes on: "And establish this custom. When the people hold festival, as compensation for your sacrifice let someone hold a knife at a man's throat and cause blood to flow, as a token of piety and that the goddess may receive honor." This is the ritual drama that did not, to our knowledge, go wrong, where the knife did not slip. It is generally supposed that the rite had something to do with initiation and that the "man" was a young one and underwent mock sacrifice on behalf of his age-group (problematic though the concepts are of "representative initiation" and, in an Attic context, of male initiation itself). But no other source mentions the practice, and we are shooting largely in the dark. Comparable if less intense must have been the experience of participants in cults in which an original human sacrifice had supposedly been replaced by that of an animal or mitigated in some other way.[160] At a rite on Tenedos, the idea of substitution was very vividly dramatized. Aelian tells us that

> they rear a pregnant cow for Dionysus the manslayer, and when it has given birth they treat it like a new mother. As for the newborn baby, they put buskins on it and sacrifice it. The individual who has struck it with the ax is pelted with stones by all present, and flees to the sea.[161]

This rite has often been aligned with others that supposedly illustrate guilt experienced about sacrifice. But, at the level of religious idea, it is not a

---

158. See the opinions cited in Jost, *Arcadie,* 434. The sole source is Paus. 8.23.1. On two late antique festivals involving bloodletting, see Nilsson, *Griechische Feste,* 416–17. "Whipping the gods under the earth," Paus. 8.15.3 (priest of Demeter Kydaria at Pheneos), is surely quite a different thing.

159. *IT* 1449–61; cf. Hughes, *Human Sacrifice,* 81 [+].

160. E.g., Paus. 7.19.8 with 20.1; 9.8.1–2.

161. Ael. *NA* 12.34: Τενέδιοι δὲ τῷ ἀνθρωπορραίστῃ Διονύσῳ τρέφουσι κύουσαν βοῦν, τεκοῦσαν δὲ ἄρα αὐτὴν οἷα δήπου λεχὼ θεραπεύουσι. τὸ δὲ ἀρτιγενὲς βρέφος καταθύουσιν ὑποδήσαντες κοθόρνους. ὅ γε μὴν πατάξας αὐτὸ τῷ πελέκει λίθοις βάλλεται δημοσίᾳ, καὶ ἔστε ἐπὶ τὴν θάλατταν φεύγει.

sacrifice at all but an act of child killing: its place is with all the other evocations of child killing in Dionysiac myth. And a belief that human victims had once been sacrificed to Dionysus Omadios on the island (and on Chios) is duly attested.[162]

One may wonder also about those attending the festival of Zeus on Mount Lykaion, about which Plato reports the story that "he who tastes of the piece of human entrails that has been cut up along with others from other victims must necessarily become a wolf." Despite Arcadia's reputation for isolation, this was no obscure local rite, but an important athletic festival that attracted participants and spectators from much of Greece, the central focus indeed of Arcadian identity. Did the assembled Panhellenes subject themselves to this Arcadian version of Russian roulette? Or, if the sacrifice in question was shared only by a restricted group, an Arcadian *genos* perhaps, did the other Greeks nonetheless cheerfully attend a festival at which human sacrifice was believed to be practiced? Or was this conflation of Arcadian werewolf legends with the old myth of Lykaon, who served up his son to Zeus, just a story told by those who had never visited Mount Lykaion and never intended to?[163]

The sending out of pairs of scapegoats, *pharmakoi,* "cures/drugs," was not a story, though there were many stories relating to the practice; it must certainly be mentioned in any study of grim and sadistic elements in Greek festivals.[164] The sources claim that *pharmakoi* were originally dispatched ad hoc, in response to crises, but the practice also became embedded in festivals, the Ionian Thargelia in particular, and we have evidence for it only in its calendrical and not its ad hoc form. The Thargelia was a festival of Apollo that had some relation to the ripening corn, and scholars used to see the dispatch of scapegoats as an agricultural prophylactic measure: one purifies the city at a time when the crop is at an especially delicate stage, or perhaps the *pharmakoi* (who were whipped with plants on the genitals) were themselves corn spirits undergoing purification. These points may not be wholly invalid (for rituals can operate at many levels), but since the late twentieth century, studies have stressed that the practice is, above all, a form of scapegoating in

---

162. Euelpis of Carystus ap. Porph. *Abst.* 2.55.3. The details do not fit entirely: the god's epithet differs slightly, and Euelpis speaks of "tearing apart" (ἔθυον...διασπῶντες), which is not reflected in Aelian's rite. But as reported, Euelpis's primary focus was on Chios, with Tenedos added en passant.

163. So roughly Hughes, *Human Sacrifice,* 96–107 [+], at 106 (on Pl. *Resp.* 565D). Arcadian identity: T. H. Nielsen in *Defining Ancient Arkadia,* ed. T. H. Nielsen and J. Roy (Copenhagen, 1999), 27–29.

164. See Burkert, *Structure and History,* chap. 3; J. N. Bremmer, "Scapegoat Rituals in Ancient Greece," *HSCP* 87 (1983): 299–320 = *Oxford Readings,* 271–93 [+].

the modern sense, of reinforcing group solidarity by victimizing weak individuals onto whom collective ills are loaded. The luckless persons chosen, of the lowest status, might be fed at public expense for a period in advance, and normally suffered no permanent harm (they seem to have been driven beyond the boundaries, not killed):[165] to this degree only was the cruelty of the practice mitigated. As usual, we observe events from a distance; a close-up view of the social dynamics of the institution escapes us. Nor do we know when if at all it fell into disuse.

Festivals and Role Ascription

In a rough way, the discussion has had two parts: first the plots of festivals, occurrences at the imagined level such as the advent or disappearance of gods; then doings at the human level such as gift bringing to the gods, role reversals and ritual abuse, scapegoating and the rest. The two levels constantly intersect, since occurrences at the imagined level are regularly simulated through actions at the human level: the god arrives in the city when humans carry in his statue. The inventory of human actions has been far from covering all the festival activities known to us, which are in turn a tiny selection of all those that actually occurred (think of a thousand or so poleis, each with a full festival calendar, and all their subgroups...). Lysimache, long-serving priestess of Athena Polias at Athens, refused the mule drivers who had brought the sacred vessels a drink, "for I fear it will become ancestral tradition."[166] Almost anything could get into a ritual. But these twin levels of analysis, things imagined and things done, fail to capture much of what actually happens (one might say) at a festival. "Women at the Thesmophoria learn about, enact, and partially resist their role as citizen wives" is a proposition that goes beyond a mere description of what they do at the festival. But the perspective that it embodies is close to being a truism among contemporary students of ritual: "Communal religions... consist of ritually-enforced role-ascription, of a kind of religious orchestration of a social organisation," wrote Ernst Gellner.[167]

---

165. This was shown by the publication of the diegesis to Call. *Aet.* fr. 90.

166. Plutarch, *De vitioso pudore* 14, 534B–C, an anecdote activated by J. Z. Smith, *Imagining Religion* (Chicago, 1982), 53–54.

167. *Plough, Sword and Book* (London, 1988), 98; "Community-oriented traditional religions ... used ritual, not script, and were primarily concerned to underwrite and fortify communal organisation and the rhythm of communal life," ibid., 75. Not a particularly recent insight: cf. A. R. Radcliffe-Brown, *Structure and Function in Primitive Society* (London, 1952), 157, summarizing a conclusion of his thesis of 1908: "Rites can be seen to be the regulated symbolic expressions of certain sentiments. Rites can therefore be shown to have a specific social function when, and to the extent

Much of what precedes has implicitly looked at "things done" in that perspective. At this level there is inevitably a political dimension to festivals. If festivals are showcases in which society displays what it regards as being most valuable, the decision about what to display in the showcase cannot but be political. Civic/military processions give prominence to cavalry and hoplites, not to light-armed troops and oarsmen; thus they reinforce the perception that the rich, who provide their own mounts and armor, contribute most to the defense of the state. A remarkable poem written by Pindar for the Theban Daphnephoria shows how a civic festival might be exploited to celebrate, much as in an epinician, the whole family of the well-born youth who took the principal ritual role;[168] we have already noted that actual epinicia could also apparently find a niche for performance at civic festivals. The poetic inscription that Isyllus of Epidaurus dedicated to Apollo Maleatas and Asclepius in his homeland late in the fourth century begins with frank praise of aristocracy and goes on to describe his successful proposals for processions in honor of the two gods; "The best men of this city of Epidaurus, those who have city-protecting courage and shame in their breasts," are to be selected and to process "with their hair long" and make prayers on behalf of the citizen body at large; their prayers are to be for health, lawfulness (*eunomia*), peace, blameless wealth, and permanent nobility (*kalokagathia*).[169] At Epidaurus, as at Athens, long hair was probably a badge of the rich; "lawfulness" and "nobility" were oligarchic code words. The common people of Epidaurus are likely to have attended and enjoyed the festivals in question too, but that was precisely the point: to go along with such tiered inclusiveness in festivals was to accept the whole social order. Festivals existed that one can perhaps classify as "nonhierarchic," but whether any can be described as antihierarchic is very doubtful.

Festivals and History

This discussion has been static, but the world of festivals was far from being so. The whole character of festivals changed, it has been argued, in the late classical and Hellenistic period: they became less rumbustious and

---

that, they have for their effect to regulate, maintain and transmit from one generation to another sentiments on which the constitution of society depends."

168. *Partheneion* 2 = fr. 94b Snell-Maehler, on which see L. Kurke in *Visualizing the Tragic*, ed. C. Kraus et al., 63–101 (Oxford, 2007). Epinicia: n. 11 above.

169. Powell, *Coll. Alex.*, 132–33, A and B; A. Kolde, *Politique et religion chez Isyllos d'Épidaure* (Basel, 2003).

spontaneous, more an orchestrated and orderly performance, a self-display by the city (or a monarch).[170] Whatever the validity of that general thesis, there was certainly innovation at the level of individual festivals. The power of Hellenistic monarchs to write new festival programs was unique: "When Ptolemy [Philopator] was establishing all sorts of festivals and sacrifices, particularly concerning Dionysus," begins an anecdote by his contemporary Eratosthenes.[171] But constant changes occurred other than at the whim of monarchs, in ways that help explain what the festivals meant to the celebrating communities. New festivals were created or existing festivals expanded to celebrate historical events: the Hellenistic evidence is abundant[172]—the paradigm example is the creation of the Delphic Soteria, which celebrated the repulse of the Gauls from Greece in 279 BC—but there is no reason to doubt that the underlying thought pattern is older. "To this day the Athenians celebrate in a festival the battle at Marathon, and the Thebans that at Leuctra, and we that of Daiphantus at Hyampolis, as you know, and Phocis is full of festivals and honorific rites," writes Plutarch. The Klazomenians established a festival Prophthasia ("Getting in First") to commemorate the trick by which they secured possession of the town Leuke, disputed between them and Kyme, in 383 BC. The Eretrian Artemisia and Dionysia seem both to have been redesigned to commemorate particular moments in the city's troubled history in the second half of the fourth century.[173]

Even without being redesigned, existing festivals could be associated with great historical events and thus acquire an added meaning that might become dominant. It is a striking detail that the date of the battle of Salamis came to be identified, quite unhistorically as it seems, as Mounichion 16, the day of the festival of Artemis Mounichia: this is just one example of the multiple ways in which the Athenian festival program came to commemorate the great victories of the Persian wars.[174] Odd ritual practices of the kind

170. See n. 105 above; to similar effect, J. Köhler, *Pompai: Untersuchungen zur hellenistischen Festkultur* (Frankfurt, 1996). Among Hellenistic festivals, Chaniotis, "Sich selbst feiern?" 161, also distinguishes those organized by cities, requiring participation, and by monarchs, requiring admiring spectatorship (on participants and spectators, cf. Köhler, *Pompai,* 147–53).

171. *FGrH* 241 F 16 ap. Ath. 7, 276A–C; cf. P. M. Fraser, *Ptolemaic Alexandria* (Oxford, 1972), 1:203–4.

172. For seventeen epigraphic examples, see Chaniotis, "Sich selbst feiern?" 151 n. 33, summarizing his "Gedenktage der Griechen," in *Das Fest und das Heilige,* ed. J. Assmann, 123–45 (Gütersloh, 1991); two obscure literary examples are in Paus. 8.47.4, Ath. 13, 561F.

173. Plutarch: *Non posse* 18, 1109E–F. Leuke: Diod. Sic. 15.18.2–4, accepted as historical by Nilsson, *Griechische Feste,* 175, and Graf, *Nordionische Kulte,* 385. Eretria: RO no. 73, with commentary.

174. See Parker, *Athenian Religion,* 187: a key passage on Athenian commemorative festivals (on which see W. K. Pritchett, *The Greek State at War* [Berkeley, 1979], 3:168–84) is Plut. *De glor. Ath.* 7, 349E–350A.

usually explained with reference to myth occasionally receive pseudohistorical explanations, creditable to the community concerned, which have probably replaced aitia of the commoner type. Why does one group of young people snatch food from another in a festival on Samos? Herodotus gives the answer: certain Corcyraean youths who had been sent by the wicked Corinthian tyrant Periander to be castrated took sanctuary in the temple of Artemis on Samos, and to feed them the pious Samians caused choruses (!) of their own young people to file past bearing food that could be seized.[175] The primary source of legitimation for festivals remains the legendary past. But festivals are also the most natural of all vehicles to commemorate great events or noble deeds (real or imaginary) in a city's history. The age of heroes and great historical feats both embody that elevation above the mundane and transitory that is one part of the meaning of the festivals.

Another aspect of the relation of history to festivals is more controversial. The search for "survivals," the argument that ritual acts understood in one way by their agents, or not understood at all, "originally" meant something quite different, the attempt to get back from a murky and mysterious present of rituals to a past when all would have been clear and comprehensible—all this is methodologically thoroughly discredited. There is no pure and pristine state of rituals to be got back to;[176] and the essential postulate in studying rituals is that they made a kind of sense to those who performed them, even if not one that they could readily formulate in words; that they were not numbly going through a succession of meaningless acts in mindless obedience to tradition. All the same, Levi-Strauss's notion of bricolage needs to be attended to. This is the idea that mythmakers and ritual makers do not fashion new myths and rituals from whole cloth, ordered specially for the purpose. Rather, like handymen, they put together the materials they find ready to hand in their workshops, left over perhaps from quite different projects. When the Athenians designed a new ritual for the new goddess Bendis, the element "torch race," one might say, was one that they found ready fashioned for other ritual purposes. But they adapted it by making it in this case a torch race on horseback, appropriate to the "horse-loving Thracians."

---

175. Hdt. 3.48; cf. p. 28 above. Dionysus's ship-cart at Smyrna was explained by reference to a sea battle against the Chians, Aristid. *Or.* 21.4 Keil; a festival "Fast" at Tarentum is explained by a siege situation in Ael. *VH* 5.20. For a nice early modern parallel, see W. R. Halliday, *BSA* 16 (1909–10): 213–14.

176. See J. Z. Smith in *Take Judaism, for Example,* ed. J. Neusner (Chicago, 1983), 223–24: "In culture, there is no text, it is all commentary; there is no primordium, it is all history; all is application." Wittgenstein's critique of Frazer, as discussed by S. J. Tambiah, *Magic, Science, Religion and the Scope of Rationality* (Cambridge, 1990), 54–64, is relevant.

And obedience to tradition is not necessarily mindless, because local tradition means also local identity: the foreigner who questioned the Boeotian custom of sacrificing Kopaic eels was told that it was an ancestral custom, and one that needed no defense before outsiders.[177]

Perhaps the most bizarre of Greek rituals, though paradoxically one of the most fully described, is the ritual of Daidala, which according to Pausanias existed in two forms or two parts, the Small Daidala conducted at uncertain intervals by the Plataeans, the Great Daidala by the Boeotians collectively every sixtieth year (!).[178] A *daidalon* was a wooden image of roughly female shape, cut at the Small Daidala from an oak tree at Alalkomenai that was picked out by an elaborate ritual procedure. At the Great Daidala, fourteen *daidala* prepared at successive celebrations of the lesser rite were distributed among different Boeotian cities or groups of cities. But apparently one of these *daidala* was "chief *daidalon*" and played the chief ritual role. It was dressed as a bride and accompanied by a bride attendant and given a bridal bath in the Asopos. According to the myth, it commemorated a make-believe wooden bride whom Zeus had pretended to marry in order to arouse Hera's jealousy at a time of estrangement; on discovering the deception, Hera laughed and cheerfully assumed the role of bridesmaid. The *daidala* were then taken in a procession—the participating groups cast lots to determine their place in it—to the summit of Mount Kithairon; there, on an elaborately constructed wooden altar, sacrificial victims, publicly and privately brought, and the *daidala* were all burned together, in the most spectacular bonfire known to Pausanias.

It is as if elements from several different rituals have become blended together in a confused dream. A complicated ritual process is applied to select the precise oak tree from which a *daidalon* is to be made. But the *daidalon* serves in the end only to be burned. The festival honors the goddess of marriage, Hera, who is honored under epithets that evoke marriage; but the marriage in question is a simulated one and is never consummated. The combination of the motifs "deity's anger" and "wooden image" suggests the constellation of themes associated by Burkert with Telepinus; but

---

177. Agatharchides *FGrH* 86 F 5 ap. Ath. 7, 297D, cited in this context by A. Chaniotis in *Kykeon,* 42. Note, however, the defensiveness of this: he might well in a different context have had a story to tell about the custom. Bendis: Pl. *Resp.* 328A.

178. What followed is based, with many refinements and complications omitted, on two innovative studies: A. Chaniotis, "Ritual Dynamics: The Boiotian Festival of the Daidala," in *Kykeon,* 23–48, and D. Knoepfler, "La fête des *Daidala* de Platées chez Pausanias: Une clef pour l'histoire de le Béotie hellénistique," in Knoepfler and M. Piérart, *Éditer, traduire, commenter Pausanias en l'an 2000* (Geneva, 2001), 343–74. The sources are Plut. fr. 157.6–7 Sandbach = *FGrH* 388 F 1; Paus. 9.2.7–9.3.8.

the theme "prosperity restored" seems to be missing. All ends in a frenzy of destruction. Much here sounds archaic, and has often been treated as such. But the vicissitudes that the festival must have undergone are evident even from Pausanias, who explains its sixty-year periodicity (unpersuasively) by reference to the Plataeans' "exile" from their own city (two such exiles occurred, neither lasting sixty years). The festival as we know it is Pamboeotian; even at the Small Daidala the Plataeans leave their own territory to cut the wood at Alalkomenai, in the central area where two Boeotian federal sanctuaries were located. The fourteen *daidala* for fourteen groups should reflect the organization of Hellenistic or possibly even Roman Boeotia.[179] Perhaps the bizarre amalgam that we observe was product of a Pamboeotian bricolage, the creation in or after the Hellenistic period of a federal festival that put together elements from various local Boeotian practices.[180] It made sense because it spoke of Boeotian cooperation, a pooling of Boeotian ritual resources. The Pamboeotian element was so strong that the inconsequentiality of the amalgam created by bricolage was not felt to be problematic. Even the aition telling of the reconciliation of Zeus and Hera may have been emblematic. No history of the Daidala can claim to be true, but something on these lines may well be like the truth.

Divine advents and disappearances; the city celebrating itself; hierarchical processions leading magnificent sacrificial animals; human scapegoats; masters waiting on slaves; dirty dancing; special food; fasting; laments for dead heroes; nubile maidens carrying baskets; old women wielding sickles; Aristippus at dalliance with Phryne; the scrap of human flesh in the casserole—generalization about Greek festivals is clearly somewhat hazardous (though one should note that the most exotic items in the preceding list are by a long way the least common). I eschew it therefore, and end instead with something unique, an account of a Greek festival by its creator, Xenophon. He is describing the land he bought at Skillous in the Peloponnese with a tithe of spoils "taken out" for Ephesian Artemis.

> He [Xenophon] built an altar and temple from the sacred money, and afterward he always tithed the seasonal products of the estate and held a sacrifice for the goddess, and all the local citizens and men and women

---

179. Knoepfler, "La fête des *Daidala*" (n. 178 above), argues strongly for "Hellenistic," but Albert Schachter has kindly shown me an unpublished lecture in which he makes a case for the second century AD.

180. For a similar, rather speculative argument in relation to the Theban Daphnephoria, see Kurke, in *Visualizing the Tragic* (n. 168).

of the region took part in the festival. The goddess supplied them as they camped there with barley meal, loaves, wine, dried fruits, and a portion both of what was sacrificed and of what was caught from the sacred land. For Xenophon's sons and those of the other citizens conducted a hunt for the festival, and such adults as wished hunted too. And game was caught from the sacred estate itself and also from Pholoe, pigs, gazelle and deer.... In the sacred estate there are a meadow and wooded hills, capable of feeding pigs and goats and cattle and horses, so that the pack animals of those attending the festival could eat well too. Around the temple itself was planted a grove of cultivated trees such as provide edible food in season. (*Anab.* 5.3.9–12)

This idyllic and idealized picture of a fête champêtre differs somewhat from most of what has been discussed hitherto, though there are familiar elements: the broad participation, the integration into the preparations of the enjoyable activity of hunting, and the stress on food. Where normally the deity is summoned to attend the festival, here she acts as hostess; but some credit evidently redounds on Xenophon himself (festival as patronage, a topic not touched on here). What is typical of the Greek festival, or at any rate not untypical, is the relaxed blend of piety with evident relish for the simpler good things of this world.

❧ CHAPTER 7

The Varieties of Greek Religious Experience

The title of this chapter is an obvious echo of *The Varieties of Religious Experience* by the great psychologist and philosopher William James, brother of Henry.[1] But having followed William James as far as my title, I must at once part company with that distinguished and eloquent guide. The religious experience that interested James was interior and individual: it had nothing to do with ritual, nothing to do with religion as a collective phenomenon. What is more, he was only interested in the minority of intense believers: "I speak not now of your ordinary religious believer, who follows the conventional religious observances of his country.... His religion has been made for him by others, communicated to him by tradition, determined to fixed forms by imitation, and retained by habit." James's concern was with "individuals for whom religion exists not as a dull habit but as an acute fever."[2] After all that has preceded, it is unnecessary

---

1. (London, 1902). There is a large secondary literature: see, e.g., Donald Capps and Janet L. Jacobs, eds., *The Struggle for Life: A Companion to William James's "The Varieties of Religious Experience"* (West Lafayette, 1995).

2. James, *Varieties,* 6, in previous note. The contrast with Durkheim's *The Elementary Forms of the Religious Life,* published ten years later, is manifest (see, e.g., R. A. Rappaport, *Ritual and Religion in the Making of Humanity* [Cambridge, 1999], 374–81). But for points of contact and influence, see S. Stedman Jones, "From Varieties to Elementary Forms," *Journal of Classical Sociology* 3, no. 2 (2003): 99–121.

to elaborate the reasons why it is impossible to study Greek religion from a Jamesian perspective: though there may have been a minority of individuals for whom religion existed as an acute fever (persons "seized by the Nymphs," for instance)[3], they were unusual and without influence, while the idea that religious practice lost value through being communicated by tradition would have seemed very odd to a Greek. The varieties within Greek religious experience do nonetheless require to be emphasized. The point is perhaps exaggerated by the plural in the title of an excellent introduction, *Religions of the Ancient Greeks:*[4] the ritual of sacrifice, for instance, was much the same everywhere, Zeus had some role in every Greek community; but it has long been recognized that these constants were surrounded by numerous variables.

Two types of variety are in question. First are those deriving from the individual's situation: How does the religious experience of an Athenian differ from a Spartan, of a man from a woman, of a free person from a slave? Second are the variations actually or potentially available in any individual's religious experience; in particular, we need to ask what options were available, how, if at all, an individual could choose particular kinds of relation to the gods.

Place

I start with the first set of issues, the variations dependent on who you were. The most obvious form of variation is the local. No two Greek communities worshipped the same set of gods; individual gods had very different prominence and roles in different places. Artemis, for instance, assumes an unwonted role almost at the center of civic life in Achaea; Demeter dominates Sicily.[5] We are confronted with an almost infinite number of variations on a theme: the extent of the variations became clear when the Copenhagen Polis Centre for the first time counted the number of Greek poleis, and reached

3. Cf. W. R. Connor, "Seized by the Nymphs," *ClAnt* 7 (1988): 155–89.

4. Price, *Religions.* Rudhardt, *Essai,* 56 makes the point that Herodotus contrasts Greek religious practice with non-Greek, while drawing no such sharp internal divisions; "Pausanias présuppose l'existence d'un arrière-plan partagé, formant la trame sur laquelle se tissent les particularités locales," Pirenne-Delforge, *Pausanias,* 248, cf. 349. θεοὶ Ελλήνιοι: Hdt. 5.49.3, 5. 92 η 5; cf. Paus. 4.32.1.

5. Osanna, *Acaia,* 306–7; Hinz, *Demeter auf Sizilien,* esp. 19–30, with a plausible down-to-earth explanation: the agricultural importance of Sicily caused the cult to grow, and it thereby became a central element in the Sicilian self-image.

for the archaic and classical periods alone the remarkable total of 1,035.[6] This fact is universally acknowledged; the follow-up question that is very seldom posed, because ways of answering it are so hard to envisage, is that of the differences this made to the religious experience of the worshippers concerned. Artemis of the Ephesians was a very strange goddess both in appearance and in the organization of her cult—she was served by a eunuch priest with a Persian title, Megabyxos, and there were other singularities in the priestly structure that surrounded her—catholic too in her clientele; but no hypothesis has been advanced, to my knowledge, as to how, from the point of view of her worshippers, she differed from an ordinary Artemis.[7] The relevant differences relate in principle not merely to the gods worshipped; political arrangements should matter too, the ways in which access to the gods may have differed under tyranny, oligarchy, and democracy, the ways in which the whole ethos of a state was reflected in its religious life. The difficulty that always arises is that of finding good evidence for states other than Athens and, to a limited extent, Sparta, and for the detailed shape of religious life under any constitution other than the democratic. All that can be done here is to offer some illustrations of the kinds of issue that might arise.

I begin with the example of Asclepius at Messenia, which can serve as something of a cautionary tale. Excavations at Messenia in the southwest Peloponnese have been among the most spectacularly successful of recent times, and one of the most striking discoveries was a very large monumental precinct of Asclepius, so large and impressive that it was initially supposed to be the agora of the city; quite a number of civic decrees were in fact uncovered there. What was not found (or not identified) was any trace of the normal equipment of a healing sanctuary. The hypothesis was accordingly advanced and widely accepted that Asclepius in Messenia had been transformed from

---

6. M. H. Hansen and T. H. Nielsen, eds., *An Inventory of Archaic and Classical Poleis* (Oxford, 2005). There have been many regional studies of cults in recent years: Graf, *Nordionische Kulte;* Jost, *Arcadie;* C. Antonetti, *Les Étoliens: Image et religion* (Paris, 1990); Osanna, *Acaia;* Parker, *Athenian Religion* and *Polytheism;* M. L. Zunino, *Hiera Messeniaka* (Udine, 1997); K. Sporn, *Heiligtümer und Kulte Kretas in klassischer und hellenisticher Zeit* (Heidelberg, 2002); M. B. Savo, *Culti, sacerdozi e feste delle Cicladi* (Rome, 2004); Prent, *Cretan Sanctuaries;* Chiekova, *Pont gauche.* Seeking parallels for ill-known local cults from others better known elsewhere in the Greek world, such local studies have, paradoxically, a built-in tendency to normalize and homogenize.

7. See W. Burkert, "Die Artemis der Epheser: Wirkungsmacht und Gestalt einer grossen Göttin," in *100 Jahre österreichische Forchungen in Ephesos,* ed. H. Friesinger and F. Krinzinger, 59–70 (Vienna, 1999); J. N. Bremmer, "Priestly Personnel of the Ephesian Artemisium: Anatolian, Persian, Greek and Roman Aspects," in *Practitioners of the Divine,* 37–53 (where the tendency is to assimilate the goddess functionally to a standard Artemis); on her image, *ThesCRA* 4:56 no. 11 [+]; U. Muss, ed., *Der Kosmos der Artemis von Ephesos* (Vienna, 2001). Clientele: see A. Bammer, *RA* (1991): 66 ("Cimmerian" offerings), 72 (Semitic donkey-sacrifices).

a healing to a political god: the Messenians had long claimed Asclepius as a Messenian and as an ancestor, and it was argued that this role as a political symbol blotted out the function as a healer that he exercised in the rest of Greece. But there had always been skeptical voices, and in the 1990s deeper soundings did after all turn up the most characteristic mark of a healing cult, votive objects imitating body parts; the Messenian Asclepius can now be seen as much more like the Asclepius of the rest of Greece.[8]

I introduce this negative history in order to draw a line that is unlikely to be crossed: it is not difficult to suppose that Asclepius could have been both a healer and (in the particular case, for the reasons given) an important deity of the state, a civic symbol; but to suppose that he could have shed his original and basic role as a healer is to postulate a degree of variability that the Greek pantheon probably did not have. Were it true, I note in passing, that Hera at Croton had no association with marriage, despite being manifestly the leading goddess of that city, the line would certainly have been crossed, and the Hera of Croton would have broken decisively with her Panhellenic image (or never come into contact with it). But the argument is inevitably *ex silentio*,[9] and inconclusive.

From the negative example I turn to a positive one, one revealed or suggested by what have now been computed, in the long-awaited definitive publication, as the 5,360 fragments of at least 1,204 clay votive tablets, or *pinakes,* of the first half of the fifth century recovered from (it is generally agreed) the celebrated sanctuary of Persephone at Locri Epizephyrii.[10] It is the exceptional survival of this huge mass of religious documents that opens a window on a remarkable local divergence from the Panhellenic norm; one is left to wonder how drastically our picture would alter had other sites yielded material of like abundance. Inevitably I must greatly simplify. Of the 197 iconographic types identified, thirty-three types expressed in 413 tablets (more than a third of the whole, that is) depict the abduction of a young woman, sometimes from amid startled companions. In a minority of types the abductor is the familiar bearded Hades/Plouton, and the victim is evidently Persephone. Much more commonly the abductor is a youthful

---

8. P. Sineux, "À propos de l'Asclépieion de Messène: Asklépios poliade et guérisseur," *REG* 110 (1997): 1–24 (an early skeptic); J. W. Riethmüller, *Asklepios: Heiligtümer und Kulte* (Heidelberg, 2005), 2:156–67; M. Melfi, *I santuari di Asclepio in Grecia* (Rome, 2007), 1:247–89. Asclepius as Messenian ancestor: Hes. fr. 50, cf. Paus. 4.3.12; Luraghi, *Ancient Messenians,* 270 n. 80 [+].

9. It is therefore introduced with due caution by its proponent, M. Giangiulio, *Ricerche su Crotone arcaica* (Pisa, 1989), 63–64.

10. In the fifteen volumes of *Pinakes di Locri.* Persephone's Locrian sanctuary was for Diod. Sic. 27.4.2 "most celebrated (ἐπιφανέστατον) of the temples in Italy"; on it see Hinz, *Demeter auf Sizilien,* 203–6.

beardless figure; details from the familiar myth, however—a dropped basket of flowers, terrified companions—suggest that the victim is still Persephone. In some scenes of both types, Persephone reacts with horror and outrage; but in others it has been argued, though not uncontroversially,[11] that she has accepted the situation, being shown, for instance, standing tranquilly beside her abductor in the chariot (see figure 6).

Such a large number of tablets depicting the same subject must have been dedicated for a purpose and on an occasion. That occasion, it has been powerfully argued, was marriage:[12] at Locri, the seizure of Persephone had been reevaluated positively, no longer as separation from the mother and, in fact, a form of death, but as access to a position of authority in the husband's household and thus as a positive divine model for human marriages. The plaques would meld the contemporary human marriage with its divine prototype: the human kore retains traits of Kore, but the aged Pluton is replaced by a beardless figure more consonant in age with the human groom. (There is no need, therefore, to postulate an otherwise unknown local myth in which Kore was carried off for Hades by a younger man.)[13] Perhaps in Locri as in certain other Greek states some ritual gesture was made to the idea of "marriage by capture."

Whether this interpretation of the abduction tablets is right or not, all recent critics agree that the idea of marriage is evoked by very many of the other tablet types: scenes, for instance, in which girls surrender childhood toys to Persephone, or show to the goddess what looks like a marriage crown. A great majority of all the scenes can be seen as appealing to women approaching or involved with marriage in some way (but not to men in the same position; the world of the tablets is an intensely feminine one, from which males other than the two rapists/husbands are all but excluded).[14] One important series of types shows a child, apparently of either sex, sitting or standing in a basket in the presence of a goddess; a further female may also be present. What is shown, it has been suggested, is the kind of presentation of a child to a god or

---

11. See M. Cardosa in *Pinakes di Locri,* 1.2.247, arguing that none of the rapes are consensual.

12. See C. Sourvinou-Inwood, "The Young Abductor of the Locrian Pinakes," *BICS* 20 (1973): 12–21; "Persephone and Aphrodite at Locri: A Model for Personality Definitions in Greek Religion," in her *"Reading" Greek Culture,* 147–88 (slightly revised from *JHS* 98 [1978]: 101–21).

13. The possibility that the beardless figure could be a variant depiction of Hades was long excluded on the grounds that tablet type 2/30 showed the "young abductor" and a bearded Hades together. Note, however, that R. Schenal Pileggi in *Pinakes di Locri,* 1.2.256, has raised the possibility that the bearded figure of 2/30 is not Hades.

14. Inscriptions and weapon dedications show, however, that the sanctuary was also frequented by men (Hinz, *Demeter auf Sizilien,* 206). Hinz therefore treats Persephone at Locri as an archaic "total goddess," but I would rather see her as having expanded her role through emerging as the "special goddess" of the city (cf. p. 86).

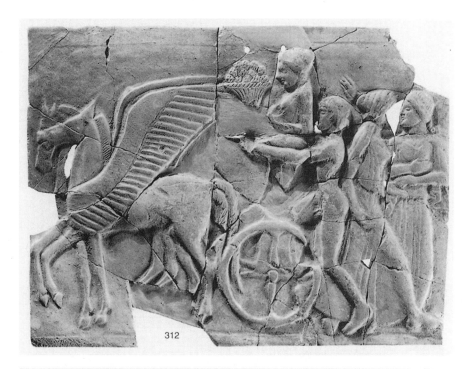

312

1

FIGURE 6. "Peaceful" and "violent" Locrian rapes: (a) "young abductor" and bride on a Locrian pinax, Reggio, Museo Archeologico, 59163/Caulonia; (b) the violent version, Reggio, Museo Archeologico, 58017+58018, reproduced from *I Pinakes di Locri Epizefiri* by permission of the Società Magna Grecia.

FIGURE 7. Goddess and child in a basket on a Locrian pinax. Reggio, Museo Archeologico, 61045/
Can, reproduced from *I Pinakes di Locri Epizefiri* by permission of the Società Magna Grecia.

goddess (in this case Persephone) well attested in the cult of other deities in
other cities; the point is to put the child under the deity's protection.[15]

---

15. Sourvinou-Inwood, *"Reading" Greek Culture,* 169–75. She insists on the point that the
child can be female, which is crucial in excluding a mythological reading of the scene. F. Barello in
Pinakes di Locri, 3.3.556–612, esp. 556–59, assumes a male child in every case, without (that I can
see) detailed argument.

The theoretical interest of all this is in the divergence between Perse-phone's role at Locri and in the standard Panhellenic representation. In that representation she is mistress of the underworld and, in close association with her mother Demeter, has something to do with the growth of crops. At Locri she still has both those roles (plaques show her seated on her underworld throne holding a sheath of corn), but she acquires a new one as patroness of marriages; she is also, if the interpretation of the "child in a basket" scenes is correct, invoked as a "child-nurturer," *kourotrophos,* to protect the growing child. In contrast to the Messenian case, therefore, Persephone has not shed functions but has gained new ones; and she has done so on the basis of the fa-miliar myth of the rape. The novelty is just that the myth has been reevaluated in positive terms. The effect that the expansion of Persephone's sphere might have had on those of other goddesses is the tantalizingly unanswerable next question. Aphrodite is not suppressed: she supposedly had a temple of her own at Locri, and she appears on some of the tablets where she embodies, it is suggested, the physical and uninstitutional eroticism that finds control within marriage.[16] Demeter apparently had no place in the Persephoneion, and very little on the tablets. It used to be supposed, drastically, that Persephone had simply blotted her mother out. (Some even dispute that Persephone was "originally" envisaged as Demeter's daughter; they do not explain, however, whose daughter she was.) But a sanctuary of Demeter Thesmophoros has now been identified in a different region of Locri.[17] Hera, the goddess who "holds the keys of marriage" in the Panhellenic representation, is thus far un-attested in the city in any role. But the example of Demeter just mentioned cautions against concluding that she was completely excluded.

A critic might protest that studies of this kind merely illustrate a kind of musical chairs in the divine world. When the music stops, different god-desses find themselves in different places; but the social functions that are discharged—patronage of marriage, care for the growing child, and so on—are the same whatever goddess performs them. Redfield, however, has tried to go further by relating the cultic singularities to the broader singular-ity of Locrian culture.[18] Locri, according to Redfield, was an oligarchy in which descent was traced through the mother: this was one reason for which so much emphasis was laid on a marriage, that of Persephone and Hades, in which the female was more important than the male. Locri was also,

---

16. See, e.g., Redfield, *Locrian Maidens,* 359–67, who suggests that the Locrian "pre-marriage offerings" may have been made to Aphrodite and Hermes at a small shrine within the Perse-phoneion.

17. Hinz, *Demeter auf Sizilien,* 206–8.

18. Redfield, *Locrian Maidens,* 346–85, 405–8. I fear my summary does poor justice to this subtle and eloquent writer, whose discussion is a most useful introduction to the tablets.

according to Redfield, a society in which the kind of hopes about the afterlife normally associated with a marginal group, the Orphics, were common cultural property: we owe to Aristotle's *Constitution of the Locrians* the remarkable information that the Locrians did not weep at funerals, but feasted.[19] For most Greeks, Persephone's marriage was a marriage to death and so could not serve as a model for human marriage: the Locrians, not fearing death, could see her destiny in a uniquely positive light. Because Locrian marriages were more "equal" than those in most Greek states and because the Locrians did not fear that symmetry between marriage and death that all Greeks perceived, marriage could be imagined as a foretaste of the blessings of the afterlife, and those blessings could be imagined in marital terms. This would be why (we might add) the cult of Persephone could become, uniquely, the chief cult of the city, important for men as well as for women.[20] Redfield's interpretation is a model of the ideal, in the sense of an approach that gives the study of cults real bite in relation to study of the society at large. Whether it is true is unfortunately another question; the matrilineal thesis is fragile,[21] the Orphic thesis rather narrowly based on a single fragment of Aristotle, the postulated Locrian idealization of marriage beyond proof.

As an illustration of the frustrations of trying to realize that ideal one might take the case of Sparta.[22] Did the city presented by Thucydides as Athens' antithesis in outlook and values have a significantly different religious culture also? Spartan extremism in certain areas of religious life has often been noted, even by the ancients: respect for oaths, respect for festivals, unwillingness to march out in defiance of bad omens were certainly not attitudes exclusive to Sparta, but were particularly pronounced there. Links between divination and power are found at Sparta of a kind that did not exist in democratic Athens: the kings had specially designated assistants, the Pythioi, who consulted Delphi on their behalf; conversely, one passage of Plutarch conveys the extraordinary information that every nine years the ephors were entitled to watch the skies on a clear night: if a shooting star appeared, this proved that a religious offense had been committed by one of the kings and he could accordingly be deposed, "until an oracle from Delphi or Olympia

19. Fr. 611.60 Rose.

20. Cf. n. 10 above.

21. See G. Lloyd's acute (but in my view too grudging) review, *TLS* 5272, April 16, 2004, 9.

22. For detail see R. Parker, "Spartan Religion," in *Classical Sparta*, ed. A. Powell, 142–72 (London, 1989); Parker, "Demeter, Dionysos and the Spartan Pantheon," in *Early Greek Cult Practice*, 99–104.

came to vindicate him."[23] But some of the most interesting questions do not allow ready answers. Much of the religious experience of women in most Greek states centered on the cult of Demeter, the goddess of corn; but Spartans did not cultivate their own fields, and one might expect the cult of Demeter to have diminished in prominence accordingly. Spartan women did, however, honor Demeter in some degree, and the extent to which their religious life had a different shape from that of most other Greek women is impossible to calibrate. Again, Sparta lacked a theater until the late first century BC,[24] but how many other aspects of the cult of Dionysus did the city lack? When, if ever, could a Spartiate go wild, behave outrageously? Moses Finley once memorably said of a segment of the Spartan population, "I am frankly unable to visualise these people," and the difficulty applies to the whole of Spartan society.

Another case, like that of Locri, where a rich iconographic find reveals an unsuspected world is that of a sanctuary at Kato Symi on the southern side of Mount Dikte in southern Crete, continuously used from the Bronze Age to the Roman period and attracting (once the Hellenistic epigraphic evidence begins, at least) worshippers from several different cities.[25] Among the many finds the most striking are ninety-five thin bronze plaques of the archaic and early classical periods, perhaps hung as votives in trees; there are also important bronze figurines of even earlier date. The plaques show, above all, beardless, often naked young men engaged with the native wild goat (agrimia): though they often carry bows, the emphasis is not on the hunt; rather they are shown wrestling with the goat, carrying it (alive or wounded or dead or already dismembered) on their backs. Once again, the scene that receives such recurrent emphasis should have ritual meaning; and an obvious possibility is that catching the agrimy was a rite of passage for ephebes, much like snaring the wild boar without nets in Macedonia. One plaque shows a second, bearded hunter face-to-face with the youth and clutching his arm: Ephorus's famous description of same-sex couples hunting together in the

---

23. Pythioi: Hdt. 6.57.2–4, Xen. *Rep. Lac.* 15.5. Shooting star: Plut. *Cleom.* 11.3–6; note, too, ibid. 28.3 and 9.1–4 on ex officio consultation of the incubation oracle of Pasiphae by the ephors.

24. There remains no evidence on the site of the Augustan theater or on any other for a predecessor (A.J.S. Spawforth, personal communication). Finley: "Sparta and Spartan Society," available, e.g., in his *Economy and Society in Ancient Greece* (London, 1981), 24–40, at 34.

25. Excavated and interpreted by A. Lebessi in many articles and in her Τὸ Ἱερὸ τοῦ Ἑρμῆ, vols. 1 and 3; cf. Prent, *Cretan Sanctuaries,* 572–91. For the initiatory interpretation see Τὸ Ἱερὸ τοῦ Ἑρμῆ, 1:188–98; for recent accounts see N. Marinatos, "Striding across Boundaries: Hermes and Aphrodite as Gods of Initiation," in *Initiation in Ancient Greek Narratives and Rituals,* ed. D. B. Dodd and C. A. Faraone, 130–52 (London, 2003); A. Chaniotis, "Heiligtümer überregionaler Bedeutung auf Kreta," in *Kult-Politik-Ethnos,* ed. K. Freitag et al., 197–209 (Stuttgart, 2006), at 200–202.

FIGURE 8.   Young hunter and older man on a 7th c. bronze plaque from Kato Symi. Louvre, Br. 93 (ex sylloge Castellani); photo © RMN/Hervé Lewandowski.

Cretan countryside for a fixed period of two months has accordingly been adduced, and the gifts given in conclusion by the older man to his young partner (a striking military suit, a bovine, a cup) have been identified on the plaques and figurines. Ephorus's institution was not, at least in his description of it, a rite of passage,[26] and should perhaps be left out of account; but the case for associating the plaques with maturation rituals can stand independently of it.

What is surprising is again the identity of the deities concerned.[27] "Hermes of the Cedar" (Kedrites) is mentioned on two dedications, one of the Roman period and one (?) Hellenistic, but he appears unmistakably much earlier on the plaques (once seated in a tree); a graffito dedication to Aphrodite was also found, and, though the evidence for her presence is much more sparse, it is possible that the cult association of Hermes and Aphrodite (which somehow issued in the figure of the hermaphrodite) finds here its earliest attestation. Nobody in the voluminous literature on Greek initiation rites had ever assigned a place of any importance in them to Hermes (nor was he known to have any connection with hunting), though it is true that he acquired an important role (itself not well explained) from late classical times as patron of the gymnasium. Can one say that, as god of spatial transitions, Hermes is also a natural patron of status transitions?[28] Or is this just a play on the ambiguity of the word "transition"? It is not clear either how the idea of "unrestrained sexuality" that seems to underlie the pairing of Hermes with Aphrodite might relate to the growing up of Cretan youths. The reliefs shed brilliant illumination on a scene in the foreground, behind which is darkness.

Variation by region is not a matter just of the role of particular gods. The practice of assigning priesthoods by sale, for instance, is common in Asia Minor and the islands off its coast (though not universal even there) but reaches its farthest westward point in Andros. Manumitted slaves are put under the notional protection of a god ("sacral manumission") in some cities but not in others.[29] In western Macedonia there develops or survives a form whereby the ex-slave acquires certain cultic obligations and the surrender of the slave is therefore in part a gift by the owner to the god like any other: owners can vow to give a young slave to the god and incur divine punishment for not

---

26. See J. Davidson, *The Greeks and Greek Love* (London, 2007), 300–315, on Ephorus *FGrH* 70 F 149 ap. Strabo 10.4.21, 483–84. Wild boar in Macedonia: Hegesandros ap. Ath. 1, 18A; cf. Amm. Marc. 31.9.5 on the Taïfali.

27. For the inscriptions see A. Lebessi, *ArchEph* (1981): 1–24, at 4–5; for Hermes shown in a tree, see her Ἱερὸ τοῦ Ἑρμῆ, 1:146–53, on plaque A 21 (*ThesCRA* 3:316 no. 58 [cf. 59], with pl. 59).

28. So, ingeniously, Marinatos, "Striding across Boundaries," in n. 25 above. For thoughts on Hermes and Aphrodite, see ibid.; Sourvinou-Inwood, *"Reading" Greek Culture,* 177–78; Redfield, *Locrian Maidens,* 366–67. Lebessi interprets Hermes Kedrites in terms of a pre-Greek substrate (e.g., Τὸ Ἱερὸ τοῦ Ἑρμῆ, 1:137, 163–87): a dubious approach, but possibly receiving some support from the "in the tree" iconography (n. 27 above).

29. Sale: see chap. 2 n. 29. Manumission: see now R. Zelnick-Abramowitz, *Not Wholly Free* (Leiden, 2005).

doing so, and exceptionally even a free child can be so consecrated.[30] Here as so often it is the existence of a large corpus of homogeneous nonliterary documents (epigraphic in this case) that renders the regional singularity vivid. How a "Geography of Greek Religion" might be written to go alongside the many "Histories" is a tantalizing question. The units involved are too many (those 1,035 cities, and their subdivisions), and the variations cannot be tidily herded into regional or (like dialects) ethnic groupings. But the god-by-god approach of the canonical histories inevitably obscures diversity, while regional monographs lack the comparative dimension.

Social Position

I leave that probably insoluble problem, and move on: to differences linked to social position. It has often been supposed that Demeter and Dionysus are virtually absent from Homer's poetry because the warrior aristocracy for whom epic was written despised them as "people's gods." But no ancient source provides more than faint support for the idea of such class distinctions on Olympus.[31] The rich sacrificed more than the poor, made more and richer dedications, were much more likely to hold priesthoods, but did not address a different set of gods. Poor Athenians often made dedications to Pan and the nymphs, but a fine recent specimen was commissioned by one

---

30. See above all the superb corpus of material *Leukopétra*. Those texts are of the second/third century AD, but comparable dedication of a slave to a goddess is already attested in Edessa apparently in the early second century BC (*SEG* 43.388; cf. *Leukopétra*, 36 n. 6). For a well-argued attempt to deny that these cases represent manumissions at all, see M. Ricl, "Donations of Slaves and Freeborn Children to Deities in Roman Macedonia and Phrygia: A Reconsideration," *Tyche* 16 (2001): 127–60. ("Phrygia" in her title refers to the cult of Apollo Lairbenos, in which the consecration of children by their parents is not uncommon: *EpigAnat* 32 [2000]: 1–86; ibid., 41 [2008]: 91–111.) But she seems to me to overstate the extent of the deity's claim over the consecrated person, which never extends beyond "service on the regular days," and thus to understate the degree of extra freedom achieved; contrast M. S. Youni, *Provincia Macedonia* (Athens, 2000), 54–115. (For the rare requirement of such service from sacrally manumitted slaves in other regions, see L. Darmezin, *Les affranchissements par consécration en Béotie et dans le monde grec hellénistique* [Paris, 1999], 219–21.) M. B. Hatzopoulos, *Cultes et Rites de Passage en Macédoine* (Athens, 1994), 113–19, notes that most of the consecrated ex-slaves are young and that the gods to whom such consecrations are made are ones who might be involved in "*rites de passage*": he suspects a mutation of an institution in which freeborn children were bound to temple service (like, for instance, the "bears" of Artemis at Brauron).

31. See Parker, *Athenian Religion*, 75. Hecker's conjecture whereby the "small god among the small" (ἐν σμίκροις ὀλίγος θεός), Tychon, would describe himself as δημοτέρων (ms. δημογέρων) θεός in *Anth. Pal.* 9.334 (Perses 8, Gow-Page, *HE*) is uncertain, since δημότερος seems to mean "local," not "popular" (see the 1996 supplement to LSJ). I cannot recover the source for an apophthegm of Wilamowitz once quoted to me by a senior colleague: "*inter deos nulli nobilitatis gradus.*" For the other view, see, e.g., Nilsson, *Geschichte*, 565.

of the richest; conversely, a washerwoman could dedicate to Athena on the acropolis.[32]

Another negative is that there were no slave cults in Greece, or almost none. Slaves had a religious life, if a very meager one, but it was largely conducted on the fringes of their masters' and addressed to their masters' gods. There was no role and no meat for them at festivals in their public aspect, though they might get their share, occasionally a guaranteed share, on the private side, and benefit from the general cessation of work. They could be initiated into mysteries: A recognition of their basic humanity, or of the need for practical reasons to allow slaves into mystic sanctuaries for menial services?[33] In the Hellenistic period, probable slaves are found as members of private religious societies, *thiasoi,* but it is almost never clear that such a group was made up specifically of slaves rather than of "little people" more generally. Slaves and free could mix, therefore; but the converse is that slaves did not develop their own religious forms through worshipping by themselves. One flourishing society of this type in Attica honored a non-Greek god, the Thracian Bendis, but the cult of Bendis had been brought to Athens by free Thracians, presumably metic merchants; there is no clear case of a cult introduced to Greece by slaves.[34]

The possible exceptions to this dependence on other people's gods come from contexts where slaves lived in clusters: there are traces of slave-only

---

32. Nymphs: Parker, *Athenian Religion,* 167. Washerwoman: *IG* 1³.794.

33. On the fringes: cf. Parker, *Polytheism,* 16 n. 33, 169, 202, 294; F. Bömer, *Untersuchungen über die Religion der Sklaven in Griechenland und Rom,* vol. 3, *Die wichtigsten Kulte der griechischen Welt,* 2nd ed. (Mainz, 1990). Much of Bömer's longish monograph is devoted to the Roman period, or to such phenomena as the tasks performed by sacred slaves: his verdict on the religious life of slaves in classical Greece is extremely bleak (e.g., 61, 238). I know no reason to deny that a slave who could afford it was free to make dedications in any sanctuary (except those few to which slaves were explicitly denied access); but demonstrable instances are few (see following notes). For the release of slaves from work at major festivals, and for their privileged role at certain festivals of reversal, see pp. 176, 211–13; they might also share in the entertainment provided by benefactors at Hellenistic festivals, but as it seems exceptionally only, and on a lesser scale than citizens (Schmitt Pantel, *Cité au banquet,* 399–401). Mysteries: Bömer, *Untersuchungen über die Religion* (in this note), 109–12 (Andania; Eleusis); 145–49 (Samothrace). For consultations by slaves at the oracle of Dodona, see Eidinow, *Oracles, Curse and Risk,* 100–104.

34. Slaves in *thiasoi:* the names suggest this for two *thiasoi* of Bendis on Salamis (known from five mid–third century texts now republished by M. J. Osborne, *Horos* 17–21 [2004–9], 657–672; cf. *Martini P. Nilsson opuscula selecta* [Lund, 1960], 3:72–73), and for two honoring uncertain gods at Eleusis (*SEG* 24.223, "second half of fourth century"; *SEG* 24.156, c. 238/7; cf. L. Robert, *ArchEph* [1969]: 14–23 = *OMS* 7.720–29, *SEG* 32.149); for non-Attic evidence, see F. Poland, *Geschichte des griechischen Vereinswesens* (Leipzig, 1909), 328. The Rhodian society of "[Diosatabyr?]iasts slaves of the city" is a rare example of an all-slave society, *IG* 12.1.31; but it is a restricted professional grouping, not a meeting place for slaves of every kind. Bendis brought to Athens: Parker, *Athenian Religion,* 170–75.

religious groupings among the mines at Laurion in Attica; and it is interesting to speculate, though that is all that one can do, about the cults of the helots of Messenia and of other serf-like populations elsewhere.[35] But none of this develops into anything remotely resembling a distinctive slave religion; "slave gods" exist at most in the weak sense of "gods in whom slaves often take an interest."[36] The strange Chian cult of the "Friendly Hero" Drimakos is thought to be rooted in the special conditions of Chios, an island with a uniquely large slave population that always posed problems of control. In life, according to legend, Drimakos had been leader of a band of runaway slaves living by plunder in the hills, but had also established a certain modus vivendi with the city and had sent back slaves who fled to him without due cause; in death too he had a foot in both camps, receiving firstfruits from the spoils of the marauding bands, but also thank offerings from their masters, whom he warned in dreams of forthcoming troubles with their slaves. So even Drimakos is more a symbol of an uneasy coexistence than an out-and-out slave hero. Leaders of slave revolts regularly claimed divine signs and support,[37] but slaves never rose up in the name of a particular non-standard god.

Another class on the fringes of mainstream religious life in Greece were resident foreigners, metics. In a society where one's religious life was based on the social groups one was born into, it must have been difficult to live away from those groups. Women at marriage were snatched away, it was said, from their ancestral gods; so too were men who traveled. (Leocrates, who fled Athens in terror after the defeat at Chaeronea, had sent to him in Megara, to Lycurgus's

---

35. Laurion: see S. Lauffer, *Die Bergwerksklaven von Laureion,* 2nd ed. (Wiesbaden, 1979), 128–30, 185–92 on *IG* 2².2937–38, 2940 (dedications by slave *eranistai* from Laurion); the recipient is unfortunately not clear, and we cannot know whether they were made at a sanctuary/sanctuaries founded by themselves (like the much later *IG* 2².1365–66 = *LSCG* 55). On 178 he lists five further pre-Roman dedications (to hero, Artemis [bis], Men [but the slave status of the dedicants here, *IG* 2².4684, is doubted by Bömer, *Untersuchungen über die Religion der Sklaven,* 196–97, in n. 33 above], and Athena) from the Laurion/Thorikos region by presumptive mine slaves; again the problem arises whether these were at slave-founded shrines (and of what gods underlie the names). For evidence of worship of Bendis in the region, see P. Themelis, *Horos* 7 (1989): 23–29 (Parker, *Athenian Religion,* 174 n. 74). Helots: see N. Deshours, *Les Mystères d'Andania* (Bordeaux, 2006), 154–58; Luraghi, *Ancient Messenians,* 202.

36. E.g., the nymphs, to whom there are two Attic dedications by groups who, to judge from their names, include some slaves or ex-slaves (*IG* 2².2934, offered by πλυνῆς; *IG* 2².4650; but cf. a similar dedication by probable citizens, *IG* 2².4832); Bendis; perhaps Men.

37. Diod. Sic. 34.2.5; 36.5.1–3; 36.7.1; cf. Dickie, *Magicians,* 113–14; W. Burkert in *ThesCRA* 3:44, who notes Hdt. 6.83.2, where a seer incites the ex-slaves of Argos to revolt. Drimakos: Nymphodorus of Syracuse (late first century), *FGrH* 572 F 4 ap. Ath. 6, 265C–266E, well discussed by Graf, *Nordionische Kulte,* 121–25. Nymphodorus speaks of Drimakos living "shortly before our time," which many doubt; an obscure concluding statement by Athenaeus that "in many copies I did not find him mentioned by name" has been taken as showing that the identification of "Friendly Hero" with Drimakos was secondary (on both points see Jacoby ad loc.).

great outrage, such of his "ancestral sacred things" as were portable; but he could not take the altars of phratry and deme and city that were also "ancestral" to him.)[38] Where British travelers could satisfy their weekly needs with a single "Protestant church in Rome" or wherever it might be, Greeks were used to receiving cuts of meat from animals offered to many different gods. By the Hellenistic period, it can be argued, there were ways for wealthy metics, at least, to meet most of their religious needs. They could become members of private religious associations. In Rhodes in particular these achieved spectacular popularity, over a hundred such picturesquely named groupings ("Hermaistai Athanaistai Haliadai Haliastai," and the like) being attested in the second and first centuries; the place of citizens in these societies is controversial, but it is certain that they had a predominantly non-citizen membership.[39]

No doubt the needs that the Hellenistic societies met were only in part, sometimes only in small part, religious. But amid the multifarious functions that they performed (sociability, networking, guaranteed burial) they provided a focus of religious activity, a limited cult group to which one belonged by right, for those who felt the need of one. In the Hellenistic period it also became regular for metics (and occasionally even temporary visitors) to be included by cities or benefactors in the invitation to public banquets, and to walk in the processions that preceded them. And in Athens, in the late Hellenistic period, the old strict line of division became permeable, at least to the wealthy, to the extent that non-citizens could serve as "performers of sacred rites" or even acquire citizenship and become priests.[40]

What of earlier centuries? Metics were better off than slaves in that, at Athens at least, they were assigned portions of meat at a certain number of public sacrifices; at the Panathenaea they were given a place in the procession, and at the Bendidea there was a special torch race on horseback conducted by Thracians. Metics could watch, and enjoy the general mood of festivity, at many more. Throughout Greece they could probably bring sacrifices

38. Lycurg. *Leoc.* 25–26, 56. Women: Soph. fr. 583.8 (*Tereus*); Eur. fr. 318.4 (*Danae*).

39. See G. Pugliese Carratelli, "Per la storia delle associazioni in Rodi antica," *ASAtene* n.s. 1–2 (1939–1940) [1942]: 147–200, and V. Gabrielsen, *The Naval Aristocracy of Hellenistic Rhodes* (Aarhus, 1997), 123–29; for the earliest evidence, Pugliese Carratelli, 187. The controversial issue is whether persons designated "Rhodioi" without demotics are full Rhodian citizens (so Gabrielsen, 120–21, against most previous scholarship). Note that in *SEG* 39.737 (contributions by members of a society) such "Rhodians" are in a clear minority. Gabrielsen argues, *ClassMed* 45 (1994): 152–54, that simultaneous membership of several associations was possible. On Athenian societies see Parker, *Athenian Religion,* 338–42. A new synthesis to replace the learned but dyssynoptic work of F. Poland (n. 34 above) is needed; J. S. Kloppenborg and S. G. Wilson, eds., *Voluntary Associations in the Graeco-Roman World* (London, 1996), mostly treats a later period.

40. Banquets: Schmitt Pantel, *Cité au banquet,* 389–96; S. Krauter, *Bürgerrecht und Kultteilnahme* (Berlin, 2004), 73–80 (also on processions). *Hieropoioi* and priests: Parker, *Athenian Religion,* 267.

and make dedications at all public sanctuaries except a small number from which foreigners were formally banned; and they could sacrifice in their own houses.[41] Permanent religious associations that admitted Greek non-citizens (whether exclusively or alongside citizens), however, do not appear until the third century (ethnic associations, of Thracian worshippers of Bendis or Egyptian of Isis or Cypriot of Aphrodite, go back further, to the fourth and probably the fifth century).[42] The formal associations with constitutions and premises and funds probably, it is true, had informal predecessors in some cities: Would the organizer of a "revel band" in fourth century Athens, for instance, have insisted on proof of citizen status from every individual willing to pay to participate? But participating in a temporary *thiasos* might not have given a sense of belonging as one belonged, say, in a phratry at home. How cramped a metic would have felt in the classical period is hard to say; it is the kind of social question to answer which we would need the evidence of (to be unrealistic) a novel with a metic protagonist. We do not know how numerous were the "certain number of sacrifices" mentioned above at which metics were full participants. There were certainly serious exclusions. A metic wife could enjoy the Adonia, a festival celebrated in private houses, to the full. But to the Thesmophoria, most important of women's festivals, she was (on the commonest view)[43] not admitted.

Gender

That example leads on to another variety of religious experience determined not by choice but by birth, that based on gender. Even Martin Nilsson, long before the feminist revolution, spoke of a "deep gulf" between men's and women's religious experience; the ancients already had their own negative

---

41. For Athens see Parker, *Polytheism,* 67, 170–71 (where the corresponding obligations of metics in respect of liturgies are also mentioned). The evidence for other classical cities is poor, but Spartan and Thessalian festivals at which *xenoi* were feasted are attested (see pp. 211–12). The general view that *xenoi* could sacrifice only with the assistance of a *proxenos* is much weakened by Krauter, *Bürgerrecht und Kultteilnahme* (n. 40 above), 81–93; see ibid., 58–64, 80, for the rare absolute exclusions. Rights of the *xenos* to sacrifice and "receive portions" (if that is the force of λαγχάνειν here) in E. Locri (less probably in Naupaktos) are attested by ML 20 (*Nomima* 1:43) 1–4; but we do not know how restricted or extensive these rights were.

42. The question is whether the Thracian association of Bendis worshippers attested in the third century (*IG* 2².1283) is already implied by the role of Thracians in the cult in the fifth (Pl. *Resp.* 327A). Isis and Aphrodite: RO 91.

43. See Parker, *Polytheism,* 271 n. 4.

stereotypes of female religiosity.[44] The topic merits a book of its own and can only be touched on here. It has become something of a cliché to say that, though women were excluded from citizenship in the sense of political rights, they possessed "cultic citizenship": an Athenian woman, say, is likely to have felt that she was Athenian, different from the wives of non-citizens, above all because of the cults she was entitled to participate in (chief among them the Thesmophoria); the chorus in Aristophanes' *Lysistrata* demonstrate their debt to the city by listing the ritual roles that they have discharged (638–48). Inequality is redressed in the religious sphere, therefore; and in some ways the religious possibilities were the same for both genders. It is of crucial symbolic importance that priestesses were as numerous and as conspicuous as priests. The same modes of communication with the gods were in principle open to both genders: like men, women could pray, make dedications, pay for and participate in sacrifices.

A necessary qualification to the last point is, however, that women in fact sacrificed and ate of sacrificial meat much less often than did men. The religious order depended on the political and social order, and most publicly financed sacrifices took place within political and social groupings (city, deme, phratry) to which women did not belong. Even in the domestic context they probably sacrificed much more rarely than men. In a poignant scene in the *Odyssey* where Penelope prays to Athena, she holds a basket full of barley grains in her hand, in a kind of gesture to sacrifice; she raises the excited cry, *ololugē,* typically raised by women in accompaniment to sacrifices performed by men; but she brings no offering, and she bases her appeal on past sacrifices made by Odysseus rather than by herself.[45] With dedications too, it seems to be the case that women made fewer, at least at the expensive inscribed level that allows gender identification, than did men.[46]

To turn to differences, one that was strongly felt by women (at least as represented by male writers) has already been noted: men stayed all their lives

---

44. *Geschichte* 783, cited by Cole, *Landscapes,* 94 n. 19, who comments "such a division, although sometimes discernable, is not easy to define." Stereotypes: H. S. Versnel, *Ter Unus* (Leiden, 1990), 121 n. 101.

45. Hom. *Od.* 4.759–67; on the *ololygē* see p. 161 n. 141. For the equality of principle, see R. G. Osborne, "Women and Sacrifice in Classical Greece," *Classical Quarterly* 43 (1993): 392–405 (reprinted in *Oxford Readings,* 294–313); cf. M. Dillon, *Girls and Women in Classical Greek Religion* (London, 2002), 241–46; for the practical exclusions, Schmitt Pantel, *Cité au banquet,* 397–99; Cole, *Landscapes,* 93, 98–100; Goff, *Citizen Bacchae,* 42; Parker, *Polytheism,* 165, 167–68. On the question whether women actually wielded the knife, see Pirenne-Delforge in *ThesCRA* 5:16.

46. On women as dedicators see Dillon, *Girls and Women,* 9–36, in n. 45 above; for their statistical underrepresentation, see Cole, *Landscapes,* 98–100, 114; but for some expensive dedications, see Goff, *Citizen Bacchae,* 70–71.

with their ancestral gods, whereas women were required to change them at the time of their marriage. But throughout their lives women and men had dealings with different gods—not absolutely, but there is a marked difference of emphasis. It is emblematic that oaths by certain gods were confined to one gender or the other: we learn this above all from several transvestite scenes in Aristophanes where disguised characters betray themselves by a wrong choice of god. There is a broad consensus[47] that the ritual life of ordinary women— though the case may have been different for priestesses—related closely to their role as wives, housekeepers, and mothers, potential and actual: everyday female activities such as water carrying, food preparation, feeding, weaving, and washing constantly reappear in ritual contexts; women's dedications are, much more often than men's, made "for their children"; and the third day of the greatest of women's festivals, Thesmophoria, was called "Fair Birth." This is, then, in good measure what Gellner calls "ritually-orchestrated role ascription." Even aischrology, dirty talk, which in ritual is commoner in the mouths of women than of men, may relate to their role as carriers of fertility, though in a much more complicated way than was postulated by the once-popular hypothesis that "smut makes the crops grow."[48]

A question that remains open is whether this ritual play on standard feminine roles served merely to reinforce the stereotypes or also, and if so to what extent, provided a context for women to develop a distinctively feminine perspective on these roles, as brilliantly argued by the late Jack Winkler.[49] Certainly the form of women's rituals could be very different from those performed by men. There was nothing in male ritual experience comparable to day two of the Thesmophoria, at which citizen women sat on the ground all day, fasting, in imitation, perhaps, of Demeter fasting for her daughter. Eva Stehle has contrasted the standard civic ritual based on animal sacrifice with this mimetic, empathetic female ritual; she speaks of the latter as "not spectacle for the god's enjoyment but integration into the god's experience." A different kind of ritual activity more characteristic of women than of men might be that based on neighborhood sociability: the Adonia was a group

47. See, e.g., Cole, *Landscapes,* 95, 98, 113; Goff, *Citizen Bacchae,* 47–48 (dedications), 51–61. Oaths: Ar. *Eccl.* 155–59, 189–91; *Thesm.* 594; cf. Parker, *Polytheism,* 270; A. H. Sommerstein, *Talking about Laughter and Other Studies in Greek Comedy* (Oxford, 2009), 18–21.

48. See p. 217 above (Gellner); pp. 208–9 (aischrology).

49. Goff's *Citizen Bacchae* is explicitly (15–17, 123, 143) an attempt to combine these approaches: on 124 she quotes M. Miles for the view that religion "makes available tools with which women may create a degree of spiritual, political and personal autonomy....If we look only for oppression we will miss the creativity with which women—never the primary shapers of their cultures—have foraged in their cultural environments for the tools with which to make their lives" (introduction to *Immaculate and Powerful: The Female in Sacred Image and Reality,* ed. C. Atkinson et al. [Boston, 1985]). Winkler: see p. 208.

festival celebrated by women on the roofs of private houses; a woman in Aristophanes speaks of slipping round to a neighbor's for a rite of Hecate.[50]

The great question mark and the great exception concerns women's rites of Dionysus, wild midwinter mountain rites in particular. The idea of the maenad seems to play on a negative stereotype of female irrationality, sensuality, potentiality to create disorder. The myths find no virtue in the maenads' extreme experience. Women fleeing the home, female against the male, mothers killing and even eating their children: horror is heaped on horror. Yet the rituals were allowed to take place; for the god was irresistible. How many cities hosted such rituals, how many women and of what condition went to the mountains, what happened when they got there: precise details on all these points unfortunately escape us. (Nor is it very clear what Dionysiac experience other than mountain dancing was widely available to women.) We have just two vivid snapshots in Plutarch of the Delphic college of Thyiades, who engaged in such mountain dancing: in one, the women stray in their trance to Amphissa and fall asleep in the agora, full of threatening males, from whom the local women protect them; in another, they are cut off in the mountains by a gale and snowstorm and have to be rescued.[51]

Whatever the scale of historical maenadism and whatever the social level of the participants, the phenomenon is clearly not one of "ritually orchestrated role ascription." It was seen rather, by men, as a safety valve, an inoculation. As for how it was seen by women, all that can be said with confidence is that service to the god was surely for some a duty and an honor. That it was also enjoyable and welcome is a general assumption, though even this is beyond proof. Whether it was welcome as a necessary but temporary escape from the shackles of an intolerably restricted existence, or (more positively) as an extension of experience, an expansion of the imaginative horizon, whether therefore "madness" is a form of protest or of self-discovery, we cannot unfortunately (in the absence again of novels, or diaries) go on to determine.[52] The answer may well have varied (it should be added, however predictably) from individual to individual and also over the long history of the phenomenon.

---

50. E. Stehle, "Thesmophoria and Eleusinian Mysteries: The Fascination of Women's Secret Ritual," in *Finding Persephone: Women's Rituals in the Ancient Mediterranean,* ed. M. Parca and A. Tzanetou, 165–85 (Bloomington, 2007); Ar. *Lys.* 700–701.

51. *De mul. vir.* 13, 249E; *De primo frigido* 18, 953D. On historical maenadism, see J. Bremmer, "Greek Maenadism Reconsidered," *ZPE* 55 (1984): 267–86. The "Lenaea vases," usually taken as a prime if enigmatic source for women's Dionysiac rituals (not on a mountain) in Athens (see refs. in Parker, *Polytheism,* 306–12), have been associated with Delphic rites instead by Sourvinou-Inwood, *Hylas,* 213–40 (cf. p. 184 n. 51).

52. For these possibilities see the useful anthropological update in Goff, *Citizen Bacchae,* 271–79.

Special Needs: Achilles, Diomedes, and Seafarers

There are other subgroups whose religious activities could be discussed, sailors and soldiers above all;[53] I will merely touch briefly on an aspect of "sailors' religion" that recent discoveries have illuminated, and pass on. It has long been known that Achilles from an early date enjoyed godlike status along the northwest coast of the Black Sea.[54] In the Roman period he was officially honored by the city of Olbia as "Achilles ruler of Pontos," but he was already "Achilles who rules Scythia" for Alcaeus c. 600, and evidence for his cult begins soon thereafter; the personal name Achillodoros, "gift of Achilles," is already attested in the region in the sixth century. The epicenter of the cult was always the uninhabited (or all but) island of Leuke, though it is also attested early at an ever-growing number of mainland sites; an early fifth-century graffito addresses him as "Achilles ruler of Leuke," a dedication as "Achilles who rules the island."[55] The main clientele of a cult so situated is likely to have consisted of sailors, and the rich though late sources that report the legends of the cult stress the hero's solicitude for men of the sea and their affection for him: the hero appears in dreams to sailors (or even visibly on the mast) as they approach the island and guides them to the safest anchorage; if they are driven to the shore by a storm without suitable sacrificial animals, they can catch one of the island's goats and offer that (the hero will fix a price by an oracular response); the island is a "hospitable hearth for ships"; Pontic sailors report that "when they catch sight of the island, since they are crossing an unending sea, they embrace one another and shed tears of delight, and sail to the land and greet it and walk to the shrine to pray and sacrifice to Achilles."[56] Such earlier evidence as bears on the character of the cult tends

---

53. On soldiers see M. Launey, *Recherches sur les armées hellénistiques* (Paris, 1949, reissued with addenda 1987), chap. 15; Mikalson, *Hellenistic Athens,* 155–60; A. Chaniotis, *War in the Hellenistic World* (Oxford, 2005), 149–54; on sailors, M. R. Recio, *Cultos marítimos y religiosidad de navegantes en el mundo griego antiguo* (Oxford, 2000).

54. See above all *Achilleus-Kult,* which gives very valuable access to the work of Russian and Ukrainian scholars; for the inscriptions, *IPE* 1².26, 34.30, 53, 130–46, 325–32, 672–73, 685, supplemented/replaced by *IGDOlbia* 48–53, *SEG* 26.812; 30.869–76, 927, 929,? 931; 32.742–44, 765–68; 37.635–39; 43.502, 505, 507; 49.1028; 50.715bis; 52.749; 53.789, and the catalog of Achilles Pontarches dedications in *Achilleus-Kult,* 215–33.

55. *Achilleus-Kult,* 74 with pl. 10.7 = *IGDOlbia* 48b (similarly *IPE* I² 326 = *IGDOlbia* 49); *IPE* 1².672. Alcaeus: fr. 354 L/P (so too probably a fifth-century graffito from Tyras, *SEG* 52.749, *Achilleus-Kult,* 155). Achillodoros: *IGDOlbia* 23. On the Achilles Pontarches cult, reestablished after the Getan destruction of Olbia and to be distinguished from what preceded, see J. Hupe in *Achilleus-Kult,* 165–234.

56. Arr. *Peripl. M. Eux.* 22–23.2; Philostr. *Her.* 54.10, 56.4; cf. Max. Tyr. 9.7 pp. 109–10 Hobein. It seems that the island was originally under the control of Olbia (*IPE* 1².325); when Olbia was supplanted (first/second century?) in this role, it reidentified Berezan, which had long hosted an

in the same direction: sites of his cult have yielded coins from a great variety of cities; a graffito addresses the hero as "Achilles savior."[57] Other factors too very probably propelled the cult, but the devotion of sailors was in all seeming the most important.

A kind of mirror image of this cult has recently appeared in the Adriatic. The myth of Diomedes' flight or exile to that region was already told, as it seems, in early poetry, and many traditions attaching to him are later found on both sides of the Adriatic, including a tradition of the "islands of Diomedes." But it was only in the early 1990s that the legend of his islands came into sharp focus with the discovery of thousands of shards of classical and Hellenistic Greek pottery, including some bearing dedications to Diomedes, on the larger of the two waterless islands of Palagruža in the middle of the Adriatic. Palagruža was evidently an important stopping point on the transadriatic trade route; it is so central that from it both shores of the Adriatic can be seen. Like the Black Sea cult of Achilles, then, the Adriatic cult of Diomedes had as its hub (we may suppose) an uninhabited island important only to sailors, though like that of Achilles it also extended to the shores (in this case on both sides of the Adriatic).[58]

Achilles was the greatest warrior to fight at Troy, Diomedes the second greatest; an Attic drinking song declared that they were both on the Islands of the Blessed. It can scarcely be coincidence that their cults came to mirror one another so extensively. Both islands, devoid of human inhabitants, even enjoyed the service of miraculous birds: those of Diomedes cleaned the shrine and repelled from it non-Greeks (or the wicked); those of Achilles merely sprinkled the shrine each day.[59] How the two great warriors on land made this turn to the sea is not beyond all guessing. The process probably began with Achilles, whose mother was a sea nymph, Thetis. There was also

---

Achilles cult, as his actual island (cf. S. B. Ochotnikov in *Achilleus-Kult,* 83–86; J. Hupe, ibid., 168–69, argues that Dio Chrys. 36.9 still refers [archaistically?] to Leuke, but the hymn *Achilleus-Kult,* 218 no. 7, clearly locates Achilles on Berezan). Arrian's description should still refer to Leuke, though, where cult continued; Philostratus's is probably largely literary.

57. Coins: *Achilleus-Kult,* 102–8, pl. 3.1; "savior": *IGDOlbia* 50. Note too the Roman-period (?) votives from sailors *IPE* 1².331–32.

58. On all this see B. Kirigin and S. Čače, "Archaeological Evidence for the Cult of Diomedes in the Adriatic," *Hesperìa,* 9, *Studi sulla Grecità di occidente* (Rome, 1998), 63–110; cf. *SEG* 48.692–94. For a probable cult of Diomedes at Cape Ploča in Dalmatia, see ibid., 72–74; for the various cults attested in literary sources on the east coast of Italy, ibid., 70–71 and 79 n. 78; for the Adriatic Diomedes traditions in general, I. Malkin, *The Returns of Odysseus* (Berkeley, 1998), chap. 8. Early poetry: Mimnermus fr. dub. 22 West; Ibycus fr. 13 (294) *PMG* (speaking of "worship as a god" on his island).

59. Diomedes: multiple sources (Kirigin and Čače, "Archaeological Evidence," in n. 58 above, 66–70), e.g., Plin. *HN* 10.126–27. Achilles: Arr. *Peripl. M. Eux.* 21.3–4. Drinking song: *PMG* 894.

an early myth that he was translated post mortem (as befitted the greatest of heroes) to the Isle of the Blessed, an isle that came to be identified as, precisely, Leuke.[60] So he was actually there, ready to help sailors, on the island that greeted them as they approached the northwest shore of the Black Sea. Sailors carried with them the taste for such a mighty island-dwelling helper to the West; finding the great Diomedes already associated with the region, they recast him in the role. Such may have been the development, one that requires no postulate of pre-Greek substrata, nor that the heroes known from the epic tradition had once been gods.[61] It was surely the greatness displayed by Achilles and Diomedes in their epic role that made them also so effective, in sailors' imaginings, in their new one.

The Variety within "Public" Religion

I pass now to my second broad division, the variety of religious experiences available to an individual. Paul Veyne has distinguished between "set menu" and "à la carte" religion, and it may seem at first sight that variety is to be sought on the à la carte side of the menu, among private cults as opposed to cults of the state or its subunits, those that the individual joined by choice rather than being born into. But a little thought shows that this is not quite right.[62] Variety of experience is built into polytheism. Processing solemnly to the acropolis is different from getting drunk with one's friends at the

---

60. Achilles taken to the Isle(s) of the Blessed: Pind. *Ol.* 2.79–80, *PMG* 894, Pl. *Symp.* 179E, 180B; to Leuke, Arctinus p. 47.28 Davies *EGF;* cf. Pind. *Nem.* 4.49–50; the two places are identified in Plin. *HN* 4.93 and Avienus, *Descriptio orbis terrae,* 722–29.

61. Substrata are generally rejected today (cf. S. B. Bujskich in *Achilleus-Kult,* 147–53), but some accept H. Hommel's case that Achilles was by origin an underworld god (*Der Gott Achilleus, Sitzb. Heid. Ak.* [1980]: 1). His argument, based inter alia on the expression "Achilles ruler of…" (8–13; cf. n. 55 above), that Achilles was treated like a god in the region (as Dio Chrys. 36.14 states explicitly), has some force; but formally he seems to have stayed a hero (Arr. *Peripl. M. Eux.* 22.4; 23.4; the dedication *IOlbia* 90 = *Achilleus-Kult,* 217–18 n. 6; note too the geographical restriction on Achilles' power observed by Arrian *Peripl. M. Eux.* 23.2), and Hommel has failed to show that this "god" was ever conceived as being anyone other than the son of Peleus and Thetis who fought at Troy, i.e., a hero who rose. A striking shard from Cape Bejkuš (*Achilleus-Kult,* 140, with pl. 35.1, 36.1) appears to show him as a hoplite; as such he "has often been seen by sailors," according to Max. Tyr. 9.7 p. 109 Hobein. The extraordinary cult complex at Cape Bejkuš (numerous cultic pits spread over a large area: Bujskich in *Achilleus-Kult,* 133–43; cf. J. Hupe, in ibid., 236) is to my knowledge unparallelled in the cult whether of gods or heroes, though taken indiviudally the pits seem heroic. The "horse race" (*IPE* 1².34.30) is not unheroic. Remarkable early evidence for worship of Achilles on Thera has recently been uncovered (*SEG* 51.1031–46), but I see no difficulty in the view that this is a further expression of sailors' religion.

62. So rightly Price, *Religions,* 108. Veyne, *Writing History,* trans. M. Moore-Rinvolucri (Manchester, 1984), 113.

Dionysia, different again from being solemnly presented to Heracles in his temple at the end of one's adolescence; rites celebrated within the domestic circle differ from those held in public space[63]—and so on. Again, public cults are those that the state was happy to see citizens participating in, not in which participation was obligatory. No individual could in fact have participated actively in all the publicly recognized cults, even in a small place such as Erythrae. Individuals chose what publicly celebrated rites to take part in; they also chose, what is still more important, which publicly recognized gods to become involved with at a private level. A couple with young children decide to put them under the protection of Artemis at Brauron; a washerwoman makes an expensive dedication to Athena on the acropolis as a tithe; a family takes a sacrificial picnic in a shrine of Pan; a well-known politician suffering a long illness decides first to give up on doctors and to try a healing power, and second makes a choice among the various healing powers and experiences available, and travels to Epidaurus.[64] These examples are Athenian, but the phenomenon is general: the sacrificial tariffs from many locations that distinguish the fees due from "the city" and from private individuals show that offerings were brought to the same sanctuaries by both categories. Father A. J. Festugière wrote a book on *Personal Religion among the Greeks*[65] and found rather little, because he was looking for something internal and spiritual; at a more humdrum level the scope for individual choice within polytheism was very large.

Private Societies

It might be objected that the variety offered by civic polytheism was rather like that offered by a bad supermarket: a bewildering diversity of wrappings for what is essentially the same product. Whatever sanctuary you approached, the procedures (dedication, sacrifice) were much the same. There was also, the objection would go on, an appetite for a more intense form

---

63. On household rites see Parker, *Polytheism*, 13–20, and C. A. Faraone, "Household Religion in Ancient Greece," in *Household and and Family Religion in Antiquity*, ed. J. Bodel and S. M. Olyan, 210–28 (Oxford, 2008); D. Boedeker, "Family Matters: Domestic Religion in Classical Greece," in ibid., 229–47. There were, however, no Greek expressions for household rites or household gods: I maintain my position on that point despite the objection of Faraone, "Household Religion," 225 n.7, who does not mention the, in my view, decisive texts that I cite in its favor on 20–21. They were subsumed within the "ancestral."

64. van Straten, *Hierà Kalá*, 80–81; *IG* 1³.794; Men. *Dysk.* 400–401 and passim; *CEG* 776.

65. Berkeley, 1954. Sacrificial tariffs: e.g., *NGSL* 20.2–7 (Chios); *LSA* 1.5–8 (Sinope); ibid. 73.9–14 (Halicarnassus).

of religion, and this had to seek satisfaction outside the civic structures, in informal revel bands and private societies. The objection underestimates the variety of civic polytheism, and oversimplifies the complicated issue of private societies, which were not all devoted to the wilder kind of god.[66] But it is certainly right to emphasize that there was much enthusiasm for intense religious experiences, of the kind found in the cult of Dionysus and Sabazius and the Mountain Mother and the Mother's attendants, the Corybantes, the kind associated with excited dancing, wild movements, loud percussive music, and often with cross-dressing. There is a passage in Strabo in which he groups together cults of this type and applies words from the ὀργι-root seven times, from the ἐνθουσι-root six (an "enthusiast" is etymologically a person "in the grip of a god" or perhaps "with a god inside"); they were recognized as distinctive in antiquity.

The various associations of such cults with madness are revealing: joining a Dionysiac band could be described as temporarily "going mad," the Mountain Mother was known as a sender of madness, and the cult of the Corybantes actually functioned as a cure for the affliction, evidently of a homoeopathic kind. Admission to such rites was sometimes described as an "initiation" (τελεῖσθαι); their intensity is suggested by the initiates' cry (at least in Demosthenes' satirical portrayal) "I have escaped the bad, I have found the better."[67] It is also true that private cult groups, though not confined to honoring the gods of "enthusiasm," were particularly often associated with them. In the classical period they tended to be temporary and informal and so are hard to track; but in the third century there emerge, for instance, a society of worshippers of Mother from Piraeus and of Dionysus from Callatis on the Black Sea, both of which survived for several centuries.[68] The Dionysiac society met in a kind of (probably) artificial cavern, a way of stressing the abnormal character of Dionysiac experience; whereas

---

66. Cf. p. 239 n. 39 on private associations. One should note too the role, in Athens at least, of hereditary religious groups (genē, orgeōnes), which, though not open to all, were certainly (genē) or arguably (orgeōnes) part public in function (Parker, *Athenian Religion,* 65, 110–11).

67. Strabo: 10.3.7–16, 466–71. Dionysiac band: Hdt. 4.79.3 (ibid. 4, "initiate"); Mother: Eur. *Hipp.* 141–44; Corybantic initiations: Dodds, *Greeks and the Irrational,* 77–80; cry: Dem. 18.259. Fritz Graf has argued (in *Sanctuaire grec,* 159–99) that incubation, too, being individual, in a different way broke with the norms of civic religion. But it was perceived as a distinctive form of healing rather than (except perhaps by Aelius Aristides) as a distinctive form of religious experience.

68. Informal societies: Parker, *Athenian Religion,* 161–63. Mother: ibid., 192–93. Dionysus: A. Avram, "Der dionysische Thiasos in Kallatis," in *Religiöse Vereine in der römischen Antike,* ed. U. Egelhaaf-Gaiser and A. Schäfer, 69–80 (Tübingen, 2002), and Chiekova, *Pont gauche,* 88–96, on *IGLSM* 35–36; 42–46 (for the cavern see 44.42) = Jaccottet, *Choisir Dionysos,* nos. 54–60.

FIGURE 9.   Ecstatic dancing in an unknown cult: further around the vase a procession approaches a god and goddess enthroned in a shrine. Attic red figure krater, group of Polygnotos. Ferrara, Museo Nazionale, T 128: photo museum.

innumerable Greek decrees specify that they are to be displayed "in the most conspicuous spot in the sanctuary," this group rather quaintly made use of "the most conspicuous spot in the cavern."

It might be tempting to conclude that these private societies flourished because standard civic polytheism was too formal and restricted to satisfy all the religious needs of the individual, but that claim is true only in a limited sense. The role of the small private group in such cults relates more to the way in which civic religion was structured than to hostility on the part of the city to such types of experience. The primary function of priests and priestesses was to look after their sanctuaries, not to lead revel bands: if there were to be many such, they had to be led by individuals other than the public priests, but their activities could take place with the approval of the city. In Athens, the cult of the Corybantes was wholly private, whereas in Erythrae there were public priests and priestesses who took a percentage of the fee from private initiators; in Cos, the priestess of Dionysos Thyllophoros was licensed to subcontract the right of initiating for Dionysus to women

operating in individual demes; the position of the priestess of Dionysos
Bacchios in Miletus was very similar.[69] Dionysus and Mother were, of course,
worshipped publicly, and, even if the more "enthusiastic" sides of their cult
were often left to private enterprise, there were public *thiasoi* of Dionysus in
many cities; Pan too, a god honored with lively and noisy rituals, was admitted to the public Athenian pantheon. So this variety of religious experience
was not intrinsically anticivic or countercultural. The myths showed that
a city that rejected Dionysus faced disaster. "Private" societies, it has been
argued, played their part in averting it.[70]

The question of how widespread was the appetite for this more intense
kind of cultic activity is unfortunately very difficult to answer. Should we
imagine Pericles going mad for Dionysus, or Demosthenes waving a tym-
panon for the Mother? Pindar, the one Greek poet whom Gilbert Murray
regarded as, in religious terms, a black reactionary, was an enthusiast for the
Mother and for Pan. Menander shows us a good bourgeois family honoring
Pan, and there are passages in fourth century literature that imply that it was
common for young Athenians of good family to go in for private initiations. Much later, a Platonic philosopher called Demetrius was slanderously
charged before Ptolemy "Dionysus" with not being willing to dance in drag
at the Dionysia; the senior Macedonian general Polyperchon, by contrast,
had always been happy even in old age to revel in a yellow dress.[71] Probably
we should not restrict involvement too much.

Mysteries

One might ask whether honoring a god within a restricted group, a *thiasos,*
had in itself a special character that could be isolated as a variety of religious
experience; the chorus of Euripides' *Bacchae* declare blessed the man who

---

69. Corybantes: *SEG* 47.1628 (cf. 52.1147; the new text, ibid. 1146 treats similar topics); Cos:
Iscr. Cos 216 A 13–21, B 8–10; Miletus: *LSA* 48 (Jaccottet, *Choisir Dionysos,* no. 150) 18–20. For the
blurring of the private-public distinction in Hellenistic cults of Sarapis, see B. Dignas in *Practitioners
of the Divine,* 73–88.

70. A. F. Jaccottet, "Dionysos entre le 'privé' et 'l'officiel,'" in Ἰδίᾳ καὶ δημοσίᾳ, 191–202; she
suspects that the Callatis society (n. 68 above) had a quasi-official role. At Miletus, both the public
thiasos of Dionysus and an unspecified number of private *thiasoi* participated in the festival Katagogia
(*LSA* 48.21–24, as explained by V. Suys in Ἰδίᾳ καὶ δημοσίᾳ, 209–11, with other examples).

71. Pindar *Pyth.* 3.97–99, fr. 95–99 S/M (for G. Murray on Pindar see *A History of Ancient
Greek Literature* [London, 1897], 110–11, 225); Men. *Dysk.* 400–22, etc.; initiations: Pl. *Euthyd.* 277D,
with Dodds, *Greeks and the Irrational,* 99 n. 104; Dem. 18.265; Theoph. *Char.* 16.11; Demetrius,
Polyperchon: Lucian *Cal.* 16; Ath. 4, 155C.

performs the rites of Dionysus and the Mother with purity and "joins the *thiasos* in his soul" (θιασεύεται ψυχάν).[72] A cluster of relevant variables at once suggest themselves: temporary against permanent *thiasoi;* different combinations (or lack of combination) of ages, sexes, civic statuses within them; *thiasoi* that honored the wilder kinds of god, and those that honored the tamer. I veer away from an arduous research that would be ill supplied with evidence before and even within the Hellenistic period, and turn instead to mysteries.[73]

Two mystery cults were of more than local importance in the classical period, those of Demeter and Kore at Eleusis near Athens, and those of the Great Gods (or Kabiroi, as Herodotus already called them) on the island of Samothrace in the northern Aegean. The "sacred truce" that allowed safe travel to Eleusis for initiation was proclaimed throughout Greece; in the Hellenistic period, public delegations went to Samothrace from a large number of cities mostly in the northern or eastern parts of the Greek world, and the cult was already generally familiar in the fifth century.[74] Both these cults differed from most civic cults in being open to anyone who understood Greek: citizens and non-citizens, men and women, free and slaves (though most slaves will have lacked the leisure and money to exploit the privilege). But both were in fact under the administrative control of cities, Athens and Samothrace; so once again we are dealing with variety within what cities offered, not beyond those bounds. Later there emerge a considerable number of lesser local mystery cults; Pausanias, for instance, knows thirteen in Arcadia alone.[75] Many are likely to have originated much earlier than they are first attested, and our ignorance of their history is a great barrier to any attempt to understand the mystic phenomenon as a whole. Was the Greece of (say) the sixth century full of mystery cults, amid which Eleusis and Samothrace

---

72. Eur. *Bacch.* 75.

73. Burkert, *Mystery Cults,* is the indispensable vade mecum, to be supplemented by his "Concordia Discors: The Literary and the Archaeological Evidence on the Sanctuary of Samothrace," in *Greek Sanctuaries,* ed. N. Marinatos and R. Hägg, 178–91 (London, 1993) (cf. Burkert, "Greek Margins: Mysteries of Samothrace," in Λατρείες στην περιφέρεια του αρχαίου ελληνικού κόσμου, ed. A. Avagianou, 31–63 [Athens, 2002]); various essays in *Greek Mysteries;* the sourcebook P. Scarpi, ed., *Le religioni dei misteri,* vol. 1, *Eleusi, dionisismo, orfismo* (Fondazione Valla, 2002); and the exhibition catalog A. Bottini, ed., *Il rito segreto: Misteri in Grecia e a Roma* (Milan, 2005); on Eleusis, Parker, *Polytheism,* 342–68 [+].

74. Hdt. 2.51.2–4; Ar. *Pax* 277. Truce: *IG* 1³.6b (*IEleusis* 18). Delegations: Dimitrova, *Theoroi and Initiates.* Hdt. 7.153.3 by his reference to hierophants seems to assume early mysteries in Gela; another early initiatory cult is that apparently taken over from local inhabitants by Athenian settlers on Lemnos (cf. R. Parker in *Ritual, Finance, Politics,* 344–45).

75. See M. Jost, "Mystery Cults in Arcadia," and F. Graf, "Lesser Mysteries—Not Less Mysterious" in *Greek Mysteries,* 143–68 and 241–62. Little is known of most of them.

FIGURE 10. Vase fragments from the Kabirion showing on the right "Kabiros" and "Child"; whether the figures on the left, Pratolaos, Krateia, and Mitos (note the grotesque features of the two former), are also deities is disputed. After P. Walters and G. Bruns, *Das Kabirenheiligtum bei Theben,* pl. 44.1.

somehow achieved preeminence? Or were they "the original and still the best," which inspired local imitations? Almost the only lesser cult of which it is possible to speak in the classical period is that at the Kabirion at Thebes, which emerges from the general gloom through the chance fact that special drinking cups, the so-called Kabirion ware, were apparently produced in the sanctuary; some of these cups depict in burlesque guise ritual scenes that should have some connection with the cult itself.[76]

It is difficult to say anything useful about mysteries in short compass (or indeed in long). The central point about Eleusis seems to be the combination of an "extraordinary experience"—title of the final chapter of Burkert's book on *Ancient Mystery Cults*—with an extraordinary claim: the extraordinary claim—extraordinary in terms of Greek religion, with its emphasis on this world—is that initiation in the cult will bring the initiate a better lot in the afterlife. The two things go together: it is the departure from normality in experience that makes the ambitious claim about the afterlife seem credible. (But it should be noted that, though the cult makes a confident claim, the initiate goes away with, at best, "good hopes"—the tentative "if" accompanied almost all propositions about the afterlife even in Attica, where most people had probably been initiated.)[77] The extraordinary experience is closed

76. See n. 82 below.
77. Confident claim: *Hymn. Hom. Dem.* 480–82 (with N. J. Richardson's note ad loc.). "Hopes": Isoc. *Paneg.* 28–29; "if": Parker, *Polytheism,* 364.

to us: the best that can be done is to quote, once again, a famous fragment of Plutarch in which he compares the experience of death to that of mystic initiation. The soul at death, he writes,

> has an experience like those who are being initiated in great rites... at first wanderings and exhausting goings around and uneasy journeys in the dark with no fulfillment, then before the consummation every kind of horror, trembling and terror and sweat and shock. But after this an extraordinary light meets them and open territory and meadows receive them, full of voices and dancing and the dignity of sacred sounds and august visions. Amid which the one who is now perfect and initiated, free and unconstrained, goes around and revels, a crown on his head, and mixes with holy and pure persons.[78]

But the special character of the Eleusinian experience did not just lie in the intense, multisensual, disorienting final nighttime revelation in the middle of a large and excited crowd. There was also the division of the process into several stages—lesser mysteries, pre-initiation, initiation, final revelation—which had to be undergone on different occasions; there were prolonged preparations leading up both to initiation and final revelation—a build up, an extension in time, a concentration of attention, quite unlike anything in normal Greek religious experience.[79]

About the clientele of the Samothracian Mysteries we know a great deal, about the experience that they underwent regrettably little. The process was divided into two stages, initiation and final revelation, probably in imitation of Eleusis; but it differed in that the mysteries were celebrated not just once a year but, it seems, recurrently during the sailing season, so that numbers at each celebration will have been much smaller. The most remarkable single fact known is that candidates for initiation were apparently asked to identify their most lawless act, though we are left to guess what use was then made of that interesting information.[80] Until very recently it was believed that

---

78. Plut. fr. 178 Sandbach. Cf. Dio Chrys. 12.33, who speaks of sights, sounds, and alternations of light and darkness as characteristic of mysteries. The opposition between cults based on regularly repeated teaching and those based on occasional intense, often terrifying, experiences (without propositional content) is the central theme of H. Whitehouse, *Arguments and Icons: Divergent Modes of Religiosity* (Oxford, 2000). Consulting the oracle of Trophonius at Lebadea was another shattering form of experience: Paus. 9.39.5–14; P. Bonnechere, *Trophonios de Lebadée* (Leiden, 2003).

79. See K. Clinton, "Stages of Initiation in the Eleusinian and Samothracian Mysteries," in *Greek Mysteries*, 50–78.

80. Lawless act: the source is a roving Spartan anecdote, [Plut.] *Apophthegmata laconica* 217C, 229D (where the Spartan is "consulting the [unattested] oracle at Samothrace"), 236D. Burkert

Samothrace differed drastically from Eleusis in that the tangible benefit that it offered to initiates was not afterworld felicity but protection in storms at sea. It certainly did offer that, and the popularity of the cult is a striking illustration of the sheer terrors of sailing in the Aegean in the premodern world.

The position changed with the publication in 2003 of an epitaph of the second/first century BC for one Isidoros, recording that he had been initiated at both Samothrace and Eleusis and ending with a request that he be granted access to the "place of the pious" in the underworld.[81] So it looks as if Samothrace may, by the second/first century, have come to offer double benefits, in this world and the next. Whether both promises were made earlier remains unknown. Still less can be said about the local Theban mysteries at the Kabirion, but they raise one complicating possibility.[82] The vases made at the sanctuary have a strong grotesque, parodic element: some characters are given black African features and exaggerated genitalia, some seem to be wearing grotesque masks. No one knows what to make of this phenomenon, but it is possible that these mysteries shunned the path of the conventionally beautiful and the sublime, deviating from normality instead via what was considered grotesque and ugly and laughable, at least for a stage. That would be a variety of Greek mystic experience, though not one that we can make much of.

The mystery of all the mysteries is the origin of the form itself. It is sometimes said that agricultural societies, accustomed to "postponed gratification," tend to nurture hopes for the afterlife, and it is indeed the goddesses of grain growing who preside at Eleusis. The Greeks were, even in the Dark Ages, agriculturalists; but any deep roots that mystic ideas may have had among them have left no traces. There is nothing after death to nurture

argues that the effect was conspiratorial (transgression as a bond), not confessional: "Concordia Discors" (above n. 73), 184–85. Frequency of initiation: Dimitrova, *Theoroi and Initiates,* 245–48.

81. C. Karadima and N. Dimitrova, *Chiron* 33 (2003): 335–45; now also in Dimitrova, *Theoroi and Initiates,* 83–84, no. 29. Formally the conclusion does not follow, because Isidoros's claim to a place of privilege in the afterlife could be based on initiation at Eleusis only. But the editors' argument that "the place of the pious" in the epitaph picks up the standard designation of Samothracian initiates as "pious *mystai*" is plausible, and strengthened, as they point out, by the occurrence of the same phrase in an afterworld context in C. Austin and G. Bastianini, eds., *Posidippi Pellaei Quae Supersunt Omnia* (Milan, 2002), 43.1. Protection at sea: Theophr. *Char.* 25.2 with J. Diggle's note ad loc.

82. "What the mysteries were about, what benefits initiation was thought to bring, this we will never know," is the gloomy verdict of Schachter, *Cults,* 2:110. See too his "Evolution of a Mystery Cult: The Theban Kabiroi," in *Greek Mysteries,* 112–42; he notes, 130, that it is uncertain whether the open-air "theater" was used for plays (to which the vases might relate) or only for the rites. M. Daumas, *Cabiriaca: Recherches sur l'iconographie du culte des Cabires* (Paris, 1998) is a very speculative treatment of the vases; for their possible derivation from a broader Boeotian burlesque tradition, see D. Walsh, *Distorted Ideals in Greek Vase-Painting* (Cambridge, 2008), 58–60.

cheerful hopes about in Homer, except for a few outstanding individuals. Use of the site at Eleusis only resumes, after a long interval, in the eighth century; it only becomes recognizably the seat of an initiatory cult, with an initiation hall, early in the sixth. Did Greek culture then take an eschatological turn early in the sixth century, and if so, why? That question has long been posed, though not very satisfactorily answered, in relation to the doctrine of metempsychosis first attested in the second half of that century.[83] But it may also be relevant to the slightly earlier emergence of mysteries, if emergence there was—though no easier to answer.

Death as Birth: High Hopes for the Afterlife

"Metempsychosis" introduces another and very important variety of Greek religious experience, that of the world renouncers (E. R. Dodds's "Puritans"),[84] the Pythagoreans and those, if there were any, who followed so-called Orphic, vegetarian lives, the circles in which there was talk of transmigration of souls and of being oneself a fallen but redeemable deity. But I pass by this variety hastily, partly because it is a whole large subject in itself, and partly because, for ordinary religion in mainland Greece, Pythagoreans were unimportant: from a plain man's perspective they were freaks, and they failed even to exercise perceptible pressure from outside on those ordinary practices on which they had turned their backs. (The reservation "in mainland Greece" is necessary because the case may have been different in southern Italy, where for a period Pythagoreans were a real political force.) Pythagoras's great interest for the religious history of classical Greece lies perhaps in a negative. There can have been few religious systems from which charismatic individuals—prophets, wonder-workers, healers, ascetics—were so comprehensively excluded as that of classical and Hellenistic Greece: between Empedocles in the early fifth century BC and Apollonius of Tyana in the late first century AD, it is all but impossible to identify a single candidate for the title. Though in one sense there were no

---

83. Dodds, *Greeks and the Irrational,* 139. C. Sourvinou-Inwood, "Reconstructing Change: Ideology and the Athenian Mysteries," in *Inventing Ancient Culture,* ed. M. Golden and P. Toohey, 132–64 (London, 1997), argues for a major change in the character of the Eleusinian cult in the late seventh/early sixth century. Non-Greek origins for the north Aegean mystery cults are possible, even if the site on Samothrace, unlike that on Lemnos (n. 74), shows no pre-Greek material (Burkert, "Greek Margins," n. 73 above, 37), but we do not know that they made eschatological promises.

84. Dodds, *Greeks and the Irrational,* chap. 5, "The Greek Shamans and the Origin of Puritanism."

religious institutions in Greece, in another all the space that in a different system might be claimed by individuals was taken up by them—state sacrificial calendars, fixed oracles, healing shrines. Archaic Greece was different, if we allow the claims of the picturesque if only distantly observable figures whom E. R. Dodds brought together as "the Greek shamans," names such as Epimenides of Crete and Hermotimus of Clazomenae and Aristeas of Proconnesus.[85] Pythagoras and his follower Empedocles were the last of a kind, the last aspirants Greece was to know for centuries to a form of charismatic religious leadership. That variety came therewith to an end.

A conduit existed, however, by which unorthodox ideas about the afterlife were made more generally available. Plato in a famous passage tells how:

> Wandering collecting-priests (ἀγύρται) and seers go to the doors of the rich and persuade them that they have a power derived from the gods, if anyone has done wrong himself, or if one of his ancestors has, to make it good by sacrifices and spells along with pleasure and feasting.... They present a hubbub of books of Musaeus and Orpheus, offspring of the Moon and the Muses, as they say, in accord with which they make offerings, persuading not just individuals but also cities that there are forms of release and purifications from wrong-doing through sacrifices and play, effective both during life and also after death; these they call initiations—they free us from evil there [in the underworld], but if we do not sacrifice, a terrible fate awaits us. (*Resp.* 364B–E)

Other sources give us the name "Orpheus initiators" for such practitioners. According to a common though not uncontroversial view, the "books of Musaeus and Orpheus" in question will have contained ideas of the divine origin of humans, our collective fall through an ancestral crime, and

---

85. Dodds's beautiful hypothesis (previous note) is, alas, ill founded: Bremmer, *Afterlife,* 27–40. But Empedocles was unquestionably a man with a religious message who claimed a special personal destiny and thaumaturgic powers (Dodds, *Greeks and the Irrational,* 145–46). The seminal work on Pythagoreanism is W. Burkert, *Lore and Science in Ancient Pythagoreanism* (Cambridge, Mass, 1972); see too, in brief, Burkert, *Greek Religion,* 301–4, and now C. Riedweg, *Pythagoras,* trans. S. Rendall (Ithaca, NY, 2005). Recent discoveries, above all the papyrus published by A. Martin and O. Primavesi, *L'Empédocle de Strasbourg* (Berlin, 1999), have put Empedoclean scholarship on a new basis: see O. Primavesi, "Empedocles: Physical and Mythical Divinity," in *The Oxford Handbook of Presocratic Philosophy,* ed. P. Curd and D. W. Graham, 250–83 (Oxford, 2008). The closest Hellenistic approaches to charismatic religious leaders are perhaps the leaders of slave revolts (n. 37 above).

the possibility of redemption through a blend of ritual and conduct: ideas analogous in very broad terms to those of the world renouncers of the previous paragraph. But even if that view of the content of the books is correct, we do not know what commitment an ordinary client of the Orpheus initiators invested in this alternative worldview (very little, Plato implies, but he is scarcely an unprejudiced witness); whether, for instance, Orpheus initiators urged their clients to lead a vegetarian "Orphic life."[86] On a minimalist view, to undergo Orphic initiation in addition to initiation at Eleusis would have been merely the eschatological equivalent to carrying a second credit card.

Then there are the gold leaves, the passports to the underworld found in graves in many parts of the Greek world (southern Italy and Sicily; Crete; Macedonia and Thessaly; strangely not Attica) and displaying shared formulas that imply a Panhellenic mechanism of distribution such as wandering initiators.[87] On the leaves, the dead individuals make claims ("I am of heavenly descent," "I have escaped from the dire cycle of deep grief") or have claims made about them ("Now you have died and now you have been born, thrice blessed, on this day"; "You have become a god from a mortal") that go well outside the modest aspirations of normal Greek speech about the human condition. This is one reason why the gold leaves have often been associated with the activities of Orpheus initiators, on the contested assumption mentioned above that the "books of Orpheus" that these deployed contained similar hyperbolic claims. Internal references show that "initiations" of some kind certainly underlie the gold leaves. Those who dissociate the leaves from Orpheus initiators connect them, on the basis of two leaves that mention Dionysus or *bacchoi,* with initiations to Dionysus. If they are right, a third credit card was available for those anxious about the afterlife! But the mentions of Dionysus in fact support a connection of the leaves with Orpheus initiators, since early allusions show that the rites that they administered typically

86. For the concept, see Pl. *Leg.* 782C; cf. Eur. *Hipp.* 952–54. For the issues I here skirt, see the conspectus of views in my "Early Orphism," in *The Greek World,* ed. A. Powell, 483–510 (London, 1995); cf. now Graf and Johnston, *Ritual Texts,* 66–93, and on one important source, G. Betegh, *The Derveni Papyrus* (Cambridge, 2004), chap. 3. Orpheus initiators: see Theophr. *Char.* 16.12, with J. Diggle's note ad loc. That Plato's men were precisely Orpheus initiators can be doubted (Dickie, *Magicians,* 331 n. 65), but the two types certainly overlap extensively.

87. Conveniently now available in Graf and Johnston, *Ritual Texts for the Afterlife;* fuller are A. Bernabé and A. I. Jiménez San Cristobal, *Instructions for the Netherworld* (Leiden, 2008) and "Orph." 474F–496F. The geographical range is extended to the Peloponnese if one includes gold leaves that contain a simple proper name or proper name plus μύστης.

honored, precisely, Dionysus.[88] (There is therefore no difficulty in the view
that a fifth-century cemetery plot at Cumae that was reserved for "those
who have undergone the bacchic rite" could have been meant for clients of
Orpheus initiators.)

More important than the name to be put on the ritual, however, is the
fact that during it the initiand will have heard and uttered bold unortho-
doxies of the kind quoted above, and not in the abbreviated or garbled
form in which they often survive on the written leaves. The tantalizing
further question is what kind of exegesis may have accompanied those bold
claims, what understanding of them, therefore, the initiand may have taken
away. He or she will also have heard and repeated various mystic formulas
("I have fallen a kid into the milk," and the like) found on the leaves; the
ritual, being Dionysiac, will have been excited. What lasting reconfiguration of the initiand's thoughts about human life may have occurred in such
conditions is an open question. Were any Greek cults "transformative," or
were they merely "complementary," add-ons to ordinary religious experience? The burial plot at Cumae reserved for "those who have undergone
the bacchic rite" is of some importance here.[89] It might imply lasting association between "those who have undergone the bacchic rite," regular
meetings that could have fostered common understandings of what "becoming a god from a man" might mean. But even if we take a maximalist
view—that the Orpheus initiators and (if different) the gold-leaf initiators
taught heterodox doctrines and recommended heterodox values, and that
these doctrines and values made a serious impression on their clients—it
will remain quite unclear what proportion of the population will have been
influenced thereby.

---

88. Eur. *Hipp.* 952–54; Hdt. 2.81, probably the Olbia bones (Graf and Johnston, *Ritual Texts,*
185–87); cf. Plut. *Alex.* 2.7, and, e.g., "Orph." 350F, 497 T–505 T. Dionysus on gold leaves: texts
1.16 and 26 in Graf and Johnston, *Ritual Texts.* "Initiations for Dionysus" are certainly attested (e.g.,
Hdt. 4.79.3–4; Ar. *Ran.* 357), but it is not established that they brought with them promises about the
future life, alongside fun in the present one. The economical hypothesis is that "Orphic initiations"
were "Dionysiac initiations" with an eschatological twist, and that the postulate of eschatological
Dionysiac initiations distinct from Orphic is redundant; contrast, however, C. Calame in *Kernos* 21
(2008): 299–311, esp. 301. Cumae: *LSS* 120 (cf. *SEG* 36.911).

89. Above, n. 88. Important too is the question whether bone tablets from Olbia attest persons calling themselves "Orphics," or merely "Orphic rites": see Graf and Johnston, *Ritual Texts,*
185–87. On transformative cults see Beard, North, and Price, *Religions of Rome,* 287–91. The cult
of Isis in its later manifestations could be transformative; whether that or any other cult (except
possibly the Orphic) known to the Greeks before the Roman Empire was so experienced is very
doubtful.

Binding and Bewitchment

The collecting priests and seers attacked by Plato in the passage quoted above supposedly also promised, should anyone want to harm an enemy, "to hurt him, just or unjust alike, at little expense by certain 'bringings against' and bindings (ἐπαγωγαῖς τισιν καὶ καταδέσμοις), persuading the gods, as they say, to do their bidding." Plato was much more concerned than any other surviving writer to patrol the boundaries of proper religious practice and to stigmatize varieties lying beyond them as "impious"; he is full of claims about the psychology of those who foster the bad practices, whom he regards as in fact crypto-atheists.[90] But a series of pejorative terms in general use (μάγος, γόης, ἐπῳδός, φαρμακεύς) show that he was not alone in distinguishing acceptable from suspect religious activities and practitioners, even if there was no agreement on where the line of division was to be put: "suspect" here is deliberately ambiguous between "of doubtful propriety" and "of doubtful efficacy; fraudulent." The practitioners in question will normally have described themselves, if men, as "seers"; women might be "priestesses" (of private revel bands), very occasionally seers, or something like "purifiers, anointers." People making their living under these names might or might not also offer the suspect practices to their clients. The capacities supposedly claimed by such people include attacks on enemies through "sending" of spirits "against" them, or through binding spells; inducing or perpetuating love through philters, or obstructing it through binding spells; propitiation of angry gods; healing by means of purifications and incantations; raising the spirits of the dead; "wonder-working"; drawing down the moon, effacing the sun, causing or allaying storms.[91]

Some elements in this list, such as dimming the sun, evidently represent big talk, or magic as a thing imagined, not done, or some kind of display. At the other end of the spectrum are those that sit very close to ordinary religious (or medical) practices and would have been accepted as such by many. Propitiation of angry gods by sacrifice, so offensive to Plato when performed by individuals, was the regular recourse of an afflicted city; purifications and initiations were common forms of ritual action, and the idea that pollution caused disease was familiar; Odysseus is shown "raising the spirits of the dead" in *Odyssey* 11. Between these extremes are the various techniques for influencing or harming other individuals: bewitchments, binding spells,

---

90. See Pl. *Leg.* 908B–909D. For the practices Plato has in view, see 908D, 909B, 933D–E. For the pejorative terms see Dickie, *Magicians*, 33. On magic at Athens, Parker, *Polytheism*, 121–35.

91. On all this see Dickie, *Magicians*, chaps. 2–3; for claims of meteorological control, see Hippoc. *Morb. sacr.* 1.9 Jouanna (1.29 Grensèmann; 4 p. 144 Jones).

love philters. A term that covers them all but also extends far beyond is φαρμακεία,[92] which in different contexts indicates what we would distinguish as "medical treatment through drugs," "poisoning," "administration of a love philter," "attack through spells." These multiple possibilities are not chance products of semantic history but express continuing ambiguities of experience: what was meant to be a love philter might turn out a poison; if all one knew or suspected was that an enemy had made one ill, there was no way of knowing whether the thing had been done by drugs or by spells.

The ever-growing number of surviving curse tablets allows us to write at least the rudiments of a social history of Greek magic. By their clustering around particular topics they reveal certain "pressure points" of Greek society. They refute decisively the notion that cursing is a prerogative of the poor and uneducated: more curses relate to litigation, an expensive activity, than any other, and well-known figures appear among their targets, presumably attacked by their peers. They refute also Dodds's etiquetting of the practice under the rubric "rationalism and reaction," whereby the rationalism of the fifth century provoked, by reaction, the cursing culture of the fourth. Written curses emerge earlier than Dodds knew, and in place and time (Sicily and Attica, fifth century) they more or less track the emergence of popular courts and of forensic rhetoric: rhetoric and forensic curses, it can be argued, are both by-products of the rewards to be won by success in the new courts.[93]

What the surviving curses cannot show is how society evaluated the practice. We should reclassify cursing, it has been suggested, away from the "dark arts," and see it instead as a normal mode of action in an intensely agonistic culture.[94] That it was normal in the sense of being commonplace, engaged in by people neither psychologically damaged nor abnormally wicked, is very likely true. But would one admit to engaging in it, and if so, to whom? There were no doubt some who would have scrupled to curse

---

92. Cf. Pl. *Leg.* 933D: καταδέσεσιν ἢ ἐπαγωγαῖς ἤ τισιν ἐπῳδαῖς ἢ τῶν τοιούτων φαρμακειῶν ὠντινωνοῦν.

93. Pressure points: so Eidinow, *Oracles, Curses and Risk* (which gives access to the large bibliography; add now F. Graf in *ThesCRA* 3:264–70), passim, esp. 225–32. Well-known figures: Parker, *Polytheism,* 129–31; the rereading of the longest of all Attic curse tablets by D. R. Jordan and J. Curbera, *ZPE* 166 (2008): 135–50, is important. Dodds: *Greeks and the Irrational,* 194–95. On Macedonian curses see n. 95 below.

94. So, e.g., C. A. Faraone, *Ancient Greek Love Magic* (Cambridge, Mass., 1999), 18, "Nor would most Greeks dismiss magical practices as a form of 'bad (i.e., unorthodox) religion,'" and works cited by H. S. Versnel, "Beyond Cursing: The Appeal to Justice in Judicial Prayers," in *Magika Hiera,* ed. Faraone and D. Obbink, 60–106 (Oxford, 1991), at 62 (who disagrees). Dickie, *Magicians,* 36–38, notes the scruples felt (but overcome in extremis) by respectable women in tragedy about the use of love philters.

in a way they would not have scrupled, say, to approach a healing god when ill. (Probably there were also those who regarded buying the services of a curse writer as a waste of money; but not everyone will have believed in the efficacy of healing gods either.) Most curses present themselves as a simple, and anonymous, attack. The minority of cursers, however, who stress that they have been wronged may have seen their injuries as a justification; it was, after all, quite normal for individuals, and even cities, to utter oral curses against those who wronged them. It is hard not to sympathize with the female writer of a fourth-century curse from Pella in Macedonia who, perhaps facing a very bleak future, curses all rivals for her lover's affections and prays, "May I and no other woman grow old with Dionysophon." A concubine in late fifth-century Athens who accidentally poisoned her lover with what was meant to be a love philter administered it to avoid being put in a brothel.[95]

Those who believed themselves to be victims of magical attack, however, will certainly not have been very sympathetic. Plato speaks of the fear that the sight of wax figurines used for such purposes could evoke, and two recently published tablets have revealed that the oracle of Dodona could be approached not only about ordinary crime but also with the question whether X has used *pharmaka* (spells/potions/poisons) against Y (and his wife and family). Another recently published document shows an individual "binding back" (ἀντικαταδεσμεύω) any persons who may have made binding spells against him; and several tablets from the sanctuary of Demeter at Cnidus in which those accused of **φαρμακεία** "consecrate" their accusers to the gods for punishment reveal, though much later (? first century BC), the intensity of feeling possible on both sides.[96] The legal position is frustratingly unclear even in Athens, almost wholly unknown elsewhere. **φαρμακεία** through spells was actionable in Plato's *Laws* and might have been so, as a form of

---

95. Anonymous: for rare exceptions see Eidinow, *Oracles, Curses and Risk,* 287 n. 16. Minority: see H. S. Versnel, "Beyond Cursing" (previous note) and "An Essay on Anatomical Curses," in *Ansichten griechischer Rituale,* ed. F. Graf, 218–67 (Stuttgart, 1998), at 217–46. Pella: *SEG* 43.434; cf. E. Voutiras, *ΔΙΟΝΥΣΟΦΩΝΤΟΣ ΓΑΜΟΙ: Marital Life and Magic in Fourth Century Pella* (Amsterdam, 1998) (who lists Macedonian curse tablets on p. 1). Concubine: see Antiphon 1, passim.

96. Pl. *Leg.* 933B; Dodona: Lhôte, *Lamelles,* 125 and 125 bis; ἀντικαταδεσμεύω: *SEG* 49.320; Cnidus: *Def. Tab.* Audollent IA, 4A, 8 (= *IKnidos* 147A, 150A, 154), discussed by Dickie, *Magicians,* 104–6. For protection against what is probably magical attack, see already *Hymn. Hom. Dem.* 227–30 and the hexameter charm cited by Dickie, *Magicians,* 48. For curses against supposed perpetrators of magical killings, see *GVI* 1875 (Alexandria,? first century BC), *Syll.*³ 1181 = *Inscr. Délos* 2532 (Jewish community on Delos,? second century BC), and later instances cited by F. Graf, "Untimely Death, Witchcraft and Divine Vengeance," *ZPE* 162 (2007): 139–50.

"criminal damage" (βλάβη), in Athens; but, perhaps significantly, no actual case is known.

Such a prosecution, had one occurred, would have related to a particular instance of harm. No general form of action comparable to the Roman *Lex Cornelia de sicariis et veneficis* is known, but a passage in Plato's *Meno* suggests that in some cities action could be taken against blatant practitioners of magical wonder-working, γοητεία, and at Athens φαρμακεία apparently played a part in some accusations of "impiety."[97] The view that cursing was just part of the rough-and-tumble of everyday life seems, in the light of these possibilities, too relaxed. But no Greek equivalent to the prosecution of Apuleius for magic is known; there is no sign that the matter was ever perceived as a serious social problem. Magic in the classical Greek world was imaginatively underdeveloped, one might say. Though its practitioners might talk of bringing down the moon, for its users it was an object not of contemplation but of use, a tool to employ in a tight situation. It was a variety of religious action more than of religious experience.

What You Will

I turn now to a final variety, the most important, or perhaps it should be called the source of infinite variety. We happen to learn from an inscription that at Athens at some time in the 140s a series of Stoic philosophers served as "performers of sacred rites," *hieropoioi,* in a public festival; among them was the famous Panaetius of Rhodes.[98] There is nothing surprising about this, except the late Hellenistic opening of the role of *hieropoios* to non-citizens. In the Hellenistic period Stoic philosophers were esteemed public figures; they were often sent on embassies and might be honored with honorary citizenship, gold crowns, and so on. Stoics were socially acceptable because they believed in virtue and duty and because they taught that the world was governed by divine providence; they even argued that the workings of providence could be tracked in advance through divination. But they were certainly not polytheists in any traditional sense; God for them was a single divine reason or providence pervading the universe, and, though they made

---

97. Legal position: Parker, *Polytheism,* 132–33 [+]; Pl. *Meno* 80A–B.

98. *IG* 2².1938, with T. Dorandi, *ZPE* 79 (1989): 87–92. The festivals in question (Ptolemaia, Rhomaia) were not addressed to Olympians, but I very much doubt whether this made a difference. Cf. C. Habicht, "Hellenistic Athens and Her Philosophers," in his *Athen in hellenistischer Zeit* (Munich, 1994), 231–47. For Epicurean priests see p. 38 n. 93.

a concession to plurality by allowing the single divine reason to have sub-aspects, they ridiculed the personal gods of poetry and myth; it is controversial whether there is any justification within their system for acts of worship or prayer, or for a providence that would benefit individuals. Nonetheless they supported and practiced traditional cult wholeheartedly. Accept the traditional forms of cult and see behind them gods who satisfy your own conception of what a god should be: in behaving like this, Stoics merely illustrate the normal attitude of Greek philosophers to religion since the beginnings of philosophy.[99] In Plutarch, Platonist, priest of Apollo at Delphi, and author of Pythian dialogues full of the most unrestrained speculation, we find the philosophical compromise displayed at length. Exactly the same freedom was available to ordinary worshippers too. So the final variety might be described in Shakespearean terms as "As you like it" or "What you will."

In a sense what we see here is what happens in all religions all the time. To survive, religions must always mutate: every age needs a god in its own image, as William James observed, and in the twentieth century Christianity underwent a remarkable process of what its advocates called demythologization. But some religious structures are more resistant to mutation than others. The demythologization of Christianity has not occurred without much anguish and much contestation, whereas, after a period of tension around the time of the trial of Socrates, philosophers settled into an easy relationship with the gods of the city. To explain the "as you like it" option—an option open to all, not just an educated elite—it is necessary to recall some themes from the first chapter. For all worshippers, not just the philosopher, there was a certain level of understanding for which the whole of traditional mythology was a gorgeous but deceptive facade behind which lay, not nothing, but "the divine," real and powerful but unknowable. Is it one, is it many, what relation does it bear to human stories told about it? We mortals do not know the answer to any of these questions, because no one has ever told us. But fortunately we do not need to know, because the traditional forms of cult, emended from time to time on oracular instruction, serve our needs. Bernard de Fontenelle's characterization of Greco-Roman paganism as "act like the others and believe what you please" sounds cynical and dismissive, as if paganism were a matter of outward conformism wholly detached from the life of the mind.

---

99. For excellent accounts see Babut, *Religion des philosophes,* and now in brief G. Betegh in *A Companion to Ancient Philosophy,* ed. M. L. Gill and P. Pellegrin, 625–39 (Oxford, 2006), with bibl. For the lively current debate on Hellenistic theology, see D. Frede and A. Laks, eds., *Traditions of Theology: Studies in Hellenistic Theology, Its Background and Aftermath* (Leiden, 2002); on the Stoic position, contrast D. Frede, "Theodicy and Providential Care in Stoicism," 85–117 in that volume, with R. W. Sharples, ibid., 24 n. 112.

But the effects of this detachment were permissive: it allowed free play to the life of the mind, made this religion without a church into the broadest of churches, excluded nobody or almost nobody. This book has not been intended as a work of apologetics on behalf of Greek religion, but it can end with a modest statement of that religion's virtues. Greek religion provided a strong framework of social cohesion; it met a human need by opening channels of communication with that unseen world that most humans believe to exist; but it did these things without insisting on any particular set of speculations about the character of that unseen world.

✍ APPENDIX 1

Seeking the Advice of the God
on Matters of Cult

Socrates in Plato's *Republic*[1] declares that in the
ideal city Apollo of Delphi should be consulted on all questions concerning "the establishment of shrines, sacrifices, and other forms of cult for gods
and *daimones* and heroes; and also the graves of the dead and the service
we must do them to have their favor," since "this god is the ancestral ex-
egete for all mankind on such matters and expounds them to them, seated
on the *omphalos* at the center of the earth." That recommendation certainly
bears some relation to actual practice; yet, as was noted above, it is not the
case that Greeks sought oracular advice on every issue that came up in the
"sacred" division of the agenda. Some empirical investigation is called for.
Inscriptions quite often state that this or that practice is conducted "in accord
with the oracle of the god," or some similar formula,[2] but it is usually impossible to know whether an oracle so mentioned was a response to a specific

---

1. 427 BC.
2. For instances, see Fontenrose, *Delphic Oracle,* responses H 2 (the Praxiergidai (?) should put
on the peplos and make sacrifices); 30 (the Athenians should spread a couch for Pluto and adorn
a table); *LSCG* 178 (fees for drinking from the spring of Halykos); [Plut.] *X Orat.* 843F–844A
(gilding of altar of Apollo). For still vaguer cases, see *IEleusis* 28a (*IG* 1³.78; *LSCG* 5; ML 73: Eleusinian first-fruits decree); *LSS* 14.11, 16, 24 (Apollo should be honored as Patroos); *IEleusis* 138
A 10 (*Agora* 16:56; *LSS* 12: Eleusinian sacred truce?); RO 97 (*LSS* 115, purifications at Cyrene);
LSA 42 (cult of Heracles), ibid. 67 B 11. The same difficulty applies to cults that are designated as
pythochrēstos: J. Robert and L. Robert in the best treatment (*Fouilles d'Amyzone en Carie* [Paris, 1983],

Table 2. Public Oracular Consultations on Questions of Cult

	CITY/MONARCH/GROUP	ORACLE	QUESTION	DATE (BC)	SOURCE
1	Clisthenes of Sicyon	Delphi	Should he expel (the cult of) Adrastus?	6th century	Hdt. 5.67.2
2	All the Greeks	Delphi	Were the spoils they had sent full and pleasing?	479	Hdt. 8.122
3	Athens	Dodona?	Should Bendis be served by a Thracian priestess or by one chosen from all the Athenians...? (?)	mid–late 5th century	IG 1^3.136. 29–30 (LSS 6)
4	Thracians at Athens	Dodona	May they buy land and found a shrine of Bendis?	? mid–late 5th century[1]	$LSCG$ 46 (IG 2^2.1283) 6
5	Athens	Delphi	Should they cultivate or leave unworked the currently unworked portions of the sacred *orgas* outside the boundaries?	352/1	$IEleusis$ 144 (RO 58; $LSCG$ 32)
6	Athens	Delphi	Should Demon dedicate his house and garden to Asclepius and be appointed priest of Asclepius? (?)	mid-4th century	IG 2^2.4969
7	Acharnae	Delphi	Should they build altars of Ares and Athena Areia?	mid-4th century	SEG 21.519
8	Chios, Klytidai	By sacrifice[2]	Should they (1) build a common house and move the ancestral *sacra* thither from private houses, and (2) move the ancestral *sacra* permanently or on the day of the sacrifice only?	c. 335	RO 87 ($LSCG$ 118)
9	Athens	Delphi?	Should they make the holy adornments larger and finer for Artemis or leave as they are now? Ditto for Demeter and Kore and for further unidentifiable gods.	c. 335	IG 2^2.333.24–31 (ZPE 154 [2005]: 141)
10	Chaones	Dodona	Should they resite the temple of Athena Polias?	330–320?	Lhôte, *Lamelles oraculaires*, 11
11	Alexander	Ammon	Should Hephaistion be sacrificed to as a god?	324	Arr. *Anab.* 7.14.7
12	Rhodes	Ammon	Should they honor Ptolemy as a god?	304	Diod. Sic. 20.100.3–4

13	Cos	?	About the posthumous cult of Arsinoe II (possibly just about the site of the temple)	early 3rd century	M. Segre, *Bull. Soc. Alex.* 31 (1937): 286–98.
14	Tanagra	an Apollo (Ptoios?)	Should they move the temple of Demeter and Kore to a new site?	3rd century	LSCG 72.3–8
15	Miletus	Didyma	Should they conduct the collections for Artemis Skiritis Boulephoros as the Skiridai expound or as now?	*Milet* VI.3. 1225 (*LSA* 47)	"before 234/3?"
16	Sicyonians	Delphi	Should they bury Aratus within the walls, despite the rule forbidding it?	213	Plut. *Arat.* 53.1–4.
17	Koinon of Mondaiatai	Dodona	Should they lend out the money of Themis?	3rd/2nd century?	Lhôte, *Lamelles oraculaires*, 8B
18	Istria	Apollo at Chalcedon	"About Sarapis, what…"	3rd c.	IHistriae 5 (*RICIS* 618/1101)
19	Herakleia under Latmos	? Didyma	Should they sell the priesthood of Latmian Athena for life or elect a priest annually?	early 1st century	*Chiron* 20 (1990): 19–58 (*SEG* 40,956)

1. The document mentioning the grant is of the third century, but the oracle should have been issued around the time when the cult came to Athens in the second half of the fifth.
2. I include this instance, though not an oracular consultation, because the sacrificial divination employed so exactly fulfills an oracle's function.

question concerning that practice, or to a more general inquiry on the lines of "How might we fare well/by sacrificing to which gods might we fare well both now and in the future?"[3] Unfortunately this distinction that we cannot draw makes a real difference: the evidence for oracular authorization being sought for specific reforms increases or decreases depending on how many or how few such "in accord with an oracle" cases derived from specific questions. We are left with a quite restricted number of undeniable or highly probable consultations by cities, monarchs, or public groups (table 2). I list here the cases I have found from before the Christian era. (I omit, however, the quite frequent inquiries seeking to confirm a sanctuary's status as inviolable and a festival's as "crowned": the primary aim here was Panhellenic validation, not the allaying of local scruples.)[4] To construct a parallel list of decisions that were made without consultation of an oracle is scarcely practicable, but cases will be mentioned in what follows. Much relevant material has surely escaped me; I present this appendix in order to pose the question.

Two inquiries relate to the terms of tenure of a priesthood: inquiry 3 in table 2 concerns a new priesthood for Bendis, and the issue seems to have been as fundamental as whether the woman appointed to it should be a Thracian or a democratically elected Athenian; the text is fragmentary, and some supplements even make the choice one between a Thracian woman and Athenian man. Inquiry 19 offers the god a choice between two options for the priesthood of Athena Latmia, of which the one chosen—annual election—is certainly an innovation. Whether the rejected alternative, sale for life, is the system in operation hitherto is uncertain, but the god's rejection of that option, so favored in the region at this date, is surprising, and suggests that the issue may have been controversial.[5] Against these two inquiries can be set the very numerous texts that in one way or another regulate priesthoods but make no mention of a consultation. Priestly perquisites, duties, and privileges must have been a matter for human decision, not divine; the quantity of evidence for unreferred decisions on such topics is overwhelming.

It is less clear how often the more fundamental questions about the kind of occupant required were so settled; many priesthoods are advertised for

---

1:110–13), suppose that a specific inquiry has often been made, but their 112 n. 122 illustrates the other possibility.

3. See, e.g., Lhôte, *Lamelles oraculaires,* 1–5, 7; *IKaunos* 56.

4. In this category I include also *LSCG* 73b, a question to Trophonius about various Boeotian festivals.

5. See the first editor, M. Wörrle, *Chiron* 20 (1990): 43–48. Annual election an innovation: a list of occupants follows, beginning with an individual marked out as the first holder. For a much later inquiry about a priesthood, see Fontenrose, *Didyma,* 199 no. 25; note too 192 no. 17, which shows some form of oracular selection of the prophetess at Didyma.

sale without reference to an oracle, but since in most cases the documents concern the refilling of an established priesthood, the omission is not decisive. Still, some documents appear to show the establishment of a priesthood without oracular consultation: those of Athena Nike in Athens, of Eumenes in Miletus, of Artemis Pergaia in Halicarnassus, for instance; or a priesthood can be transferred to a family that agrees to meet the expenses of the cult, again without consultation.[6] Many changes in the tenure of priesthoods from permanent to annual are recorded in Rhodian inscriptions, without any mention of oracular authorization.[7] But one can imagine that there were limits to the kind of change that a city felt able to make on its own account. In the first century AD, Sidyma in Lycia resolved to appoint a virgin, not as thitherto a married woman, as *neōkoros* of Artemis, "after investigation and in accord with a god's oracle" (which is quoted). It is plausible that such a drastic change would have required oracular sanction in earlier centuries too, but dependable evidence in either direction is not to hand.[8]

There are two inquires about relocating a temple (10, 14), and a pair (together in 8) about relocating sacred objects in a new "house" to be built to receive them. The only relocation conducted without such sanction that I can confidently point to is that of the image of Artemis Leukophryene to her Parthenon in Magnesia on the Maeander; and here the magnificence of the new temple, and of the ceremony by which the goddess was brought to it, perhaps provided the necessary justification. There must also be doubt whether Seleukos II (?) sought oracular authorization before ordering the relocation of a precinct of Soteira on the island of Failaka; but kings had an unusually free hand.[9] It is interesting that the two inquiries of the Klytidai about transferring their sacred objects (8) are followed by a third decision

---

6. *IG* 1³.35 (M/L 44, *LSCG* 12 A), cf. ibid. 36 (M/L 71, *LSCG* 12 B); *IstMitt* 15 (1965): 96; *LSA* 73; transfer *LSCG* 61; *LSA* 13. I use the argument from silence in such cases with confidence in the belief that any oracle that had been sought would certainly have been mentioned. Maiandrios's bid for a priesthood too implies that it was in the Samians' gift (Hdt. 3.142.4).

7. See H. J. Wiemer, *Chiron* 33 (2003): 308 n. 314.

8. There are stories of priesthoods being transferred from older women to virgins in consequence of rapes (Diod. Sic. 16.26.6; Paus. 8.5.12), apparently by simple decision of the community, but they are not historically reliable. Sidyma: *SEG* L 1356.71–112 (*TAM* 2.174; *SEG* 28.1222).

9. *LSA* 33 (Magnesia); *SEG* 35.1476 (see M. Petropoulou, *EpigAnat* 39 [2006]: 139–47: Failaka). There is no knowing whether the temple transfer that an Athenian is honored for carrying out in *Syll.*³ 587.6–25 (Peparethus, c. 196 BC) had oracular sanction. In the imperial period an issue about the relocation of a temple in Nicomedia came to Pliny's attention and was referred by him to Trajan, who sanctioned the change (Plin. *Ep.* 10.49–50); whether Pliny became involved through a question put to him by the Nicomedeans is not clear. Dio Chrys. *Or.* 47.16–17 implies that relocations were frequent, though they could be controversial; he reveals nothing about procedures. On the Roman procedure of *exauguratio,* see *ThesCRA* III, 271–72.

taken without inquiry. They resolve that their new "house" is to be open to none but Klytidai. The issue of inclusion/exclusion is, in this case at least, one for human decision. And decisions about works to be conducted in a sanctuary (building a spring; even building a shrine to a different deity)[10] do not seem necessarily to require divine sanction. Nor does the transfer of a sanctuary from control by one community to another, whether it happened through conquest or by agreement.[11]

One question each is asked about two familiar practices, the loaning of sacred money (17) and the agricultural exploitation of sacred land (5). The latter concerns the most special case that can be imagined, the ever-controversial "sacred *orgas*" on the borders of Attica and Megara; it would have been extraordinary if the Athenians had considered bringing part of that land into use without special authorization. But they make an analogous decision about the precinct of Codrus on their own responsibility.[12] As for the loaning of sacred money, the one inquiry is isolated amid the abundant evidence for the practice. And though cities were careful to observe the form of charging interest, even when lending to themselves, it was they who determined the rate at which it was charged. Sacred fines and sacred dues and the like were also in the control of cities: they took their responsibility seriously in the sense that formal remission was unusual,[13] but we do not find the gods involved through oracles in this area of activity.

Greek cities often asked general questions about their future well-being, and the response would often take the form of advice to sacrifice to a particular god or gods; this will be the origin, or one of the origins, of the epithet *pythochrēstos,* "by order of Pythian Apollo," borne by some gods. But it is unclear how often proposals to institute new sacrifices or build a new altar were taken to Delphi for approval. A verdict on this point depends in part on the ambiguous allusions mentioned above to action undertaken "in accord with an oracle." Inquiry 7 appears to be one example,[14] and there were no

---

10. *LSCG* 75; ibid. 129 (where the question is "where?" not "whether?").

11. For the former see Thuc. 4.98.2–3, with Sourvinou-Inwood, "Polis Religion," 18–19; for the latter, *IG* 9².1.2.583 (*LSS* 45).

12. *IG* 1³.84 (*LSCG* 14), cf. *LSCG* 47.

13. Interest: for Athens during the Peloponnesian War, see ML p. 215. In *Ilion* 10 (*LSA* 10) 13–19 (? 77 BC), arrears of interest due to Athena Ilias are canceled and a nominal rate is introduced for ten years. Fines and dues: the Athenians exacted the sixtieth for Athena even when they absolved allies from the substantive tribute payment, *IG* 1³.61(ML 65) 5–9, 29–32; the Eleans offered to pay themselves a sacred fine from which they proposed, on conditions, to exempt the Spartans, Thuc. 5.49.5.

14. But, since only the answer is preserved, it is possible that the question was not a request for simple authorization but posed alternatives.

doubt others; but there are certainly many instances of decisions by cities to establish or adjust sacrifices and festivals on their own initiative.[15] No sacred calendar presents itself as having received oracular approval, and it is clear that Nicomachus's revision of the Athenian calendar at the end of the fifth century had not, or he could not have found himself prosecuted in consequence. Nor is there any mention of an oracle in the decree that records the sacrificial calendar of Mykonos as extensively revised after the island's synoecism.[16] It is not just, then, that day-to-day decisions about expenditure on particular cults were of necessity taken locally; thoroughgoing revisions of a sacred calendar could also be entrusted to human intelligence.

The introduction of new gods was, we know from the trial of Socrates, a sensitive area. But less oracular involvement is attested than might have been expected. It was "in accord with the response from Dodona" that the Athenians "granted to the Thracians alone of all foreign peoples the right to acquire land and found a shrine" (of Bendis), those Thracians announce (inquiry 4: the same response as that concerning the priestess of Bendis, 3? The point is not clear.). But an identical decision in favor of the Citian worshippers of Aphrodite was taken by the Athenian assembly in 333/2 on its own authority. Number 18 is an inquiry from Istria "about Sarapis"; but the question may have been "how to honor" him, not "whether." The Egyptian cults spread widely without leaving any other traces of oracular consultation about them; the coming of Sarapis to Delos aroused controversy, but it was settled by litigation and (on the pious view) a miracle,[17] not by reference to an oracle. Against the two questions posed to oracles about ruler cult (12, 13) can be set the many decisions to honor rulers taken directly by the cities.

It is difficult to identify a topic, except perhaps the relocation of a sanctuary, on which consultation is mandatory; topics on which it never occurs, on the other hand, such as sanctuary discipline or priestly emoluments, can readily be found. The conclusion seems to follow that, on the issues where consultation may or may not occur, it is not routine; the case is problematic or controversial in some way that debars a human decision on the basis of tradition and precedent. It is easy to see what is exceptional about certain cases not yet mentioned: abolishing an existing cult (1) would have been a very drastic action, as was permitting an intermural burial (16); the repulse of the

---

15. Chaniotis's list, "Sich selbst feiern?" 164–68, provides very numerous examples.

16. *LSCG* 96. Nicomachus: see Lysias 30, passim. As example of an arbitrary decision that became law, Aristotle chooses "sacrificing a goat and not two sheep," *EN* 1134[b] 22.

17. *IG* 11.4.1299 (*RICIS* 202/0101); cf. H. Engelmann, *The Delian Aretalogy of Sarapis* (Leiden, 1975). Citian Aphrodite: RO 91 (*LSCG* 34).

Persian invaders was a sufficiently extraordinary collaborative achievement to justify checking whether it had been adequately, and fairly, given thanks for (2). Inquiry 9 by contrast seems banal, at least given the tendentious way in which it is formulated: it would be odd for the god to oppose the preparation of larger and finer adornment! Dedication management was a routine procedure, and small objects were melted down to make larger ones without greater precaution than a propitiatory offering.[18] It is a little surprising too that the Milesian assembly did not feel able to make up its mind on the Skiridai's proposal (15) concerning collecting in their cult, even if it involved a change. Perhaps local conditions are relevant in both cases. Inquiry 9 was proposed by Lycurgus, the educator of the Athenians in religious propriety;[19] as for 15, Miletus was unusual in having a major oracle on its doorstep and under its control, and made conspicuously free use of it in this period not in the religious sphere alone.[20]

---

18. *LSCG* 41, 42, 70. Note, however, Paus. 3.16.1 (a young woman deterred by a dream from modernizing the adornment of a statue).

19. From the list in n. 2 above, Fontenrose H 30 (*IG* 2².1933, "330–320") and [Plut.] *X Orat.* 843F–844A (explicitly linked to Lycurgus) may well also reflect specific consultations from the Lycurgan period; note too the sacrifice of a propitiatory offering on Lycurgus's motion in *IEleusis* 177.431. Item 7 in the list in the text could also be Lycurgus-influenced.

20. See Fontenrose, *Didyma*, 181–83, nos. 5–7.

❦ APPENDIX 2

Accepting New Gods

The decision to allow a new god into the city was evidently one of special importance and sensitivity, given the prejudice expressed in the accusation brought against Socrates that he "introduced new powers" (*daimonia*). New gods, or old gods worshipped under new epithets, did nonetheless very regularly arrive. The fact is clear; the process is less so.[1]

One possibility was direct revelation by the god in question that he desired to be admitted. Pan in 490 appeared to the runner Philippides (while carrying an important public message—this is surely relevant) and reproached the Athenians for "neglecting him although he was well disposed to them and had often been helpful to them, and would be so again." Perhaps comparable was the aid given by Boreas to the Athenians in 480 in answer to a prayer: though in this case the god did not request cult, he showed that he deserved it, and a sanctuary was founded for him beside the Ilissus. One can imagine that in these cases, if we accept Herodotus's accounts (which there is no reason to doubt), a simple proposal was made to the assembly to honor the god in return for favors received. Perhaps it was on the same basis that

---

1. On the Athenian cases, which as so often predominate, see R. Garland, *Introducing New Gods: The Politics of Athenian Religion* (London, 1992); Parker, *Athenian Religion,* chap. 9. In the passage quoted on p. 15 (*Leg.* 738B–C) Plato supposes that cults arise either by oracular instruction or through a form of epiphany. He looks with equal favor on cults so arisen whatever their geographical origin.

Themistocles argued for the foundation of a temple of Artemis "of Best Counsel" after the repulse of the Persian invasion.[2]

The commonest mechanism was doubtless a recommendation by an oracle in answer to an inquiry, whether general ("How/by sacrificing to what gods will we prosper?") or specific (about plague, portents, etc.). Acceptance by the city would then have been automatic. In attested cases, oracles seem to have been cautious in their advice; they might recommend giving a familiar god an epithet that he already bore elsewhere in Greece, making Poseidon "Asphaleios," for instance.[3] There is no sign that oracles propagated radically new cults, not at least of gods.

A form of acceptance (but not normally acceptance into the public pantheon) was the granting to a society of foreigners of the right to buy land on which to build a sanctuary of their native god. Bendis, Isis, and a Cyprian form of Aphrodite all gained a footing in Athens in this way, Bendis apparently after consultation of an oracle, Isis and Aphrodite without.[4] The point at issue was, formally at least, one of law and not of religion: foreigners could not own land without special permission. Whether permission was ever denied, and if so on what grounds, is unknown. The case of Bendis is exceptional in that the goddess was in fact also incorporated into Athenian public cult, at or near the same date, and a question was put to an oracle about the priesthood. We can only guess about the special circumstances, and detailed mechanisms, that led to this unique development.

These three procedures are very far from explaining all the introductions that occurred. A fourth is the one so much disapproved of by Plato, private initiative, the activities of those lamentable individuals who "fill every house and every village" and open spaces too with "altars and shrines."[5]

---

2. Pan: Hdt. 6.105. Boreas: Hdt. 7.189, cf. 6.44.2. Artemis: above, p. 47. Several cults are associated by ancient sources with help given during the great plague of 430–426, sometimes spontaneous (Paus. 2.32.6, dream advice of Pan Lyterios at Troizen), sometimes solicited in obedience to an oracle (Paus. 1.3.4), sometimes without the mechanism being specified (Paus. 8.41.8–9; Σ Ar. *Ran.* 501; on chronological difficulties, see Parker, *Athenian Religion,* 186 n. 121).

3. To judge from such texts as *LSCG* 180; *IG* 12.5.913.9–14; *IKaunos* 31 (= *LSA* 87: recognized as an oracular response by Lupu, *NGSL,* 35 n. 162); *SEG* 45.912; cf. Dem. 21.52; 43.66. Sometimes a simple instruction to sacrifice to a major Olympian seems to have led to a new cult of that god with the epithet *pythochrēstos* (p. 265 n. 2 above). Hero cults are often introduced on oracular advice, in legend at least. But adding a new hero to a state's list was no more drastic than giving a god a new epithet. Delphi's involvement in dramatic cult introductions to Rome (Magna Mater, Asclepius) is not historical (E. Schmidt, *Kultübertragungen* [Giessen, 1909], 113).

4. See above. For a similar case on Athenian Delos, see *Inscr. Délos* 1519.11–16 (Tyrian Heracles). On the mystery of Bendis, cf. Parker, *Athenian Religion,* 170–75.

5. See p. 59 above; and cf. A. Purvis, *Singular Dedications: Founders and Innovators of Private Cults in Classical Greece* (NY, 2003).

Artemidorus of Perge is an extreme example of the altar-founding type: he set up a dozen or so, several to gods probably not hitherto there honored, in Thera in the third century BC. As far as we can tell, private initiative was the vehicle for the diffusion of the two cults that spread most conspicuously in the historical period, those of Asclepius and of Isis and Sarapis. By his own account it was as an independent agent that one Telemachus brought Asclepius, certainly a new god, to Athens in 421 BC, and found himself required to fight off a counterclaim to the site of his sanctuary by one of the Eleusinian priestly *genē*. It has, it is true, been doubted whether Telemachus could have established the expensive precinct in a prime site under the acropolis without some form of authorization or agreement. But the form such an agreement could have taken is hard to divine.[6] Cults of Asclepius at Naupactus, Sicyon, Elis, Lebena, and the famous one at Pergamum all passed as having been introduced by private individuals, though the details are sometimes fabulous;[7] there is by contrast no instance of a Greek city doing what the Romans supposedly did, summoning the god publicly in a time of crisis. Such accounts as there are of the "coming of Sarapis" are full of dreams and miracles, but the agents here too are individuals, and private associations of Sarapiasts demonstrably existed in many places. Egyptian gods might, we suppose, be introduced either by citizens who became acquainted with them while traveling as traders or soldiers, or by immigrants from Egypt.[8]

Such associations of Sarapiasts are a reminder of all the private revel bands and religious associations that must fall under the heading of "established by individual initiative." There is no sign that a person wishing to establish such a group was required to seek permission to do so, or that there was any authority from which such permission could be sought. (But the impossibility of acquiring a legal charter for such a band does not mean that it was exempt from attack in the courts for being unlawful.) Here too belong cults of their

---

6. Artemidorus: *IG* 12.3.421–22; *IG* 12.3 *Suppl.* 1333–50; cf. *IG* 12 *Suppl.* 86; cf. Wilamowitz, *Glaube,* 2:382–85; F. Graf in *Stadtbild und Bürgerbild im Hellenismus,* ed. M. Wörrle and P. Zanker, 107–12 (Munich, 1995). Telemachus: Parker, *Athenian Religion,* 175–85, 216, 345 [+].

7. Paus. 2.10.3 (Sicyon), 2.26.8 (Pergamum), 6.21.4 (Elis), 10.38.13 (Naupactus); Melfi, *Lebena,* appendix 1 no. 10 (= *IC* 1 17 8+10+7). According to pious myth, the cult at Halieis was public from the start, but through response by the city to the god, not an independent initiative: a sacred snake came to the city uninvited on the wagon of a pilgrim returning from Epidaurus, and performed a cure; Delphi, consulted about the event, advised establishing a sanctuary (in *IG* 4².1.122, cure 33; Edelstein and Edelstein, *Asclepius,* vol. 1, T 423). For the likelihood that Archias son of Aristaichmos who introduced the cult to Pergamum was a politically influential figure, see R. E. Allen, *The Attalid Kingdom* (Oxford, 1984), 161–64.

8. Cf. P. M. Fraser, *Op. Ath.* 3 (1960): 24, 32. Accounts: *IG* 11.4.1299 (cf. p. 271 n. 17); *IG* 10.2.255 (*RICIS* 113/0536); cf. P. Cair. Zenon 59034 (*RICIS* 314/0601). Sarapiasts: see *RICIS,* 1:6.

native gods established by foreign residents who did not seek permanent ownership of property on which to found a shrine. An Egyptian who was prosecuted on Delos for building an unauthorized sanctuary of Sarapis had conducted the cult previously on a rented site without arousing protest.[9] All this activity apparently took place without license or regulation.

Some such private cults, whether established by Greeks or foreigners, eventually achieved public recognition through a public priesthood. One can suppose—but unfortunately no case study presents itself—that familiarity will have eased a proposal's path through the assembly; there is little trace of oracular consultation in such a situation.[10] The process was irregular—thus the cult of the Corybantes was public in Erythrae but apparently remained private in Athens[11]—but it was probably by this route that the cults of Asclepius and the Egyptian gods eventually acquired public status in many cities.[12] An alternative scenario would be the following: a citizen would propose that a cult that was obviously proving beneficial in a neighboring city should be introduced directly to his own city too as a public cult; perhaps he might offer to meet some of the expenses himself. That would obviously have been an initiative open only to a figure of considerable standing and self-confidence. By a variation on the alternative scenario, a prosperous citizen would offer a sum of money to fund a recurrent sacrifice to a new god: by voting to accept the endowment, the city would also accept the god. Whether the alternative scenarios were actually played out is uncertain;[13] so too, therefore, whether they would have required reference to an oracle.

To sum up: the decision to add a god to the existing public pantheon must always have been made in the assembly. Sometimes the assembly's decision will have been rendered easy and automatic by oracular advice or by the god's manifest services to the city. Sometimes a case may have had to be made for the god on the grounds that he/she was already being honored privately in the city without harm, or in neighboring cities with benefit. In such a case an

9. *IG* 11.4.1299 (*RICIS* 202/0101); cf. H. Engelmann, *The Delian Aretalogy of Sarapis* (Leiden, 1975).

10. But see 3 and 18 in table 2 on pp. 266–67 above.

11. Athens: Dodds, *Greeks and the Irrational,* 77–79; Erythrae: *IErythrai* 206 (*LSA* 23) with *SEG* 47.1628 (LSA 23); what difference this distinction in formal status made in practice is another issue (B. Dignas, *EpigAnat* 34 [2002]: 29–40).

12. Cf. L. Robert and J. Robert, *BÉ* 1963, no. 169.

13. But see above, on the possibility that Telemachus's introduction of Asclepius to Athens was less wholly private than he represents it. Endowments for sacrifices are commonplace, but usually relate to existing cults. Note, however, *IHistriae* 1.15–18, which conceivably introduced a cult of the Muses to the city; and it was Xenophon's endowment which brought Artemis of Ephesus to Skillous (*Anab.* 5.3.4–13).

oracle might reasonably have been consulted, but evidence is largely missing, to an extent that makes it doubtful whether consultation in such cases often occurred. The assembly also ruled on applications by foreign groups to buy land on which to build shrines. Beyond this assembly-controlled central area there was a hinterland where private cults and gods, both Greek and foreign, came and went freely; some of them would eventually become sufficiently recognized to acquire a public priesthood. The hinterland was beyond detailed surveillance by the assembly, though not, so to speak, beyond occasional police raiding if it suited an individual to bring a prosecution for impiety.

✹ APPENDIX 3

Worshipping Mortals, and the Nature of Gods

Several points are now widely agreed after various important contributions.[1]

1. The paying of cult to mortals was not a product or a symptom or a cause of the decline of traditional Greek religion. The cult paid by Hellenistic cities to kings was caused by their new situation of dependence on the actions of individuals external to themselves with life-and-death power over them. But the cult of traditional gods carried on alongside that of monarchs; where a city felt itself to have been saved from a crisis without the involvement of a monarch, it thanked the gods with just the same forms as were used for honoring kings; and the various ways in which kings were worked into divine cult—through festivals or temples shared between god and king, or by assimilation of the king to a particular god—show how the cult of mortals was in fact dependent on the cult of immortals.

---

1. Preeminent are C. Habicht, *Gottmenschentum und griechische Städte,* 2nd ed. (*Zetemata* 14, Munich, 1970); S.R.F. Price, *Rituals and Power: The Roman Imperial Cult in Asia Minor* (Cambridge, 1984), 7–52; also very useful are F. W. Walbank, "Monarchy and Religion," *Cambridge Ancient History* i² (Cambridge, 1984), 7:84–100; A. Chaniotis, "The Divinity of Hellenistic Rulers," in *A Companion to the Hellenistic World,* ed. A. Erskine, 431–45 (Oxford, 2003) [+]. Many important insights go back to A. D. Nock. My concern here is with the cults established by cities, not the slightly later phenomenon of dynastic cults organized by monarchs themselves (on this important distinction, see Walbank, cited in this note.)

2. The cult of mortals was made possible by various aspects of established religion:

   a. The post-mortem cult of mortals, in the form of heroes, had long been practiced; the continuity is particularly clear between the cult traditionally paid to founders and that of monarchs honored as founders.

   b. Expressions such as "You are my Zeus Phanaios" or "I will pray and sacrifice to you as to the gods"[2] had always been possible in excited popular speech as ways of expressing intense gratitude; cult translated such figures of speech into action.

   c. The standard Greek equivalent to our "worshipping" the gods was "honoring"; there was no verbal distinction between worship, an act confined to gods, and honoring, as commonly done to mortals. It is true that one strand of Greek thought insisted on a distinction within honors between those appropriate to gods and to mortals; but it was also possible to see honors as an unbroken continuum within which godlike honors were just the highest grade of honor.[3] Monarchs, through their power, were able to confer benefits much greater than those bestowed by ordinary benefactors; it was necessary, therefore, to go right to the top of the scale of honors.[4]

   d. The concept of the "godlike man," who somehow approaches godhead, goes back to Hesiod and occurs in a variety of contexts.[5]

3. The institution of cults by cities, initially at least, was a response to specific actions benefiting them by monarchs, not small actions but ones affecting their freedom or very existence.[6] These were just the situations in which thanks were offered to city-protecting gods: the monarch has brought to the city a benefit such as traditionally could only have been conferred by gods. Because the benefit came first, the city was not "making a god" of the mortal; it was expressing thanks for a godlike act that had already occurred. What mattered was particular actions of the monarch, not his general character. So the phenomenon was not one of charisma (and the

---

2. See, e.g., Aesch. *Supp.* 980–82; Eupolis fr. 384.6; Eur. *Rhes.* 355; for similar language in epic, see Currie, *Cult of Heroes,* 178–80; at Rome, I. Gradel, *Emperor Worship and Roman Religion* (Oxford, 2002), 44–49.

3. As Arist. *Rhet.* 1361a 28–37 suggests; cf. Nock, *Essays,* 241–42; Gradel, *Emperor Worship,* 25–35, in n. 2 above.

4. Cf. P. Gauthier, *Les cités grecques et leurs bienfaiteurs* (Paris, 1985), 42–45.

5. Currie, *Cult of Heroes,* 172–78.

6. This is the central and crucial insight of Habicht, *Gottmenschentum,* in n. 1 above.

importance of "godlike men," 2(d) above, and such charismatic predecessors as athletes who became heroes should not be overplayed).
"The kings" (of Macedon) to whom cult was paid by the Samians
who returned to their island c. 322 after almost half a century of
exile were the infant son and mentally defective half-brother of
Alexander the Great, because formal credit for the great restoration
was theirs.[7]

4. The mortals who received cult were both assimilated to gods and
   separated from them. In terms of cult actions they were sometimes
   assimilated completely: they were honored with temples, priests, and
   sacrifices, and the word "god" could be used of them even during their lifetime. But though the word was used of them, it was
   not normally used to them, in direct address; nor did they so describe
   themselves. It was still necessary to make sacrifices for their welfare to
   the traditional gods; they themselves still prayed and sacrificed. Cities resolved by decree to confer "god-equal" honors on them, not to
   "honor them as gods" or add them to the gods. The decrees in question only occasionally hint at the godlike character of the benefits
   conferred,[8] and are in the main cast in the same dry pragmatic tone as
   ordinary civic decrees for ordinary benefactors: religious enthusiasm
   may have been sometimes displayed in hymns to the monarchs, but
   not in the decrees.

5. The cults were useful to both kings and cities; they were a mode of
   interaction that suited both sides in an unprecedented situation.[9]
   This mode of interaction had close parallels in cities' dealings with
   lesser benefactors: honors were given in gratitude for favors received,
   in hope of more favors to come (a hope which could be openly
   expressed); it also had parallels in traditional ways of dealing with
   the gods, which worked on just the same basis. The cults gave the
   city a certain leverage: at a certain point the Achaean League voted

---

7. *IG* 12.6.42.64–5; Habicht, *Gottmenschentum* (in n. 1 above) 222–23.

8. Note, e.g., the simple but pregnant ascription to Antiochus III and Laodike III of the typically
divine capacity to "give good things" in the Tean decrees for them (Ma, *Antiochus III,* dossier 17.52,
18.95–96). But for the restrained norm, see Chaniotis, "Divinity of Hellenistic Rulers," 440 (in n. 1
above): "not . . . recognition of superhuman godlike achievements, but . . . of past services."

9. This insight is one of the main achievements of Price's fundamental *Rituals and Power* (in
n. 1 above); cf. Chaniotis, "Divinity of Hellenistic Rulers" (in n. 1 above), 440. Price puts the issue
in terms of cognitive adjustment, but as has been observed (W. Liebeschuetz, *JRS* 75 [1985]: 263;
Lane Fox, *Pagans and Christians,* 686 n. 42), that is too intellectualist (unless "cognitive" is understood in a very broad sense): the power of the kings was easy to understand but hard to know how
to deal with, practically and also perhaps emotionally and psychologically.

to scale down the honors it had accorded to King Eumenes II of Pergamum not, they explained, out of hostility, but because they had been out of proportion to the benefits he had actually conferred.[10] The many splendid festivals suited the hellenistic appetite for entertainment, and might help to efface memories of earlier less happy phases in the dealings between the king and city in question.[11]

What remains problematic[12] is how to interpret the ambiguity of 4 above, the position of the monarch as both god and mortal.[13] Was 'mortal' the real perception of celebrants, 'god' a metaphor or convenient fiction? Or have we a compromise between an awestruck response to power/benefaction perceived as being on a truly superhuman scale, and awareness that its agent was after all mortal? (And how relevant was the thought that death was not the end for exceptional mortals?) Did the intensity of the ritual experience obliterate for its duration awareness of the recipient's mortality? Answers to these questions are likely to have varied according to time, place, and individual.

---

10. Polyb. 28.7.11 with 27.18.1–3; for graded rewards, cf. Diod. 20.100.2–3. "Openly expressed": see, e.g., Ma, *Antiochus III,* dossier 17.29.

11. See the brilliant section of Ma, *Antiochus III,* 219–26, "Ruler cult as social memory."

12. There also remain many uncertainties about the detailed history of the phenomenon before the Hellenistic norms were established early in the reigns of the first Successors: for a survey, see K. Buraselis in *ThesCRA* 2:164–71; and cf. now M. Mari, "The Ruler Cult in Macedonia," *Studi Ellenistici* 20 (2008) 219–51.

13. S. R. F. Price points out (*JHS* 104 [1984]: 79–81) that the question "Is x a god?" like the question "Is x a person?" is one that admits of borderline cases. But immortality is such a standard and central feature of the typical image of a god that the lack of it might be thought immediately to exclude a candidate from the category.

✍ APPENDIX 4

Types of Chthonian Sacrifice?

This appendix continues the argument of p. 84 above.

The case for replacing the exploded single concept of "chthonian sacrifice" with a cluster of types of chthonian sacrifice runs roughly as follows:[1]

a. The following are the most diagnostic non-standard traits in sacrifice (not a complete list, but the most identifiable features): burning of the victim whole, or burning of more than occurs in normal Olympian sacrifice; wineless libations; pouring of the blood into the ground; black or pregnant victims; the requirement to consume the meat on the spot.

b. Not every sacrifice to a chthonian will display any of these traits, because all Greek gods including chthonians had a double aspect, favorable as well as frightening, and the separation/marking of difference created by the nonstandard features was not obligatory; sometimes the two aspects might be evoked successively in a single ceremony. But any chthonian will predominantly receive rites that show some of the diagnostic traits.

---

1. Scullion, "Olympian and Chthonian."

c. All or almost all the non-standard forms of sacrifice listed in (a)
   occur in one of two contexts (inevitably, given the character of our
   evidence, there are one or two irresoluble cases): they are made
   either to a chthonian god, or to a god in whose cult other forms of
   reinforced sacrificial action are also found or might be predicted.
   "Other forms of reinforced sacrificial action" here refers to those
   (what A. D. Nock termed *heilige Handlungen*) used in crises such
   as storms or a forthcoming battle; they stress killing, renunciation,
   and immediate ritual efficacy (the two black lambs to stay a storm)
   rather than feasting and a long-term relation of reciprocity with
   a god. The non-standard forms can serve as mitigated variants, in
   regular cult, of these more drastic destruction sacrifices. In both cases
   (when addressed to chthonians; when serving as mitigated *heilige
   Handlungen*) the non-standard forms evince a similar attitude of ner-
   vousness vis-à-vis the recipients.[2]

Proposition (b) depends heavily on the claim that the requirement to eat
the meat of a sacrificial victim "on the spot" marks out a special form of
sacrifice with a special mood in the same sense as does, say, a ban on libations
of wine. The claim is necessary in order to show that the cult of one class
of chthonians, the heroes, was ritually differentiated from that of Olympian
gods. "On the spot" rules were frequent and perhaps universal in heroic cult;
those aside, the forms of heroic cult are often indistinguishable to our eyes
from those of divine cult.[3] Against the argument that "no carry out" rules
had special ritual significance, it has been objected that eating the meat on
the spot was the norm, to judge both from literary descriptions and from the
banqueting rooms so abundantly attested archaeologically in Greek sanctuaries. Such rules would therefore not mark out a special class of sacrifices,
but make obligatory in particular cases what was anyway common; the motive would be to encourage/discourage the active participation of particular
classes of worshipper.[4] The objection is inconclusive: even if "on the spot"

---

2. "Recipients of the various ritual features traditionally assembled under the rubric 'chthonian'
almost always display a connection with the earth; those who do not will fall into a restricted class of
beings, including weather gods of the heights and recipients of wartime *sphagia* or mythical human
sacrifice, who are in temperament similar to the chthonians": Scullion (previous note), 116.

3. To preserve a difference, one will need to postulate (not wholly unreasonably, but quite unveri-
fiably) distinctions, such as in the treatment of the blood, which sacred calendars seldom had reason
to record: cf. R. Parker in *Greek Sacrificial Ritual*, 41–43.

4. So Ekroth, *Sacrificial Rituals*, 310–25. She also (313) adduces two instances of sacrifices to heroes that she argues were certainly "carried out"; but in the one case (*LSS* 19.19–24) the issue seems
to me indeterminable, and in the other she relies on a doubtful reading in *SEG* 33.147 (*NGSL* 1) 27
(see Jameson, "The Spectacular and the Obscure," 329 n. 29).

dining was the norm, the carrying away of some part of the meat even after such communal banquets was doubtless very frequent. Proof positive, however, that an "on the spot" rule gave the banquet a special, chthonian intensity is not available. And the adoption of such rules as a criterion opens the door uncomfortably wide. They are found in many cults of gods as well as of heroes, of whom some can be explained as chthonian or otherwise formidable but a few create real difficulty.[5]

As for proposition (c), it is an attempt to maintain the diagnostic value of the non-standard forms of sacrifice. The epigraphic discoveries of the twentieth century showed that these could occur in the cult of manifest non-chthonians such as Zeus Overseer (Epopetes) or Zeus of the Heights (Epakrios).[6] Proposition (c) seeks to isolate the exceptions within a single class, so that the occurrence of a non-standard form will indicate one of two things: the god in question will either be of the type for whom "reinforced sacrificial action" (*heilige Handlung*) is appropriate, or he will be a chthonian. But even if we allow the first part of this either/or (non-standard sacrificial forms serving as a weakened form of *heilige Handlung*),[7] the second part (all other recipients of non-standard forms chthonian) can be doubted. "Sober offerings," for instance, were supposedly made to the nymphs and to the Muses in Attica. But there is nothing obviously chthonian about Muses and nymphs. On the other hand, non-standard forms of sacrifice cluster in the cults of certain gods, Zeus above all, but are absent from those of others (e.g., Apollo), in a way that suggests that the character of the god is indeed relevant. The preliminary offering to Zeus of the City (Polieus) before his great festival on Cos, for instance, was a piglet, burned whole; an interpretation in terms of an oppositional logic within the ritual (the pig burned as a preliminary contrasts with the ox sacrificed in the normal way the following day) has been influential, but a good case has been made that Zeus Polieus on Cos had, in fact, a strong connection with agriculture not revealed in his

---

5. No proof positive: but Scullion, "Olympian and Chthonian," 102, adduces an Old Testament parallel and a passage of the Orphic *Lithika* (699–747, esp. 732–33 Abel; 693–741 Hermann). Real difficulty: in particular Apollo Lykeios (whom Scullion struggles to explain, "Olympian and Chthonian," 109–10). The table in Ekroth, *Sacrificial Rituals,* 156, is useful.

6. See Ekroth, *Sacrificial Rituals,* 156.

7. It was argued in chap. 5 that "sacrifices" divide into those that are cast in an alimentary idiom and those that are simple killings: on this view, a holocaust accompanied by sober libations to Zeus the Overseer, for example, belongs to a quite different category from, say, the slaughter of black lambs to the winds, whereas Scullion sees the former as a mitigated form of the latter. I also note the different recipient in the two cases.

epithet "of the City" and so was an appropriate "chthonian" recipient of the small holocaust.[8]

The main offering to Zeus Polieus in that Coan festival was accompanied by the offering of a pregnant sheep to Athena Polias. That is the detail that, above all, suggests that these gods of the city were also concerned with the city's fields; for the connection between pregnant victims and agricultural growth is, surely, one of the rare transparent elements in Greek ritual.[9] It is, however, startling, here and in one Attic instance, to find none other than Athena as recipient of the pregnant victim. What should we then say? That Athena (Polias) is a (part) chthonian? That she has a chthonian aspect? It might be easier merely to say that here, unusually, she has an association with agriculture. And here lies the weight of the case for describing as chthonian only the limited number of gods so described in ancient sources. To establish that the cult of Zeus Polieus has an association with agriculture advances our knowledge. To label it chthonian merely substitutes for that precise description a vaguer one.

---

8. RO 62 (*LSCG* 151 A) 29–38; see Scullion, "Olympian and Chthonian," 81–89, dissenting from Graf, "Milch, Honig und Wein." Muses and nymphs: Suda v 356 = Polemon of Ilium fr. 42 Preller.

9. Though for a different view, see J. N. Bremmer in *Greek Sacrificial Ritual,* 155–65. Athena Polias on Cos: RO 62 (*LSCG* 151 A) 55–56; Athena Skiras receives a pregnant sheep in *LSS* 19.93 (Salaminioi, Attica).

❧ APPENDIX 5

The Early History of Hero Cult

           The first principle in the study of ancient religion should be to observe what can be observed, and refrain from fantasizing about "origins" that are not open to investigation. But the cult of heroes is a special case, because it is arguable that its origin, or at least a radical change of direction, is indeed available for inspection. The topic is highly obscure, but also highly important, because here for once the word "history" found in the titles of Histories of Greek Religion may have a justification: a key transformation in the very hierarchy of the divine world perhaps occurs before our eyes.

    The conception of hero cult as a phenomenon stretching back into the mists of time (still found, for instance, in Brelich's *Gli eroi greci* of 1958) has been problematic since archaeologists observed that, in several areas of the Greek world, Mycenaean tombs, unused for centuries, were reopened for cult purposes in the late eighth century; the new cult was often evanescent, but in a few cases continued for several centuries.[1] Classical sources speak of the typical location of a hero cult as the hero's tomb, and it is intuitively plausible

---

1. The phenomenon was first emphasized by J. N. Coldstream, "Hero-Cults in the Age of Homer," *JHS* 96 (1976): 8–17. The archaeology is now surveyed by Antonaccio, *Ancestors,* and Boehringer, *Heroenkulte.* Written sources treating tombs as location for hero cult: R. Seaford, *Reciprocity and Ritual* (Oxford, 1994), 114–23.

that men of the eighth century, who disposed of their dead differently, imagined impressive Mycenaean tombs as harboring individuals from the age of demigods; it is therefore widely supposed that these offerings at Mycenaean tombs provide our first archaeological evidence for the cult of heroes. In parallel with the new cults at ancient tombs, we can perhaps observe archaeological instances of historical individuals who received continuing, and apparently collective, cult after death. Both types of hero—the mythological and the recently dead—would therefore emerge archaeologically at about the same time. A complicating factor is that reuse of Mycenaean tombs for contemporary burials had also occurred sporadically from the eleventh century. Where cult seems to imply respect and a sense of distance, reuse suggests relaxed familiarity.[2]

Even prior to these archaeological discoveries, literary evidence had often been thought to create a difficulty about retrojecting the cult of heroes to primeval time. But the difficulty can perhaps be got round. The silence of Homer on the subject need not be the obstacle that it has been taken to be: in strict verisimilitude Homer's characters cannot pay cult to the heroes if they themselves are those heroes, the men of the age of ἡμίθεοι; there were not yet any heroes available for them to worship. One allusion to the worship of a past mortal does appear to slip in, if only in the Catalog of Ships: the "youths of the Athenians" bring sumptuous offerings to Erechtheus, though in a temple, not at a grave.[3]

It is more disconcerting that, in his myth of five ages in *Works and Days*, Hesiod fails to assign any cultic function to "the divine race of the heroes, those who are called ἡμίθεοι" and who fought and died at Thebes and Troy. Instead, Zeus transported them to the Isles of the Blessed, where they now live, "fortunate heroes," free from care (170–73). Hesiod does know of quondam mortals who live on in the human sphere as gods in a small way, but they are not the heroes: it is the men of the golden age who are now "reverend

---

2. Cf. C. Sourvinou-Inwood, "The Hesiodic Myth of the Five Ages and the Tolerance of Plurality in Greek Mythology," in *Greek Offerings,* ed. O. Palagia, 1–21 (Oxford, 1997), at 6. Reuse is much emphasized by Antonaccio, *Ancestors;* cf. in brief Antonaccio, "Archaeology of Ancestors," 49. Historical individuals: see references in Parker, *Athenian Religion,* 37, and A. Seiffert in *ThesCRA* 4:25; but interpretation of the prime exhibit, the "hero shrine at the West Gate" of Eretria, remains controversial (Antonaccio, *Ancestors,* 228–36). Certain or plausible cases of long-lasting cult at Mycenaean tombs come from Menidi and Thorikos in Attica (Boehringer, *Heroenkulte,* 48–59), Mycenae (ibid., 164–66), Tiryns and Berbati (ibid., 178–84), and now Metropolis (n. 12 below).

3. *Il.* 2.546–51. For further arguments to indicate Homer's knowledge of hero cult, see Currie, *Cult of Heroes,* 48–59. Brelich, *Eroi,* 387, robustly argues that the word ἥρως, commonly taken to mean "lord, warrior" in Homer, already has its later sense: so too H. van Wees, *Status Warriors: War, Violence and Society in Homer and History* (Amsterdam, 1992), 8. But the debate on that issue rumbles on… (Currie, *Cult of Heroes,* 60–70; Bremmer, "Hero Cult," 17–18).

powers (*daimones*) upon the earth, good, averters of evil, guardians of mortal men, wealth-givers" (122–23, 126), while those of the silver age "are called blessed mortals under the earth, second [to the golden age men], but honor accompanies them too" (141–42). That distribution of functions is not one with which we are familiar from the classical period. But Hesiod was a spec-ulative theologian, seeking to reconcile a myth of metallic generations that succeeded one another with the separate tradition of an age of heroes; one could speculate that, in order to assign a properly honorable post-mortem destiny to the men of the golden and silver ages, he split up the patrimony of the heroes.[4] It is significant that he attests for the first time the conception of the "divine race of the heroes" as belonging firmly to the past. Homer too, however, has the conception of a great lost age: not only does he often con-trast the feeble men of today with those of the past, but in the one exceptional passage of retrospect that opens book 12 of the *Iliad* he speaks (line 23) of the "race of half-divine men" (ἡμιθέων γένος ἀνδρῶν) as having perished in the dust of the plain of Troy. The conceptual underpinning for a cult of heroes (if not necessarily under that name)[5] is present in both authors.

The weight of the case for a decisive change reverts therefore to the much-discussed archaeological evidence. After a period of energetic theorizing, a certain pessimism has emerged about the possibility of developing a unified explanation to account for it: the phenomenon occurs in parts of the Greek world that were historically in very different conditions;[6] even within a single region, the types of offering may seem to indicate worshipping groups of different character;[7] and serious uncertainties exist not only about the inter-pretation of particular cases but also about the proper description (tomb cult? ancestor cult? hero cult?) of whole classes of activity. The emphasis in this debate has mostly lain on the eighth-century phenomenon rather than on the history of hero cult in a longer view. In relation to that longer view, the

---

4. Cf. Sourvinou-Inwood, "Hesiodic Myth" (n. 2 above), 6–9. She argues, by a different route, that the Hesiodic passage is compatible with cult paid to heroes (but not to men of the silver age). Lane Fox, *Travelling Heroes,* 367–68, challenges the widespread view that Hesiod's myth of ages is a borrowing from Near Eastern sources.

5. Bremmer has argued, "Hero Cult," 15–26, that (1) the term "hero" in a religious sense is not attested before the sixth century, and accordingly (2) we should not speak of hero cults before then. "Surely we can speak of hero-cults only when there is a clear concept of heroes" (17). But on his own showing, 24–25, a clear concept of "demigods" existed much earlier.

6. J. Whitley, "Early States and Hero-Cults: A Reappraisal," *JHS* 88 (1988): 173–82. For surveys of the debate see Kearns, *Heroes of Attica,* 129–32; Parker, *Athenian Religion,* 36–39; Boehringer, *Heroenkulte,* 13–15.

7. A main theme of the valuable detailed study of Boehringer, *Heroenkulte:* see, for instance, 103 on the contrast between three Attic cults (Thorikos, Menidi, and the "sacred house" at Eleusis).

best that can be done at the moment is to identify the possibilities that seem to be available, and the difficulties that confront them.

1. What we observe is not the emergence of hero cult but a huge increase in its popularity under the impulse of Homeric epic. This was the view of J. N. Coldstream, to whom much of the credit for identifying the eighth-century phenomenon belongs. That the epic tradition had some influence on cult in the archaic period appears certain; it would be a strange coincidence otherwise that Achilles and Diomedes, the two greatest warriors of the *Iliad,* became in particular regions such godlike figures, or, to take a small example, that a naval hero at Phaleron should be identified as a "Phaiacian hero" (in tribute to the naval skills of Homer's Phaiacians).[8] But many objections have been advanced to the specific claim of a sudden surge of influence in the eighth century.[9]

2. Hero cult existed before the eighth century (cf. the Homeric Erechtheus, honored in a temple), but at this point assumed a new and for the first time archaeologically visible form, attaching itself to tombs. The difficulty here is obviously that of explaining the new form. But the uneven archaeological visibility of hero cult, typically conducted on a fairly small scale, is a complication that must always be taken very seriously.[10]

3. Hero cult did indeed emerge for the first time in the eighth century, under strong new social pressures. The problem of identifying those pressures has already been mentioned. The extraordinary diversification that the cult then underwent would also remain to be explained; a particular issue would be how the connection with real or supposed tombs with which the cult began could have become optional.

---

8. I do not understand Burkert's argument, *Greek Religion,* 204–5, that Achilles' Black Sea cult depends on his birth from the sea goddess Thetis and is therefore independent of Homer: he is her son in the *Iliad.* On Diomedes and Achilles, see pp. 244–46; on "Phaiacian hero," Kearns, *Heroes of Attica,* 38–39. Coldstream: n. 1 above.

9. Currie, *Cult of Heroes,* 49 n. 14, cites twelve countervoices.

10. I do not know that archaeologically one could prove that heroes were worshipped in fourth-century Attica at all. It would be interesting to compare archaeological and literary/epigraphic evidence for hero cult region by region: I anticipate that great disparities would emerge. The tripod dedications beginning in the ninth century in the Polis cave at Ithaca would prove the preexistence of a different form of hero veneration, if one could be sure that they honored Odysseus (see I. Malkin, *The Wanderings of Odysseus* [Berkeley, 1998], chap. 3). M. Deoudi, *Heroenkulte in homerischer Zeit* (BAR international series 806, Oxford, 1999) (critically reviewed by G. Ekroth in *OpAth* 28 [2003]: 204–7) accepts more phenomena as clear evidence for hero cult than most scholars and so takes the archaeological evidence back earlier, but still detects a great intensification in the late eighth century (27, 39, 62).

4. The cults of the eighth century at Mycenaean tombs have nothing to do with hero cult. What they attest is "ancestor cult": such hero cults as existed at this date were celebrated in sanctuaries; the partial coalescence of hero cult with cult at tombs was a later development. This view has acquired considerable support.[11] But ancestor cult as it is known from many ethnographic descriptions did not take place in Greece; and the closest Greek equivalents to ancestors, the Tritopatores, were not normally worshipped at tombs though they might be worshipped near them. The explicit evidence that cult at reopened Mycenaean tombs might be addressed to heroes used to rest on a single fifth-century shard inscribed "I belong to the hero" and found in the region of Grave Circle A at Mycenae. That shard has now been joined by a roof tile of the seventh/sixth century, from a most impressive new instance of continuing cult paid to a reopened tomb at Metropolis in Thessaly (a region where the phenomenon had hitherto been unknown). The tile is inscribed]EAIATIIONE[(last letter doubtful); within these letters a reference to a shrine, Aiation, of the Thessalian hero Aiatos has been identified. A slight doubt lingers, because one of the iotas is redundant and no obvious way of supplementing the whole presents itself. The counterargument, however, that early hero cults were never practiced at tombs is based on a limited number of cases,[12] and depends on the exclusion of precisely those cults at tombs of which the character is in debate. One might rather suppose that, as later, some hero cults were located at tombs, others not.

5. A reconfiguration of the supernatural world occurred.[13] There had always been mortals, figures of legend, who remained powerful after death, but hitherto their status had been ill defined or they counted

---

11. Advocated especially by C. Antonaccio, at length in *Ancestors,* briefly and clearly in "Archaeology of Ancestors"; accepted, e.g., by Bremmer, "Hero Cult," 20 and in part by F. de Polignac, *Cults, Territory, and the Origins of the Greek City-State* (Chicago, 1995), 140–41. Tomb/ancestor cult in Antonaccio's broad definition goes back to the tenth century (see *AJA* 98 [1994]: 402–3). For dissent see Boehringer, *Heroenkulte,* 42–45, 47 n. 4. On Tritopatores see Jameson, Jordan, and Kotansky, *Selinous,* 107–14: I write "not normally" to allow Selinous as a possible exception.

12. Antonaccio in fact allows only one certain case, the Menelaion at Sparta ("Archaeology of Ancestors," 62)—which the ancients treated as divine, not heroic! The postulated cult of Phrontis on Cape Sounion (Antonaccio, *Ancestors,* 166–69) is an early instance of a hero cult at the place believed, however wrongly, to be the site of the hero's tomb. Shard from Mycenae: *IG* 4.495; Antonaccio, *Ancestors,* 51. Aiatos: B. G. Intzesiloglou, "Aiatos et Polycléia: Du mythe à l'histoire," *Kernos* 15 (2002): 289–95 (*SEG* 52.561); for the hero, see Polyaenus, *Strat.* 8.44.

13. For varieties of this approach, see Kearns, *Heroes of Attica,* 129–37; Burkert, *Greek Religion,* 204–5; Bremmer, "Hero Cult," 19.

vaguely as gods; they were now accorded a specific status as demigods or heroes, and the fact that, unlike gods, they had passed through death might be stressed by the link with a tomb. Some "gods in a small way" also entered the class, and were therefore given, insofar as anyone cared to inquire into the matter, human parentages; but they did not necessarily acquire also a tomb. The putative reconfiguration, it should be noted, was not carried through very effectively, since, as we saw, heroes were often loosely spoken of as "gods," though not gods as heroes.

A firm choice between these options can scarcely be made in the present state of research. Some element of "pick and mix" among them is doubtless possible. A problem that arises in almost all cases is that of the relation between hero cults that were and were not conducted at supposed tombs. ("Supposed" is crucial here; for Greek understandings, the question whether the supposed tombs were real ones is quite irrelevant.) Many of our uncertainties about hero cult hover around that relation. From the Attic cult calendars there is unfortunately no way of telling the kind of emplacement at which each offering was made, and thus the relative frequency of the two kinds. This uncertainty may interconnect with the problematic issue of the forms of hero cult, which often closely resembled those of divine cult, but were sometimes assimilated more to the cult of the dead.[14] Were offerings at tombs more likely to involve destruction of the victim, those at little sanctuaries to be made "as to the gods"? The question hangs in the air. What it confirms, thus suspended, is the mixed character of the heroes, mortals by biography, small gods in power.

---

14. See p. 110. The process of equipping hitherto tombless heroes with tombs continued into the Hellenistic period: see Pirenne-Delforge, *Pausanias,* 230–32, on Phoroneus at Argos (citing M. Piérart) and on Paus. 2.23.7–8. Heroes spoken of as gods: see p. 110.

✺ BIBLIOGRAPHY

Abbreviations of periodicals and works of reference aspire to be those recommended for use in the *American Journal of Archaeology* at http://www.ajaonline.org, with a few supplements listed below. For ancient authors, standard source collections, and works of reference not listed by *American Journal of Archaeology,* the abbreviations in S. Hornblower and A. Spawforth, eds., *The Oxford Classical Dictionary*³ (1996), supplemented by those in Liddell, Scott, and Jones, *A Greek English Lexicon with a Revised Supplement* (Oxford, 1996), have been followed, with a few trivial divergences. Abbreviations of epigraphical corpora are from Liddell, Scott, and Jones (with some supplements listed below). Comic fragments are cited from R. Kassel and C. Austin, *Poetae comici Graeci* (Berlin, 1983–), tragic from B. Snell, R. Kannicht, and S. Radt, *Tragicorum Graecorum fragmenta* (Göttingen, 1971–2004).

On much-debated topics, I sometimes cite only a recent contribution, adding the symbol [+] to stress that this work refers to earlier studies that remain important. What follows is not a list of all works mentioned in the notes, but of those cited by an abbreviated title (author plus title for monographs and journal articles; title only for collections of inscriptions and of essays).

Achilleus-Kult = J. Hupe, ed. *Der Achilleus-Kult im nordlichen Schwarzmeerraum.* Rahden, 2006.

Ancient Greek Cult Practice = R. Hägg, ed. *Ancient Greek Cult Practice from the Epigraphical Evidence.* Stockholm, 1994.

Antonaccio, C. "The Archaeology of Ancestors." In *Cultural Poetics,* 46–70.

———. *An Archaeology of Ancestors.* Lanham, Md., 1995.

Babut, D. *La religion des philosophes grecs.* Paris, 1974.

Beard, M., J. North, and S. Price. *Religions of Rome.* Vol. 1, *A History.* Cambridge, 1998.

Bickerman, E. J. "Cutting a Covenant." In *Studies in Jewish and Christian History,* 2nd ed., 1:1–31. Translated by B. McNeil. Leiden, 2007. First published in French as "Couper une alliance" in ed. 1, Leiden, 1976.

Boehringer, D. *Heroenkulte in Griechenland von der geometrischen bis zur klassischen Zeit.* Berlin, 2001.

Brelich, A. *Gli eroi greci: Un problema storico-religioso.* Rome, 1958.

Bremmer, J. N. *Greek Religion.* Oxford, 1994. Reprinted with addenda, 1999.

———. *The Rise and Fall of the Afterlife.* London, 2002.

———. "The Rise of the Hero Cult and the New Simonides." *ZPE* 158 (2006): 15–26.

Burckhardt, J. *Griechische Kulturgeschichte.* Vol. 1, *Staat und Religion.* Edited by J. Oers. Berlin, 1898. Reprint, Leipzig, 1929. Page references are to the 1929 edition.

Burkert, W. *Ancient Mystery Cults.* Cambridge, Mass., 1987.

——. *Greek Religion: Archaic and Classical.* Translated by J. Raffan. Oxford, 1985. First published in German in 1977.

——. *Homo Necans: The Anthropology of Ancient Greek Sacrificial Ritual and Myth.* Translated by P. Bing. Berkeley, 1983. First published in German in 1972.

——. *Structure and History in Greek Mythology and Ritual.* Berkeley, 1979.

Casabona, J. *Recherches sur le vocabulaire des sacrifices en Grec.* Aix-en-Provence, 1966.

Chaniotis, A. "Sich selbst feiern? Städtische Feste des Hellenismus im Spannungsfeld von Religion und Politik." In *Stadtbild und Bürgerbild im Hellenismus,* edited by M. Wörrle and P. Zanker, 147–72. Munich, 1995.

Chiekova, D. *Cultes et vie religieuse des cités grecques du Pont gauche.* Bern, 2008.

City of Images = C. Bérard et al. *A City of Images.* Translated by D. Lyons. Princeton, 1989. First published in French in 1984.

Cole, S. G. *Landscapes, Gender and Ritual Space.* Berkeley, 2004.

Companion = D. Ogden, ed. *A Companion to Greek Religion.* Oxford, 2007.

Connelly, J. B. *Portrait of a Priestess: Women and Ritual in Ancient Greece.* Princeton, 2007.

Cuisine et autel = S. Georgoudi, R. Koch Piettre, and F. Schmidt. *La cuisine et l'autel: Les sacrifices en questions dans les sociétés de la méditerranée ancienne.* Turnhout, 2005.

Cuisine of Sacrifice = M. Detienne and J. P. Vernant. *The Cuisine of Sacrifice among the Greeks.* Translated by P. Wissing. Chicago, 1989. First published in French in Paris, 1979.

Cultural Poetics = C. Dougherty and L. Kurke, eds. *Cultural Poetics in Archaic Greece: Cult, Performance, Politics.* Cambridge, 1993.

Currie, B. *Pindar and the Cult of Heroes.* Oxford, 2005.

de Heusch, L. *Sacrifice in Africa: A Structuralist Approach.* Translated by L. O'Brien and A. Morton. Bloomington, Ind., 1985.

Dentzer, J.-M. *Le motif du banquet couché dans le proche-oriente et le monde grec du viie au ive siècle avant J.-C.* BEFAR 246. Rome, 1982.

Detienne, M. *Apollon le couteau à la main.* Paris, 1998.

Detienne, M., and J. P. Vernant. *Cunning Intelligence in Greek Culture and Society.* Translated by J. Lloyd. Chicago, 1991. First published as *Les ruses de l'intelligence: La mètis des grecs,* Paris, 1974.

Dickie, M. W. *Magic and Magicians in the Greco-Roman World.* London, 2001.

Dignas, B. *Economy of the Sacred in Hellenistic and Roman Asia Minor.* Oxford, 2002.

——. "Rhodian Priests after the Synoecism." *Ancient Society* 33 (2003): 35–52.

Dimitrova, N. *Theoroi and Initiates in Samothrace: The Epigraphical Evidence.* Hesperia suppl. 37. Princeton, 2008.

Dodds, E. R. *The Greeks and the Irrational.* Berkeley, 1951.

Ducat, J. *Spartan Education: Youth and Society in the Classical Period.* Translated by E. Stafford, P.-J. Shaw, and A. Powell. Swansea, 2006.

Early Greek Cult Practice = R. Hägg, N. Marinatos, and G. C. Nordquist, eds. *Early Greek Cult Practice.* Stockholm, 1988.

Edelstein, E. J., and L. Edelstein. *Asclepius: A Collection and Interpretation of the Testimonies.* 2 vols. Baltimore, 1945.

Eidinow, E. *Oracles, Curses and Risk among the Ancient Greeks.* Oxford, 2007.

Ekroth, G. "Burnt, Cooked or Raw? Divine and Human Culinary Desires at Greek Animal Sacrifice." In *Transformations in Sacrificial Practices: From Antiquity to*

Modern Times, edited by E. Stavrianopoulou, A. Michaels, and C. Ambos, 87–111. Berlin, 2008.

——. "Meat, Man and God: On the Division of the Animal Victim at Greek Sacrifices." In Μικρὸς Ἱερομνήμων: Μελέτες εἰς μνήμην *Michael H. Jameson,* edited by A. P. Matthaiou and I. Polinskaya, 259–290. Athens, 2008.

——. *The Sacrificial Rituals of Greek Hero-cults.* Liège, 2002.

——. "Thighs or Tails? The Osteological Evidence as a Source for Greek Ritual Norms." In *Norme religieuse,* 125–52.

Evans-Pritchard, E. E., *Nuer Religion.* Oxford, 1956.

Flower, M. *The Seer in Ancient Greece.* Berkeley, 2008.

Fontenrose, J. *The Delphic Oracle.* Berkeley, 1978.

——. *Didyma: Apollo's Oracle, Cult and Companions.* Berkeley, 1988.

Foucart, P. *Le culte des héros chez les Grecs.* Mémoires de l'Académie des Inscriptions et Belles-Lettres 42. Paris, 1918.

Gebauer, J. *Pompe und Thysia: Attische Tieropferdarstellungen auf schwarz- und rotfiguren Vasen.* Münster, 2002.

Gibson, T. *Sacrifice and Sharing in the Philippine Highlands.* London, 1986.

Goff, B. *Citizen Bacchae.* Berkeley, 2004.

Graf, F. "Milch, Honig und Wein: Zum Verständnis der Libation im griechischen Ritual." In *Perennitas: Studi in onore di Angelo Brelich,* edited by G. Piccaluga, 209–21. Rome, 1980.

——. *Nordionische Kulte.* Rome, 1985.

Graf, F., and S. I. Johnston. *Ritual Texts for the Afterlife.* London, 2007.

Greek Mysteries = M. B. Cosmopoulou, ed. *Greek Mysteries.* London, 2005.

Greek Sacrificial Ritual = R. Hägg and B. Alroth, eds. *Greek Sacrificial Ritual, Olympian and Chthonian.* Stockholm, 2005.

Halliwell, S. *Greek Laughter.* Cambridge, 2008.

Harrison, T. *Divinity and History: The Religion of Herodotus.* Oxford, 2000.

Hero Cult = R. Hägg, ed. *Ancient Greek Hero Cult.* Stockholm, 1999.

Hinz, V. *Der Kult von Demeter und Kore auf Sizilien und in der Magna Graecia.* Wiesbaden, 1998.

Hubert, H., and M. Mauss. *Sacrifice: Its Nature and Function.* Translated by W. D. Halls. London, 1964. First published as *Essai sur la nature et la fonction du sacrifice* in *L'Année sociologique,* 1898.

Hughes, D. D. *Human Sacrifice in Ancient Greece.* London, 1991.

Ἰδίᾳ καὶ δημοσίᾳ = V. Dasen and M. Piérart, eds. Ἰδίᾳ καὶ δημοσίᾳ: *Les cadres "privés" et "publics" de la religion grecque antique.* Liège, 2005.

IEleusis = K. Clinton. *Eleusis: The Inscriptions on Stone.* Vol. 1A, *Text.* Athens, 2005.

IGDOlbia = L. Dubois. *Inscriptions grecques dialectales d'Olbia du Pont.* Geneva, 1996.

IGLSM III = A. Avram. *Inscriptions grecques et latines de Scythie Mineure.* Vol. 3, *Callatis et son territoire.* Bucharest, 1999.

IKaunos = C. Marek. *Die Inschriften von Kaunos.* Munich, 2006.

Iscr. Cos = M. Segre. *Iscrizioni di Cos.* Vol. 1. Rome, 1993. All references are to the decrees (ED in Segre's numeration).

Jaccottet, A. F. *Choisir Dionysos: Les associations dionysiaques ou la face cachée du Dionysisme.* 2 vols. Zurich, 2003.

Jameson, M. H. "The Spectacular and the Obscure in Athenian Religion." In *Performance Culture and Athenian Democracy,* edited by S. Goldhill and R. Osborne, 321–40. Cambridge, 1999.

Jameson, M. H., D. R. Jordan, and R. D. Kotansky. *A Lex Sacra from Selinous. GRBM* 11. Durham, N.C., 1993.

Jost, M. *Sanctuaires et cultes d'Arcadie.* Paris, 1985.

Kearns, E. *The Heroes of Attica. BICS* suppl. 57. London, 1989.

Konaris, M. "The Greek Gods in Nineteenth-Century German and British Scholarship." D. Phil. diss., Oxford University, 2009.

Kowalzig, B. *Singing for the Gods.* Oxford, 2007.

Kykeon = H. F. J. Hortstmanshoff et al., eds. *Kykeon: Studies in Honour of H. S. Versnel.* Leiden, 2002.

Lane Fox, R. *Pagans and Christians.* London, 1986.

——. *Travelling Heroes: Greeks and Their Myths in the Epic Age of Homer.* London, 2008.

Larson, J. *Greek Heroine Cults.* Madison, Wis., 1995.

Lebessi, A. Τὸ Ἱερὸ τοῦ Ἑρμῆ καὶ τῆς Ἀφροδίτης στὴ Σύμη Βιάννου. Vol. 1, Χάλκινα κρητικὰ τορεύματα. Athens, 1985.

——. Τὸ Ἱερὸ τοῦ Ἑρμῆ καὶ τῆς Ἀφροδίτης στὴ Σύμη Βιάννου. Vol. 3, Τὰ χάλκινα ἀνθρωπόμορφα εἰδώλια. Athens, 2002.

Leukopétra = P. M. Petsas, M. B. Hatzopoulos, L. Gounaropoulou, and P. Paschidis. *Inscriptions du sanctuaire de la Mère des Dieux Autochthone de Leukopétra (Macédoine).* Athens, 2000.

Lhôte, E. *Les lamelles oraculaires de Dodone.* Geneva, 2006.

Lloyd, G. E. R. *Magic, Reason and Experience: Studies in the Origins and Development of Greek Science.* Cambridge, 1979.

LSA = F. Sokolowski. *Lois sacrées de l'Asie Mineure.* Paris, 1955.

LSCG = F. Sokolowski. *Lois sacrées des cités grecques.* Paris, 1969.

LSS = F. Sokolowski. *Lois sacrées des cités grecques, supplément.* Paris, 1962.

Lupu, E. *Greek Sacred Law: A Collection of New Documents.* Leiden, 2005. A citation of this work (abbreviated *NGSL*) without the author's name refers to the number of one of the documents there edited.

Luraghi, N. *The Ancient Messenians.* Cambridge, 2008.

Ma, J. *Antiochus III and the Cities of Asia Minor.* Oxford, 1999. "Dossier" plus a number refers to the texts in his epigraphic dossier.

Malkin, I. *Religion and Colonization in Ancient Greece.* Leiden, 1987.

McClymond, K. *Beyond Sacred Violence.* Baltimore, 2008.

Melfi, M. *Il santuario di Asclepio a Lebena.* Athens, 2007.

Meuli, K. *Gesammelte Schriften.* Edited by T. Gelzer. Basel, 1975.

——. "Griechische Opferbräuche." In *Phyllobolia: Festschrift für P. v. der Mühll,* edited by O. Gigon et al., 185–288. Basel, 1946. Reprinted in Meuli, *Gesammelte Schriften,* 907–1021.

Mikalson, J. D. *Athenian Popular Religion.* Chapel Hill, N.C., 1983.

——. *Religion in Hellenistic Athens.* Berkeley, 1998.

NGSL. See Lupu, E.

Nilsson, M. P. *Geschichte der griechischen Religion,* vol. 1 (3rd ed.) and vol. 2 (2nd ed.). Munich, 1967 and 1961. The reference is to vol. 1 unless otherwise stated.

——. *Griechische Feste von religiöser Bedeutung mit Ausschluss der attischen.* Leipzig, 1906.

Nock, A. D. *Essays on Religion and the Ancient World.* Oxford, 1972.

Nomima = H. van Effenterre and F. Ruzé. *Nomima: Recueil d'inscriptions politiques et juridiques de l'archaïsme grec.* 2 vols. Paris, 1995–96.

Norme religieuse = P. Brulé, ed. *La norme en matière religieuse en Grèce ancienne.* Kernos supplement 21. Liège, 2009.

"Orph." = A. Bernabé, *Poetarum epicorum Graecorum testimonia et fragmenta.* Vol. 2. *Orphicorum et Orphicis similium testimonia et fragmenta.* Vols. 1 and 2. Munich, 2004–5.

Osanna, M. *Santuari e culti dell'Acaia antica.* Naples, 1996.

Oxford Readings = R. Buxton, ed. *Oxford Readings in Greek Religion.* Oxford, 2000.

Pagan Priests = M. Beard and J. North, eds. *Pagan Priests.* London, 1990.

Parker, R. *Athenian Religion: A History.* Oxford, 1996.

——. *Miasma: Pollution and Purification in Early Greek Religion.* Oxford, 1983.

——. "New Problems in Athenian Religion: The 'Sacred Law' from Aixone." In *Myths, Martyrs, and Modernity: Studies in the History of Religions in Honour of Jan N. Bremmer,* edited by J. Dijkstra, J. Kroesen, and Y. Kuiper, 193–208. Leiden, 2009.

——. *Polytheism and Society at Athens.* Oxford, 2005.

Pinakes di Locri = *I Pinakes di Locri Epizefiri.* Parte 1, 4 vols. Rome, 1999 (= *Atti e Memorie della Società Magna Grecia,* Quarta Serie 1 [1996–99]); Parte 2, 5 vols. Rome, 2003 (= *Atti e Memorie,* Quarta Serie 2 [2000–3]); Parte 3, 6 vols. Rome, 2007 (= *Atti e Memorie,* Quarta Serie 3 [2004–7]). These volumes were edited by E. L. Lissi Caronna, C. Sabbione, and L. V. Borelli but written by E. Grillo, M. Rubinich, R. Schenal Pileggi (all parts), M. Cardosa (parts 1 and 3), and F. Barello (part 3).

Pindar's Poetry = S. Hornblower and C. Morgan, eds. *Pindar's Poetry, Patrons and Festivals.* Oxford, 2007.

Pirenne-Delforge, V. *L'Aphrodite grecque.* Liège, 1994.

——. *Retour à la source: Pausanias et la religion grecque.* Liège, 2008.

Pironti, G. *Entre ciel et guerre: Figures d'Aphrodite en Grèce ancienne.* Liège, 2007.

Plut. *Non posse* = Plutarch. *Non posse suaviter vivi secundum Epicurum.*

Practitioners of the Divine = B. Dignas and K. Trampedach, eds. *Practitioners of the Divine.* Washington, D.C., 2008.

Prent, M. *Cretan Sanctuaries and Cults.* Leiden, 2005.

Price, S. *Religions of Ancient Greece.* Cambridge, 1999.

Pulleyn, S. *Prayer in Greek Religion.* Oxford, 1997.

Rappaport, R. A. *Ritual and Religion in the Making of Humanity.* Cambridge, 1999.

Redfield, J. M. *The Locrian Maidens: Love and Death in Greek Italy.* Princeton, 2003.

RICIS = L. Bricault. *Recueil des inscriptions concernant les cultes isiaques.* 3 vols. Paris, 2005.

Ritual and Communication = E. Stavrianopoulou, ed. *Ritual and Communication in the Graeco-Roman World.* Liège, 2006.

Ritual, Finance, Politics = S. Hornblower and R. Osborne, eds. *Ritual, Finance, Politics: Democratic Accounts Rendered to D. M. Lewis.* Oxford, 1994.

RO = P. J. Rhodes and R. Osborne, eds. *Greek Historical Inscriptions, 404–323 BC.* Oxford, 2003. Reference unless otherwise noted is to inscription number, not page.

Robertson Smith, W. *Religion of the Semites.* 2nd ed. London, 1894.

Rudhardt, J. *Du mythe, de la religion grecque, et de la compréhension d'autrui.* Geneva, 1981.

———. *Essai sur la religion grecque.* In *Opera Inedita,* 35–156. Liège, 2008.

———. *Thémis et les Hôrai: Recherches sur les divinités grecques de la justice et de la paix.* Geneva, 1999.

Rutherford, I. *Pindar's Paeans.* Oxford, 2001.

Sacred and the Feminine = S. Blundell and M. Williamson, eds. *The Sacred and the Feminine in Ancient Greece.* London, 1998.

Sacrifice antique = V. Mehl and P. Brulé, eds. *Le sacrifice antique: Vestiges, procédures et stratégies.* Rennes, 2008.

Sacrifice dans l'antiquité = *Le sacrifice dans l'antiquité. Entretiens Hardt* 27. Vandoeuvres, 1981.

Sanctuaire grec = *Le sanctuaire grec. Entretiens Hardt* 37. Vandoeuvres, 1992.

Schachter, A. *Cults of Boiotia.* 4 vols. London, 1981–94.

Schmitt Pantel, P. *La cité au banquet.* Rome, 1992.

Scullion, S. "Olympian and Chthonian." *ClAnt* 13 (1994): 75–119.

Sourvinou-Inwood, C. *Hylas, the Nymphs, Dionysos and Others: Myth, Ritual, Ethnicity.* Stockholm, 2005.

———. "Polis Religion" = "What Is Polis Religion?" In *The Greek City,* edited by O. Murray and S. Price, 295–323. Oxford, 1990; and "Further Aspects of Polis Religion." *AION* 10 (1988): 259–74; both are reprinted in *Oxford Readings,* 13–55, from which I cite.

———. *"Reading" Greek Culture: Texts and Images, Rituals and Myths.* Oxford, 1991.

Steinepigramme = R. Merkelbach and J. Stauber. *Steinepigramme aus dem griechischen Osten.* 5 vols. Stuttgart, 1998–2004.

Stengel, P. *Opferbräuche der Griechen.* Leipzig, 1910.

ThesCRA = *Thesaurus cultus et rituum antiquorum.* 5 vols. Los Angeles, 2004–5.

van Straten, F. T. *Hierà Kalá: Images of Animal Sacrifice in Archaic and Classical Greece.* Leiden, 1995.

Vernant, J. P., *Mortals and Immortals: Collected Essays.* Princeton, 1991.

Versnel, H. S. *Transition and Reversal in Myth and Ritual.* Leiden, 1993.

Veyne, P. "Inviter les dieux, sacrifier, banqueter: Quelques nuances de la religiosité gréco-romaine." *Annales* (2000): 3–42.

Wilamowitz-Moellendorff, U. von. *Der Glaube der Hellenen.* 2 vols. Berlin, 1931–32. Cited from 1959 Darmstadt reprint, which has slightly different page numbers.

Winkler, J. J. "The Laughter of the Oppressed." In his *The Constraints of Desire,* 188–209. New York, 1990.

Wörrle, M. *Stadt und Fest im kaiserzeitlichen Kleinasien.* Munich, 1988.

✹ INDEX

Greek words are positioned alphabetically as if transliterated into English.

299

Franklin Pierce University

00194586

DATE DUE

GAYLORD

PRINTED IN U.S.A.